W9-DHM-194

THE MEDIEVALIST IMPULSE IN AMERICAN LITERATURE

Twain, Adams, Fitzgerald, and Hemingway

Kim Moreland

THE MEDIEVALIST IMPULSE IN AMERICAN

LITERATURE *Twain, Adams, Fitzgerald, and Hemingway*

University Press
of Virginia
Charlottesville
& London

THE UNIVERSITY PRESS OF VIRGINIA
Copyright © 1996 by the Rector and Visitors
of the University of Virginia

First published 1996

⊗ The paper used in this publication meets the minimum requirements of American National Standard for Information Sciences—
Permanence of Paper for Printed Library Materials, ANSI Z39.48-
1984.

Library of Congress Cataloging-in-Publication Data

Moreland, Kim Ileen, 1954–
 The medievalist impulse in American literature : Twain, Adams,
Fitzgerald, and Hemingway / Kim Moreland.
  p.   cm.
 Includes bibliographical references (p.   ) and index.
 ISBN 0-8139-1658-5 (cloth : alk. paper)
  1. American literature—History and criticism. 2. Middle Ages
in literature. 3. Medievalism—United States—History—20th
century. 4. Medievalism—United States—History—19th century. 5. Twain, Mark, 1835–1910—Knowledge—Middle Ages.
6. Adams, Henry, 1838–1918—Knowledge—Middle Ages. 7. Fitzgerald, F. Scott (Francis Scott), 1896–1940—Knowledge—Middle
Ages. 8. Hemingway, Ernest, 1899–1961—Knowledge—Middle
Ages. 9. American literature—European influences. I. Title.
PS169.M45M67 1996
810.9'358—dc20   95-49141
                                                                          CIP

Printed in the United States of America

For my husband, Lee Weigle—ever encouraging, ever loving, ever loved—whose unwavering presence created a free space in which I could write
and
For my parents, Betty Hill Moreland and Joseph M. Moreland, whose love and confidence have always provided my foundation, and whose extraordinary joie de vivre offers a continuing inspiration

Contents

Acknowledgments   ix

Abbreviations   xi

1 The Once and Future America
   Reviving the Middle Ages   1

2 Mark Twain
   An Ambivalent Yankee at King Arthur's Court   28

3 Henry Adams
   The Historical Visionary as Medievalist   77

4 F. Scott Fitzgerald
   Tender Is the Knight   118

5 Ernest Hemingway
   Knighthood In Our Time   161

   Notes   203

   Works Cited   231

   Index   249

Acknowledgments

Like many books, *The Medievalist Impulse in American Literature* has been the work of years, the manuscript evolving through several discrete phases at different stages in my academic life. Its first incarnation owes much to the careful reading, astute questions, and sound suggestions of Mark Spilka, Elizabeth Kirk, and Patricia Caldwell at Brown University. My reading of the Star-Director passage of *The Great Gatsby* owes a particular debt to Patricia Caldwell, which I am happy to acknowledge.

I am very grateful to George Washington University, which enabled me in a variety of ways to undertake the task of reworking the manuscript, first by means of a Junior Scholar Incentive Award (which financially supported me for one summer of work on the manuscript), and later and more importantly by means of a sabbatical semester that provided the luxury of months of uninterrupted research and revision. I was also afforded course reductions and the occasional special course assignment (a Major Authors course on Twain and Adams, for example) that freed me to concentrate on my topic. I owe a special debt of gratitude to Judith Plotz and Christopher Sten, whose tenures as chair of the George Washington University English Department overlapped during the time I was working on this book; they each provided encouragement for my project and supported my need to step away from a demanding administrative role in the department so that I could focus more attention at a critical time on my writing and related teaching.

Such virtues as this book possesses are due in no small part to James M. Cox's extraordinarily careful readings of it in manuscript. His detailed responses included a wealth of provocative questions, fruitful suggestions, and astute criticisms, coupled with the type of encouragement that makes revision a challenge rather than a chore. His responses were invaluable to me. I also want to thank Tom Quirk, who read a later version of the manuscript and offered not only valuable suggestions concerning content (especially with regard to Chapter 1) and style, but also a useful list of additional secondary sources.

I am pleased to have the opportunity to thank Cathie Brettschneider, my acquisitions editor at the University Press of Virginia, for her considerable help. Her initial interest during our first conversation served as important encouragement; her continued enthusiasm for the project as the book took shape and then was reshaped in response to suggestions (not least of all her own) helped to sustain my own enthusiasm. I am also grateful to Gerald Trett, manuscript editor at the University Press of Virginia, and copyeditor Robert Burdette for their careful and efficient editing. They saved me from egregious errors, improved the flow of the manuscript, and rendered my prose more graceful. Their suggestions and corrections were all that one could wish in the editing of a manuscript. I want to thank my former student, Jennifer Mayne, who helped in the final stages of manuscript preparation, tracking down citations, checking references, locating books and journals—all at short notice and with good cheer. I also want to thank Deborah O'Connell-Brown for her extraordinary help in preparing the index.

Finally, I want to thank Susan Bell for her empathic understanding and wise counsel during the writing of this book. I will always be grateful for her vicarious participation, which provided me with valued support.

Acknowledgments are also due to several publications in which parts of individual chapters in somewhat different form first appeared. I owe thanks to the editors who have granted permission to reprint. "The Education of Scott Fitzgerald: Lessons in the Theory of History" first appeared in *Southern Humanities Review* 19 (1985): 25–38. "Hemingway's Medievalist Impulse: Its Effect on the Presentation of Women and War in *The Sun Also Rises*" was copyrighted 1986 by the Ernest Hemingway Society, all rights reserved, and was originally published in *The Hemingway Review* 6, no. 1 (1986): 30–41. "Courtly Love in America: Ernest Hemingway and F. Scott Fitzgerald Present the Lady and the Vamp" first appeared in *Selected Papers on Medievalism*, edited by Janet E. Goebel and Rebecca Cochran (Indiana: Indiana Univ. of Pennsylvania Press, 1988), 19–32. "Henry Adams, the Medieval Lady, and the 'New Woman'" first appeared in *CLIO* 18 (1989): 291–305.

Abbreviations

Mark Twain

CY   *A Connecticut Yankee at King Arthur's Court*

GA   *The Gilded Age*

HF   *Adventures of Huckleberry Finn*

IA   *The Innocents Abroad*

JA   *Personal Recollections of Joan of Arc*

LOM   *Life on the Mississippi*

MS   "The Mysterious Stranger"

PP   *The Prince and the Pauper*

PW   *The Tragedy of Pudd'nhead Wilson*

TS   *The Adventures of Tom Sawyer*

WM   *What Is Man?*

Henry Adams

D   *Democracy: A Novel*

E   *Esther*

EHA   *The Education of Henry Adams*

MSMC   *Mont-Saint-Michel and Chartres*

PVC   "Prayer to the Virgin of Chartres"

RPAH   "The Rule of Phase Applied to History"

TH   "The Tendency of History"

F. Scott Fitzgerald

BD   *The Beautiful and Damned*
CD   "The Count of Darkness"
CU   "The Crack-Up"
DH   "In the Darkest Hour"
DMR   "Does a Moment of Revolt Come? . . ."
EJA   "Echoes of the Jazz Age"
ES   "Early Success"
GD   "Gods of Darkness"
GG   *The Great Gatsby*
HV   "Homage to the Victorians"
KD   "The Kingdom in the Dark"
LT   *The Last Tycoon*
PT   "Pasting It Together"
TN   *Tender Is the Night*
TSP   *This Side of Paradise*

Ernest Hemingway

ARIT *Across the River and into the Trees*
BTHR "Big Two-Hearted River"
DIA   *Death in the Afternoon*
FA   *A Farewell to Arms*
FS   "Fathers and Sons"
FWBT *For Whom the Bell Tolls*
GHA   *Green Hills of Africa*
LGC   "The Last Good Country"
OMS   *The Old Man and the Sea*
SAR   *The Sun Also Rises*

John Steinbeck

AKA   *The Acts of King Arthur and His Noble Knights*
TWC   *Travels with Charley*

William Faulkner

KG   *Knight's Gambit*
M   *Mayday*

THE MEDIEVALIST IMPULSE IN AMERICAN LITERATURE

Twain, Adams, Fitzgerald, and Hemingway

1

The Once and Future America

Mid-nineteenth-century America was a place of radical and disconcerting change marked by sudden and disruptive transformations. The United States was literally wrenched apart by the Civil War, certainly the most violent of the disruptions marking American life of this era. In addition to creating a geopolitical and moral faultline between South and North, the Civil War, as military historians have long noted, served to separate the era of traditional warfare from that of modern warfare, with all the horrors attendant upon the appropriation of increasingly sophisticated technology for military purposes.

But this violent military transformation, ultimately resulting in the profound social transformation occasioned by the abolition of slavery, was only the most obtrusive of the changes altering American society and the American identity. In the economic sphere, the postbellum boom period—largely a function of the availability of liquid capital originally collected to finance the Northern armies—resulted in the consolidation of the industrial revolution and the consequent transformation of America's agrarian economy. This boom period was punctuated throughout the century's last three decades by violent busts, bursting bubbles, and financial panics, the gold rush of the last half of the century testifying to boom-or-bust economic cycles in the inherently unstable context of western mining towns. Widespread labor unrest—culminating in 1887 in the first national strike—testified to an economic instability that threatened political and social stability, robber barons and the "tramp menace" representing the two extremes of the destabilized structure.

The postbellum consolidation of the industrial revolution and the 1869 completion of the transcontinental railroad (itself in part a function of political fears that the West would separate from the United States or fall into enemy hands) resulted in the increasing urbanization of America, profoundly altering the American landscape. Between 1850 and 1870, over 131 million acres were appropriated for the railroad by federal land grants. When the first American railroad opened in 1830, it encompassed only 27 miles of track—a number that increased exponentially over the next decades, with over 2,000 miles of track in 1840, over 30,000 in 1860, over 93,000 in 1880, over 194,000 in 1900, and over 254,000 in 1916 at the railroad's peak. The American population doubled between 1860 and 1890, waves of immigrants numbering over ten million arriving during this period. Intensifying the effect of this increased population and urbanization was the disappearance of the American frontier as white settlers increasingly populated western territory. No longer could the West serve as an escape hatch, literal or psychological, for those Americans disaffected by civilization.

In government, political machines dominated a system originally founded on and guided by the principles of eighteenth-century statesmen. In religion, the rigors of Puritanism had been replaced by an increasingly flexible Protestantism resulting in the secularization of American culture, speeded along by the discoveries of modern science—particularly Darwinian biology, but also geology, anthropology, and archaeology—that challenged traditional religious views of the origin of man and the universe. In social relations, the rise of feminism—originating in the reformist sensibilities of the 1830s and 1840s, closely allied with the antebellum abolitionist movement, and developing into a powerful independent movement in the postbellum era—threatened traditional attitudes about the proper roles for women, and by extension men, just as the abolition of slavery threatened traditional attitudes about the proper roles for blacks, and by extension whites.

Many Americans embraced this period of profound disruption and transformation, responding with vitality and optimism to the progress effected thereby. But this optimistic response was mediated by a certain hesitancy and pessimism on the part of others who were uneasy about the changes and sometimes even on the part of those who generally embraced these changes yet at some level recognized their costs.

No Age to Get Cathedrals Built: Medievalism in American Culture

During this period a remarkable number of influential Americans began to focus on aspects of a culture that seems quite alien: the European Middle Ages. Particularly within the New England intelligentsia and the southern aristocracy, medieval architecture, literature, and history became topics of interest, the cultural authority of these two groups influencing contemporary and subsequent American popular culture.

Medieval architecture attracted the earliest attention. During the 1830s and 1840s, prominent American architects like Andrew Jackson Downing and Alexander J. Davis popularized the Gothic Revival style, which continued into the 1870s. After a brief period out of fashion, Gothic Revival (known also as neo-Gothic and the somewhat pejorative Carpenter Gothic) again became popular, remaining so throughout the 1920s when it was rechristened Collegiate Gothic because of its popularity on college campuses.[1] Beginning in the 1870s, American scholars like Charles Eliot Norton, then architects like Ralph Adams Cram, became fascinated by the architecture of Gothic cathedrals, traveling throughout Europe to engage in detailed primary analysis. Their interest extended beyond aesthetics to the spiritual impulse behind Gothic architecture and the culture that had given rise to it. One outgrowth of this interest was a new attention to medieval stained glass, resulting in the production of modern stained glass in America, this medium undergoing a revival in the 1890s spearheaded by John La Farge and Louis Comfort Tiffany, who were often compared to medieval artisans.

The stained-glass revival was part of the larger Arts and Crafts movement, which encouraged the founding of societies to promote the development of crafts in America, adherents modeling themselves on medieval artisans. American craft leaders, many of whom had been influenced by John Ruskin's *The Stones of Venice* (1851–53), praised the medieval artisan's creative freedom and joy in improvisation, contrasting this freedom with the rigidity of demands by Renaissance architects on their workers— a rage for order that many believed had led to the horrors of the modern factory system with its mass-production line and machine-produced goods. Because craft leaders admired the medieval artisan's rootedness in a community, various American craft communities were founded; their names, such as New Clairvaux, signaled their link with medieval religious communities or trade guilds.

A new interest in medieval literature also developed, signaled by the American translation and adaptation of texts in medieval French and

Italian and Middle English. Particularly noteworthy were the translations of Dante and the related founding of the Dante Society in 1881 (by Charles Eliot Norton, Henry Wadsworth Longfellow, and James Russell Lowell), dedicated to stimulating scholarly and popular interest in Dante. In a related development, translations of the writings of medieval mystics were published, as were popularized biographies of medieval saints—notably those by Vida Dutton Scudder, a Wellesley professor who claimed that she had a "passionate sense that the middle ages rather than the nineteenth century were my natural home" (quoted by Lears 210). Popularized biographies of chivalric knights—such as William Gilmore Simms's *The Life of the Chevalier Bayard: The Good Knight, Sans peur et sans reproche* (1847)—appeared, as did scholarly studies of the Arthurian legends and popular adaptations of medieval romances—some, such as Sidney Lanier's *The Boy's Froissart* (1879) and *The Boy's King Arthur* (1880), written expressly for children. Allusions to medieval traditions, characters, and events were often included even in texts whose subjects were not medieval. Popular periodicals like *Harper's Monthly, Munsey's,* and the *Atlantic Monthly* were the typical vehicles for medievalist fiction, often illustrated by Howard Pyle, who also illustrated *The Merry Adventures of Robin Hood* (1883), a classic text about the archetypal robber-knight of the Middle Ages.

The sheer quantity of the evidence, of which the above is a mere sampling, suggests that the medievalist impulse beginning in the mid–nineteenth century and extending into the twentieth was not merely a passing vogue, a superficial interest in the decorative aspects of an earlier age, though its effect on American culture is typically dismissed as such when it is acknowledged at all. Its frequent manifestations in widely disparate elements of American culture suggest that it derived from deeply felt needs and concerns that were often voiced only indirectly and were related to the sense of disruption and rapid transformation—and the concomitant sense of hesitancy and pessimism—experienced by many Americans during this period. The existence and persistence of the medievalist impulse in American culture suggest that the Middle Ages served some important functions for those Americans driven by it. The powerful nostalgia for medievalism that emerged in mid-nineteenth-century America functioned not in the ordinary way as an individual memory of a past experience but as a cultural memory, a trace of an earlier time that the American consciousness linked itself to in the past as source, measured itself against in the present as contrast, and aspired to in the future as ideal. Although this nostalgia was often conscious and overt, its effect was sometimes far more subtle and implicit.

With regard to the past, the Middle Ages served as a historical link between this still young nation and an older tradition. What is perhaps most surprising is the sense that Americans were not borrowing the history and traditions of another culture but were rightfully reappropriating their own, despite the geographic and historical disruption from England occasioned by the American experiment. Though America had no medieval past, many Americans felt no qualms about looking back proprietarily on the European medieval past. As Thomas Bulfinch, the nineteenth-century American popularizer of Arthurian tales and traditions, states forthrightly in his preface to *The Age of Chivalry* (1858): "We are entitled to our full share in the glories and recollections of the land of our forefathers, down to the time of colonization thence" (vi). Europe was perceived as the historical background for America—the "source from which we sprung," as Bulfinch puts it (vi)—and European cultural values were regarded as the rightful property of Americans, who inherited them not from the mother country but from their "forefathers" by virtue of patrilineage.

This backward glance into the medieval past provided matter of real interest to Americans trying to ground themselves in history. Though the Puritan colonists had identified themselves as analogues of the ancient Israelites, the New Jerusalem had failed to materialize in New England, so nineteenth-century Americans required a different set of historical analogues. The antebellum southern aristocracy chose the Cavaliers of seventeenth-century England—among the first settlers of Virginia and the Carolinas, according to the myth of the Old South—and through them the knights of the Middle Ages. T. C. De Leon thus proudly proclaims that "the Virginians and Carolinians especially were of direct descent from the rufflers of Hastings and . . . Agincourt" (quoted by John Fraser 34). However suspect the historical validity of this myth,[2] the popular identification significantly affected the way southerners viewed themselves. Southern writers invoked the myth to encourage the South in a war of secession, as in Nathaniel Beverley Tucker's inflammatory article in the *Partisan Leader* (1861), using language reminiscent of Bulfinch's to identify the Confederate soldier with "the gallant cavaliers from whom we spring" (quoted by Parrington 37). General Robert E. Lee believed, as his biographer Douglas Southall Freeman reports, that "he had in his veins the blood of conquerors, crusaders, and cavaliers" (160), and this belief powerfully influenced his military commitments and behavior. Interest in America's medieval past was not merely antiquarian, then, since it shaped contemporary American behavior.

With regard to the present, however, the Middle Ages served largely to provide a direct contrast to contemporary American life. This contrast was evaluative, many writers assuming that medieval values were superior to contemporary American values. When appointed to Harvard's chair of fine arts in 1875, Charles Eliot Norton adopted the following pedagogical objectives: "To show the significance of the fine arts as the expression of moral and intellectual conditions of the past; then to illustrate, by contrast, the barrenness of the American experience which . . . had starved the creative spirit" (Vanderbilt 125). Norton implicitly contrasts the barren American present with the golden medieval past, identified in a letter to Thomas Carlyle as one of the "tracts in history in which man has reached the highest level" (*Letters* 2:112). Another scholar of the Gothic cathedral—Brooks Adams, historian Henry Adams's younger brother—presents modern civilization as a degeneration of the civilization of the Middle Ages in his pessimistic treatise *The Law of Civilization and Decay* (1895). In this antimeliorist book, Brooks Adams contrasts the crass materialism of the modern age with the imaginative mentality, religious faith, and physical courage by which he characterizes medievalism. James Russell Lowell, a Harvard colleague of Henry Adams and Charles Eliot Norton, draws the same contrast between the medieval and the modern in his long poem *The Cathedral* (1870), inspired by Chartres, poignantly commenting about the present: "This is no age to get cathedrals built" (*Poetical Works* 59).

The contemporary evocation of medieval chivalry and courtly love in particular came to function as a standard against which modern American life was judged and found wanting. Because these traditions took the figure of the knight as their point of departure, they offered a standard against which the modern American man could be measured. According to this valuation, the modern American man did not measure up to his medieval predecessors in the martial realm since modern warfare offered fewer opportunities for glory than the rule-governed warfare of chivalry, nor did he measure up in the romantic realm since the modern American woman offered fewer opportunities for dedication and sacrifice than the medieval lady of the court. Though modern man came in for his share of criticism, the major share was reserved for modern warfare and modern woman because they no longer served as satisfying loci for masculine aspiration and achievement. Implicit in these judgments was an ideal of men, women, and war that contemporary American society was unable to achieve.

The Middle Ages had value and relevance for America precisely because medieval culture provided a model or ideal to which America might aspire in the future. Thus Andrew Jackson Downing published several books in the 1840s and 1850s exhorting the American public to adopt Gothic Revival not for cosmetic reasons but because this architectural tradition could civilize the rural American public by refining its moral and aesthetic senses. Downing's architectural descendant Ralph Adams Cram wrote in his 1913 introduction to Henry Adams's *Mont-Saint-Michel and Chartres* that he hoped that America might come to adopt medieval values as a result of the "rediscovery of this great epoch" (vi), which was typified by Adams's text and evident elsewhere in American culture (for example, in Cram's own neo-Gothic architecture like the Cathedral of St. John the Divine and the Princeton Chapel). Cram hoped that twentieth-century America might thereby aspire to become the new Middle Ages, noting in his introduction that *Mont-Saint-Michel and Chartres* not only "gives new and not always flattering standards for the judgment of contemporary men and things" but "establishes new ideals, new goals for attainment, . . . open[ing] up the far prospect of another thirteenth century in the times that are to come and urg[ing] to ardent action toward its attainment" (vii–viii). The same note was struck in a 1904 speech at the dedication of the University of Chicago's neo-Gothic Bartlett Gymnasium (its mural depicting a medieval tournament and its stained-glass window depicting the crowning of Ivanhoe by Rowena) when churchman and educator Frank Wakely Gunsaulus announced that "the age is weary of vulgar and soul-destroying success [and] it longs for knightly devotion to what often seem lost causes in politics, society, church, and state" (quoted by Block 110).

The Middle Ages served some as a cautionary exemplum, warning America just how far off the path the nation had roamed and tolling it back, before it was too late, to behavior and values consistent with the medieval codes. For the more pessimistic, the Middle Ages served as a potential beacon in the darkness ahead, a model on which to rebuild once America, along with the rest of Western civilization, experienced its inevitable apocalyptic fall. Neither set questioned the worth of the model, particularly as embodied in the traditions of "knightly devotion" known as chivalry and courtly love. Careful study of these medieval traditions, however, reveals that despite their celebrated contributions to Western civilization, they have provided standards that were not completely worthy in the European Middle Ages and are even more problematic when imported into America.

The influence of medievalism on American culture has attracted remarkably little attention, with two noteworthy exceptions: T. J. Jackson Lears's *No Place of Grace: Antimodernism and the Transformation of American Culture, 1880–1920* (1981) and John Fraser's *America and the*

Patterns of Chivalry (1982). Lears argues that the appeal of antimodernism as such, be it medievalism or Orientalism, stemmed from the American culture's drift toward "a weightless modernity" (98) caused by various trends that developed in the nineteenth and twentieth centuries: the fragmented nature of capitalist society, the upper-class fear of class degeneration, the increase in neurasthenia due to the luxury of urban life, the lack of an arena for physical and moral testing, the dissolution of rigorous Protestantism and its replacement by indiscriminate toleration, the emphasis on rationality to the exclusion of powerful emotions, the stifling effect of social and sexual propriety, and the fragmentation of the integral self. Lears suggests that this modern sense of weightlessness or insubstantiality was countered by a desire for authentic and intense experience. According to contemporary opinion, such experience was still available in the Orient but was last available in the West during the Middle Ages since the Renaissance marked the turn toward rationality and science that culminated in the modernist trends. Lears asserts that medieval culture thus held a special interest for nineteenth- and twentieth-century Americans, who saw it as a model of life lived with intensity.

John Fraser similarly argues that America has always exhibited a strong attachment to the medieval tradition of chivalry, claiming that "the history of nineteenth-century America could be seen as a progressive overlaying of Enlightenment common sense by chivalric romanticism" (8). Fraser argues that the repeated attempts in America to annihilate chivalric patterns by exposing them to rational analysis paradoxically attest to the power of the chivalric impulse in this country. Like Lears, Fraser suggests that much of the appeal of chivalry comes from its celebration of vigor and emotional intensity. He argues that chivalry appeals because it transcends the dichotomy between "solid but somehow empty reality" and "appealing but insubstantial fictions" (54)—that is, between the real and ideal. He thereby acknowledges the "shaping power of romantic fiction" (7) on American life, a power evident from the most cursory reading of American biographies. According to Fraser, the chivalric is not a mere escape from reality but serves to shape American reality in various significant ways.[3]

Lears and Fraser provide an impressive body of evidence—drawing extensively on architecture, art, film, social history, publishing history, popular culture, and political movements—to support their claims that a medievalist impulse functions in American culture, an impulse they both largely celebrate as salutary.[4] Their contention concerning the cultural import of medievalism, the focus of these two important works, is supported in part by references to American literature. It is fair to say, however, that the medievalist impulse in American literature has had even less critical attention than this impulse in American culture. The general rule among literary critics has been frequent casual mentions—a male protagonist described as knightly, a heroine described as a fair lady adored from afar—but few extended studies. The casual comments are with few exceptions peripheral to the main focus, mere asides that are never developed. Only in the past decade or so have literary critics begun to correct this neglect, as evidenced by occasional articles on American literature in collections such as *Selected Papers on Medievalism* (1988) and *Medievalism in American Culture* (1989), and especially in Leslie Workman's seminal journal *Studies in Medievalism* (which first appeared in 1979 and which has sponsored annual general conferences on medievalism since 1986). But this new attention to the role of medievalism in American literature remains tentative and fragmentary. No serious extended study takes as its central focus the influence of medievalism on American literature or traces this influence through the works of various American writers.[5]

But if medieval traditions are indeed traceable in American literature as in the culture at large, one must ask why the literary significance of this influence has so often gone unremarked, especially since the self-conscious medievalism of many nineteenth- and twentieth-century British writers has been discussed at length, culminating in the American critic Alice Chandler's *A Dream of Order: The Medieval Ideal in Nineteenth-Century English Literature* (1970). Although the cause of this omission is overdetermined, the common thread is America's absence of a medieval past, an absence that inhibits literary critics from searching for or recognizing the medievalist impulse in American literature and encourages them to interpret obtrusive evidence as idiosyncratic to a writer or text rather than part of a larger tradition. The contrasting obviousness of the medievalism of the British romantics, as well as their literary precursors and heirs, also militates against a recognition of the more subtle medievalism of American literature. The medievalism of the Keats of "The Eve of St. Agnes" and "La Belle Dame Sans Merci," the Coleridge of "Christabel," the Walter Scott of *The Lay of the Last Minstrel* and *Ivanhoe,* the Horace Walpole of *The Castle of Otranto* and Strawberry Hill, the Tennyson of *Idylls of the King,* shimmers on the very surface of their texts, yet the American transcendentalists—those writers most clearly under the influence of the British romantics—do not manifest a particular interest in medievalism.[6]

The absence of an American medieval past is accompanied by the presence of other elements that would seem to militate against a medievalist impulse in American culture and literature. American democracy con-

structs itself in opposition to the hierarchical structure perfectly represented by medieval feudalism, self-consciously displacing the power of
the aristocracy with that of the common man. America's Puritan heritage,
which privileged the individual's unmediated relationship with God, the
examination of conscience, literacy, and plain style, rejects Roman Catholicism's privileging of the priestly role and intercession of saints, for-
malized rituals, oral tradition, and powerful iconography—all of which
characterized the Middle Ages. The American commitment to progress,
particularly through science and technology, necessarily repudiates a regressive movement into a distant past marked by religious faith and
superstition. The commitment to the establishment of a national American literary tradition militates against the extension and adaptation of
exclusively European traditions. Yet each of these assumptions can be
challenged.

Despite the democratic foundation of America, the aristocratic societies of Brahmin New England and the Old South flourished, and writers
from these American aristocracies found the traditions of medievalism
particularly congenial. Such writers sometimes attempted to mediate between the concerns of the aristocracy and those of democracy, as in
Charles Eliot Norton's idiosyncratic assertion that the typical medieval
society in which cathedrals were built was actually marked more by
republicanism than feudalism. Such awkward attempts indicate an attraction to medievalism coupled with a desire to assert its relevance to American life, for Norton was self-consciously attempting to provide democratic America—with its celebration of materialism and technology, its
promotion of the common man, and its antagonism to the claims of culture—with a relevant model derived from the Middle Ages, in which high
culture was served by the common people.[7]

The nineteenth-century middle class felt a measure of fascination
with the American aristocracies of Brahmin New England and the Old
South—an attitude that continues into the present with regard to the
British royal family, the half-American (courtesy of Grace Kelly) Grimal-
dis of Monaco, and American dynasties like the Kennedys, whose American Camelot not only continues to attract popular attention but also
functions as a model for the administration of President Bill Clinton. The
middle class, to a greater extent than might be expected, was attracted by
the medievalist impulse evinced in the works of American aristocratic
writers. The medievalist impulse in a diluted form was further evinced
in the genteel sentimentalism so popular with the nineteenth-century
middle class, since sentimentalism was a domestication of the medieval

traditions of courtly love and chivalry, as Leslie Fiedler suggests in *Love and Death in the American Novel*. Yet this domestication of courtly love for the American audience was also paradoxically a reaction against it since the domestication required a negation of the sexual passion embodied within the medieval tradition.

The increasing tolerance for Roman Catholicism in nineteenth-century America permitted, even encouraged, the development of an interest in medievalism, just as the interest in medievalism encouraged a tolerance for Roman Catholicism. By the nineteenth century, the hegemony of Puritanism had declined to the extent that even scions of Brahmin New England Puritan families like Henry Adams and Charles Eliot Norton felt free to admire aspects of Roman Catholicism. Norton bemoaned in a 1901 lettter "the breaking down of its [Protestantism's] dogma" and "the fact of its having become, with the progress of science, vacant of spiritual significance," and he proposed that "the Catholic church in this country . . . would render an enormous service in standing against the anarchic religion of the unchurched multitude" (*Letters* 2:304–5).

The faith in progress and technology that was a hallmark of American culture was regarded with increasing suspicion as the nineteenth century came to a close, and this faith was almost completely undermined by 1918 when World War I finally dragged to an end. Individuals like Charles Eliot Norton, Henry Adams, and Ralph Adams Cram thus regarded the nostalgia for medievalism as offering a positive alternative to the problems inherent in a technological society rather than a regressive escape from those problems.

Despite the desire of a number of American writers to create a national American literary tradition, many others felt comfortable drawing from European literary sources. And just as Norton tried to forge a link between democratic America and the Middle Ages, James Russell Lowell chose to draw an idiosyncratic equivalence between American national literary sources and medieval sources, praising those writers who drew from either and conversely criticizing only those who drew from classical sources (thereby turning the more conventional valuation on its head). In *The Cathedral*, he unites in his poetic persona the American and the medieval when he cries out in the climactic line: "I looked, and owned myself a happy Goth" (*Poetical Works* 51).[8] Similarly, Henry Adams fancifully asserted at various times that New England and Normandy shared many characteristics and that since he was a New Englander, he necessarily had Norman ancestors. This creative genealogy provided him with many opportunities to identify with his "respectable Norman ancestors," as in an 1895 letter to John Hay asserting that "Caen, Bayeux, St. Lo, Coutances, and Mont-Saint-Michel are clearly works that I helped to build, when I lived in a world I liked" (*Letters* 4:319).

The medievalist impulse clearly runs counter to the major American cultural tradition at every point. Medievalism is feudal and aristocratic rather than capitalistic and democratic, Roman Catholic rather than Puritan, European rather than nationalist American, and regressive rather than progressive. This impulse emerged only as American culture underwent a transformation during which the traditional order broke down, a transformation whose effects we are still feeling. The medievalist impulse expresses the desire for a golden past—an age of order, stability, beauty, and faith—at a time of radical change in what seemed to many an all too gilded present. Ironically, this desire led the twelfth century to celebrate the mythic adventures of sixth-century King Arthur, just as the "various phases of the medieval revival [in England] can usually be correlated," according to Alice Chandler, "with contemporary changes or revolutions in the structure of society" (1–2)—whether "the rapid shifts in politics and religion that characterized the sixteenth century," the "depradations of Cromwell's soldiers . . . and the 'Glorious Revolution'" in the seventeenth century, the acceleration of "social and economic changes" in the eighteenth century (2), or the "degraded and impoverished condition of the industrial proletariat" in the nineteenth century (3). In longing nostalgically for the Middle Ages, American knights manqué yearned for the days when the chivalric contest gave men the opportunity to prove their worth and an appropriate arena in which to prove it, when ladies were satisfied to serve as occasions for male achievement, and when the possibilities for knightly adventure seemed limitless.

The Good Knight: Chivalry and Courtly Love in the "Dark Ages"

Of these two complex medieval traditions, chivalry is certainly the easier to examine. By devoting his *Chivalry* (1984) to a detailed exploration of this complicated tradition, historian Maurice Keen responded, wittingly or not, to Mark Girouard's earlier assertion in *The Return to Camelot* (1981) that "chivalry is not a simple phenomenon; its origin, meaning and early development call for a book, not a few paragraphs" (16). As the basis for his convincing analysis, Keen draws on many primary texts from various types of sources—notably, treatises on chivalry per se, but also ecclesiastical treatises, romances, epic chansons de geste, and genealogical histories.

Keen presents chivalry as a positive force in Western civilization that encouraged honorable behavior and individual achievement in the face of personal danger. While acknowledging that individual deviations from chivalry were inevitable, he argues that the ongoing and self-conscious "struggle of true chivalry against false knighthood" (234) bore witness to the transformative power, worth, and vitality of this ideal in medieval society. Keen suggests that chivalry "not only exercised a very powerful influence on the medieval world, but also left . . . a very deep imprint on the times that followed" (253), asserting that only in the twentieth century have chivalric values been called into question and self-consciously evincing a real regret at this modern development. In this regret he seems to be joined by Aldo Scaglione, who in the conclusion to his recent *Knights at Court* (1991) argues that his "coupling of chivalry with courtesy and courtliness lays stress on the close connection between chivalry and a universal behavioral model," this model "remain[ing] operative until the great behavioral changes that have occurred in our own century" (306).

Keen's extensive historical research leads him to conclude that chivalry was no mere literary ideal or convention but a reflection of sociohistorical reality, though he also acknowledges that the literary romances and chansons de geste served both to codify and heighten the tradition. Chivalry spread from France to Italy, Germany, and Spain, according to Keen, holding sway as a dominant and vital code of behavior from the late eleventh until the sixteenth century. Here he self-consciously differs from Johan Huizinga, whose *The Waning of the Middle Ages* (1924) is the classic text on chivalry. Indeed Keen's text can be read as a response to Huizinga's text; respectful and admiring in tone, it typically offers qualifications of Huizinga rather than rebuttals.

In contrast to Keen, Huizinga had argued that later medieval chivalry, at least, had little vitality or relevance to society, functioning instead as little more than a veneer—at best a pleasant fiction offering a respite from reality, at worst a misdirection of energies resulting in a celebration of hollow ceremonies that were completely, and ultimately destructively, out of touch with the harsh realities of the day. Mark Girouard seems to concur with Huizinga's interpretation, suggesting that the real world bore little relationship to the chivalric world described in the poems and romances of the troubadours of Provence and trouvères of northern France, but he also observes that "none the less the ideal existed and was recognized" (16), and he explores the ways this ideal continued to influence behavior even into the twentieth century.

Keen is at some pains to delineate the relationship between chivalry and Christianity (necessarily Roman Catholicism, or the "church"), arguing that chivalry was a basically secular tradition that operated within the framework of a Christian society. It therefore honored and even served to advance the goals of the church (for example, by service in the Crusades), but "religious priorities were not the driving force behind its ethic" (252). The chivalric knight's major loyalties were to his secular lord (his suzerain) and to himself—the chivalric code thus merging social responsibility with individual self-realization. Scaglione aptly notes that "what the knight errant's adventure is supposed to produce [is] a finding of one's identity by becoming worthy of the court" (125).

Chivalry is defined, according to Keen (as well as Huizinga, Girouard, and Scaglione, for there is little controversy here), as a code of behavior followed by the knight, a noble warrior skilled in horsemanship, who committed himself to serving his lord honorably and faithfully and sought opportunities (in jousts, tournaments, *pas d'armes*, and other martial adventures) to test himself and thereby gain fame. The knight was expected to manifest particular qualities: courage (*prouesse*); independence, individuality, and self-assurance (*franchesse*); loyalty (*loyauté*); generosity (*largesse*); nobility of birth and of behavior (*noblesse*); and courtesy (*courtoisie*). C. Stephen Jaeger, in *The Origins of Courtliness* (1985), lauds the Middle Ages as the period in the modern West "when knights first took it upon themselves to mitigate the violence typical in any warrior class with ideals of restraint and mercy" (261), and Keen suggests that "chivalry taught the gentleman of a succeeding age to place honour at the centre of his mental and social world" (250). Huizinga, perhaps less enthusiastically, calls chivalry "a noble game with edifying and heroic rules" (66), this reference to the game signaling the ludic foundation of his theory of chivalry. Girouard acknowledges the value of the honor to which the knight committed himself, but he calls into question the destructive excesses of behavior and the disjunction from reality to which this commitment sometimes led.

Much more than the discussion of chivalry, the discussion of courtly love is complicated by a lack of consensus about virtually every aspect of this much-disputed tradition, whether its origins, its relationship to Christianity, or its defining characteristics. Unlike "chivalry"—a term whose origin lies in the early Middle Ages (drawn from "chevalier" or "horseman")—the term "courtly love" is modern, first introduced in 1883 by Gaston Paris, a leading French romance philologist, in an article in *Romania* focusing on the figure of Lancelot.[9] Indeed the renewal of interest in this tradition was itself a striking feature of nineteenth-century scholarship. Roger Boase recounts the history of courtly love scholarship in his enormously useful *The Origin and Meaning of Courtly Love* (1977), where he also exhaustively discusses seven theories on the origin of courtly love (Hispano-Arabic, Chivalric-Matriarchal, Crypto-Cathar, Neoplatonic, Bernardine-Marianist, Spring Folk Ritual, and Feudal-Sociological) as well as five theories on its meaning (collective fantasy, play phenomenon, courtly experience, stylistic convention, and critical fantasy).

Four influential critics of courtly love, each promoting an interpretation quite different from the others, have dictated the terms of the debate during much of the twentieth century: C. S. Lewis (*The Allegory of Love*, 1936), D. W. Robertson (*A Preface to Chaucer, Studies in Medieval Perspective*, 1963), Denis de Rougemont (*Love in the Western World*, 1939; rev. ed. 1983), and Erich Auerbach (*Mimesis*, 1946). Lewis, taking the sociohistorical perspective (and influenced by the romantic scholarship of the nineteenth-century French philologists), presents courtly love as a noble and ennobling force for good in Western civilization, celebrating what he regards as a fortuitous revolution in the way society perceived love. Robertson, taking the perspective of patristic exegesis, presents courtly love as an ignoble celebration of concupiscence in place of the Christian virtue of charity (*caritas*). Rougemont, taking the perspective of mythic-psychological criticism, regards courtly love with a complex ambivalence, which explains why his *Love in the Western World*, whose self-conscious purpose is to reveal the negative impact of this tradition on Western civilization since the twelfth century, nonetheless evinces a curious attraction to the tradition. Auerbach, taking the perspective of genre criticism, is concerned largely with the influence of the courtly love tradition on literary history, regarding courtly love negatively insofar as it has had a restrictive effect on the development of literary realism. At least with regard to the continuing powerful influence of the courtly love tradition on modern culture, however, the four critics agree, Ian Watt additionally suggesting in *The Rise of the Novel* (1957) that the courtly "ideal that love between the sexes is to be regarded as the supreme value of life on earth" (135) continues to affect literature as well as life and remains the central concern of the modern novel.

All the critics grant some relationship between the courtly love tradition and sociohistorical reality, although the exact nature of this relationship is disputed, perhaps because of their concentration on almost exclusively literary rather than more narrowly historical texts. Lewis regards actual behavior at historical courts in twelfth-century Provence as the fundamental basis from which courtly love literature soon developed, the literature a reliable mirror of the rarefied society at court where the lady and her few damsels served as a refining and constraining influence on the many men (inferior nobles, unattached knights, squires, and pages) who owed feudal allegiance to their often absent suzerain and therefore service to her. Robertson, on the other hand, argues that the romances and treatises were actually satiric rather than mimetic in intent, yet it is clear that these satires must at some level be satirizing actual behavior, and Robertson grudgingly admits that society during this period became more generally interested in romantic love as such. Rougemont suggests that courtly love literature did not reflect society but described a situation that was the opposite of the social conditions of the period. The courtly ideal was "in flat contradiction with the 'stern reality' of the age" (247) where the position of women, even in Provence, was clearly inferior to that of men. He posits as the source of this tradition a contemporary religious heresy known as the Albigensian heresy, or Catharism (here drawing by way of Otto Rahn on the nineteenth-century work of Eugène Aroux and the early-twentieth-century work of Joseph Péladan), courtly love serving as the disguised medium for religious dissent rather than serving romantic ends,[10] but he acknowledges that the tradition soon affected the way society regarded and conducted actual love relationships. Auerbach assumes that the courtly romances detailed some of the actual customs of the period—particularly the love relationship, less so warfare—but he focuses on the ways the romances were constructed as literary texts rather than mirrors of reality.

These critics also address, explicitly or implicitly, the relationship of the courtly love tradition to Christianity. Lewis regards the "religion of love" (20) as a parody of Christianity, a rival of Christianity, even an escape from Christianity, yet clearly developing within its context and ultimately reuniting with it once Christian marriage was no longer merely utilitarian but could encompass romantic love (a feat accomplished, according to Lewis, by Edmund Spenser in *The Faerie Queene*). Robertson sees the popular conception of courtly love as absolutely opposed to Christianity, but since all courtly texts are for him satires, then Christianity was the ethos that these satires suggested as the ideal, most explicitly in the concluding palinode. Rougemont sees the courtly love tradition as heretical, but he indicates that it was ultimately appropriated by society and thus by Christianity, particularly in the form of the cult of the Virgin, otherwise known as Mariolatry (which he argues was initiated by the Catholic Church to counter the rise of the cult of the idealized woman in courtly love). Auerbach regards courtly love as an escape from reality into myth and fairy tale where Christianity ceased to be a relevant force.

All four critics agree that courtly love can be defined, superficially at least, as a celebration of an adored and superior lady in which the lover was ennobled by his service. The lover was expected to manifest humility (because of his inferior position relative to the lady in the social, economic, and moral spheres) and to practice courtesy (the elaborate series of rules, customs, and usages derived originally from feudalism and then ever more refined, which made of love an art);[11] once enrolled in the religion of love, he was expected to remain faithful in his passion and discreet about its object. This passion was necessarily extramarital if not necessarily consummated since a romantic idealization of love could not exist within the confines of utilitarian marriage.

Lewis celebrates these characteristics, approving even of the adulterous sexual consummation as " 'a kind of chastity,' in virtue of its severe standard of fidelity to a single object" (34). Robertson rejects the positive connotations of such characteristics, arguing that the lover was sunk into an idolatrous fixation that diminished charity and increased desire. Rougemont is ambivalent about the characteristics, suggesting that they embodied a death wish aesthetically contained by the courtly love tradition (the suffering knight ever seeking a perfect love not available in life and therefore placing obstacles in the way of sexual consummation, so that suffering was increased, with the paradoxical result that "instinct [was] excited by the very insistence on denying it" [235]). Auerbach points out that the idealistic nature of courtly love's characteristics caused them to be impractical and absolute, revealing their lack of significance and usefulness in the real world.

Although largely concentrating on the male figure of the knight-troubadour-lover, these critics also devote some attention to the figure of the lady. Lewis at least partially recognizes the severe limitations of a "courtesy [that] demands that the lovers should serve all *ladies*, not all women" (35), since not only all nonaristocratic females (the vast majority of the female population) but all aristocratic females in their role as wife are excluded because "a wife is not a superior [but] ... sinks at once from lady into mere woman" (36–37). But Lewis does not recognize that even the aristocratic lady's much vaunted "free choice in her acceptance or rejection of a lover" is sharply delimited since "only women who are 'enlisted in the soldiery of love' are praised among men" (34), and Lewis seems to concur in the judgments of, respectively, the lady who supposedly abuses her power by truly considering her own desires and the lady who "does well" by "admitting a worthy lover to her favours" (34). For all her supposed freedom, the lady must accede to male standards (Lewis glossing over who gets to define worthiness) or suffer the consequences. As occurs so often in the later courtly lyrics of the Renaissance, these consequences involve poetry itself: the woman is either written out of the poetry, denied her status as worthy subject of poetry and therefore denied aesthetic immortality, or she is censured within the poetry, condemned to remain forever characterized as the unworthy object of a great poet's love, the shallow source of a great man's suffering. In contrast to Lewis, Robertson pointedly calls into question the freedom from compulsion that supposedly characterizes courtly love, noting that if a lady allows a man to hope for her love, she must later grant it to him. Similarly, if she has agreed to engage in "pure" love—"the kiss, the embrace, and contact with the nude beloved, but with the final solace omitted" (437)—she is bound to engage later in "mixed" or consummated love if her lover requests it. Rougemont points out that the same knight who extols the ennobling influence of courtly love often views women and female sexuality negatively; the adorer of the lady is often a scorner of women.[12] And Ian Watt notes that "while courtly love provided the conventional beginning and end, the main interest of the narrative lay in the adventures which the knight achieved for his lady, and not in the development of the love relationship itself" (140), thereby alluding consciously to the critical commonplace that courtly romances were written to gratify the noble lady but unintentionally revealing that the focus on the knight's self-realization, even self-creation, betrays the egocentricity, indeed the phallocentricity, of the form.

Recent feminist critics of courtly love have thus focused much more attention on the representation of the lady celebrated in the lyrics and romances of the medieval troubadours. Noting that the twelfth-century hero moves through a fictional world dominated by women, Joan M. Ferrante observes in *Woman as Image in Medieval Literature* (1975) that these women function not as "'real people' with human problems" but as "symbols and aspects of philosophical and psychological problems that trouble the male world" or as representations of the male hero's "ideals, his aspirations, the values of his society" (1). While closely examining the image of woman in medieval literature—and discovering that there is little to distinguish one courtly lady from another—Ferrante returns repeatedly to the fact that courtly literature is largely concerned with the investigation of male emotions and impulses.

In *The Troubadour Lyric: A Psychocritical Reading* (1990), Rouben C. Cholakian explores these male emotions and impulses (the focus of most earlier criticism) from a specifically feminist-psychoanalytic perspective, engaging in a fascinating analysis of troubadour lyrics to uncover the motivations for the ambiguous portrait of the woman. Identifying the courtly lady as "*constructed*, not *real*" (9), Cholakian asserts that "the more appropriate question [is] not *who* she represents *historically*"—a question that has obsessed many scholars of courtly love—"but *what* she represents *psychologically* for her inventor" (84). Focusing on five such "inventors"—the troubadours Guillaume d'Aquitaine, Marcabru, Jaufré Rudel, Arnaut Daniel, and Guiraut Riquier—Cholakian reveals that the code of courtly love is actually concerned with masculine performance. Noting that the poetic persona "has the woman say what he wants to hear" (91), Cholakian argues that the troubadour grants only a deceptive power to his beloved by constructing an amorous discourse within which she may speak and by means of which she is praised but over which he maintains control.[13]

Like Ferrante, Cholakian discovers in the poetry a depersonalization of the woman. He points out that she is typically identified not by a name but a quality (such as "Miels de Domna," or "Better than Woman," and "Belhs Deportz," or "Lovely Pleasure") attributed to her by the troubadour, this identifying quality appearing in the poetry as a grammatically masculine *senhal*—a nickname or "sign for something necessarily and paradoxically absent" (22). In short, she has no center, no self. Cholakian argues that the woman's constructed selflessness performs a significant psychological function, "mak[ing] possible the man's selfhood and the ultimate identification of her will with his [so that] they become as one because she is his" (178). The woman is thus, according to Cholakian, "topos by absence, removed from the amorous discourse through abstraction (Rudel, Riquier) and from the self-powering *logos* through excluding obscurantism (Marcabru, Daniel [practitioners of *trobar clus*, the closed or difficult style of courtly lyric])" (188). Cholakian concludes that the courtly lyrics are "fundamentally androcentric" (181), even "misogyny[stic]" (185), despite their self-conscious identification as celebrations of women.

The Medievalist Impulse in American Literature: Where Knighthood Was Still in Flower

Although most American writers of the nineteenth and twentieth centuries were not by profession or inclination scholarly researchers dedicated to a careful study of the various details of medieval traditions so as to self-consciously incorporate an accurate version into their texts, it is noteworthy that many American writers did engage in some historical research on the medieval period. Their understanding of the courtly love tradition was typically what was commonly accepted by scholars and readers alike—the sociohistorical view later sympathetically elaborated by C. S. Lewis, who derived his theory not only from a study of the medieval texts but also from the many analyses of the tradition by nineteenth- and early-twentieth-century philologists and historians—notably Gaston

Paris (whom Henry Adams cites in *Mont-Saint-Michel and Chartres*), but also Violet Paget, Alfred Jeanroy, Joseph Anglade, and H. J. Chaytor.

It is this view to which American writers would have had easiest access, as evidenced by the popularity of Bulfinch's *The Age of Chivalry*, a mid-nineteenth-century American text clearly based in the sociohistorical perspective. This popular recounting of romances opens with a series of brief essays that admiringly describe aspects of medieval life with the purpose of educating the reader about medieval traditions, especially chivalry and courtly love. Bulfinch speaks of chivalry in high terms, stating that it "framed an ideal of the heroic character, combining invincible strength and valor, justice, modesty, loyalty to superiors, courtesy to equals, compassion to weakness, and devotedness to the Church" (14). To courtly love Bulfinch ascribes the refinements of civility and the development of courtesy, finding charming the relationship between knight and lady whereby "the service of his mistress was the glory and occupation of a knight, and her smiles . . . were held out as the recompense of his well-directed valor" (17). Lovingly describing the tournament, in which "every combatant proclaimed the name of the lady whose *servant d'amour* he was," he notes in a particularly purple passage that the knight "was wont to look up to the stand, and strengthen his courage by the sight of the bright eyes that were raining their influence on him from above" (20). Such celebratory descriptions of the medieval traditions—in the same spirit as C. S. Lewis's *The Allegory of Love*, if certainly more sentimental—would have been familiar to nineteenth- and twentieth-century American writers.

Though Lewis's seminal study must serve as a touchstone for any exploration of the medievalist impulse in American literature, the other views of chivalry and courtly love are significant since each provides important insights into the medieval traditions that are available if only subliminally to any reader of the literature of the Middle Ages. Moreover, if chivalry and courtly love have the mythic, culturewide influence that Rougemont, Auerbach, and Girouard suggest, it follows that American writers have been influenced by these traditions even when they have not read the medieval texts, even when they are not aware of the influence. Indeed, Rougemont concerns himself explicitly with the power of this influence in America specifically, noting that "no other known civilization, in the 7,000 years that one civilization has been succeeding another, has bestowed on the love known as *romance* anything like the same amount of daily publicity" (291–92). The revisionist views of chivalry and courtly love presented so polemically by patristic exegetes like Robertson and feminist critics like Ferrante and Cholakian offer a means of exploring the sometimes uncritical appropriation of these medieval traditions by American writers driven by the medievalist impulse.

These writers are legion in the nineteenth and twentieth centuries, as even a brief survey reveals. Hugh Henry Brackenridge's six-volume *Modern Chivalry* (1792–1815) offers an American Don Quixote and Sancho Panza in the characters of the idealistic Captain John Farrago and his shrewd servant Teague O'Regan. John Pendleton Kennedy's *Rob of the Bowl* (1838) is a Cavalier romance set in Maryland; William Alexander Caruthers's *The Cavaliers of Virginia* (1834–35) and *The Knights of the Horse-Shoe, a Traditionary Tale of the Cocked Hat Gentry in the Old Dominion* (1845) are Cavalier romances set in Virginia. Edgar Allan Poe's "Ligeia" (1838), "The Fall of the House of Usher" (1839), "The Masque of the Red Death" (1842), "The Pit and the Pendulum" (1843), and "The Cask of Amontillado" (1846) are set in the Middle Ages or exist in a time-less zone marked by Gothic features. James Russell Lowell's "A Legend of Brittany" (1843) recounts the love of a simple young maiden for a hard-hearted Knight Templar named Mordred, and his "Vision of Sir Launfal" (1848) offers a version of an Arthurian romance in which a knight searches for the Holy Grail. Richard Hovey's play *The Marriage of Guenevere* (1891) partakes of what Howard Mumford Jones calls the "romantic Arthurianism" (360) in vogue in the 1890s, as do, at a remove, Henry Maugham's play *The Husband of Poverty* (1897)—presenting the life of the Lady Clare, founder of the Franciscan sister order—and Louis K. Anspacher's play *Tristan and Isolde* (1904). Frank Norris's short story "Grettir at Drangey" (1892) is one of several that he modeled on medieval Icelandic tales, and he also wrote a long verse romance, *Yvernelle* (1892). Other examples are Clinton Scollard's "Taillefer the Trouvère" (1892), Edward W. Barnard's "Ballade of Chivalry" (1894), L. H. Hammond's "Knights Errant" (1898), and Bryan Hooker's numerous medieval romances, such as "Ysobel de Corveaux" and "Swanhild" (early 1900s). Charles Major's *When Knighthood Was in Flower* (1899) became a best-seller, as did George Washington Cable's *The Cavalier* (1900), later dramatized on Broadway. James Branch Cabell wrote several popular and influential medievalist novels, notably *Line of Love* (1905) and *Jurgen* (1919), as well as a collection of short stories, *Chivalry* (1909), peopled by medieval characters. Stephen French Whitman's "The Noble Family of Beaupertys" (1907), Edith Wharton's "Ogrin the Hermit" (1909), and Emily James Putnam's "The Lady of the Castle" (1910) are other medievalist short stories of the era. Over the course of twelve years, Edwin Arlington Robinson published four book-length poems on medieval figures: *Merlin: A Poem* (1917), *Lancelot: A Poem* (1920), *Tristram* (1927), and *Modred: A Fragment* (1929).

For twentieth-century writers, a minor work sometimes powerfully signals the medievalist impulse that appears more subtly in their major works, an appearance that might otherwise go unnoticed. John Steinbeck's unfinished *The Acts of King Arthur and His Noble Knights* (written in 1958–59) is a case in point. At a time in his professional life when he felt stale and blocked, Steinbeck devoted almost two years to research and two to the writing of this translation into modern American English of the Winchester Manuscript of Malory's *Morte Darthur,* an experience recounted in detail in letters to his literary agent, Elizabeth Otis, and his managing editor, Chase Horton (included in the posthumously published book). In a 1958 letter to Otis, Steinbeck explained that his objective was "to keep the content and the details but to cast them into a form for our time" (*AKA* 320). He also projected a series of explanatory essays that would draw directly on the "literally hundreds of books on the Middle Ages" (*AKA* 311) he had read, as he wrote to Otis in 1958, and on the primary research he had accomplished during extended visits to England and Italy. Steinbeck's letters bear frequent witness to how "desperately [he wanted] for this work to be the best [he] had ever done" (*AKA* 324). Judging in March 1959 that *The Acts of King Arthur* was "the best prose I have ever written" (*AKA* 330), Steinbeck was devastated to discover in May 1959 that Otis and Chase had severe reservations about the manuscript. Though continuing to work on it for another three months, he ultimately ceased writing, although maintaining the illusion that he would return to the manuscript eventually.

While still engaged in research, Steinbeck wrote to Chase in 1957 that "the parallels with our own time are crowding me" (*AKA* 302), and a year later, as he approached the beginning of the actual writing in 1958, he wrote yet more intensely that "the application with the present is very close, and also the present day with its uncertainties very closely parallels the uncertainties of the fifteenth century . . . [so that the projected work has] applications in the present day and definite roots in our living literature" (*AKA* 314). Noting that the "devilish welter of change" that Malory confronted was "so like the one today," Steinbeck asserted that Malory "tried to create a world of order, a world of virtue governed by forces familiar to him" (*AKA* 315). In escaping to that world of order that he was in the process of reconstructing via the translation, Steinbeck entered a "a curious state of suspension" (*AKA* 314), and he wrote about his manuscript in 1959, "I've dreamed too many years . . . to change direction" (*AKA* 345). Steinbeck stated in a 1959 letter to Horton: "The twentieth century seems very remote. And I would like to keep it that way for a while" (AKA 329). But he had conversely argued in a 1958 letter to Horton: "In turning over the lumber of the past I'm looking for the future. This is no nostalgia for the finished and safe. My looking is not for a dead Arthur but for one sleeping" (AKA 326–27). Steinbeck thus inextricably links the medieval past and the American present and future, though the relationship he draws is fluid and changing.

Steinbeck turned from *The Acts of King Arthur* to *Travels with Charley in Search of America* (1962), a nonfictional account of his journey to "rediscover"—and perhaps conquer?—"this monster land" (TWC 5). The chivalric impulse so prominent in *The Acts of King Arthur* has not disappeared, remaining as a subtext that occasionally emerges. The journey that Steinbeck takes with his poodle sidekick, Charley, is a pilgrimage, as emphasized by the title "In Quest of America" under which portions of the text appeared serially in *Holiday*. His vehicle is a truck that he immediately names "Rocinante, which you will remember was the name of Don Quixote's horse" (TWC 7). He jokes about "the end of the Quest" (TWC 189), hears "the wail of trumpets and the clash of arms" when a barroom brawl is threatened, and then decides, "But hell, I'm too old for it" (TWC 202), and later worries, "We're soft, Charley. Maybe it's time for a little gallantry" (TWC 221). *Travels with Charley* is a sad book, permeated by a sense of aging and loss, personal and cultural.

In his introduction to *The Acts of King Arthur*, Steinbeck had written of the magical moment in childhood when he first overcame his painful reading difficulty, a moment he associated with the Caxton version of Malory's *Morte Darthur*, "the very strangeness of [whose] language dyd me enchante, and vaulted me into an ancient scene" (AKA xii). Steinbeck discovered "in that scene . . . *gallantry*—perhaps the only single quality of man that the West has invented" (AKA xii; emphasis mine). It is gallantry that bears the greatest emotional resonance for him (as suggested by the later *Travels with Charley* reference), originating in his reading of the *Morte Darthur:* "I think my sense of right and wrong, my feeling of noblesse oblige, and any thought I may have against the oppressor and for the oppressed, came from this secret book" (AKA xii). Traces of this medieval ideal are evident in a number of Steinbeck's novels—notably *Tortilla Flat* (1935), *Of Mice and Men* (1937), and *The Grapes of Wrath* (1939)—revealing that Steinbeck the social critic is instead (or causally related to?) "John Steinbeck of Monterey, Knight" (AKA vi).

William Faulkner is another writer whose attraction to the traditions of medieval chivalry and courtly love is most powerfully signaled by a little-read minor work. *Mayday* (written in 1926) is the hand-lettered and personally illustrated book that Faulkner wrote and produced for Helen Baird; only a single copy of this personally bound book existed until a facsimile edition was posthumously published in 1977. *Mayday* is an allegorical work set in the Middle Ages in which Sir Galwyn of Arthgyl sets out on a quest to rescue a lady who has appeared to him in a dream vision. He is accompanied by the figures of Pain and Hunger, "but for [whom] no one would ever ride into this enchanted wood" (*M* 55). In questing for the lady of the dream vision, Sir Galwyn comes upon three others—the princesses Yseult, Elys, and Aelia—for each of whom he experiences an attraction that he thinks will be everlasting but discovers to be fleeting upon consummation: "'It occurs to me,' young Sir Galwyn [said] profoundly, 'that it is not the thing itself that man wants, so much as the wanting of it'" (*M* 71). Although Sir Galwyn and the romantic quest are subjected to gentle ironic undercutting, the ladies are treated somewhat more harshly. Faulkner may be revenging himself here on Helen Baird, who had refused his marriage proposal, Faulkner allegorically suggesting that Baird's appeal for him paradoxically continues only because of that refusal. Sir Galwyn ultimately discovers the lady of his dream—the lady of his dreams—in Little Sister Death with whom he unites in the conclusion. "Thus it was in the old days" (*M* 87), as the tag line announces: the courtly knight is revealed to be in love with death, as Rougemont would confirm.

In his introduction to *Mayday*, Carvel Collins points out the numerous "connection[s] between *Mayday* and Faulkner's first major work, *The Sound and the Fury* [1929]" (*M* 23), noting for example that "it is quite obvious that *Mayday* has much in common with Quentin Compson's monologue" (*M* 27). Collins argues that *Mayday* "plainly displays some of the significant elements which in *The Sound and the Fury* lie below the surface" (*M* 32). But it might be more useful to think of *Mayday* in broader terms, not simply as a source or practice run for a single novel. After all, the same author who wrote *Mayday* also wrote a collection of stories entitled *Knight's Gambit* (1932) in whose title story he explored "the tenets of that agrarian and equestrian land" (*KG* 168) called the South. And in various novels he explored the relationship between modern southern knights manqué like Quentin Compson, Gowan (Galwyn? Gawain?) Stevens, Horace Benbow, and Bayard (Le Chevalier sans peur et sans reproche?) Sartoris, and modern southern ladies manqué like Caddy Compson (the absence at the center of three male first-person narratives), Temple Drake, Belle Mitchell, and Narcissa Benbow—all revealed to be lost causes.

Clearly the medievalist impulse in American literature is no mere idiosyncratic characteristic of one or two writers. The degree to which it serves as a subtext in American literature—as source, contrast, and model—is only recently becoming evident. This heretofore unrecognized tradition is best represented by four writers, two from the nineteenth century and two from the twentieth, three canonical and one whose influence is powerful though his works are infrequently read, two at least partially associated with the South and two with the North: Mark Twain, Henry Adams, F. Scott Fitzgerald, and Ernest Hemingway.

Mark Twain's works are the best place to start because they provide a locus wherein collide spectacularly both the major cultural tradition (with its celebration of American progress, even in the face of radical change and disruption) and the counterimpulse of medievalism (with its attraction to the codes and traditions of the Middle Ages). Twain's intense and explicitly articulated objection to the medievalist tradition in American culture, coupled with his almost unwilling and frequently unacknowledged attraction to this tradition, bear witness to the power and pervasiveness of this impulse, even in a writer who regarded himself as an opponent of the medievalist revival he saw emerging in American culture. This most quintessentially American writer set three novels, one novella, and various short stories in the Middle Ages, and medieval motifs, characters, and plot devices recur even in those texts set in nineteenth-century America.

Like Twain, Henry Adams directly addressed the attraction of medievalism, but unlike Twain, he responded with a deeply felt sympathy—not, however, mere antiquarianism, for it paradoxically looked to the future, providing a way of understanding twentieth-century America. Whereas Twain figured forth the Middle Ages and nineteenth-century America as binary opposites with nineteenth-century America privileged as the superior term in the hierarchy, Adams at times simply reversed the hierarchy, at other times deconstructing it so that the two terms are no longer opposites but embedded within each other, both ages struggling with the same problem—in Adams's terms, the relationship between multiplicity and unity. In one text recounting an imaginative journey into medieval France, in another recounting an autobiographical journey into his own—and America's—recent past and the present while also projecting into its future, Adams measures these ages against each other, discovering webs of relationship that powerfully influenced subsequent generations of American writers, among them Fitzgerald and Hemingway.

Like their nineteenth-century predecessors, Fitzgerald and Hemingway sometimes overtly concerned themselves with medieval subjects,

characters, and settings, but more often the medievalist impulse functioned subtextually (as in Steinbeck and Faulkner), particularly affecting
the way they portrayed the modern American man, whose constructed
identity was in flux. As in Steinbeck and Faulkner, Fitzgerald's attraction
to the Middle Ages is signaled by an obscure text, *Philippe, Count of Darkness*, an unfinished historical novel set in ninth-century France and written at a time of personal and professional crisis, as were Steinbeck's *Acts
of King Arthur* and Faulkner's *Mayday*. However unsuccessful Fitzgerald's
attempt at a medieval novel, his modern American novels and stories are
suffused by the lost ideals of the Middle Ages. For Fitzgerald, the Middle
Ages offered a compelling model of behavior appropriate to the romantic
arena, courtly love functioning as the ideal of true love to which his male
protagonists aspire despite the historical transformation of the medieval
lady into the modern vamp. Knightly behavior offers Fitzgerald's middle-
class male protagonists a means of winning the golden girl, thereby simultaneously striking a blow against aristocratic privilege and affirming
its value in modern America.

For Hemingway, who unknowingly served as the model for Fitzgerald's
medieval Philippe and proclaimed himself the spokesman In Our Time,
a time marked by multiple wars rather than the peace that the Anglican
prayer entreats, the Middle Ages offered a compelling model of behavior
appropriate to the martial arena. Chivalry functioned for Hemingway as
the ideal of grace under pressure, an ideal that modern war renders un-
realizable. Only ritualized blood sports and the tournament-like confines
of the bullfight arena offer his male protagonists the opportunity to approach the chivalric ideal in the modern world, an opportunity that re-
cedes as they move further into the twentieth century, with powerful implications for the construction of masculine identity.

The works of Twain, Adams, Fitzgerald, and Hemingway map the lines
that the medievalist impulse has followed and continues to follow in
American literature—for example, in Walker Percy's *The Last Gentleman*
(1966) and *Lancelot* (1977). Twain, Adams, Fitzgerald, and Hemingway
repeatedly grapple—consciously or unconsciously, textually or subtextually—with various questions: What is the relationship between modern
America and the Middle Ages? Did the Middle Ages offer a mythic golden
past to which America could link itself, its abrupt beginnings in the
seventeenth-century American wilderness too stark for imaginative nour-
ishment later in its history? What is the relationship between dreaming of
the Middle Ages and the American Dream? Do the childlike qualities attributed to the Middle Ages bear a particular relevance to this youthful
nation? Do the social and martial conventions of courtly love and chivalry

offer a guide—or perhaps a reproach—to an America whose vaunted freedom renders it particularly vulnerable to abrupt changes, technological disruptions, and social upheavals? What lessons does the figure of the medieval knight have to teach nineteenth- and twentieth-century male writers and the culture in general? The works of Twain, Adams, Fitzgerald, and Hemingway reveal with particular power the various ways nineteenth- and twentieth-century writers answered these and other questions, appropriating the Middle Ages as a means of critiquing and reshaping their contemporary American reality.

2

Mark Twain

It is a commonplace of literary scholarship that Mark Twain was violently critical of medievalism—not only the actual culture of the Middle Ages as preserved in European architecture, museums, and monarchies but the medievalist revival in nineteenth-century England and America. Although the Middle Ages, however reprehensible in Twain's view, were indisputably part of the distant past, the medievalist revival constituted a contemporary threat. Twain repeatedly blamed the revival on Sir Walter Scott, criticizing in hyperbolic terms its effect on America, particularly the American South. His major objection was the revival's regressiveness, its militation against the progressivism of American culture and its militation against the progressive movement of history. This teleological perspective resulted necessarily in a consideration of the present as the apex of history, the present envisioned as a complex version of the simple past, just as an adult is a mature version of his childhood self. Indeed Twain repeatedly uses this very analogy, praising the mature and sophisticated culture of the nineteenth century by throwing it into relief against the culture of the Middle Ages, which he characterizes as childish and naive.

Yet such an analogy is peculiarly interesting in Twain's case, for he of all American writers is known as the celebrant of childhood, the creator of affirmative myths that resonate powerfully in the American psyche. These myths resonated equally powerfully in Twain's psyche, as suggested by his emotional declaration in a 1906 letter to one of his "Angel Fish"—

prepubescent girls to whom he formed emotional attachments in his last years—that "youth is the golden time" (*Aquarium* 21). Twain's "gently satirical but also affectionate" nickname was "Youth," which his wife called him despite being ten years younger, as he reported in his *Autobiography* (228).

But Twain flourished on contradictions, as suggested by the prevalence of disguises, twins, and doubles in his fiction, which repeatedly allowed him to have it both ways. His use of the child as symbol for the Middle Ages functions similarly. Connoting most obviously the primitive, undeveloped, unsophisticated, foolish, and ignorant—negative connotations supporting the critical contention that Twain was diametrically opposed to medievalism, a contention with which Twain would have readily agreed—the image of the child also connotes freedom, innocence, exuberance, imagination, and love of beauty—positive connotations militating against Twain's self-conscious criticism of the Middle Ages, suggesting that for him, this period possessed certain values that the present lacked.

A balanced judgment of Twain's surprisingly complex response to medievalism will result not merely from an examination of those explicit comments about the nineteenth century and the Middle Ages on which most critics focus but also from an examination of Twain's literary use of the child and related images. Twain's repeated conflation of child and knight also suggests a conflation of childhood and the Middle Ages, itself the childhood of Western civilization according to the nineteenth-century view. Childhood for Twain inevitably suggested his youth in the antebellum South, the childhood of America before the growth pains of the Civil War catapulted the country into postbellum adulthood.

Twain thus lived an historical irony: his "golden youth," with which he associated personal freedom, was lived in a culture of slavery that was yet for him a golden age; his adulthood, with which he associated personal constraints upon his liberty and even, as he said repeatedly, "slavery" to his business ventures and his writing (see, for example, *Autobiography* 132), was lived in a culture of supposed emancipation that he identified as a gilded age. Personal and cultural history contradicted each other, just as the teleological imperative of history collided with the romantic myth of childhood within which Twain operated. Unable to resolve these contradictions and ambivalences, Twain responded viscerally, expressing them obsessively in his writing and his life.

An Adopted Yankee Celebrates American "Sivilization"

Twain was not alone in his espousal of the teleological view of history. Many of the historians on whom he relied when writing his historical novels preached meliorism, a theory particularly well suited to America's construction of its identity. This simplistic vision of history as a progressive march through the centuries, an irrevocable movement toward perfection, resulted in a self-serving celebration of the present, narrowly defined as the post-Civil War period in the northern states. Through much of his life, Twain shared in the general optimism that prevailed about America's identity and destiny in the world. The machine, often in the form of the electric turbine known as the dynamo, became the preeminent symbol of the age of technology emerging in the postbellum North, and technology became identified with progress.[1] Twain's experiences with the Paige typesetting machine bear witness to his profound commitment to the age of technology, his youthful apprenticeship to a printer providing him with a "lifelong interest in the technology of writing" in particular (Lauber, *Making* 36). Having organized a company for the perfecting, manufacturing, and marketing of this revolutionary machine, he devoted fifteen years and much of his fortune, about $190,000, to its development.

Perhaps the most important result of postbellum industrialism was the development of an increasingly powerful middle class, whose characteristics Twain describes in *Life on the Mississippi* (1883): "From St. Louis northward there are all the enlivening signs of the presence of active, energetic, intelligent, prosperous, practical nineteenth-century populations. The people don't dream, they work. The happy result is manifest all around in the substantial outside aspect of things, and the suggestions of wholesome life and comfort" (*LOM* 321). Because this passage encapsulates a number of motifs to which Twain returns in his novels and nonfiction, it deserves careful attention. Overridingly it provides a celebration of the American common man, rhetorically effected by the piling up of honorific adjectives climaxed at "practical." This worker rises by his own efforts and superior personal qualities into the middle class, progress on the individual level replicating cultural progress. A pragmatist, he is concerned only with solving practical problems efficiently—a nineteenth-century secular manifestation of the Puritan work ethic. A capitalist, he expects his hard work to result in economic reward whose appeal is the consumption of material commodities. Above all, the middle-class man values his "wholesome" home and family, the genteel tradition of sentimentalism having displaced religion as the locus of moral values in American culture.

Many of the characteristics of middle-class life that Twain celebrates in *Life on the Mississippi* were manifested in his life. From the time of his childhood in the southwestern town of Hannibal, Missouri, he desired great success—personal, social, professional, and economic—and he determined to regain the distinction that his family had lost through his father's business reverses. Twain's adult loyalties, however, were split between his writing vocation and his business ventures, for he hoped to succeed specifically where his father had failed. The large sums of money that he eventually earned as both writer and businessman were largely devoted to his home and family. He chose to live in Hartford, a prosperous northeastern manufacturing city that he had once admiringly described in a newspaper article as "the centre of Connecticut wealth" (quoted by Kraft 106), his house an elaborate showplace filled with the latest technological conveniences like the "*first* [telephone line] that was ever used in a private house in the world" (*Autobiography* 254). He lived there with his wife Olivia and his three daughters for twenty years, a devoted husband and father.

His relationship with Olivia was from the first highly sentimental. A member of one of the richest and most respected families of Elmira, New York, she was a sheltered and innocent angel in the house,[2] a delicate and often sickly woman whom Twain sentimentally idealized while acknowledging his own unworthiness: "You seemed to my bewildered vision, a visiting *Spirit* from the upper air—a something to *worship*, reverently & at a distance—& *not* a creature of common human clay, to be profaned by the *love* of such as I" (*Love Letters* 43). Throughout their courtship Twain apostrophized Olivia as saint and sister, defusing any suggestions of sexuality. She was the most important in a series of women (including his mother and an older confidante, Mary Fairbanks) whose genteel judgment he sought.

Twain identified with the common man of nineteenth-century America—the worker who successfully attains middle-class life, adheres to middle-class values, and manifests middle-class characteristics—because his life manifested that peculiarly American pattern. He provided a fictional spokesman for this common man in Hank Morgan of *A Connecticut Yankee at King Arthur's Court* (1889). This archetypal common man—the self-proclaimed "Yankee of the Yankees" (*CY* 36) who lives in prosperous Hartford like Twain (a "Connecticut Yankee by adoption," as he identified himself in the 1881 speech "Plymouth Rock and the Pilgrims" [112])—exhibits all the characteristics celebrated by Twain in his description of the citizens of St. Louis some six years earlier.

Great energy and an appetite for work enable Hank to transform Arthurian society, making sixth-century England over in the image of nineteenth-century America, a task whose worth he considers self-evident. Indeed progress is the very "breath of life" (*CY* 219) for Hank, just as it serves to "enliven" the citizens of St. Louis. Since progress is equated with life, Hank recognizes that his removal to Arthurian England is a rare opportunity for an enterprising man. His reforms are directed at improving the situation of the masses rather than the elite, the common man rather than the aristocrat. Though unsuccessful in engineering a bloodless revolution that will replace the monarchy with a republic, he does manage to legislate the equality of all men before the law, to outlaw slavery, to develop a system of public education, and to introduce mass communication and mass transportation into Arthurian England.

Like the people of St. Louis, Hank prefers working to dreaming. Initially interpreting his arrival in Arthurian England as a dream, he characteristically demands that the dream "scatter!" (CY 63) so he can return to his factory. Just as his enthusiastic adoption of the work ethic originally led to his promotion as superintendent at the Colt Arms Factory, it contributes to his promotion as the "Boss" of Arthurian England. Proud of being "a practical Connecticut man" (CY 50) in medieval England, Hank repeatedly contrasts the pragmatism implicit in the work ethic with the aesthetic impulse, always to the benefit of the former, noting that he is "practical; yes, and nearly barren of . . . poetry" (CY 36). Upon hearing a tale at the Round Table, Hank notes only its "usual slovenliness in statistics" (CY 109), disregarding its aesthetic qualities. Because Twain himself "regard[ed] philistinism as a necessary concomitant of democracy—and thus of Americanism" (Henry Nash Smith, Fable 72), he found himself in the peculiar position of denigrating art, though an artist.

Prosperity is the result of Hank's energetic application of the work ethic for practical ends. Though he hopes to reform the Arthurian economy so that the wretchedly poor (and ironically named) freemen will be able to subsist decently, his economic efforts are also impelled by materialism. Like the citizens of St. Louis, Hank desires material commodities that derive from and symbolize prosperity. Because of his displeasure at the absence of modern conveniences in Arthurian England, Hank is oblivious to the beauty of medieval tapestries and furnishings, aggrievedly listing all the things missing from a medieval castle that would be present in a nineteenth-century middle-class home, just as Twain yearned during his 1892 residence at a Florentine villa for the "objects without number" that rendered "the American house . . . the most satisfying refuge yet invented" (Autobiography 347). After establishing himself in Arthurian society, Hank takes pride in sponsoring a dinner party that could compete with a nineteenth-century event, engaging in social one-upmanship and conspicuous consumption, proving his worth as a man by the amount of money he spends on commodities and thereby also demonstrating his middle-class respect for the new.

According to Twain, the common man desires not only the external characteristics of the middle-class household but a "wholesome life," defined by the norms of middle-class morality. The values of the domestic hearth and home prevailed over the dictates of religion in an increasingly secularized America, gentility and sentimentalism providing the standards by which Americans of the nineteenth century lived. Though Huck Finn rejects the "sivilizing" influence of the family, thereby testifying to Twain's deep-seated ambivalence about the sentimental and genteel values, Hank Morgan is more conventional.[3] In the midst of what he regards as the lasciviousness of the court, he takes pride in his genteel family life. The marriage of Hank and his medieval lady, Alisande, whom he immediately renames "Sandy" in an act of patriarchal and imperialistic appropriation, is undertaken not to satisfy the demands of passionate love but the demands of a middle-class morality that operates for no one in Arthurian England but Hank: "I was a New Englander, and in my opinion this sort of partnership [the courtly love relationship] would compromise her. . . . She couldn't see how, but I cut argument [short] and we had a wedding" (*CY* 372). The marriage develops into a sentimental relationship, an idealized friendship unmarked by sexuality. Sandy is the virtuous wife who creates a home to which Hank can retreat after the rigors of his working day. In the fashion of nineteenth-century husbands, he proclaims himself "her worshipper" (*CY* 372). That stock character of nineteenth-century sentimental fiction, the sick but adorable child, completes the sentimental tableau as husband and wife tenderly lean over her crib.

Knights-Errant and Errant Wives

Twain's celebration of nineteenth-century America was perhaps inevitably accompanied by criticism of the Middle Ages since the teleological view of history implies not only a celebration of the present but also a denigration of the past. In his preface to *Connecticut Yankee*, Twain thus posits infinite regress as a justification for his anachronistic appropriation of twelfth-century laws and customs in his sixth-century tale. William Hartpole Lecky, a contemporary historian whose works Twain carefully read, hyperbolically described the medieval period as "lower than any other period in the history of mankind" (quoted by Williams, "Use of History" 103), an evaluation that particularly impressed Twain, as evidenced by his scoring of the passage in his own copy of Lecky's text.[4]

This same evaluation is expressed in the preface to *Personal Recollections of Joan of Arc by the Sieur Louis de Conte* (1896) where the "translator"— Twain's narrative persona, with whom he is closely identified—proposes that "her century was the brutalest, the wickedest, the rottenest in history since the darkest ages" (*JA* 1:v). The Middle Ages served for Twain, as for many other historical progressivists, as the locus for a mistrust of and condescension to the past.

A satire of this period was one of Twain's major aims in *Connecticut Yankee*. Some years after writing this novel, Twain described it as an attempt "to contrast . . . the English life of the whole of the Middle Ages, with the life of . . . modern civilization—to the advantage of the latter, of course" (*Autobiography* 295). Twain's satire is two-pronged, targeting the Middle Ages and the nineteenth-century medievalist revival. Though Twain's most elaborated criticisms of the Middle Ages occur in *Connecticut Yankee*, they also appear in other works—notably *The Prince and the Pauper* (1882) and *Joan of Arc*, but also *The Innocents Abroad* (1869)—his criticisms primarily focusing on the political, social, and religious aspects of medieval culture.

Twain reserved much of his harshest criticism for the medieval aristocracy because it achieved nobility by birth rather than deeds. He traced most social problems of the Middle Ages to the hereditary privileged class that inevitably disregarded the welfare of the common people, a disregard symbolized in *Connecticut Yankee* and *The Prince and the Pauper* by the compelling scenes of slavery. Hank Morgan draws an absolute identification between the aristocrat and the slaveholder, asserting that "an aristocracy . . . is but a band of slaveholders under another name" (*CY* 226). Twain felt so strongly about the symbolic import of this identification that he skewed the facts of history to include references to slavery in these two novels.

Thus Yokel, one of the gang members in *The Prince and the Pauper*, has a moment of great dignity when he identifies himself as a slave and describes the horrifying treatment accorded him by his "superiors," who have literally branded him: "I have run from my master, and when I am found—the heavy curse of heaven fall on the law of the land that hath commanded it!—I shall hang!" (*PP* 112). Twain explains in a note that Yokel "was suffering from this law by *anticipation* [since] . . . this hideous statute was to have birth [later]" (*PP* 207 n. 10). The enslaved Hank Morgan and King Arthur also suffer "by anticipation," and the graphically described horrors that they endure on their long forced march are regarded indifferently even by those who by nature are kind. Twain thus makes the point that the moral perceptions of the aristocracy are blunted by familiarity with the institution of slavery, a point that he later makes in his *Autobiography* with regard to the white citizens of antebellum Hannibal.

To Twain's mind, the aristocrat's sense of superiority was clearly faulty since such superior individuals all too often proved themselves inferior to the people they ruled. In *Connecticut Yankee* and *The Prince and the Pauper*, Twain invokes an archetypal scene—the ruler dressing in the clothes of a commoner and henceforth going unrecognized and unhonored—to demonstrate that this sociopolitical superiority has no relation to intrinsic superiority. Clothing, not worth, makes the king. Twain's particular bête noire was the theory of divine right of kings, which to his mind was disproved by the evident inferiority of most monarchs. *The Prince and the Pauper*'s Henry VIII thus insists on the right of his seemingly incompetent son (actually the disguised Tom Canty) to be king: "He is mad, but he is my son and England's heir, and mad or sane, still shall he reign! . . . Were he a thousand times mad, yet is he Prince of Wales, and I the King will confirm it" (*PP* 35). That Tom is neither Henry's son nor a madman does not mitigate the chilling horror of Henry's pronouncement with its absolute disregard for the welfare of the common people.

The unworthiness of the aristocracy takes a particularly insidious form in *Joan of Arc*'s Charles VII of France, who embodies virtually all the character flaws that Twain attributes to aristocrats in general and whose flaws show up particularly badly when contrasted with the numberless virtues of the perfect Joan. Though France lies in ruins around him, on the brink of defeat to the British, Charles sits placidly in Tours, his personality reflected in the "tinseled snobs and dandies around him" (*JA* 1:306) and the "frivolous animal in his lap" (*JA* 1:307). Indolence and cowardice contribute to his decision to postpone marching with Joan to Rheims for his coronation, and the attack on Paris fails because the king, in contrast to the courageous Joan, "hung back and was afraid" (*JA* 2:102). Most damning is Charles's abandonment of the ever-faithful Joan to martyrdom because of his cowardice and concern for political expediency. He repeatedly earns the ironic nickname "Charles the Base" (*JA* 1:306), his ignoble character overshadowing his noble birth. Charles has none of the merits—neither seriousness of purpose, commitment, courage, nor loyalty—necessary to a good ruler, thus serving as an object lesson on the indefensibility of the divine-right theory.

Twain's criticisms of the medieval political structure were matched by criticisms of the aristocratic social conventions, the courtly love tradition attracting his particular attention. Even in the ponderously serious *Joan of Arc*, Twain provides a subplot allowing him to burlesque the actions of a courtly lover:

> I had made a poem . . . in which I most happily and delicately celebrated that sweet girl's charms, without mentioning her name. . . . It was a rash idea, but beautiful . . . [and] wonderfully pathetic, . . . with the rhyme and all to help. At the end of each verse there was a two-line refrain pitying the poor earthly lover separated . . . from her he loved so well, and growing always paler and weaker and thinner in his agony as he neared the cruel grave. . . . [This girl] cross[ed] my path, and out came the poem, and no more trouble to me to word it and rhyme it and perfect it than it is to stone a dog. (*JA* 1:238–41)

The satire here is relatively gentle, for the "poet," Joan's loyal follower and the narrator of her story, is in all other respects a sympathetic character. But in other works Twain criticized the courtly love tradition more harshly. Reacting with moral indignation to the courtly romance, which celebrated sexual passion and sympathetically portrayed illicit relationships, he was more comfortable with the celebration of the genteel family provided in the nineteenth-century novel and manifested in his life.

In *The Innocents Abroad*, Twain censures two celebrated medieval couples whose relationships did not conform to the strictures of sentimental marriage. As a public service, Twain decides to reveal the true story of Abelard and Héloïse, Twain's version resembling a nineteenth-century novel of seduction with Abelard unrecognizable as the "dastardly seducer" (*IA* 147) and "cold-hearted villain" (*IA* 143), Héloïse sentimentalized as the "misused, faithful girl" (*IA* 147), and Fulbert, Héloïse's uncle and the man who ordered Abelard's castration, revealed as the true hero of the story! Twain is particularly appalled by Abelard's violation of the "sacred" (*IA* 143) home created for Héloïse by the paternal Fulbert, with whose "abused trust" and "broken heart" and "troubled spirit" (*IA* 146) Twain sympathizes. Twain's sympathies are again oddly placed in his recounting of Petrarch and Laura's story, where he notes that "poor Mr. Laura" doubtless disliked "having another man following his wife every where and making her name a familiar word in every garlic-exterminating mouth in Italy with his sonnets to her pre-empted eyebrows" (*IA* 184).[5]

Twain's loyalties to husband and father are clear in these revisions, as is his hostility to the force that threatens the home and family—passionate love, personified by the courtly lover. When this love is not overtly sexual but refined and idealized, as with Petrarch, Twain restrains his criticism, identifying Petrarch merely as "the gentleman who loved another man's Laura, and lavished upon her . . . a love which was a clear waste of the raw material" (*IA* 183–84). When this love is overtly sexual, as with Abelard, Twain's hostility is severe, leading him to applaud the "just deed" (*IA* 145) of Abelard's castrators.

Given Twain's hostile attitude toward Abelard and Petrarch, his portraits of Héloïse and Laura are relatively generous because sentimentalized. Commenting that Héloïse's "noble, self-sacrificing love . . . [was] characteristic of the pure-souled [girl], but it was not good sense" (*IA* 144), Twain adroitly shifts the blame to Abelard. Twain's evident discomfort at the thought of female sexuality and passion is also paradoxically manifested in his forays into bawdry in works such as *1601, or Conversation as It Was by the Social Fireside, in the Time of the Tudors* (privately printed in 1880) since his frank presentation of female sexuality occurs only in a pornographic work (set in the Middle Ages as Twain expansively defined this period) that was privately circulated among his male friends, who served as the exclusive intended audience for this text. As he slyly observes in an 1884 letter to his publisher, James R. Osgood, "I have mailed you a 1601; but mind, if it is for a lady you are to assume the authorship of it yourself" (*To His Publishers* 168). Ironically, the pornographic *1601* functions in much the same way as the supposedly philogynous courtly lyrics; the female is the "subject-object for male discourse," and the "context is validation by other males" (Cholakian 57) who are its intended audience.

In those works intended for a mixed-gender audience, when Twain presents courtly relationships without sentimentalizing the ladies, his disapproval is sharp. In *Life on the Mississippi*, he cynically notes that the effect of "lax court morals and the absurd chivalry business" in the Middle Ages was that "while religion was the passion of their ladies, . . . the classifying their offspring into children of full rank and children by brevet [was] their pastime" (*LOM* 16). The rhetorical antithesis emphasizes the uneasy linkage between Catholicism and courtly love, between "the ardours of a religion that was believed" and "the delights of a religion that was merely imagined" (C. S. Lewis 21). More important, Twain criticizes the sexual activity of the ladies on the grounds of its threat to the integrity of the patriarchal family structure.

Twain's scorn for such passionate medieval ladies reaches its apex in *Connecticut Yankee*, where Hank Morgan is repeatedly confronted by women whose behavior shocks him. Sentimental Hank considers the actions of these medieval ladies coarse, indelicate, and therefore necessarily unladylike. These ladies drink alcohol publicly and tell dirty stories; they witness dogfights without shrinking back in horror at the blood and violence; they witness with similar enthusiasm, "instead of fainting" (*CY* 93), the violent encounters between knights in tournaments. Here the contrast between the courtly lady and the sentimental lady (who certainly *would* faint) remains implicit, but it is rendered explicit when Hank announces that "the humblest hello-girl [a nineteenth-century telephone operator] . . . could teach gentleness, patience, modesty, manners, to the highest duchess in Arthur's land" (*CY* 137). Again social class is revealed to bear no relationship—or perhaps an inverse relationship—to intrinsic worth.

The contrast between the courtly and the sentimental lady is economically manifested in the character of Sandy, whose shifting portrait is accompanied by a concomitant shift in tone. Sandy is initially presented as a courtly lady (Alisande la Carteloise) who originates a foolish quest on which the contemptuous Hank must accompany her. This initial portrait is unsympathetic, Hank apostrophizing her as "this wandering wench" and more harshly as "a perfect ass" (*CY* 113). She bores Hank with her long-winded tales; she embarrasses his genteel sensibility by traveling with him unchaperoned; and though "she was a handy person to have along on a raid" (*CY* 135), he considers her bravery and ingenuity marks of coarseness. Yet this unattractive portrait of Sandy as a courtly lady is later replaced by a sympathetic portrait emphasizing her domestic qualities: "Ah, Sandy, what a right heart she had, how simple, and genuine, and good she was! She was a flawless wife and mother" (*CY* 372). Sandy's final voyage of maternal mercy—traveling with her sick child in search of a healthier climate—contrasts favorably with her original quest, and the narrative tone shifts accordingly from the satiric to the affectionate, the celebratory, the honorific. The courtly lady of the Middle Ages is thus metamorphosed into the sentimental lady—wife and mother—of the nineteenth century, and in the process Twain reconstructs the definition of "lady," arguing that it is not until the nineteenth century that "the earliest samples of the real lady . . . appear[ed]" (*CY* 62).

The highest "lady" of all in medieval England was Guinevere, the queen whose passionate love for her knight is celebrated in such medieval romances as Chrétien de Troyes's *Lancelot du lac* but who is presented in *Connecticut Yankee* as simply a lascivious female. When Hank learns of her affair with Launcelot, he does not think of her as an aristocratic lady caught up in an overwhelming passion that leads inevitably to the glorious "fault" of courtly love, a sexual consummation which, though morally wrong because adulterous, results in an experience that transcends morality and thus deserves celebration in the poetry of the medieval trouvères (see Rougemont 235). Hank regards "Guenever" as simply an errant wife, his sympathies always allied with Arthur in his role as husband. Hank is troubled by the adulterous passion of Guenever and Launcelot because his commitment is to domestic harmony. When Arthur discovers the affair, domestic harmony, both marital and national, is destroyed.

The medieval tradition of the droit du seigneur served for Twain as a particular index to the sexual immorality of the Middle Ages, and he thus presents it almost obsessively in *Connecticut Yankee.*[6] Though Hank Morgan initially refers obliquely to the "last infamy of monarchical government," he later speaks of this "unprintable" (*CY* 126) right more directly, describing two incidents in which it was invoked with disastrous consequences to innocent young girls, brides both, and their honorable husbands. Though Twain's criticism was certainly warranted, its emotional intensity derived from his horror at the thought of an innocent girl involved in sexual activity.[7] The droit du seigneur, like the courtly love tradition, implied sexual behavior, whereas the sentimental marriage, for Twain and other nineteenth-century writers, simply did not. Moreover, the droit du seigneur, again like the courtly love tradition, offended Twain's moral sense because it destroyed the integrity of the patriarchal family structure by undermining the authority of the husband and the integrity of patrilineage.

In contrast to Twain's sentimentalization of Héloïse and Laura and criticism of Abelard and Petrarch, he reverses his sympathies in *Connecticut Yankee,* criticizing the lady and sentimentalizing the man. Launcelot is portrayed as a stock character of sentimental fiction, the bachelor uncle who dotes on children and honors motherhood, Hank judging him suitable for the role of nineteenth-century paterfamilias: "He was a beautiful man, a lovely man, and was just intended to make a wife and children happy. But of course, Guenever—however, it's no use to cry over what's done and can't be helped" (*CY* 369). Hank blames Guenever's powerful and dangerous sexuality, which irresistibly attracts Launcelot, for forestalling the knight's opportunities to establish the kind of marriage and family life that Hank and Sandy share.

By sentimentalizing Launcelot, the figure who in medieval romance functioned as the very archetype of the courtly knight, Twain effectively separates him from his knightly identity and thereby displaces his criticism of chivalry and courtly love onto other medieval knights. Twain particularly objected to their celebration of the martial skills and dedication to battle, which he regarded as a kind of war-mongering. He thus debunks the historical figure of Richard the Lion-Hearted in *Life on the Mississippi,* presenting him as neither a religious crusader nor a noble warrior but as the perpetrator of massacres. Twain was "bitterly opposed to war in general, perhaps because of his own disillusioning experience in the Civil War" (Denton 5), during which he served as a Confederate volunteer, deserting after only three weeks (as he recounts in his fictionalized version, "Private History of a Campaign That Failed" [1885]). His opposition is particularly clear in several works published only posthumously because of the depths of their bitterness and despair. Among these are "The War Prayer" (written in 1904–5), a harsh satire on the martial spirit, and "The Mysterious Stranger" (written in three versions between 1897 and 1905), in which Satan contemptuously reviews mankind's martial history—past, present, and future—and announces that "there has never been a just [war], never an honorable one—on the part of the instigator" (MS 667). Twain's attitude is also evident from the horrifying image of the Hundred Years' War provided by the narrator of *Joan of Arc,* who describes it as "an ogre that went about for near a hundred years, crunching men and dripping blood from his jaws" (JA 2:31). Ironically, this novel celebrates the exploits of France's greatest "knight." Yet Joan, the victor in the Hundred Years War and the single warrior whom Twain glorifies in his fiction, is sentimentalized as a gentle adolescent girl who hates war and cannot stand the sight of blood.

Twain typically attacked the "'righteous' warfare associated with Christianity" (Denton 6), criticizing not only the crusades against the Turkish infidels but knightly quests and tournaments. After hearing tales about the adventures of the knights of the Round Table, Hank Morgan ingenuously notes: "As far as I could make out—these murderous adventures were not forays undertaken to avenge injuries, nor to settle old disputes or sudden fallings out; no, as a rule they were simply duels between . . . people who had never even been introduced . . . and between whom existed no cause of offense whatever" (CY 54). The tournaments provided even less justification for combat, yet jousts and other such "games" often resulted in injuries and death. Hank is appalled by this custom, on several occasions comparing tournaments to "human bull-fights" (CY 92), thereby forging a connection that Twain's literary heir Ernest Hemingway would later extend to opposite effect. Recognizing that a replacement for the tournament, like the original, would need to provide an energy outlet, entertainment, and an exemplary model, Hank ultimately succeeds in transforming the tournament into the nineteenth-century American sport baseball. Having defused the military identity of the knight by transforming his armor into a sport uniform, Hank takes one more step toward his goal of making "knight-errantry [into] . . . a doomed institution" (CY 363).

Twain also criticized the religious conditions of the Middle Ages. A virulent agnostic throughout most of his adult life, he mistrusted organized religion in general but focused much of his mistrust on Catholicism. Revolt though he did against his mother's Calvinism, its familiarity served to defuse much of his anger, fear, and suspicion, these emotions being directed instead at the more alien Catholicism that he associated with Europe—particularly medieval Europe. Roger Salomon notes that Twain thought of the years from 300 to 1800 as "a single, unified epoch whose chief institutions were Catholicism and its bastard offspring feudalism [and] he accused these institutions of promulgating cruel laws which made people do terrible things to each other" (24).

In *Innocents Abroad,* Twain blames Catholicism for making Italy the home of "a happy, cheerful, contented ignorance, superstition, degradation, poverty, indolence, and everlasting unaspiring worthlessness" (*IA* 209). Twain considered the elaborate rituals of the mass an unsatisfactory substitute for the Puritan examination of conscience. He criticized the privileged position of the Virgin Mary in the Catholic schema, and he implicitly criticized the link between courtly love and Mariolatry (see C. S. Lewis 8; Rougemont 111), noting that the Pantheon's Venus, the goddess of sexual love, was "tricked out in consecrated gimcracks [to do] reluctant duty as a Virgin Mary" (*IA* 276).

Twain reserved his harshest criticism for the power wielded by the church in the Middle Ages. In *Connecticut Yankee,* Hank incredulously notes that the Catholic Church is stronger than the combined force of the king (representative of the aristocracy) and Hank (representative of progressive technology). Echoing observations made by Twain in various marginal notations, Hank accuses the church of promoting certain "virtues"—humility, servility, meekness—that support the unfair social hierarchy depriving the common man of power. In any power struggle, the church holds the ultimate weapon, the interdict, which when unleashed casts England back into darkness, reversing all the progressive changes implemented by Hank. The Inquisition as described in *Innocents Abroad* also reveals the destructive power of the church, Twain contrasting its horrors with the actions of the so-called barbarians to ironic effect. Noting that the Christians "did all they could to persuade [the barbarians] to love and honor [Christ]," Twain ticks off these persuasive efforts— "twisting their thumbs out of joint with a screw," "nipping their flesh with pincers," "skinning them alive," and "roasting them in public"— ending by noting with climactic irony that "they always convinced those barbarians" (*IA* 275).

Twain's tone reaches even more sustained heights of outrage in *Joan of Arc,* where the church's treatment of Joan is revealed to be contemptible from first to last. In the trial scenes, Joan is sympathetically presented as a weary child worn down by the bullying church in the grotesque person of Cauchon, with "his great belly distending and receding with each breath," "his three chins, fold above fold," "his knobby and knotty face," "his purple and splotchy complexion," "his repulsive cauliflower nose," and "his cold and malignant eyes" (*JA* 2:141). The almost hysterical rhetoric of this passage reveals Twain's visceral disgust with the medieval Catholic Church, though his curious choice of a Catholic saint as biographical subject gives pause. Even here, Twain's ambivalence reveals itself.

Agent of Infection: The Sir Walter Disease

Twain's exaggerated hostility toward a "long-vanished society" (*LOM* 266) derived from his hostility toward a contemporary threat. Twain judged the nineteenth-century imitation of medieval culture as even more reprehensible than the original because it was necessarily a falsification. In a famous passage of *Life on the Mississippi*, Twain placed the blame for this revival squarely on the shoulders of Sir Walter Scott: "Then comes Sir Walter Scott with his enchantments, and by his single might checks this wave of progress, and even turns it back; sets the world in love with dreams and phantoms; with decayed and swinish forms of religion; with decayed and degraded systems of government; with the sillinesses and emptinesses, sham grandeurs, sham gauds, and sham chivalries of a brainless and worthless long-vanished society" (*LOM* 265–66). Labeling the medievalist revival "the Sir Walter disease" (*LOM* 266), Twain hyperbolically grants Scott the distinction of doing "more real and lasting harm, perhaps, than any other individual that ever wrote" (*LOM* 266).

Twain's choice of Scott as a target increases the polemical effect of his argument by enabling him to attack an individual rather than an abstraction, thereby constructing himself as the champion of the good in a personal battle between worthy opponents—in effect, a duel. In placing the blame for the revival on Scott, Twain also shifts it from America, implying that Scott has imposed an alien sensibility on wholesome, practical, and progressive America. But Scott could not have single-handedly altered the cultural history of an unresponsive America, as even Twain must have recognized. Many influences encouraged this revival, and those Americans who welcomed it found something compatible with their interests, beliefs, and psychological needs.

Twain particularly regretted that the medievalist revival took hold so strongly in his native South. Characteristically noting that copies of Scott's *Ivanhoe* were proudly displayed in the best southern homes, Twain blamed the revival on "the debilitating influence of [Scott's] books" (*LOM* 237), arguing that were it not for the revival, the southerner's character "would be wholly modern, in place of modern and medieval mixed, and the South would be fully a generation further advanced" (*LOM* 266). Twain drew multiple implicit and explicit comparisons between the cultures of the Middle Ages and the American South,[8] revealing certain basic similarities—both societies were feudal, aristocratic, and agrarian—that made the South particularly amenable to the medievalist revival.

Hank Morgan's description of a medieval town—complete with windowless houses, thatched cabins, indifferently cultivated garden patches, crooked unpaved alleys, dogs and naked children playing outdoors, and hogs lying in wallows in the main street—is suggestive of many towns in the Deep South and Southwest. Even the castle overlooking the medieval town has its double in the southern plantation mansion. The medieval town described in *Connecticut Yankee* has a near parallel in Eseldorf, the sixteenth-century Austrian town that provides the setting for "The Mysterious Stranger," and both these medieval towns are strikingly similar to the St. Petersburg of *Tom Sawyer* (1876) and *Huckleberry Finn* (1884). These basic similarities in the landscapes of the Middle Ages and the American South were reinforced by self-conscious imitations of medieval architecture by the southern aristocracy. Public and private institutions were often housed in imitation castles, as Twain notes in *Life on the Mississippi*. The effect of the Gothic Revival movement was even perceptible in the decorative motifs used in more modest buildings, the log house of the Grangerford family boasting curtains with a decorative motif of vine-covered castles, as does the Hawkins's home in *The Gilded Age* (1873).

Twain agreed with Gothic Revival architect Andrew Jackson Downing that this movement signified more than a mere cosmetic change, that it had moral and aesthetic ramifications. But whereas Downing argued that Gothic Revival architecture embodied beauty, harmony, and truth, Twain insisted that it embodied falseness and sham. Objecting that this architecture, which he blamed on Scott, was unsuited to nineteenth-century America, Twain labeled it "a hurtful thing and a mistake" (*LOM* 238), suggesting that a better architectural model would be the New Orleans Cotton Exchange, a contemporary construction devoted to business interests.

In *Connecticut Yankee*, Hank explicitly notes that the oppressive hierarchical class structure of Arthurian England is similar to the one he has observed and deplored in the American South, where the aristocratic slave owner stands above "'poor whites'" (*CY* 277), who stand above black slaves. Hank later draws an explicit comparison between a supposed medieval law concerning the identification of freemen and a similar southern law: "'The law . . . doth not require the claimant to prove ye are slaves, it requireth you to prove ye are *not.*' . . . This same infernal law had existed in our own South in my own time . . . [resulting in] hundreds of freemen . . . be[ing] sold into life-long slavery" (*CY* 320–21). The medieval version of this law is of course unhistorical, and most of the experiences suffered by the enslaved and disguised Hank and Arthur derive from Twain's reading of autobiographical narratives written by American slaves like Charles Ball.[9] Yet Twain is not being fanciful in drawing this comparison, instead highlighting the intimate linkage between the institution of slavery and a hierarchical class structure.

Less explicit is Twain's comparison of the medieval and the southern aristocrat, though Colonel Grangerford of *Huckleberry Finn* is frequently identified as a southern aristocrat whose bright contemporary armor is a "full suit from head to foot . . . so white it hurt your eyes to look at it" (*HF* 89). Yet the Grangerfords, with their tacky parlor and bad poetry, are, as Robert Lowrey points out, "obviously only imitations of a sophisticated culture whose feet of clay show through the facade" (20). Twain accuses Scott of encouraging southern aristocrats in their assumption of inherited privilege, as signaled by their appropriation of titles like Colonel, hyperbolically asserting that "it was [Scott] that created rank and caste down there, and also reverence for rank and caste" (*LOM* 266). Twain's attitude is manifested in *Connecticut Yankee* when Hank contemptuously notes that "in a country where they have ranks and castes, a man isn't ever a man, he is only part of a man" (*CY* 298). Twain deplored this assumption of inherited privilege because it inhibited "gentlemen" from adopting the work ethic, a failure that would necessarily undermine the progress of both the individual and American society.

Twain extended his criticism of southern aristocracy to its exaggerated sense of honor. This knightly construction derived from Scott resulted, according to Twain, in excessive violence, ranging from the relatively self-contained duel[10] to the feud and finally to the Civil War. The duel involved only two men, both governed by the "code duello" (an eighteenth-century Irish formalization of the medieval code). But Twain recognized that this code had degenerated since the days when knights jousted as a way of defending their honor. The much-discussed duel between Colonel Sherburn and Boggs in *Huckleberry Finn* bears witness to this degeneration, Sherburn proving himself a man of "honor" by cold-bloodedly killing the pathetic Boggs.

However violent such debased duels, feuds were far worse, continuing for years as a point of honor. Twain refers in *Life on the Mississippi* to two historical feuds, including in a footnote a newpaper account of the Mabry-O'Connor feud, perhaps because a paraphrase would be impossible to believe—the violence described is so ludicrously excessive that the account seems more like a burlesque than a news report—and offering his own account of the sixty-year Darnell-Watson feud, an episode of which serves as the source for the murder of Buck Grangerford in the fictional Grangerford-Shepherdson feud of *Huckleberry Finn*. Since participation in feuds is one of the marks of the aristocratic gentleman, only the "uncivilized" Huck, who is sickened by the violence, finds this behavior reprehensible. The Grangerford-Shepherdson feud, like most feuds, ends only when all the male relatives have been killed. Thus the "best" southern families engaged in a suicidal destruction that guaranteed not only their own deaths but the destruction of their aristocratic families and the enfeeblement of southern society—their actions ironically sanctioned by the very society they were destroying.

Southern society faced its most serious threat in the Civil War, which Twain addresses in a chapter of *Life on the Mississippi* ironically entitled "Southern Sports"—a foreshadowing of Hank Morgan's literal transformation of the medieval tournament into baseball, but to opposite effect. Although recognizing that the South's dependence on and promotion of slavery was a cause of the Civil War, Twain blamed more harshly the southern aristocracy's exaggerated sense of honor, love of a lost cause, militarism, and self-destructiveness—all traits leading to an unhealthy indulgence in violence. Given Twain's horrifying characterization of the Civil War, his indictment of Scott as "in great measure responsible for the war" (*LOM* 266) is particularly devastating.

Twain's objections to the medievalist impulse extended to its impact on language and literature. Characterizing the medievalist style as inflated, flowery, and dependent on tag phrases, he was most passionately critical of its regressive dependence on archaisms. Concerned about the limitations this style imposed on southern writers, Twain feared that these "student[s] of Sir Walter Scott" (*LOM* 261) were at a disadvantage when compared with progressive northern writers or those southern writers— such as Joel Chandler Harris, George Washington Cable, and Twain himself—who eschewed the medievalist style for the vernacular. Twain worried that the South was losing the literary battle to the North just as it had lost the Civil War and that adherence to the medievalist style was casting the South back into a literary Dark Ages.

Nineteenth-Century American Gilt

In spite of Twain's criticism of medievalism, his contrasting celebration of nineteenth-century American culture was not absolute. As in so many aspects of his life, he was split, recognizing serious flaws in contemporary American culture that were often the reverse of aspects he at other times celebrated. Despite his early commitment to the theory of historical progress, for example, Twain often felt that the human race was incapable of progress. He could not reconcile his optimism about the possibilities for historical progress with his basic pessimism about human nature,[11] a pessimism that Lawrence Berkove has labeled "deep-rooted," "desperate," and "always central to both his inner life and his art" (12). His utopianism thus ran afoul of his cynicism. Even Hank Morgan, Twain's apologist for historical progress as represented in nineteenth-century America, grows uncharacteristically depressed at the thought of "this plodding, sad pilgrimage, this pathetic drift between the eternities" (*CY* 161), bearing witness to what William Merrill Decker calls the "nineteenth-century 'crisis of historicism'—the recognition that history entails change without necessary progress, that it is not self-evidently, much less optimistically, teleological" (185).

In contrast to historical progressivism, Twain's cynicism about human nature, when logically extended, suggests a necessary similarity between the cultures of the nineteenth century and the Middle Ages. But Twain also recognized certain ways in which American culture was inferior to earlier cultures. Fearing many of the characteristics that he at other times celebrated, Twain acknowledged an ambivalence that signaled his ebbing faith in the nineteenth century, asserting in an 1887 letter to William Dean Howells that "the change is in *me*—in my vision of the evidences" (*Twain-Howells Letters* 276).

Twain's "vision of the evidences" about technology darkened considerably over time, his fifteen years of experience with the Paige typesetter profoundly influencing his changing attitudes. He alternated between euphoric optimism and despairing pessimism about the future of this machine—an enormously complex apparatus composed of over 18,000 separate parts, which he refused to market until it was absolutely perfect. His obsessive faith in the perfectibility of this machine was neither warranted nor rewarded, and the typesetter company was dissolved before any machines could be sold, leaving Twain emotionally exhausted and financially bankrupt.[12] The disastrous failure of the typesetter seemed to foretell the fate of the century, just as this machine had once seemed the symbol of nineteenth-century progress. Twain's initial faith in the machine, whose creation he once saw as a divine mystery, turned into despair and horror, his experiences and changing responses thus microcosmically recapitulating those of the culture at large in the face of the nineteenth-century technological developments that ultimately culminated in the horrors of World War I.

More than any of his other works, *Connecticut Yankee* is informed by Twain's experiences with the Paige typesetter. At the very time when he was beginning serious work on the novel (January and February 1886), he was also beginning his most serious involvement with the machine, no longer merely a backer but an active participant in its development and manufacture. Justin Kaplan points out that for Twain, the novel and typesetter were inexorably linked, "both tests of a perfectible world" (281). Twain bore witness to this connection by his repeated announcements concerning the projected conclusion of his novel: "I want to finish the day the machine finishes" (quoted by Kaplan 281). Not least among the points of connection is the fictional Hank's position as foreman at the Colt Arms Factory in Hartford, where the Paige typesetter was being constructed even as Twain wrote the novel at his Hartford home.

The completed novel, though it begins as a paean to nineteenth-century technology, ultimately manifests Twain's increasing suspicions of technology, suspicions that were justified by those imperfections of the machine that rendered its completion impossible. As a promoter and developer of the typesetter, Twain evinced moments of enthusiasm for the machine up to its very end, but as a writer he was far more perceptive about the limitations and failures of technology. The novel's apocalyptic conclusion, with its shift in tone and unsympathetic portrait of the heretofore generally sympathetic Hank, is a function of Twain's shifting attitudes about technology.[13] In the narrowest sense, the apocalyptic end results from the adaptation of modern technology for military purposes. In contrast to the medieval knights, who were trained in the art of chivalric war and thereby given a means to structure and thus contain the martial passion aesthetically (as Rougemont persuasively argues), the students at Hank's military academy are trained in the "science of war" (*cy* 231), later using "deadly scientific war-material" (*cy* 384) in their battle with the massed host of knights. Though this battle is in one sense the culmination of Hank's campaign to end knight-errantry, its excessive violence undermines the considerable validity the enterprise once had. Hank's earlier criticism about the militarism of chivalric knights is thrown into ironic relief by his decision to "blow up our civilisation [because] it was the right move—and the natural one; a military necessity, in the changed condition of things" (*cy* 386–87).

Modern technological war is thus naturalized in Hank's world as science displaces art, paradoxically resulting in an absurd rather than a rational end as civilization is destroyed to save it. To win the Battle of the Sand-Belt—which Hank persistently calls the "episode" (CY 393, 396) with unwarranted understatement, thereby foretelling the propagandistic abuses of language in modern wartime—he employs Gatling guns, dynamite, electrified fences, flooding apparatuses, trenches, and a mined no-man's-land, this appropriation of technology for military ends resulting in the massacre of 25,000 knights, whose horrific deaths destroy their integrity as individuals, reducing them to "homogeneous protoplasm, with alloys of iron and buttons" (CY 396). Unlike the heroic deaths these knights could have expected in chivalric combat, the ignoble deaths of modern war literally and metaphorically destroy their independent identities—their *franchesse,* to use the language of medieval chivalry.

Hank's victory is Pyrrhic, however, for the technological advances that enabled him to kill so many knights paradoxically lead to disaster for his army. As Hank's second-in-command notes elegiacally, in beautifully constructed antitheses, of the epidemic caused by the wall of the dead enclosing the camp: "We were in a trap . . . of our own making. If we stayed where we were, our dead would kill us; if we moved out of our defences, we should no longer be invincible. We had conquered; in turn we were conquered" (CY 406). In providing this scene Twain was not only looking back on the horrors of the Civil War but also foretelling the devastation of World War I's trench warfare, when blown-up bodies lay bloating in no-man's-land while the war of attrition ground on.

The implicit prophecy with which *Connecticut Yankee* ends is made explicit in "The Mysterious Stranger" when Satan foretells war's "progress," revealing a future filled with "slaughters more terrible in their destruction of life, more devastating in their engines of war" (MS 662). Prophetically, the last soldiers awake in Hank's camp are the "dynamo-watch" (CY 407). Where progress "enliven[ed]" (LOM 321) the citizens of St. Louis, some six years later in *Connecticut Yankee* it proves to be linked with death and destruction, just as the "electric surprise" (CY 34) of Hank's remark to "Mark Twain" at Warwick Castle in "A Word of Explanation" is a benign version of the electric surprise that Hank prepares for the knights who come into contact with his electrified fences.

Related to Twain's concern about the appropriation of technology for destructive ends was his recognition of the problems inherent in nineteenth-century capitalism, however much his business speculations implicated him. The period that Twain and Charles Dudley Warner named the "Gilded Age" in their novel of the same title—subtitled *A Tale of*

Today, as no other Twain novel could have been—provided plenty of evidence about the dangers of laissez-faire capitalism: monopolies stifling competition, credit unsupported by assets, speculation in place of production, economic panics, unemployment, corruption in government, and the emergence of robber barons. Twain later said of one such robber baron that "the people had *desired* money before this day, but [Jay Gould] taught them to fall down and worship it" (*Eruption* 77). The money worship of the Gilded Age transformed supposedly free men into wage slaves, as suggested by Daniel Beard's illustration for *Connecticut Yankee* (approved by Twain), in which the slavedriver is a portrait of Gould. Claiming that the motto "In God We Trust" had not been true since the Civil War, Twain argued that the frenzied excesses of postbellum capitalism had led Americans to trust instead in "the dollar" (*Eruption* 50), to which they became enslaved.

Given Twain's own obsessive desire for "the dollar," these critical pronouncements are somewhat poignant, signaling one more ambivalence that informs *Connecticut Yankee*. Although Hank's business successes are generally presented sympathetically, his unattractive reduction of various virtues to economics is called into question. Hank's criticism on economic grounds of what he calls the "trade" of knight-errantry clearly misses the point: "Knight-errantry is a most chuckle-headed trade . . . but I begin to see that there *is* money in it. . . . A successful whirl in the knight-errantry line—now what is it when you blow away the nonsense? . . . It's just a corner in pork. . . . But when the market breaks, in a knight-errantry whirl, and every knight in the pool passes in his checks, what have you got for assets? . . . Give me pork, every time" (*CY* 172–73). When Hank refuses to quest for the Holy Grail because there is "no money" (*CY* 97) in it, he reduces to the economic all the spiritual, moral, and aesthetic virtues to which chivalry aspired, unconsciously revealing his own "chuckle-headed[ness]." As Henry Nash Smith points out, the "deliberate contrast between the Yankee's philistine commercialism and the idealism of the Grail quest" signals that Twain "holds back from full identification with the narrator" (*Fable* 52).

Even more pernicious is Hank's impact on the economic system of Arthurian England, resulting in the transformation of the Round Table— the locus of chivalry and therefore morality—into a stock board where seats are bought and sold on speculation instead of earned by valorous deeds and where shady dealings lead to the civil war that erupts in Arthur's kingdom, this "modern improvement" (*CY* 379) releasing destructive forces with disastrous consequences. Hank's actions are again called into question when he economically capitalizes on the medieval religious impulse, using a hermit's movement at prayer to run a sewing machine on which he manufactures shirts, which, in a stroke of marketing genius, he then sells to pilgrims. Hank's exaggerated insensitivity and his pride in this capitalist enterprise serve as an oblique commentary on the exploitation of workers in nineteenth-century sweatshops.

Yet despite Twain's sympathetic responses to the worker, a sympathy dictated by his celebration of the American democratic system, his works also manifest a scorn, fear, even hatred of the common man. Again Twain's superficial celebration of an aspect of nineteenth-century American culture is qualified by criticism, most notably in *The Prince and the Pauper, Huckleberry Finn,* "The Mysterious Stranger," and *Connecticut Yankee,* where strikingly similar scenes of mobs and mob violence are presented. The direction in which Twain's sympathies lie is evident from his hyperbolically disgusting description in *The Prince and the Pauper* of one such mob, worth citing in full:

> Around [the fire], and lit weirdly up by the red glare, lolled and sprawled the motliest company of tattered gutter scum and ruffians, of both sexes. . . . There were huge, stalwart men, brown with exposure, long-haired, and clothed in fantastic rags; there were middle-sized youths of truculent countenance, and similarly clad; there were blind mendicants with patched or bandaged eyes, crippled ones with wooden legs and crutches; . . . some of the females were hardly grown girls, some were at prime, some were old and wrinkled hags, and all were loud, brazen, foul-mouthed; and all soiled and slatternly; there were three sore-faced babies; there were a couple of starveling curs. (*PP* 109)

Physical deformity, sexual promiscuity, drunken revelry, and filth characterize this hellish scene. Some sympathy is briefly generated by a short sociological explanation in which the allegorically named Yokel indicts the larger society that supports slavery and therefore devalues the worth of the baseborn individual, however worthy his character, but this sympathy is curiously undermined because *only* Yokel seems worthy of it. The rest of the mob is composed of "base and brutal outlaws" (*PP* 121) who rob not from the rich but from those almost as poor as they. The pages of the novel are filled with "mangy mob[s]" (*PP* 194), "dirty mob[s]" (*PP* 169), "roaring masses of humanity" (*PP* 174), "degraded mob[s]" (*PP* 171), "jeering crowd[s]" (*PP* 26)—all of which threaten sympathetic characters (notably Tom Canty and Edward) and by extension the reader who identifies with them. The omniscient narrator's pejorative adjectives shape the reader's response, as does Miles Hendon's characterization of one mob as "base kennel-rats" (*PP* 65), which confirms Edward's judgment of them as a "pack of unmannerly curs" (*PP* 65). Their subsequent attack on Miles en masse testifies to the justice of these bestial epithets.

The famous mob scene in *Huckleberry Finn* where the aristocratic Colonel Sherburn is attacked has garnered much critical attention because of the inconsistent characterization of Sherburn, whose earlier murder of Boggs marked him as a villain but whose bravery before the mob demands admiration, the same admiration to which Twain later refers in a posthumously published article, "The United States of Lyncherdom" (written in 1901): "No mob has any sand in the presence of a man known to be splendidly brave" (37). Like Twain, Sherburn pointedly distinguishes between a real "*man*" and the "masked cowards" who compose a mob, granting ironically that a mob is "brave enough to tar and feather poor friendless cast-out women" (*HF* 123). Evidence of such "bravery" is later provided when another mob tars and feathers the defenseless Duke and Dauphin, American confidence men disguised as European royalty, in yet another version of Twain's archetypal change-of-clothes scene. Though Huck has borne uncomfortable witness to this pair's evil deeds, he recognizes the greater baseness of the mob's action.

Huck's double in "The Mysterious Stranger" is the sensitive Theodor, who reluctantly joins a mob whose scapegoat, "a born lady" (*MS* 664) unhistorically acting the part of nineteenth-century philanthropist to the common people, is stoned and lynched in front of her daughter. In *Connecticut Yankee*, another mob stones and burns a woman, also in front of her daughters. Twain employs the sentimental idealization of motherhood to emphasize the horror of the mobs' actions and the poignancy of the women's fate. Though sympathy is generated at other points in *Connecticut Yankee* for the plight of the individual common man in a society that oppresses him, the novel also manifests a fear of the common man en masse. In Twain's fictional worlds, the "base scum of [the] village" (*CY* 307) take any opportunity to turn on one of their own.

Twain's critical presentations of mob violence manifest his ambivalence about the common man, a figure typically celebrated by nineteenth-century American writers but described by Twain as often cowardly and weak, violent, disloyal to his fellows, and eager to follow any powerful leader. Twain thus gives voice to his latent fear that American democracy might at some time degenerate into mob rule because of inherent weaknesses in the common man and the political system based on him. The widespread riots associated with the national railroad strikes of 1877 served as cautionary evidence for Twain that the American worker was capable of a violence that could disrupt American society, perhaps resulting in a revolutionary overthrow of the government (see *To Mrs. Fair-*

banks 208–9), and Twain's subsequent descriptions of fictional mobs bear a remarkable resemblance to contemporary newspaper descriptions of the riots, which frequently imaged the strikers as criminals and animals.

The Romances of Sir Mark Twain, Duke of Hartford

Twain's ambivalence about the changes wrought by nineteenth-century progress increasingly manifested itself as a distaste for the urbanized and industrialized America that developed during the postbellum period, his celebrations of this period alternating with expressions of his desire to escape it. Most often noted is Twain's nostalgia for childhood and the antebellum Hannibal of his own childhood. More recently, critics have concentrated on Twain's desire to transcend history itself[14] by escaping into a timeless zone that often takes the form of a world of myth.[15] These two forms of escape from the present are joined by the medievalist impulse, which is typically overlooked not only because it runs counter to Twain's voiced opposition to medievalism but also because it embodies the more oft-noted forms of escape, Twain's medievalist impulse expressing his desire to escape into the recent personal past of childhood and the transcendently present mythic moment.

Twain's self-conscious hostility to medievalism disguises his lifelong fascination with it, a Clemens family legacy. In an 1899 autobiographical sketch, Twain cited his Anglo-Saxon antecedents, noting that he was descended through his father from Gregory Clemens (identified as a judge who condemned King Charles I to death), and through his mother from the aristocratic "Lamptons of Durham."[16] This family history itself signals the division in Twain's attitude. Descendant of a Puritan regicide and the loyalist earl of Durham, Twain carried in his blood the conflict that tormented him.

Twain's mother, Jane, and his brother Orion were particularly affected by their supposed aristocratic lineage. With his mother's encouragement, Orion spent much of his adult life vainly waiting to realize his fortune from the sale of land in Tennessee that his father, John Marshall Clemens (known as the "Squire"), had left to the family. Twain grew disgusted at this waste of his brother's time and talents, ultimately satirizing him in *The Gilded Age* and *The American Claimant* (1892) as Colonel Beriah Sellers, the ever-cheerful but completely ineffectual speculator cum claimant to the earldom of Rossmore.[17] Justin Kaplan identifies Sellers as an "American archetype," a "dreamer of great dreams that don't come true" (165). Sellers is thus a comic antecedent of F. Scott Fitzgerald's tragic Gatsby.

But for all Twain's disgust at his brother's pretensions, he whimsically considered that he himself might be a titled aristocrat, as he recorded in his notebook: "'Suppose I should live to be 92 and just as I was dying a messenger should enter and say—' 'You are become the Earl of Durham—' interrupted Livy" (*Notebook* 158), thereby demonstrating what he repeatedly called "mental telegraphy" in his notebook and several essays ("Mental Telegraphy" [1891], "Mental Telegraphy Again" [1895]). This fantasy—shared here with Olivia but in a deeper sense with Orion— suggests that Twain's repeated satires of Orion served as a defensive psychological mechanism distancing Twain from his own identification with the aristocracy. It also explains the affectionate nature of these satires, for Sellers is a strangely attractive figure who was enormously popular with the nineteenth-century public.

Though Twain's feelings about his aristocratic background were mixed, his attitude toward his Virginia ancestry was less so. Elmo Howell notes that Twain "traced his lineage back to Virginia and spent his formative years in a society which aspired to the standards derived from [Virginia]" (1). Twain's close friend William Dean Howells specifies in his memoir *My Mark Twain* that Missouri was marked by "the peculiar social civilization of the older South [that is, Virginia] from which his native State was settled" (149).

Twain gave fictional form to Missouri's society in the setting of *The Tragedy of Pudd'nhead Wilson* (1894). The leading citizens of Dawson's Landing are all members of the First Families of Virginia, who conscientiously "ke[ep] up [the] traditions" of their "old Virginian ancestry" (*PW* 23), traditions that are largely rendered unironically, even with regard to the duel. Virginia's aristocratic traditions powerfully influenced life in such western "frontier town[s]" (*PW* 91), resulting in a construction of the western cowboy as a contemporary incarnation of the knight, as Hank attests in *Connecticut Yankee* when he refers to knights as "cow-boys" (*CY* 136) and then transforms the medieval tournament into a rodeo at which he triumphs by means of horse, lasso, and revolver. Owen Wister later made explicit the connection between Virginia and the West in his novel *The Virginian* (1902), which recounts the Wyoming adventures of a knightly cowboy, revealing the cultural transformation of medieval knight into Virginia cavalier into western cowboy, a transformation of which Twain's literary heir Ernest Hemingway was particularly aware, given his correspondence with Wister.

Though the Clemens family moved west, it maintained its link with the southern aristocracy as a marker of superiority, Twain making clear in his biographical sketch that his family was "blood-pure and proud gentry" (Kaplan 356), their superiority by birth confirmed by their position in the southern feudal hierarchy since they then owned land and slaves. Yet Twain was bitterly aware as a child that the family fortunes were in decline, a decline that he planned to reverse. After his first important literary success, the publication of "The Notorious Jumping Frog of Calaveras County" (1865), he moved into an elegant hotel in New York City that he described in a letter to his family as "full of 'bloated aristocrats,'" noting, "I'm just one of *them* kind myself" (quoted by Kaplan 32), this single statement manifesting the two poles of Twain's attitude toward the aristocracy—the identification just as important as the ironic qualification.

Between August 1872 and July 1907, Twain spent about eleven years abroad, largely in Europe. His first extended stay, during 1872, occurred after his initial literary triumphs, and he was delighted at his warm reception by the English nobility. Though he had arrived in England planning to write a satire on English life, he chose upon his return to write *The Gilded Age,* a satire about contemporary American life and government. England, as Kaplan suggests, "offered him for the first time a baseline by which he could measure his discontent with his own country" (154). As *The Gilded Age* makes clear, Twain was particularly discontented with America's system of government. Though President Grant, who makes only cameo appearances in the novel, is never directly criticized, his administration is revealed to be riddled by corruption and plagued by scandal. In an 1877 letter to Mary Fairbanks's daughter Mollie, Twain refers to his distrust of the political judgment of the masses, who repeatedly elect unworthy politicians like the fictional Senator Dilworthy, rendering statesmen like the allegorically named Senator Noble obsolete: "You may easily suppose I hate all shades & forms of republican government. . . . Representative government, with a sharply restricted suffrage, is just as good as a Consitutional monarchy with a virtuous & powerful aristocracy; but with an unrestricted suffrage it ought to (perish, execrable) perish because it is founded in wrong & is weak & bad & tyrannical" (*To Mrs. Fairbanks* 208– 9). Though Twain later supported universal suffrage, these fierce objections reveal his ambivalence about democracy.

Twain was particularly attracted by England's long history, writing to Mary Fairbanks in 1873 during his second extended visit to England: "God knows I wish we had some of England's reverence for the old & great" (*To Mrs. Fairbanks* 175). Twain was particularly impressed by the cathedral town of York, which reminded him, as he reported in an 1873 letter, of "the heart of Crusading times and the glory of English chivalry and romance" (*Letters* 1:208). Twain was also fascinated by the aristocracy that contemporaneously personified medieval history. Having long studied the list of names in the British peerage, Twain put this hobby to good use during a visit with a squire named Broom, as he recounted with obvious relish: "On his table cutlery I noticed . . . a sprig of broom. . . . I knew that the broom-sprig (plant-a-genet) was the cognizance & gave name to the Plantagenet Kings, & so I just asked him facetiously if he wasn't a Plantagenet—but bless you he didn't notice the facetiousness of it, & simply said he *was*. . . . Why it had all the seeming of hob-nobbing with the Black Prince in the flesh!" (*To Mrs. Fairbanks* 167). Just as Twain's irony about the earl of Durham and the "bloated aristocrats" was accompanied by identification, his "facetiousness" here does not disguise excitement and admiration. In later life, Twain's aristocratic identification was similarly revealed by his nickname—Howells, Cable, and his personal secretary, Isabel Lyon, all calling him "King."

Twain's period of what Howells called "Anglomania" (13) was most pronounced during the 1870s, but its effect continued in his later life.[18] While Twain and his family made various extended trips to Europe over the years, by 1871 they had taken up semipermanent residence in Hartford, where Twain commissioned the design and construction of an elaborate neo-Gothic house decorated in part by Tiffany, a medievalist showpiece whose furniture and mantelpieces—carved with gargoyles, sphinxes, and griffins—were also neo-Gothic. The medieval effect was further emphasized in 1880 when Twain, who joined the rest of Hartford in celebrating Grant's visit, decorated his property with shields, heraldic devices, and two figures in complete armor. Shortly thereafter, while on a disastrous visit to Boston at the invitation of the *Atlantic,* he wrote Olivia a letter referring to himself and Howells as the dukes of Hartford and Cambridge, respectively. The title that Twain claimed enabled him both to satirize the pretensions of the Boston peerage by whom he felt scorned and to escape into a "reactionary fantasy" (Kaplan 186) that assuaged his hurt feelings.

Just as the medievalist impulse in Twain's life was complicated, and for many critics completely disguised, by the irony that signaled his ambivalence, it is sometimes difficult to perceive in his work, but the obsessive attention that he paid to medievalism is an important index of his interest. Twain refers at some length to medieval history, literature, and architecture in such works of "journalism" as *The Innocents Abroad* and *A Tramp Abroad* (1880), sometimes even recounting medieval legends and tales. The Middle Ages provide the setting for several short stories (among them, "A Medieval Romance" [1870]), one short and obsessively reworked novel ("The Mysterious Stranger," subtitled "A Romance"), and three novels (*Connecticut Yankee, The Prince and the Pauper,* and *Joan of Arc*). Twain spoke of the latter two novels with particular pleasure, describing *The Prince and the Pauper* as "a historical tale, of 300 years ago, [written] simply for the love of it—for it will appear without my name—such grave & stately work being considered by the world to be above my proper level" (*To Mrs. Fairbanks* 218) and describing *Joan of Arc* in strikingly similar terms as "private & not for print, . . . written for love & not for lucre, & to entertain the family with" (*To Mrs. Fairbanks* 269). In both cases Twain's motive for composition was love of his subject. His comments about *Connecticut Yankee* in an 1886 letter, though less emotionally charged, are also relevant: "I am writing it for posterity only; my posterity: my great grandchildren. It is to be my holiday amusement for six days every summer the rest of my life. Of course I do not expect to publish it" (*To Mrs. Fairbanks* 258). In all three cases he attempts to deny the relationship between his public persona as humorist "Mark Twain" and the novel, as though this identification would trivialize these works—one of which, *The Prince and the Pauper,* his wife and daughters' favorite; the other, *Joan of Arc,* his own unlikely favorite.

In addition to an overt dependence on medievalism for subject matter and setting, many of Twain's works "abound," according to Louise Schleiner, "in the stock motifs of medieval romance, which often serve as structurally essential elements of his plots" (330). Schleiner points out the prevalence of aristocratic foundlings, interchanged babies, separated twins, identity quests, lofty ladies, errant knights, royal progresses, tests, wilderness trials, forest hermits, and other-world strangers. Twain's sources for these motifs and plot conventions were medieval and Renaissance romances and nineteenth-century medievalist literature. Careful documentation of Twain's reading leaves little doubt as to his familiarity with such texts. Perhaps his earliest acquaintance was with Cundall's version of the Robin Hood legends, *Robin Hood and His Merry Foresters.*[19] Among Twain's favorite boyhood books, ironically, was Scott's *Ivanhoe,*[20] as well as other popular melodramatic romance novels, pirate tales, and Gothic magazine fiction. In *Innocents Abroad,* he refers to "those gorgeous knights we read about in romances of the Crusades" (*IA* 396), and a later comment suggests that he first read these romances[21] as a boy: "The plain old sword of that stout Crusader, Godfrey of Bulloigne . . . stirs within a man every memory of the Holy Wars that has been sleeping in his brain for years" (*IA* 563). Though some irony informs the long passage about the sword that follows, Twain clearly retains much admi-

ration for "these splendid heroes of romance," among whom he lists
"great Richard of the Lion Heart" (*IA* 563)—a figure who is criticized at
other points in Twain's works.

There is much evidence that Twain read other works that contributed
to his knowledge of the Middle Ages, though it is sometimes difficult to
date his first acquaintance.[22] The most important of these was Malory's
Le Morte Darthur. It is generally accepted that Twain was first introduced
to Malory's work in December 1884 by George Washington Cable, with
whom he was browsing in a bookstore during a lecture tour. Both Twain
and Cable later referred to the incident, and Twain's designated biographer, Albert Bigelow Paine, provided a dramatized account: " 'Cable,'
he said, 'do you know anything about this book, the Arthurian legends of
Sir Thomas Malory, *Morte Arthure?*' Cable answered: 'Mark, that is one
of the most beautiful books in the world. Let me buy it for you. You will
love it more than any book you ever read' " (790).

Alan Gribben notes, however, that Twain's first acquaintance with
Malory's Arthurian characters probably occurred somewhat earlier in a
nineteenth-century version edited for children by Sidney Lanier, *The
Boy's King Arthur, Being Sir Thomas Malory's History of King Arthur and
His Knights of the Round Table* (1880; see "Master Hand" 34). Two copies
were purchased—on 18 November 1880 and 13 December 1880—by a
member of the Clemens household, Gribben noting that Twain's "habits
of reading aloud to his family and of perusing his daughters' book
collections . . . lend significance to these acquisitions" ("Master Hand"
34). At Twain's death, his personal library contained another of Lanier's
Arthurian popularizations, *The Boy's Mabinogion, Being the Earliest Welsh
Tales of King Arthur in the Famous Red Book of Hergest* (1881). The sheer
amount of literature that Twain read suggests this period's appeal for him,
since "someone who keeps Malory at hand for bedtime reading does not
do so in order to torture himself," as Louise Schleiner commonsensically
points out (331). Indeed Twain wrote his daughter Susy in 1884 that the
Morte Darthur "is the quaintest and sweetest of all books" (quoted by
Emerson 155), and he told Paine in 1906 that it was "one of the most
beautiful things ever written in English" (1320). When asked in 1888 to list
his favorite authors, Twain cited Malory's *Morte Darthur* in a list of nine
authors or works (Lauber, *Inventions* 120). It was this work that served as
the inspiration for *Connecticut Yankee,* and as Robert H. Wilson documents, the novel evinces many "straightforward borrowings" (185) from
Malory, including personal and place names, incidents, archaic diction,
and even extended quotations. Though Hank, as Wilson points out,

sometimes criticizes weaknesses in the medieval literary techniques—prolixity, plot repetitions, and flat characters—he also acknowledges its peculiar beauty—simplicity, quaintness, and dignity.

Shortly after reading the version of the *Morte Darthur* provided by Cable, Twain recorded a note in his journal that was the germ of his novel: "Dream of being a knight errant in armor in the Middle Ages. Have the notions and habits of thought of the present day mixed with the necessities of that" (*Notebook* 171). Initially conceived as a good-humored burlesque, the developing novel was carefully distinguished from harsh satire in a revealing letter that Twain wrote to Mary Fairbanks in 1886:

> The story isn't a satire peculiarly, it is more especially a *contrast*. It merely exhibits under high lights, the daily life of the time & that of to-day; & necessarily the bringing them into this immediate juxtaposition emphasizes the salients of both. . . . Of course in my story I shall leave unsmirched & unbelittled the great & beautiful *characters* drawn by the master hand of old Malory. . . .—I am only after the *life* of that day, that is all: to picture it; to try to get into it; to see how it feels & seems. (*To Mrs. Fairbanks* 257–58)

These comments must be read with an eye to Twain's special relationship with Mary Fairbanks, but however much he may have been attempting here to assuage her fears about his tendency to lapse into dreaded vulgarity, Twain reiterated the gist of these comments in a variety of other contexts. Nine months earlier he had written to Charles L. Webster, his nephew by marriage and factotum, that he had "saturated [him]self with the atmosphere of the day & the subject" before beginning the story, "whose scene is laid far back in the twilight of tradition" (*Business Man* 355). In such comments, which construct the Middle Ages not as the Dark Ages but as the "twilight of tradition," there is no indication of the ironic distance and sense of superiority that the satirist must maintain toward his subject. Instead, as James D. Williams points out, "even [when] the novel [was] half finished, Mark Twain insisted that 'fun' was its primary purpose and planned to accompany it with a free copy of Malory" ("Revision" 289). For Twain, the "fun" was effected in part by an imaginary identification with the figure of the knight, whose armor and life he "tr[ied] to get into" by the act of writing—an act that he later apostrophized as "literary dreaming" in the context of writing *Joan of Arc* (*To Mrs. Fairbanks* 269), thereby returning full circle to the "dream of being a knight errant" that inspired *Connecticut Yankee*.

Given the obvious criticisms of the Middle Ages that occur in the completed novel, critics have tended to give Twain's comments short shrift, accusing him of exaggerated ingenuousness about his motives. But though Twain's attitudes about the novel shifted during composition, clearly one of his motives was to provide a backhanded tribute to the Arthurian legends. The tonal shifts between satire and celebration are thus a function of Twain's dual motives and dual perspectives.[23] For Twain, there were two Middle Ages: the historical period, marked by the social, political, and religious evils that he abhorred, and the mythic period, whose beauties he admired. His tone at any given moment is dependent on how he is envisioning and therefore constructing the Middle Ages.[24] Though even here Twain is not absolutely consistent, his harshest criticisms are generally reserved for aspects of the historical culture of the Middle Ages, and his gentle burlesques and explicit celebrations are generally reserved for the mythic world represented in this novel by Arthurian legends. Twain "appears to hate the reality of the Middle Ages but to love the ideality of it," as Lesley Kordecki points out (339).

Twain's dual vision of the Middle Ages is embodied in the very structure of *Connecticut Yankee*. It begins with an authoritative preface by the author Mark Twain (specifically dated "Hartford, July 21, 1889") attesting to the "historical" quality of the "ungentle laws and customs touched upon in this tale" (*CY* 29). But the novel proper begins with a frame story in the manner of dream visions, to which medieval genre *Connecticut Yankee* is closely related,[25] in which the character "Mark Twain" (the narrator of the frame story) and Hank Morgan meet while touring Warwick Castle. The scenes composing the frame story are concerned less with historical detail than imagery of enchantment, magic, reverie, and dream. Hank seems not merely from another historical era but from another ontological realm, and his influence is so strong that "Twain" (it is tempting here to identify narrator and author) is imaginatively transported there in a significant early passage: "As he [Hank] talked along, softly, pleasantly, flowingly, he seemed to drift away imperceptibly out of this world and time, and into some remote era and old forgotten country; and so he gradually wove such a spell about me that I seemed to move among the spectres and shadows and dust and mould of a grey antiquity, holding speech with a relic of it! . . . He spoke of . . . [the] great names of the Table Round—and how old, old, unspeakably old, and faded and dry and musty and ancient he came to look as he went on" (*CY* 33).

Hank's story, with its echo of the "once upon a time" opening of fairy tales, seems to have magical properties, transforming both him and his listener, "Mark Twain," and inviting the reader to suspend his disbelief. The initial piling up of mellifluous adverbs has a hypnotic quality, effecting a change that is both psychological and physical. The parallel massing of adjectives that ends this passage offers a double meaning, emphasizing Hank's literal chronological age while also revealing his historical identification with the Middle Ages. The effect of the "spell" lasts even after Hank's initial disappearance, "Twain" spending his evening "steeped in a dream of the olden time" (CY 34). He purposely extends this mood of dream and reverie by reading another magical narrative, "old Sir Thomas Malory's enchanting book" (CY 34), which affects "Twain" in the same way as Hank's "spell." Drinking the book in "for a night-cap," feeding at its "rich feast of prodigies and adventures," and breathing in "the fragrance of its obsolete names," "Twain" consumes and inhales the Middle Ages, and "dream[s] again" (CY 34). The Middle Ages are now part of "Twain," just as Hank is part of the Middle Ages. Indeed Hank reappears to "Twain" at the magical hour shortly after midnight, as if summoned by "Twain"'s reading of Malory's "How Sir Launcelot Slew Two Giants, and Made a Castle Free" (itself included in the text). After four whiskeys, the intoxicated Hank in effect takes up where Malory left off, describing his own capture by Sir Kay, who, as Malory described, was dressed in Launcelot's armor.

Surprisingly, given the portrait drawn of him as a pragmatist, Hank at this point reveals himself to be an artist, offering "Twain" the book he has written about his experiences. An adaptation of Malory's Arthurian legends, this book is a palimpsest, written on top of "old monkish legends" (CY 38). Not a careful history but art—legends upon legends upon legends—brings to life the mythic world of medieval England. The aesthetic and mythic impulses are thus united in the dream vision (introduced by a Daniel Beard illustration captioned "The Tale of the Lost Land") that forms the core of the novel.

Though Hank offers a quasi-scientific explanation for his presence in the mythic world, the magical nature of the transformation is not disguised. When Hank collapses at the Colt Arms Factory, "the world went out in darkness" (CY 37), but upon awakening he finds himself in a mythic landscape that is "beautiful and broad" (CY 37), "soft [and] reposeful" (CY 41), and "lovely as a dream" (CY 41), Hank thus describing himself more truly than he knows as "mov[ing] along as one in a dream" (CY 41). Such lyrical moments repeatedly punctuate the narrative, even at the least likely points.[26] In "Slow Torture," a chapter dedicated to a gentle burlesque of knight-errantry (focusing on the discomfort of wearing armor), the mythic landscape is invoked in a significant passage: "Straight off, we were in the country. It was most lovely and pleasant in those sylvan solitudes. . . . From hilltops we saw fair green valleys lying spread out below, with streams winding through them, and island-groves of trees here and there, . . . and beyond the valleys we saw the ranges of hills, blue with haze, stretching away in billowy perspective to the horizon, with at wide intervals a dim fleck of white or grey on a wave-summit, which we knew was a castle" (*CY* 118). Like Huck Finn on the Mississippi or Mark Twain on "the shining river . . . [that is] as tranquil and reposeful as dreamland, and has nothing this-worldly about it" (*LOM* 329), Hank has "left the world behind" (*CY* 118) and entered a mythic realm that brings him peace and contentment, a place of healing where he can recover from the wounds inflicted by nineteenth-century American society.

The comparison of Huck and Hank is peculiarly apt, given the water motif that informs this passage:[27] most notably, the castles imaged as flecks of foam on a sea of haze, but also the prevalence of literal streams and metaphoric "island-groves" of trees. Like Huck and Jim "drifting down the big still river" (*HF* 55), Hank and Sandy "crossed broad natural lawns sparkling with dew" (*CY* 118). And as Hank and Sandy travel through this mythic landscape, they become mythic figures—again like Huck and Jim—"mov[ing] like spirits, the cushioned turf giving out no sound of footfall . . . [and] dream[ing] along through glades in a mist of green light" (*CY* 118). But just as Huck and Jim must leave the Mississippi at regular intervals for the "sivilized" shore, so must Hank and Sandy leave the mythic landscape, "swing[ing] again into the glare" (*CY* 118) of reality where they immediately confront personal and social problems.

Within *Connecticut Yankee,* Hank and Sandy are not alone in their dual functions as mythic and realistic characters, and the consistent shifts in characterization may explain a troubling shift in tone. King Arthur is perhaps the most telling example of these shifts. He is presented both as a medieval man—an uncompassionate aristocrat, ineffectual leader, and cuckolded husband—and as a mythic figure of Arthurian legend. In his role as representative medieval ruler, he is satirized mercilessly; in his role as mythic figure, he is celebrated extravagantly. This split leads to certain contradictions, Hank at one point slighting Arthur's intelligence—"He wasn't a very heavy weight, intellectually" (*CY* 263)—but a few short pages earlier praising it—"It was a wise head" (*CY* 257). In another sense, however, no real contradiction results, for Hank's attitudes are governed by whether Twain is constructing Arthur as a medieval and thus necessarily ignorant man or a mythic and thus necessarily transcendent figure.

Arthur is praised most extravagantly in the chapter "The Smallpox Hut." Up to this point in the travels of Hank and the disguised king, Arthur has largely acted the part of buffoon, repeatedly getting into trouble from which Hank must extricate him. But suddenly he rises to surprising heights of nobility, risking his life against Hank's advice to aid the helpless: "It were shame that a king should know fear, and shame that belted knight should withhold his hand where be such as need succour. Peace, I will not go [from the hut]. It is you who must go" (CY 266). The very sentences—balanced, symmetrical, marked by parallelism and repetition—signal that Arthur is now speaking as a figure of myth, especially since his usual rhetoric is markedly different—so turgid, convoluted, and "lubberly" that it exacts "distinct distress" (CY 311) from his audiences. And Hank, recognizing that Arthur is absolutely firm when acting on the basis of "his knightly honour" (CY 266), which specifically requires knights "to defend widows and orphans and help the poor" (Scaglione 71), watches with admiration and even reverence as the king bears the infected daughter to her dying mother: "Here was heroism at its last and loftiest possibility, its utmost summit; this was challenging death in the open field unarmed. . . . He was great, now; sublimely great" (CY 267–68). Hank pronounces Arthur's nobility not in his typical vernacular style but in a rhetoric that identifies him with Arthur, as though the very witnessing of this scene has ennobled him.

Immediately after this incident, however, Arthur disconcertingly shifts from a hero who is larger than life to a man all too limited by the constraints of medieval culture. Upon overhearing several peasants discussing their escape from a cruel noble, his only impulse is to return them to their master, this shift demonstrating the cruelty and selfishness of the medieval aristocracy: "[Arthur] was born so, educated so, his veins were full of ancestral blood that was rotten with this sort of unconscious brutality" (CY 272). Yet the polemical point is murky since it seems to blame both blood and training, a confusion that frequently recurs in Twain's work, most disturbingly in *Pudd'nhead Wilson*.

Despite Hank's harsh criticisms, however, he is ultimately most affected by Arthur's heroic stature. After the two are rescued from execution, Hank is compelled to admit that "there *is* something peculiarly grand about the gait and bearing of a king" (CY 352), even when he is dressed in rags, this acknowledgment undermining the point made earlier in *Connecticut Yankee* and also in *The Prince and the Pauper* that in medieval society it is clothing, not merit, that makes the king. When Arthur is killed in a battle with Mordred several years later, it is not the man limited by his medieval environment but the larger-than-life Arthur, the mythic hero, whom Hank mourns: "It had not seemed to me that any wound could be mortal to him" (CY 384). This reverent tone is consistent with Twain's earlier comments to Mary Fairbanks in an 1886 letter:

I shall hope that under my hand Sir Galahad will still remain the divinest
spectre that one glimpses among the mists & twilights of Dreamland
across the wastes of the centuries; & Arthur keep his sweetness & his purity, & Launcelot abide & continue 'the kindest man that ever strake the
sword,' yet 'the sternest knight to his mortal foe that ever put spear in the
rest;' & I should grieve indeed if the final disruption of the Round Table,
& the extinction of its old tender & gracious friendships, & that last
battle—the Battle of the Broken Hearts, it might be called—should lose
their pathos & their tears through my handling. (*To Mrs. Fairbanks* 258)

It is most telling that the mythic world gains the last word. *Connecticut
Yankee* concludes not with a final polemic against the historical culture of
the Middle Ages, an acknowledgment of the limitations of modern technology, or even a celebration of nineteenth-century America, but with an
invocation of a mythic world in which "all is well, all is peace, and I
[Hank] am happy again" (*CY* 409). In the delirium of his final illness,
Hank rejoices at finding himself once more at Camelot: "A bugle? . . . . It
is the king! The drawbridge, there! Man the battlements!—turn out
the—" (*CY* 410). Maria Ornella Marotti's discussion of Twain's experiments in the genre of fantasy is relevant here, for she argues that "Twain's
fantastic is an exploration of the powers of the imagination that leads
eventually to the assertion of the power of dream over reality" (70).
With regard to the complicated ending of *Connecticut Yankee*—Hank's
dream vision "Tale of the Lost Land" is followed first by "A Postscript by
Clarence" and then by a "Final P.S. by M.T." in perfect symmetry with
the opening structural layers of the "Preface" and "A Word of Explanation"—Marotti rightly notes that "the return to the waking state in the
frame leaves the reader with no doubts as to the real nature of the events
portrayed in it" but that "what could be regarded as the dismissal of the
unreal proves to be its opposite [since] the Yankee is unable to adjust
himself to the reality of his time, . . . the language of dream reveal[ing] an
unsuspected power" (101). Dream triumphs over reality; myth triumphs
over history; Camelot triumphs over not only the Middle Ages but postbellum America; and "Twain" triumphs over Twain.

Twain's perspective similarly shifts between the mythic and the historically realistic in his other two medieval novels, his preface to *The
Prince and the Pauper* explicitly foregrounding these two ways of interpreting the Middle Ages: "I will set down a tale as it was told to me by
one who had it of his father, which latter had it of *his* father, this last
having in like manner had it of *his* father, and so on, back and still back,
three hundred years and more, the fathers transmitting it to the sons and

so preserving it. It may be history, it may be only a legend, a tradition. It may have happened, it may not have happened; but it *could* have happened" (*PP* 13). Like history, *The Prince and the Pauper* includes written documents and describes historical people, places, and events; like myth, its source is the oral tradition, and it is informed by motifs and characters typical of romance. *Joan of Arc* is similarly a mixture of history and myth, partaking of the literate and oral traditions with a protagonist who is both a historical personage and a Catholic saint.

In celebrating the mythic figure of the knight embodied in King Arthur and others, Twain granted this figure a superiority that he denied at other times. Yet Twain was attracted by the knightly virtues, particularly admiring the knight's individualism and bravery. As in courtly romance, Twain's knightly figures are set into relief against the "despised *vilain*" who are their "antithesis" (Scaglione 123). In *The Prince and the Pauper*, the aristocratic Miles Hendon, dubbed knight by the disguised Edward,[28] single-handedly defends the prince from mobs. And Edward, like King Arthur when standing on the executioner's scaffold, "defie[s] the mob right royally" (*PP* 65) though unable to overcome it physically. Twain provides a female version of the knight in Joan of Arc, who not only leads her army to victory in battle but also withstands the psychological tortures inflicted on her by a mob of ecclesiasts. When Colonel Sherburn of *Huckleberry Finn* turns back the Arkansas mob, he behaves as a nineteenth-century version of these knights, acting on the basis of the same code. When the Grangerfords fight another "clan of aristocracy" (*HF* 90), they too act on the basis of the knightly code, which inculcates a desire for death before dishonor, love of adventure, and respect for ritualized behavior and fine manners. And however much the Grangerford-Shepherdson feud is called into question, the Grangerfords themselves, and particularly Colonel Grangerford, are granted a measure of respect. Despite the comic exaggeration of their names, so are *Pudd'nhead Wilson*'s Judge York Leicester Driscoll ("fine and just and generous," "respected, esteemed, and beloved" [*PW* 23]), Percy Northumberland Driscoll, Pembroke Howard ("fine, brave, majestic" [*PW* 23]), and Colonel Cecil Burleigh Essex—the "aristocracy" (*PW* 93) of Dawson's Landing. When the supposed Thomas à Becket Driscoll (actually the slave Valet de Chambre in disguise) takes a personal dispute with an Italian count to a court of law instead of the field of honor, all the sympathetic characters—not only the aristocrats Pembroke Howard (a lawyer) and York Driscoll (a judge) but also the middle-class Pudd'nhead Wilson (a lawyer) and the slave Roxana (mother to the disguised Valet de Chambre)—regard this breach of honor with disgust. Reminding Valet de Chambre of his paternity—

his father is the aristocrat Essex—and her own genealogical linkage to "Cap'n John Smith, de highest blood dat Ole Virginny ever turned out, . . . Pocahontas de Injun queen, . . . [and] a nigger king outen Africa," Roxana scorns his cowardly "slinkin' outen a duel en disgracin' our whole line" (*PW* 109). Elmo Howell rightly notes that "when Mark Twain comes face to face with an individual who lives by the code, his irony fails" (2). In *Pudd'nhead Wilson,* only the wildly unsympathetic Thomas à Becket (the disguised Valet de Chambre) does not live by the code, a lapse that foreshadows his later moral failures, notably his murder of his supposed uncle (Judge Driscoll), his attempt to incriminate an innocent man for the crime, and most heinously, his selling his mother down the river.

Just as Twain's medievalist impulse is manifested in his escape into elements of myth—whether language, setting, plot, or character—so is it associated with the escape into childhood. Many of Twain's works— *Tom Sawyer, Huckleberry Finn, The Prince and the Pauper, Joan of Arc,* and "The Mysterious Stranger"—present a child as protagonist, the first three written expressly for an audience of children. Childhood itself had a mythic resonance for Twain (as it did for other nineteenth-century figures, notably Wordsworth and Rousseau), and the cultural changes that took place after the Civil War, irrevocably dividing the antebellum Hannibal of Twain's youth from the postbellum America of his adulthood, only sharpened this sense. Twain's nostalgia for the "child's world of possibility and romance" (Harrison 7) had important links to not only his nostalgia for antebellum America but his attraction to the Middle Ages, and these three golden ages (each serving as an objective correlative for the others) had their opposites in the gilded ages of adulthood, postbellum America, and the modern age.

Twain was first exposed to medieval ballads and romances and medievalist novels and poetry as a child. No mere passive affair, his reading actively nourished his imagination, as evidenced by his manner of play. In an 1870 letter to his childhood friend Will Bowen, Twain wrote nostalgically: "We used to undress and play Robin Hood in our shirt-tails, with lath swords, in the woods on Halliday's Hill" (*To Will Bowen* 19). This memory evoked powerful feelings in Twain, who later recapitulated his childhood behavior in that of Tom Sawyer, the fictional description remarkably like the epistolary: "Tom flung off his jacket and trousers, . . . [located] a rude bow and arrow, a lath sword and a tin trumpet, and . . . bounded away, barelegged, with a fluttering shirt. . . . [Tom and Joe Harper, as Robin Hood and Guy of Guisborne respectively] took their lath swords, . . . struck a fencing attitude, foot to foot, and began a grave, careful combat" (*TS* 59–60). Tom imitates not only Robin Hood's actions but his language, demanding of his playmates that they act and talk "by the book" (*TS* 60), and he provides a detailed if idiosyncratic explanation of this mythic figure's significance, contrasting him with the nineteenth-century American man: "He was the noblest man that ever was. They ain't any such men now" (*TS* 157). For the boys of St. Petersburg, but especially for Tom, the medieval Robin Hood—knightly in his behavior, living by a code of honor—is a hero worthier of emulation than any provided by the modern age.

The juvenile reader is likely to identify with Tom's assertions and approve of his manner of play, but the adult reader may object to both. Tom's insistence that his way is the only right way proves irritating, and his adherence to authorized texts, whose subtleties he cannot recognize, is often ridiculous. Huck's refusal in the early scenes of *Huckleberry Finn* to continue playing the Don Quixote game as directed by Tom thus garners applause from most critics.[29] Yet the affection with which these childhood games are described, particularly in *Tom Sawyer* but even in *Huckleberry Finn,* must not be ignored. However irritating Tom may sometimes be as he directs these games, he also shows himself to be a precocious, intelligent, and imaginative boy, a natural leader whose adherence to the knightly code absorbed from his reading enables him to succeed in several real adventures where "unromantic men" (*TS* 212) have failed—notably, the discovery of the gold and the rescue of Becky Thatcher from the cave.

While acknowledging that childhood was not exempt from sorrows, Twain points with pleasure in *Innocents Abroad* to games like Tom's: "We look back upon [schoolboy days] regretfully because . . . we have forgotten all the sorrows and privations of that canonized epoch and remember only its orchard robberies, its wooden sword pageants and its fishing holydays" (*IA* 585). The pervasive religious imagery of Twain's memory, so like his 1887 description of *Tom Sawyer* as "simply a hymn" (*Letters* 2: 477), bears nostalgic witness to the mythic nature of childhood and helps to explain the motivation behind his hagiography of Joan of Arc.

Even Tom's habit of talking by the book, however false and irritating it may seem to modern critics, has near parallels in Twain's adult life, for he and Cable persisted in speaking a form of "medieval" English while on their lecture tour,[30] as Twain explained in an 1885 letter to Olivia. They also sent a telegram signed "Sir Mark Twain" and "Sir George W. Cable" to Ozias Pond—here called "Sir Sagramore" after a character in the *Morte Darthur*—assuring him that his friends "will well that thou prosper at the hand of the leech, and come lightly forth of thy hurts, and be as thou were tofore" (quoted by Turner 96). Of course, the adult Twain's game has elements of parody, and Tom Sawyer's game is an ingenuous form of hero worship. Yet parody is a manner of talking "by the book," with the addition of the ironic sense that comes with age. In his childhood world, Tom persistently acts the part of a medieval knight as well as he can, and the narrator's attitude toward his attempts is a mixture of amusement at Tom's shortcomings, gentle mockery of his pretensions, and admiration for his adventurousness.

This prepubescent knight seems most silly in his "courtship" of Becky, first described in a chapter that mock-heroically alludes to the chivalric and courtly traditions in its title, "Busy at War and Love." After successfully engaging in a highly ordered "battle" (*TS* 18) Tom falls in love with the "Adored Unknown" (*TS* 22) at first sight (rather like Twain falling in love with Olivia at first sight of her miniature portrait) since "as a romantic Tom Sawyer sees girls as . . . [a] necessary part of the fantasy adventure" (Parkison 32). Having studied the behavior dictated by his books, Tom performs those services for his "lady" that are possible under his reduced circumstances. And like the worthy knight engaged in the ritual known as *domnei* or *donnoi* (which relates courtly love to the feudal tradition of vassalage), Tom earns a token as his reward—in this case, a pansy thrown over the fence. Tom's identification with the courtly knight, hinted at throughout the chapter, is conclusively revealed by the description of his departure from Becky's house: "Finally he *rode* home reluctantly, with his poor head full of visions (*TS* 19; emphasis mine). Of course, Tom has actually walked to Becky's house. Although the narrative description may refer to Tom's fantasy of himself as a chevalier, Twain's indulgent humor permitting the reader to enter into and to stand above that fantasy, it may more provocatively reveal that Twain identified Tom so closely with the knight at this point that he unconsciously visualized Tom astride a horse as he left his "lady."

Though Tom's relationship with Becky derives from the courtly love tradition, it is overlaid by the sentimental tradition that had absorbed and domesticated romantic love.[31] Tom and Becky become "engaged"; Becky hides behind her apron before shyly submitting to a ritualistic kiss; and Tom, curiously combining the typical activities of the middle-class businessman and the knightly adventurer, quests for buried treasure so that he can "get married" and buy "a sure-'nough sword" (*TS* 152). John E. Bassett suggests that "Tom's test to win Becky, in a sense, is to show he can convert his child-world skills of piracy and chivalry into [adult] real-world skills of money-making and wife-protecting" (15). In *Tom Sawyer*,

Twain presents an affectionate picture of a child aspiring to be a knight—
or more exactly, any one of a number of romantic heroes, all of whom
(including the sentimentally domesticated husband) abide by a code derived from the chivalric and courtly traditions. This "history of a *boy*"
(*TS* 217) concludes with a tag phrase of medieval romance, including
decorative capitals, as in an illuminated manuscript: "So ENDETH this
chronicle" (*TS* 217).

Twain rings various changes on his presentation of the child-as-knight.
Most startlingly, he first identifies the child with the slave—representing
the slave as the child's companion (the two in flight from adult masters)
and constructing the slave as intrinsically childlike—and then, by means
of an associative link, affiliates the childlike slave paradoxically with the
medieval knight, as in the case of Jim in *Huckleberry Finn,* who becomes
for Tom "the hero of a historical romance, a peer of the Man in the Iron
Mask or the Count of Monte Cristo" (Henry Nash Smith, "Sound Heart"
96), complete with a coat of arms because "all the nobility" (*HF* 217) has
one. A child who repeatedly hides from his school-"master" (*TS* 46, 47)
to avoid "going into captivity and fetters" (*TS* 39) thus transforms the
escape of a southern slave into the "evasion" (*HF* 224) of a medieval aristocrat—all three figures characterized by their faith in magic and superstition. But the association is too strained (an easier association is the one
drawn in *Connecticut Yankee* between the southern slave and the medieval
slave-freeman), hence the uncomfortable burlesque quality of the episode. Jim's intrinsic nobility is smothered by the aristocratic nobility that
he is compelled to assume during this childplay. The very compulsion,
effected by a child who is and is not his "master," problematizes the equation drawn among child, knight, and slave.

In *Pudd'nhead Wilson,* the amazing reversal of Thomas à Becket Driscoll and Valet de Chambre's identities, accomplished again by a change of
clothing, enables a more complex equation among child, knight, and
slave wherein the "slave," Chambers (actually the master, Tom), protects
his "master" so well on the playground that his "master" could have
"changed clothes with him, and 'ridden in peace,' like Sir Kay in Launcelot's armor" (*PW* 42). These reversals of identity self-consciously prob-
lematize the identities of aristocrat and slave, pointing up the arbitrary
nature of that identification, repeatedly termed a "fiction" (*PW* 29, 41).

The initial transformation recalls those scenes where a medieval aristocrat adopts the identity of a slave in *The Prince and the Pauper* (with
which Twain compares *Pudd'nhead Wilson* in his author's note) and *Connecticut Yankee,* learning lessons that will make them better rulers, though

no such happy lessons are learned in *Pudd'nhead Wilson,* rightly titled a *Tragedy.* At the conclusion, the supposedly "white" Tom is revealed to be the "black" Chambers and is sold down the river in an act of poetic justice, given his sale of Roxana down the river, that nonetheless uncomfortably confirms antebellum morality, and the supposedly "black" Chambers is revealed to be the "white" Tom and is condemned to isolation from the black community with only limited possibilities for integration with white society.

Twain knew that miscegenation in the Old South was socially validated by the droit du seigneur and resulted in the mixing of blood of aristocrat and slave, these seemingly opposed identities merging, however much southern society attempted to keep them distinct via "a fiction of law and custom" (PW 29). In *Pudd'nhead Wilson,* Twain deconstructs the binary opposition of aristocrat and slave, white and black, more directly than in any other work, repeatedly pointing out the absurdity of the social fiction by deft touches: the fair-complexioned Roxana disguises herself upon escaping from slavery by blackening her face; Roxana's son "become[s] her master" (PW 41) because of her machinations, intended to keep him from being sold down the river but ultimately resulting in exactly that fate, and her master's son becomes her son's slave; Tom "blacked his face with burnt cork" (PW 140) before robbing and murdering his "uncle," then disguises himself as a girl to make his escape;[32] Tom's face turns "ashen" and his lips turn "white" when his true identity as Chambers, "Negro and slave" (PW 163), is revealed; Chambers is simultaneously revealed to be the aristocrat Tom and immediately becomes "white and free" (PW 163), but his inability to read or write, his "speech, . . . his gait, his attitudes, his gestures, his bearing, his laugh, . . . his manners" (PW 166) continue to mark him as "black" and "slave."

But despite these incidents exploiting the fictionality of the binary opposition, the suppressions and gaps in *Pudd'nhead Wilson* are sometimes more telling than the text's surface. The logical reason for the veritable twinship of Tom and Chambers (born on the same date in the same household) is that they share a father, but Twain avoids this culturally dangerous territory, only hinting at its possibility by paralleling the fates of the two fathers—Percy Driscoll and Cecil Burleigh Essex—both leading citizens of Dawson's Landing, both slaveholding aristocrats, and both dead in the fall of 1845. Much later, when the adult Tom refuses to fight a duel, Roxana disgustedly proclaims: "It's de nigger in you, dat's what it is. Thirty-one parts o' you is white, en on'y one part nigger, en dat po' little one part is yo' *soul*" (PW 109)—a judgment with which the omniscient narrator earlier seemed to concur in noting that "the 'nigger' in him assert[ed] its humility" (*pw* 75). But this narrator repeatedly notes of Roxana, who is fifteen parts white and one part black, that she has a "masterful attitude" (*pw* 65) and that "her nature needed something or somebody to rule over" (*pw* 77) without asking the corollary question whether this need to be master is the "white" in her. This puzzling late work falters since blood, as well as training, is invoked to explain the selfishness, cowardice, disloyalty, and "native viciousness" (*pw* 43) of Tom (the "black" slave Chambers in disguise) and the generosity, courage, and loyalty of Chambers (the "white" aristocrat Tom in disguise).

Twain is on somewhat safer cultural ground when he projects his deconstruction of the binary opposition between master and slave, white and black, onto the Italian Capello twins, "exact duplicates" (*pw* 51) except for their coloring—Angelo a blond, and Luigi (the "brown one" [*pw* 110] with the "dark face" [*pw* 86]) a brunet. These counts "of the old Florentine nobility" (*pw* 52) were orphaned and left in debt, which they repaid by means of "slavery, . . . receiving no wages" (*pw* 53) for their musical performances. Having "escaped from that slavery" (*pw* 53), they become recognized "masters" (*pw* 56) of music. Later accused by the aristocratic Judge Driscoll of being "back-alley barbers disguised as nobilities" (*pw* 127), they are ultimately revealed as "heroes of romance" (*pw* 165)—an appropriate assignment of identities since the "candy-striped pole" is a signifier of "nobility . . . [in] Venice," though it signifies only "the humble barbershop . . . [in] Dawson's Landing" (*pw* 22). The many transformations in the identitites of the Capello twins, "Italian noblem[e]n or barber[s]" (*pw* 143), comically replicate the tragedy of Tom and Chambers, this projection enabling Twain to grapple with his complicated feelings about the antebellum South with its personal and cultural associations of childhood freedom, aristocratic independence, and "grotesque" slavery (*Autobiography* 32).

In *Joan of Arc* and *Connecticut Yankee*, Twain reverses the child-as-knight relationship developed in *Tom Sawyer* and *Huckleberry Finn*, presenting the knight-as-child—literally in the first case, metaphorically in the second. Though Joan leads her army to victory in battle while dressed in knightly armor, her youth is repeatedly emphasized, indeed exaggerated, by Twain, who according to his own account was a boy when he first learned her story, having discovered by chance a leaf torn from a biography of Joan.[33] Although seventeen during the battles and nineteen at her death, she is repeatedly apostrophized as the "girl," the "child," the "Maid," even the "small darling." Based on Twain's favorite daughter,

Susy, Joan is an "idealization of non-sexual young womanhood" (Kaplan 315), for Twain believed that Joan remained always prepubescent, never menstruating. Twain's identification of this knightly figure as a child serves to foreground certain characteristics that he values: innocence, vitality, idealism, love of beauty, and emotional sensitivity. In idiosyncratically representing the knightly Joan as a child, Twain also defused the revolutionary significance of her gender, rendering her sexless by presenting her not as a woman-knight but a child-knight.[34]

The medieval knights of *Connecticut Yankee* are similarly imaged as children, though the comparison is not always complimentary. Just as Twain refers in *Life on the Mississippi* to "romantic juvenilities" (*LOM* 237) and "jejune romanticism" (*LOM* 266) in order to criticize the medievalist impulse, Hank Morgan criticizes medieval culture by describing "the childlike improvidence of this age and people" (*CY* 123), thus ascribing immaturity and primitivism to medievalism. But even the ever-practical Hank must recognize that other, more positive connotations also derive from this image: "Yet there was something very engaging about these great simple-hearted creatures, something attractive and lovable. There did not seem to be brains enough in the entire nursery, so to speak, to bait a fish-hook with; but you didn't seem to mind that, after a little, because you soon saw that brains were not needed in a society like that, and, indeed, would have marred it, hindered it, spoiled its symmetry— perhaps rendered its existence impossible" (*CY* 54). Though their values are absolutely alien to Hank, he must ruefully acknowledge that the knights, "a childlike and innocent lot" (*CY* 53), have charmed him, and he bears reluctant witness to their exuberance, spontaneity, trustfulness, imagination, and emotionalism—all characteristics lacking in adult postbellum America according to Twain.

These "big children" (*CY* 132) of the Middle Ages also share with children an instinctive love of beauty, both admiring fine spectacles that the practical nineteenth-century man would scorn. Particularly when describing the medieval pageant, Twain gives free reign to his love of beauty and spectacle[35]—one of the "mental and material peculiarities and customs proper to a much younger person" (*Autobiography* 228) that he self-consciously retained into adulthood. Indeed *The Prince and the Pauper* is itself a kind of spectacle wherein Twain describes numerous medieval pageants in elaborate detail, sometimes attributing these descriptions to an "ancient chronicler" (*PP* 103). But his most revealing narrative ploy occurs in his presentation of the coronation day pageant, which is provided in the first-person plural and present tense, as though narrator and reader are present:

Stir and life, and shifting color [is] everywhere. . . . We have seen that this massed array of peeresses is sown thick with diamonds, and we also see that it is a marvelous spectacle. . . . A shaft of sunshine . . . drifts slowly along the ranks of ladies, and every rank it touches flames into a dazzling splendor of many-colored fires, and we tingle to our fingertips with the electric thrill that is shot through us by the surprise and the beauty of the spectacle! . . . We catch our breath, the glory that streams and flashes and palpitates . . . is so overpowering. (*PP* 185–86)

Both narrator and reader are placed in the position of awestruck tourists, as emphasized by the breathless tone. With its detailed presentation of beautiful spectacles and its skillful manipulation of narrative strategy and reader response, *The Prince and the Pauper* "satisfied deep imaginative longings, starved in Victorian America" (Lauber, *Inventions* 50), thus guaranteeing its popularity.

Though Twain's attitude toward the medievalist impulse is more hostile in *Life on the Mississippi* than in any other work, his pro forma criticism of the New Orleans Mardi Gras, identified as a modern imitation of the medieval pageant, is qualified by much admiration: "I saw the procession of the Mystic Crew of Comus . . . with knights and nobles . . . clothed in silken and golden Paris-made gorgeousnesses . . . and in their train all manner of giants, dwarfs, monstrosities, and other diverting grotesquerie—a startling and wonderful sort of show" (*LOM* 264). The southern aristocrat responds both emotionally and aesthetically to the Mardi Gras, paralleling the response of the knight to the medieval pageant but also that of the child to a contemporary spectacle, the circus.

Huck Finn spends some of his happiest hours on shore at a circus watching equestriennes who look "just like a gang of real sure-enough queens, and dressed in clothes that cost millions of dollars, and just littered with diamonds" (*HF* 124). Echoes of the medieval coronation day pageant are evident in this description of the nineteenth-century circus, each serving as the other's mirror image. The reverse is often true as well, allusions to the circus occurring in Twain's presentations of medieval spectacles. Hank Morgan's first sight of the convocation of the Round Table is a case in point: "It was as large as a circus ring; and around it sat a great company of men dressed in such various and splendid colours that it hurt one's eyes to look at them" (*CY* 52). But Hank tends to scorn this aesthetic aspect, crying out to Sir Kay, "Get along back to your circus" (*CY* 37), dismissing him as a mere "circus man" (*CY* 41), and noting that Sir Dinadan is "worse than the clown in the circus" (*CY* 60). Yet Hank must acknowledge his love of the spectacular, theatrical, and stylish, though ruefully identifying it as "the crying defect of my character" (*CY* 346). Insofar as Hank acts upon what he self-consciously identifies as "the circus side of my nature" (*CY* 129), he is similar to the medieval knights he mocks and bears a striking resemblance to young Tom Sawyer, who also approves only of stylish gestures, gaudy effects, and theatrical escapes, and particularly loves "play[ing] circus" (*TS* 139).

The figures of the medieval knight and the contemporary child merge here, the Middle Ages and childhood serving as loci for the yearnings of nineteenth-century man. Tragically, childhood, whether that of Western civilization or the individual man, implies possibilities that inevitably go unrealized. Hank's army of boys ultimately defeats the host of knights in a presumed defeat of the medieval by the modern, the South by the North, the aristocratic masters by the slaves and freemen, and inescapably adulthood by childhood. But because the knights are themselves metaphorically boys, the supposed contrast becomes identification—hence the poetic inevitability of the self-destructive conclusion, which is a tragic version of the many childish battles (often imitative of medieval models) recounted comically in *Tom Sawyer* and *Huckleberry Finn*. In his fictions, then, Twain repeatedly transgresses the boundaries between child, knight, and slave, presenting childlike knights and knightly children, childlike slaves and children enslaved to the adult world, knightly slaves and knights enslaved to medieval codes, superstitions, and monarchs.

As a child, Twain had various ambitions, including becoming a circus clown, but "the ambition to be a steamboatman always remained" (*LOM* 37), this adventurous life holding a special appeal. In *Life on the Mississippi*, the officers are repeatedly described in aristocratic terms, Twain speaking of "the lordly steamboatman" (*LOM* 42), comparing the mate to a "monarch" (*LOM* 42) who "felt all the majesty of his great position" (*LOM* 43), and describing the pilot as an "absolute monarch" (*LOM* 94) who drew "a princely salary" (*LOM* 40). Twain claimed that his years as a pilot were among the happiest of his life because "a pilot . . . was the only unfettered and entirely independent human being that lived in the earth" (*LOM* 93). Given his elucidation of the aristocratic, independent, and adventurous nature of pilots, his ultimate titling of these men as "knights of the tiller" (*LOM* 100) is peculiarly appropriate.

Yet these knights, like their medieval counterparts, do not triumph forever. The railroad, corruption in the pilots' association, and the Civil War (like the civil war that destroyed Camelot) are the primary villains in *Life on the Mississippi*, but a share of the blame is apportioned to technology and government regulations—all disruptions signaling the shift to the modern era. Because many of the circumstances resulting in the destruction of the steamboat industry were closely tied to American progress, Twain was torn in his responses. But his struggle to acknowledge the preeminence of progress over even the steamboat ends in failure, and he nostalgically recalls the golden age when "the steamboatmen [were still] . . . an aristocracy" (*LOM* 142).

Twain's emotional allegiance is to the noble past and not the progressive future, to his childhood dreams and not the adult realities of postbellum nineteenth-century America, as is clear from his bitter rumination about the changes:

> This [regulation requiring lamps at crossings] has knocked the romance out of piloting. . . . It and some other things together, have knocked all the romance out of it. For instance, the peril from snags is not now what it once was. The government's snag boats go patrolling up and down, in these matter-of-fact days, pulling the river's teeth. . . . Formerly, if your boat got away from you, on a black night, and broke for the woods, it was an anxious time with you; . . . but all that is changed now—you flash out your electric light, transform night into day in the twinkling of an eye, and your perils and anxieties are at an end. . . . The Government has taken away the romance of our calling; the Company [which restricted the pilot's independence] has taken away its state and dignity. (*LOM* 171–72)

Though the pilot's lot was improved in safety, comfort, and efficiency, Twain clearly regrets the changes. Such an attitude seems bizarre given the danger of the occupation that claimed the life of Twain's brother Henry, for whom he had procured a job on the steamboat on which he was himself a cub pilot,[36] and whose gruesome death in a steamboat explosion is given fictional form in that of *The Gilded Age*'s Henry Worley. But for a knight, who necessarily courts danger for its own sake since "trial through adventure is the real meaning of the knight's ideal existence" (Auerbach 134), such considerations would not signify, and Twain develops throughout this passage a metaphoric pattern identifying the pilot, steamboat, and river as analogues for the knight, his horse, and the dragon that must be conquered in a test of the knight's mettle. Of course, Auerbach argues that the "perilous [knightly] adventures called *avantures . . .* have no experiential basis whatever" (134) and that problems necessarily result whenever the chivalric tradition is viewed not as an ideal but as a practical response to reality—a view with which Henry Clemens would no doubt agree. Yet Twain expresses keen regret that "these matter-

of-fact days" have "knocked the romance out of piloting," an elegiac refrain in this passage.[37]

In the antebellum section of *The Gilded Age*, a steamboat trip was for
the Hawkins children and slaves "a glorious adventure, a royal progress
through the very heart and home of romance" (*GA* 40–41), just as in
Pudd'nhead Wilson Roxana's "wonderful travels . . . [and] adventures" as
a steamboat chambermaid make her "a heroine of romance" (*PW* 61) to
the childlike slaves of Dawson's Landing. Given the negative connotations
attached to "romance" in so much of Twain's work, its positive valence
here suggests a different set of allegiances. Indeed the many complex and
convoluted associations between childhood and knighthood in Twain's
works suggest that his allegiance to nineteenth-century America and all
that it represented—technology, democracy, materialism, pragmatism,
and, above all, progress—was more qualified and tenuous than is often
assumed. Just as in childhood, so in the Middle Ages Twain discovered,
almost in spite of himself, certain valuable characteristics lacking in
nineteenth-century American culture. However contradictory his responses and complicated his allegiances, Twain was clearly attracted to
medievalism and to that which, in his complex mind, was associated with
it: myth, childhood, the steamboat, the western frontier, the antebellum
South with its undeniable ties to slavery. His criticism of medievalism
notwithstanding, Twain yearned at times to escape imaginatively into that
very period, as into his own childhood, and thereby to escape from what
he termed "the drive and push and rush and struggle of the raging, tear-
ing, booming nineteenth century" (*Speeches* 145). The tragedy that Twain
grasped only occasionally was that the Middle Ages were not the absolute
opposite of modern America but the ground of the modern world,
the very "ground-connection" (*CY* 388) that made the medieval knights
of *Connecticut Yankee* vulnerable to the electric charge that Hank sent
through them in the apocalyptic conclusion. That Twain, who seemed so
clearly a man of his time, should have experienced the medievalist impulse bears witness to the power of this countercurrent in American
culture.

It remained for a man who was *not* of his time—a man who was less
ambivalent in his response to nineteenth-century American culture and
more aware of the complex relationship between the Middle Ages and
modern America—to give voice to this impulse in an explicit and overt
manner, thereby paradoxically revealing himself to be yet more modern
in sensibility, a twentieth-century man. Twain's early notes for the conclusion of *Connecticut Yankee* imaged the Yankee as "mourn[ing] his lost
land" that had been "so virgin" (quoted by Kaplan 294–95) before he

destroyed it via the electric surprise of the dynamo-charged fence. Henry Adams, no innocent abroad, placed the figures of the Virgin and the dynamo at the very center of his intellectual and literary journey into a "world that is lost" (MSMC 227), rigorously exploring their equivalences as well as their contrasts for clues about America's future.

3

Henry Adams

THE HISTORICAL VISIONARY AS MEDIEVALIST

In Mark Twain's *What Is Man?* (written in 1905–6 and posthumously published in 1917), a character named Henry Adams is described as the "unhappiest" man, "cheerless, hopeless, despondent" (*WM* 106)—a judgment with which the real Henry Adams seems all too often to have agreed. Whereas Mark Twain succeeded as a humorist in the Gilded Age and presented himself as an apologist for nineteenth-century America (whatever his ambivalences), the pessimistic Henry Adams insisted upon his own failure and openly expressed his criticisms of American culture. Twain characteristically celebrated St. Louis as the archetypal progressive northern city. Adams dismissed it as "a third-rate town . . . without history, education, unity, or art" (*EHA* 466). Twain worshiped the desexualized Angel in the House. Adams rejected the "sexless" (*EHA* 446) American woman as "a failure" (*Letters* 5:701).

However, these two contemporaries shared a fascination with the Middle Ages, though differing in their explicit evaluations, Twain presenting the medieval period largely as a satirical butt and Adams as an ideal. Twain thus emphasized the destructive power of the medieval Catholic Church; Adams presented it as a compelling force for unity and creativity, as represented by the Gothic cathedral. Twain derided courtly love as an agent of immorality, reviling Pierre Abelard as a dastardly seducer and recuperating Héloïse by sentimentalizing her; Adams celebrated its passionate energy and productive impact on literature and manners, praising Abelard's courtly devotion to Héloïse and the Virgin

Mary and lauding Héloïse as "the immortal and eternal woman" (*MSMC* 221) who "unites the ages" (*MSMC* 287) by her intense passion. Even behind Adams's criticism of the modern city of St. Louis stands his affectionate portrait of King Louis IX of France, known as St. Louis, whom he characterizes as "the most devoted of all" (*MSMC* 151) to the Virgin of Chartres.

Adams's two greatest works—*Mont-Saint-Michel and Chartres* (1913; privately printed in 1904), which defines the medieval sensibility, celebrates twelfth-century unity, and constructs a female reader as its ideal audience, and *The Education of Henry Adams* (1918; privately printed in 1907), which defines the modern sensibility, criticizes twentieth-century multiplicity, and constructs a male reader as its ideal audience—emphasize this polarity, for he perceived them as a pair, each implicitly commenting on the other, just as each age is highlighted when placed in relief against the other. For Adams, the twelfth and twentieth centuries served as magnetic poles, one attracting and the other repelling him, in a reversal of Twain's hierarchy. Yet Adams also recognized that the twelfth and twentieth centuries were inextricably linked in a historical whole that included past, present, and future. The twelfth century was not wholly Other to Adams, as Twain generally succeeded in constructing it.

Because Twain was concerned largely with two terms, past and present, he inevitably placed them into binary opposition—an approach with which Adams would have been sympathetic, given his "double nature" and early conviction that "life was a double thing" composed of "irreducible opposites" (*EHA* 9). But Adams complicated the mathematics by adding a third term, the future. No simple linear development, progressive or regressive, but a "triangulation," to use one of Adams's characteristic metaphors, was the basis of his dynamic theory of history. Adams associated the medieval past with unity and the modern era, both present and future, with multiplicity, but he recognized that all ages ultimately had to grapple with these two forces, which he powerfully imaged as the Virgin and the dynamo. Yet Adams's medievalist impulse was trivialized by a number of early readers, who regarded it as simple antiquarianism, charming but ultimately irrelevant to life in the nineteenth century. The avuncular persona adopted by Adams in *Chartres* encouraged such an interpretation. This elderly American gentleman pottering ineffectually about European cathedrals while trailed by an inattentive niece inspired affection in early readers, but many questioned the historical accuracy of his descriptions, and few felt personally challenged by his devotion to the culture of the Middle Ages.

In retrospect, however, Adams seems one of the most modern of nineteenth-century writers. Whatever his self-deprecating comments, his discomfort at life in the nineteenth century resulted less from an outmoded sensibility and inability to keep up with the times than a too clear vision of the future.

Though some elements of escapism mark his fascination with the Middle Ages, Adams was concerned with getting back to the medieval source of modern culture largely to analyze the direction of future historical developments, to triangulate from past and present into the future. Trigonometric triangulation, the Holy Trinity, medieval Scholastic philosopher Guillaume de Champeaux's "universal equilateral triangle" and his "common crystal" composed of "perfect equilateral triangle[s]" (*MSMC* 297), and the "triangle of churches" (*MSMC* 56) composed of Notre Dame de Mantes, de Paris, and de Chartres all serve for Adams as examples of the complicated relationship between unity and multiplicity, the essential and accidental, the universal and individual, the infinite and finite, order and chaos, "the universe and the atom" (*MSMC* 350)—indeed the universe and Adams.

Man had long assumed the primary existence of unity, first in the context of religion and then science, attempting to solve the "eternal and primary problem of the process by which unity could produce diversity" (*MSMC* 304), all roads ultimately leading to unity until the twentieth century. But for Adams, who experienced and foresaw the fragmentation of the modern world, the dynamo paradoxically generated the Virgin insofar as his contemporary experience of multiplicity led him to desire her. The medieval Virgin effected unity, yet she was paradoxically multiple, marked by contradictory qualities and various constructed identities. Whether in the form of the Virgin of Chartres, the Virgin of Dreux, the Virgin of France, or the Greek Virgin—whether the Virgin as queen, empress, or madonna—for Adams, the Virgin idiosyncratically represented the inertial force of sex. While for Twain, genteel convention required that all births derive from immaculate conceptions, for Adams, the Immaculate Conception (proclaimed as Catholic dogma in 1854) paradoxically "lays bare the whole subject of sex" (*MSMC* 198). Adams subverts the nineteenth-century Angel in the House—maternal without being sexual—by his portait of the medieval Virgin in her shrine—sexual because maternal. Rather than the pale sentimental heroine (as figured in Twain's fictional incarnations of his wife, Olivia), Adams's Virgin was a sexual generator, a "Unity [that] . . . explain[ed] and include[d] Duality, Diversity, Infinity—Sex!" (*MSMC* 261). Adams constructs the Virgin as feminine principle and the dynamo as masculine principle, contrasting sexual force with dynamic force, inertia with intensity, sexuality with electricity, reproduction with mechanization, arithmetical with geometrical progression. Yet they are not mere opposites but "interchangeable forces on man" (*EHA* 388), the Virgin the "animated dynamo" (*EHA* 384) that stands at the center of Adams's Middle Ages, providing clues about America's future as directed by the electric Virgin known in the modern era as the dynamo.

Dynamo or Dynamite?

Written during his late sixties, Adams's autobiography, *The Education of Henry Adams*, offers the events of a lifetime in the nineteenth and early twentieth centuries, but his descriptions of his younger self, or selves, are inevitably shaped by his contemporary perspective and ideological agenda, despite his idiosyncratic use of the distancing technique of the third person with its suggestion of objectivity.[1]

Repeatedly emphasizing that he was never at home in his own time, Adams insists that his strongest allegiance was to the eighteenth century, the period of his family's greatest triumphs in the persons of his great-grandfather John Adams and grandfather John Quincy Adams. Just as the young Twain absorbed the antebellum atmosphere of Hannibal, Adams images himself early in the *Education* as a child inhaling the eighteenth-century atmosphere surrounding him, particularly in Quincy at the family house inhabited for generations by Adamses (whose history was bound to the history of America itself) but also in Boston near his Brooks relatives. Adams immediately alerts us to his double vision by offering us two childhood homes, the focus of the first two chapters, "Quincy" and "Boston," but he discusses both homes in both chapters rather than segregating his discussion, as the chapter titles would suggest.

Quincy is Adams's Jackson's Island (or Glasscock's Island), associated with summer holiday, nature and sense impressions, "liberty, diversity, [and] outlawry"; Boston is his St. Petersburg (or Hannibal), associated with "winter confinement, school, rule, discipline," civilization, "restraint, law, [and] unity" (*EHA* 7–8). Adams initiates the binary opposition that structures the *Education* and *Chartres* but gives fair warning that this opposition is not to be understood simplistically.[2] Though Quincy is the preferred home, indeed the lost Eden, as suggested by references to the "garden" (*EHA* 39) and his habit of punning on his name, it is associated not with unity but multiplicity—the term that Adams typically devalues. He further complicates the opposition by noting that "winter [read Boston] represented the desire to escape and go free [read Quincy]" (*EHA* 8), one term implying the other, presence implying absence. In another turn of the screw, Adams paradoxically associates Quincy with the medieval home of Abelard—author of an autobiography ("Story of Calamity" [*MSMC* 311]) that Adams translates in the "Abélard" chapter of *Chartres.* Abelard's Oratory of the Paraclete was located "in the parish of Quincey" (*MSMC* 307) in twelfth-century France, and Abelard "start[ed] from the atom" (*MSMC* 294)—the Adam or Adams?—in order to reason from multiplicity to unity rather than the reverse.

Adams associates his allegiance to the eighteenth century with fragility and sickness, the childhood bout with scarlet fever that slowed his physical development symbolizing his inability to succeed in the nineteenth century. His eighteenth-century models particularly affected his attitude toward government. As a boy, he learned the distinction between statesmen, the eighteenth-century ideal, and politicians, the nineteenth-century reality, while proofreading John Adams's *Novanglus and Massachusettensis* for his father (who was editing the *Works*) in the same room where Charles Francis Adams and his friends gathered to discuss the antislavery Free-Soil Party they had founded: "It was the old Ciceronian idea of government by *the best* that produced the long line of New England statesmen. . . . The little group of men in Mount Vernon Street were . . . statesmen, not politicians; they guided public opinion, but were little guided by it" (*EHA* 32). The ideal statesman was ruled by benevolence, integrity, and morality, concerned with means as well as ends, and assumed that fixed principles could be determined by the application of reason and that all social and political problems could be solved by reference to these principles. The young Adams learned that the statesman proposed to accomplish perfection in the political and social spheres, the only instruments required being "Suffrage, Common Schools, and Press" (*EHA* 33)—the very instruments Hank Morgan so hopefully employed in *Connecticut Yankee*, though to paradoxically disastrous effect. Belief in meliorism linked the eighteenth-century statesman with nineteenth-century thinkers like William Hartpole Lecky, the historian who influenced Twain, though in most other respects the eighteenth- and nineteenth-century sensibilities conflicted, as Adams learned when it came time for him to take his place in the political arena.

As a member of one of the ruling American dynasties, he assumed that his future political success (and succession) was a given: "The Irish gardener once said to the child: 'You'll be thinkin' you'll be President too!' The casualty [*sic*] of the remark made so strong an impression on his mind that he never forgot it. . . . That there should be a doubt of his being President was a new idea. What had been would continue to be" (*EHA* 16). The irony is that what had been would not continue to be. Though the childish Adams protagonist merely thinks it strange that anyone might not grant his right to rule, the mature Adams narrator recognizes that the eighteenth-century fashion of governing—a democratic version of noblesse oblige—was becoming obsolete even as the gardener spoke.

As power shifted away from the Adamses and what they represented, it shifted ever more directly into the hands of the common people, here represented by the figure of the immigrant. The note of derision in the Irish gardener's comment signals the triumph of one class over another, one concept of government over another, one century over another—a triumph that the aristocratic Adams reprehended, as signaled by the ethnic slurs that mark his writing. The "swarm of blackguards from the slums" (EHA 42) battling the Latin School boys on Boston Common prefigures not only the Civil War—"the two hostile forces were called North-Enders and South-Enders" (EHA 41)—but the increasing power of the "dark mass" (EHA 41) of immigrants, imaged as a mob "threatening total annihilation" to "the aristocratic element in society" (Tanner 165).

Adams came closest to attaining political power when serving as private secretary to his father, then minister to England. Charles Francis Adams's mission was to maintain England's neutrality in the Civil War, countering powerful forces inclining England toward an alliance with the South. His diplomatic success was a deciding factor, perhaps second only to Lincoln's leadership, in the North's ultimate victory. During the four years that Henry assisted his father,[3] he held "a position at the centre of action, with his hands actually touching the lever of power" (EHA 210).

Yet the control suggested by this image is revealed to be illusory. Adams presents the Civil War as "an unknown energy which played with all his generation as a cat plays with mice" (EHA 98), imaging it variously as a thunderstorm, firestorm, and wild ocean—all natural energies beyond human control. He identifies the war as a historical rupture that caused many "to be set adrift in a world they would find altogether strange" (EHA 208), a world "so changed as to be beyond connection with the past" (EHA 209). However much he tried to incorporate the Civil War into the political and social scheme established by his Adams forefathers, he recognized that a cataclysmic shift had rendered both the original scheme and his family obsolete.[4]

The unhappy position of the Adamses was made clear to Henry in 1870 when President Grant announced the composition of his cabinet. Not only was Charles Francis Adams not rewarded for his diplomatic service with an appointment, but those who were appointed betrayed a dedication to materialism, expediency, and political manipulation, revealing that "the eighteenth-century fabric of *a priori*, or moral, principles [had broken down because] politicians had tacitly given it up" (EHA 280–81), rejecting idealism in favor of the political machine. That the eighteenth-century system no longer worked was for Adams a negative commentary on nineteenth-century life and a tacit acknowledgment of flaws inherent in the eighteenth-century system that led to the Civil War.

Adams's political hopes had centered around the possibilities for reform (for which Twain in *The Gilded Age* also called, although he later became an admirer of Grant), but his failure to play an active part in politics freed him to undertake an activity for which he was better suited temperamentally: observing and analyzing the direction of modern life. He thus answers the question "What could become of such a child of the seventeenth and eighteenth centuries, when he should wake up to find himself required to play the game of the twentieth?" by stating anticlimactically, "He never got to the point of playing the game at all; he lost himself in the study of it, watching the errors of the players" (EHA 4). Repeatedly imaging himself as passive observer and helpless victim, he characteristically ends the chapters of the *Education* anticlimactically, announcing yet another failure, but his pessimistic interpretation of various nineteenth-century "errors"—social, political, scientific, and technological—results in a number of disturbingly accurate predictions about the twentieth century. Whether these errors were free or determined, marked by multiplicity or unity, is a question he cannot answer, though he repeatedly returns to it via the pervasive gambling imagery in the *Education*, as well as in his second novel, *Esther* (1884), where he ironically names a priest Hazard, repeatedly alludes to bluffing at poker and bridge, and images life as a risky horse race or billiard game.

Adams called into question certain foundational beliefs of the nineteenth century, notably meliorism. Darwin's theory of evolution was often invoked as a justification for belief in absolute progress, America representing the best social example, but Adams found little to convince him that nineteenth-century America was the apex of uniform and unbroken progress. In "A Letter to American Teachers of History" (written in 1909 and dated 16 February 1910), he cited, as Ferman Bishop notes, "the number of suicides, the increase of alcoholism, the increase of disease as signs of loss of vitality in the body politic" (123). He appealed to the second law of thermodynamics—which states that all energy tends to dissipate, entropy thus tending to the maximum—to explain scientifically "the rapid atrophy of the social mind" (*Letters* 6:495), thereby using theoretical physics to combat the social application of Darwinian evolution, just as Twain put the paradigms of nineteenth-century physics to literary use in

the fabulistic writings of his later years.[5] Once the second law of thermodynamics is appropriated, "the historian can no longer in good faith represent human experience as a progressive and ameliorative process," as
William Merrill Decker states (80). In an 1897 letter to Lucy Baxter,
Adams observes more personally that he can "see no great hope of going
back to the prosperous days of 1850–60 when we began life with an idea
that the world was made new and man dead-sure of perfection" (*Letters*
4:461). As these dates suggest, the Civil War provided Adams with a powerful counterargument to the theory of "moral evolution" (*EHA* 229).

Adams's rejection of social and moral progress was consistent with his
rejection of political progress (belied by the failure of political reform), as
is evident from his derisive treatment of President Grant, culminating
in his assertion that "the progress of evolution from President Washington to President Grant, was alone evidence enough to upset Darwin"
(*EHA* 266). He characterizes Grant as "inarticulate, uncertain, distrustful
of himself, still more distrustful of others, and awed by money" (*EHA* 297)
as well as simpleminded, archaic, and a member of the Stone Age. In
Adams's first novel, *Democracy* (1880)—part political satire, part roman-
à-clef, and part novel of manners—he identifies his fictional president
with Grant by means of clever wordplay, noting that he was called " 'the
Stone-cutter of the Wabash' " and " 'the Hoosier Quarryman' " but that
"his favorite appellation was 'Old Granite' " (*D* 108), and he satirizes
him mercilessly. Politically naive, Old Granite abdicates his presidential
responsibilities when he allows himself to be manipulated by corrupt
politicians—notably, Senator Ratcliffe, based largely on James G. Blaine,
a senator involved in scandals during the Grant administration.

The index of the fictional president's inferiority is marked by an ironic
comparison with George Washington, always Adams's standard of the
great statesman.[6] The inferiority of contemporary society is revealed by
its evaluation of Old Granite as Washington's equal. Yet this misguided
comparison actually reveals a measure of respect for Washington, an attitude that Ratcliffe rejects, refusing even to pay lip service to the quality
of Washington's leadership. Ironically, when Ratcliffe criticizes Washington—"no politician at all, as we understand the word" (*D* 93)—and
praises contemporary politicians—"If virtue won't answer our purpose,
we must use vice, or our opponents will put us out of office" (*D* 94)—the
effect is quite different from what he intends. Rather than diminishing
Washington's achievements, Ratcliffe reveals that democracy has not lived
up to the ideals on which it was founded. As power shifted into the hands
of the masses ever more directly, the Old Granites and Ratcliffes, the

Grants and Blaines, were chosen over the Washingtons—and by exten-sion, the Adamses. Implicit is Adams's criticism of this change in which the masses select the mediocre over the best, the politician over the statesman.

Adams's criticisms of American government in *Democracy* are not un-like Twain's some seven years earlier in *The Gilded Age*, but ultimately *The Gilded Age* is a more buoyant novel, the portrait of Dilworthy soft-ened by that of his partner, Colonel Sellers (briefly mentioned in the *Edu-cation*), whose irrepressible dynamic energy is presented with comic affection in contrast to the more ruthless portrait of Ratcliffe, whose cor-ruption is revealed in all its ugly specificity. *The Gilded Age* ends optimis-tically, the melodramatic conclusion of the Laura-Selby courtship plot supplanted by the sentimental conclusion of the Ruth-Philip plot (en-abled by the successful silver speculation of the allegorically named Philip Sterling, which recuperates the Gilded Age while implicating him in its values). *Democracy*'s courtship plot ends gloomily, Madeleine Lee prop-erly rejecting Ratcliffe yet refusing to accept the clearly worthy Carring-ton, an honorable Virginia lawyer and "type . . . of George Washington" (*D* 17) whose statesmanly qualities are now passé. Written during the same year as *Democracy*, Adams's admiring biography *The Life of Albert Gallatin* (1879) "focused on Gallatin what increasingly had become [Adams's] despair over the opportunities for statesmanship in American experience," as Decker points out (141).

In the *Education* and *Democracy*, Adams makes the same point by ex-tending the comparison between Washington and Grant to a comparison between Mount Vernon and the city of Washington, which he had first visited as a boy while traveling with his father. Washington was marked for Adams by the taint of slavery, but Mount Vernon stood apart as a place to which "people made pilgrimages" (*EHA* 47), rather like the Adams house on the suggestively named Mount Vernon Street in Boston. Adams appropriately felt at home at Mount Vernon, which he lyrically described in pastoral terms. "Always remain[ing] where it was, with no practicable road to reach it" (*EHA* 48), Mount Vernon served for Adams as an ideal against which the unattractive reality of American democracy was necessarily measured. In *Democracy*, a similar pilgrimage is under-taken to Mount Vernon, Madeleine Lee—who like Adams wants to "touch with her own hand the massive machinery of society . . . [and so get] to the heart of the great American mystery of democracy and govern-ment" (*D* 9)—immediately recognizing that Mount Vernon represents political, moral, and aesthetic sensibilities intrinsically more admirable than those represented by the city of Washington. Because Madeleine lives in Washington and socializes with politicians, she feels tainted when she looks at pastoral Mount Vernon.

Just as the movement from George Washington to Ulysses S. Grant implied regression and thereby undermined Darwin according to Adams, his attitude toward the biographical and geographical Washingtons replicating his attitude toward the biographical and geographical St. Louises, so did the shift from Mount Vernon to the city of Washington. Yet Adams acknowledged that George Washington, a fixed principle or "ultimate relation like the Pole Star" (EHA 47), was also a problematic figure insofar as his personal implication in slavery undermined his moral stature and laid the groundwork for the Civil War—a puzzle that Adams could not solve.

The objections that Adams raised to absolute historical progress— social, moral, or political—were joined by objections to the science that was invoked as a justification of meliorism. As a young man, Adams had made a considerable study of Darwin, particularly his *Origin of Species* (1859) and *Voyage of the "Beagle"* (1840), just as Mark Twain had studied Darwin's *The Descent of Man* (1871) shortly after its publication (which Twain asserted had "startled the world" [*Autobiography* 105]). Again like Twain, Adams had studied the works of geologist Charles Lyell, writing an essay in 1866 to introduce Lyell's *Principles* to an American audience.

The theories of Darwin and Lyell appealed to the young Adams because they "seemed to lead somewhere—to some great generalization" (EHA 224)—namely that "steady, uniform, unbroken evolution from lower to higher" (EHA 226) was the cause of all change and that perfection was thus attainable. Adams initially welcomed the theory of evolution, though many of his contemporaries were horrified by its implicit challenge to religious faith. Many years later, in "The Tendency of History" (an address dated 12 December 1894, sent in letter form to a meeting of the American Historical Society during Adams's tenure as president), he referred to the "cheerful optimism which gave to Darwin's conclusions the charm of a possible human perfectibility" (TH 130), though no longer regarding this optimism as an appropriate response. The mature narrator of the *Education* thus ironically notes of his complacent younger self that "such a working system for the universe suited a young man who had just helped to waste five or ten thousand million dollars and a million lives" (EHA 225) in the Civil War.

Yet even when the young Adams first espoused a belief in evolution, he recognized flaws and inconsistencies in the process. He learns from Lyell that certain simple forms of life have not evolved into more complex forms, while other more complex forms of life seem not to have evolved from earlier, simpler ancestors. Adams was similarly troubled with regard to geology since Lyell failed to incorporate the catastrophic glacial epoch convincingly into a theory of uniform change. As Mark Twain sardonically noted, "Glacial epochs are great things, but they are vague—vague" (*LOM* 120). Given such unanswered questions and able to prove not evolution but only change, Adams determined that the theory of evolution was "pure inference, precisely like the inference of Paley, that, if one found a watch, one inferred a maker" (*EHA* 230).

Adams's comparison of Lyell's theory with deism enables him to suggest that contemporary science is the new orthodoxy, replacing religion as the locus of belief in modern life, but also to suggest that science is no more liable to proof than religion. Hence George Strong, *Esther's* representative scientist, notes that "there is no science which does not begin by requiring you to believe the incredible, . . . [with] the doctrine of the Trinity . . . not so difficult to accept for a working proposition as any one of the axioms of physics" (*E* 317). Like Strong, who does not believe science is "true" but only interesting, Adams must admit that "he was a Darwinian for fun" (*EHA* 232).[7] He emphasizes the relationship between science and religion by repeatedly referring to medieval Scholastic philosophy as "science" (*MSMC* 288), asserting that in the Middle Ages "faith in science was strong" (*MSMC* 288), Adams's cross-textual pun revealing a modern slippage from the twelfth century when "words had fixed values" (*MSMC* 290).

Adams selected the electric turbine, called the dynamo, as the most appropriate symbol for the modern age since it would "shape the 20th century as steam had shaped the 19th" (Hamill 8). Twain seems to have shared Adams's vision, as signaled by the scene in *Connecticut Yankee* where the last soldiers awake in Hank's camp are the "dynamo-watch" (*CY* 407). Much more powerfully than Twain, however, Adams recognized the revolutionary nature of the dynamo and the energy produced by it, asserting that "they gave to history a new phase" (*EHA* 342). The dynamo became for Adams "a modern scientific image representing ultimate energy and infinite force" (Koretz 69). Adams was particularly struck by what he called its "occult mechanism" (*EHA* 381), since the production and transmission of electricity seemed almost magical to him, as is clear from this famous passage: "He found himself lying in the Gallery of Machines at the Great Exposition of 1900, his historical neck broken by the sudden irruption of forces totally new" (*EHA* 382). Suspicion and fear, signaled by the violent image of the broken neck, an image repeatedly recurring in his letters of this period, tempered his excitement at the release of this occult power by the dynamo, which "can generate energy but not life" (Diggins 168). Just as for Twain, the equivalence between energy and life has broken down, to be replaced by its opposite. The violence of Adams's images suggests his fear that these new energies will ultimately generate death, sexual reproduction inevitably giving way to dynamic production just as religion has given way to science.

Adams therefore grew obsessed with plotting the direction the energies would take and the rate at which they would accelerate, an obsession documented in numerous letters of the 1890s and early 1900s, especially to his younger brother Brooks. As a historian, Adams had spent much of his life committed to determining cause-effect relationships, yet he was repeatedly frustrated in his attempts, feeling that he could never get back to a true cause or origin, nor could he fix "a necessary sequence of human movement" (EHA 382). Some sixty years before Michel Foucault, who looked "for beginnings, not origins . . . [because] origins imply causes [while] beginnings imply differences" (O'Brien 37), Adams was intensely aware of the difficulty, perhaps impossibility, of discovering origins instead of mere sources without causality, mere sequences without necessity. Lois Hughson argues that those chapters of the *Education* "in which he wrestles with imperfectly understood laws of science and mathematics in an attempt to transform historical studies" (5) are his response to his dissatisfaction with the various current historical theories—whether grounded in the individual great man, institutions, politics, or evolution.

In frustration at his failure to determine a necessary historical sequence, Adams turned to a more basic unit of measure—force, energy, power—to determine its necessary sequence,[8] just as Foucault later placed "at the heart of [his] history of Western civilization . . . the organizing principle of power [so that] culture is studied through technologies of power—not class, not progress, not the indomitability of the human spirit" (O'Brien 34). Adams ultimately coupled his study of the sequence of force with his historical studies into a new and idiosyncratic theory, the dynamic theory of history, which "defines Progress as the development and economy of Forces . . . [and] defines force as anything that does, or helps to do work" (EHA 474). Again like Foucault's theory of history, the dynamic theory denied the classical notion that history was "the product of the conscious actions of man," instead focusing on "objective forces independent of men," so that history becomes "the embodiment of power itself" (Diggins 176–77). Adams ultimately asserted that the historian's job was "to follow the track of the energy; to find where it came from and where it went to; its complex source and shifting channels; its values, equivalents, conversions" (EHA 389).[9] He was thus fascinated by translation (understood literally and metaphorically) and border areas, often imaged as bridges (notably the *"pons seclorum"* [*MSMC* 33] or bridge across the ages), portals, parvis (covered-porch anterooms to cathedrals), douanes (custom houses), stairways, and transitional states (notably the Gothic Transition, the period when "the quiet, restrained strength of the [masculine] Romanesque [is] married to the graceful curves and vaulting imagination of the [feminine] Gothic" [*MSMC* 33] but also the transition between the square base and the octagon of the flèche, to which Adams devotes many pages of the chapter "Towers and Portals").

According to Adams's theory, the mechanical and electromagnetic forces both developed within and characterized the nineteenth century, but these forces also resulted in the fragmentation of modern industrial life. Throughout the *Education,* as in *The Gilded Age* and so much other literature of the period, the railroad serves as an important symbol of this new industrial world. Adams recognized that industrialism on the scale undertaken in America implied not only technological changes but vast social and economic changes. Acknowledging the huge influx of capital required, he objected to the methods of the capitalistic system that America adopted, such as the imposition of protective tariffs, the incorporation of businesses, the consolidation of trusts, and the development of trade unions—in short, "the whole mechanical consolidation of force, which ruthlessly stamped out the life of the class into which Adams was born, but created monopolies capable of controlling the new energies that America adored" (*EHA* 345). This mechanical consolidation of force was one of the types of unity—Adams repeatedly conflating the railroad with the medieval church and the Virgin—that Adams found unappealing.

However mortgaged to the railways his generation was, Adams could be of no use, unlike the lowly mechanic with whom he repeatedly compares himself. Ironically, his older brother, Charles Francis Adams, Jr., eventually became president of the Union Pacific Railroad but surrendered its management in 1890 to Jay Gould because of insufficient working capital. Henry Adams regarded his brother's situation as more evidence of the shift in America's direction, as he revealed in an 1891 letter to Elizabeth Cameron: "[I wish in twenty-five years] to continue my history, and show where American democracy was coming out. . . . As yet we can but guess, and Jay Gould has much to tell us. Unfortunately I am cursed with the misfortune of thinking that I know beforehand what the result must be, and of feeling sure that it is one which I do not care to pursue; one with which I have little or no sympathy, except in a coldly scientific way" (*Letters* 3:382). Granted that Adams felt uncomfortable with the forces associated with industrialism and the social and economic changes precipitated by it, he more intensely feared what might next develop in the twentieth century, as this letter implies.

To Adams, who hyperbolically characterized the locomotive steam engine, the electric tram, and the automobile as "terrible," "destructive," and a "nightmare" (EHA 380), respectively (though using them all for transportation), the "wholly new" (EHA 381) force of radioactivity seemed particularly frightening. Adams was struck that even the physicist Samuel Pierpont Langley was unsettled by this new force, calling it "anarchical" and "parricidal" (EHA 381). The image of radium as "parricidal" is particularly revealing, suggesting that this new force will destroy the preceding generation (those eighteenth-century Adams forefathers), creating a rift that cannot be healed. Man had brought into existence something that he could not understand—Adams notes "the stupor of science before radium" (Letters 5:627)—which resulted in his "translat[ion] . . . into a new universe" (EHA 381), Adams imaging man in the atomic age as wandering about in a universe gone insane, "physics stark mad in metaphysics" (EHA 382), where increased knowledge would lead paradoxically to less control.

Yet modern man aspires to this hollow victory, as Adams represents him in his "Prayer to the Virgin of Chartres" (a 1901 poem in which is embedded "Prayer to the Dynamo," which presents a dialogue between man and the atom), Adams's twentieth-century version of a twelfth-century Adam's (de Saint Victor) "prayer to the Virgin" (MSMC 329):

> Seize, then, the Atom! rack his joints!
> Tear out of him his secret spring!
> Grind him to nothing!—though he points
> To us, and his life-blood anoints
> Me—the dead Atom-King! (PVC 130)

Man's scientific zeal is revealed as a manifestation of an excessive will to power: "Though we destroy soul, life and light, / Answer you shall—or die!" (PVC 130). Because "Atom" homophonously recalls "Adam," and therefore "Adams," its identity as individual and multiplicitous energy is emphasized, implicitly contrasting with the divine unity of the Virgin.[10]

Just as the mechanical forces were directed toward fragmentation and multiplicity, the atomic forces seemed by extension to be directed toward destruction, calamity, catastrophe. Like Twain, who speculated in his fable "Sold to Satan" (1904) that "if atomic power were unleashed, 'the world would vanish away in a flash of flame and a puff of smoke'" (Cummings 44–45), Adams determined to discover where these new forces were blindly leading America. Noting that "the new American" (EHA 349) sometimes sensed that the changes warranted hesitation, Adams also notes that the halfhearted attempts to slow things down had paradoxically the opposite effect since "the movement, once accelerated by attempting to impede it, had the additional, brutal consequence of crushing . . . [all] that stood in its way" (EHA 349). Therefore, not only the kind of energies but the rate at which these energies developed, exponential rather than arithmetical, seemed ominous to Adams. Because man's control decreased as their rate of acceleration increased, a point would arrive, Adams suggested, when forces would control man more than man controlled them: "The throb of fifty or a hundred million steam horsepower, doubling every ten years, and already more despotic than all the horses that ever lived, and all the riders they ever carried, drowned rhyme and reason" (EHA 408). The very rhythm of this sentence reiterates the acceleration it describes, an acceleration that causes Howard Munford to ask provocatively, "Is Adams suggesting that although man is responsible for his own world he is also immutably its victim?" (149).

Looking to history for an answer, Adams found a civilization that sufficiently paralleled American society to justify further study. Because the Roman Empire—with its Pax Romana, civil laws, free trade, and transportation system—seemed an analogue for America, he used the dynamic theory as a tool for determining the causes of the decline and fall of Rome, discovering in the language of his theory that the empire had developed energies without economizing them. Like Rome "torn to pieces by acceleration" (EHA 478), New York in 1904 seemed to be coming apart because of an excess of uncontrollable energies, as Adams describes in this remarkable passage:

> The outline of the city became frantic in its effort to explain something that defied meaning. Power seemed to have outgrown its servitude and to have asserted its freedom. The cylinder had exploded, and thrown great masses of stone and steam against the sky. The city had the air and movement of hysteria, and the citizens were crying . . . that the new forces must at any cost be brought under control. Prosperity never before imagined, power never yet wielded by man, speed never reached by anything but a meteor, had made the world irritable, nervous, querulous, unreasonable and afraid. . . . A traveller in the highways of history . . . felt himself in Rome, under Diocletian, witnessing the anarchy, conscious of the compulsion, eager for the solution, but unable to conceive whence the next impulse was to come or how it was to act. (EHA 499–500)

Such a description throws into ironic relief Adams's characterization of his friend John Hay's accomplishments as secretary of state: "A true Roman *pax* was in sight" (*EHA* 503). The treaties and agreements laboriously worked out by Hay to create "a working system" and an "intelligent equilibrium" (*EHA* 503) among world powers fell apart shortly thereafter, as Adams foresaw.

Adams's dynamic theory and a later theory also derived from science—"The Rule of Phase Applied to History" (written in 1908, dated 1 January 1909 by Adams, and published only posthumously)—led him to predict that a crisis would occur soon:

> Supposing the Mechanical Phase to have lasted 300 years, from 1600 to 1900, the next or Electric Phase would have a life equal to [the square root of] 300, or about seventeen years and a half, when—that is, in 1917—it would pass into another or Ethereal Phase, which . . . would last only [the square root of] 17.5, or about four years, and bring Thought to the limit of its possibilities in the year 1921. . . . But even if the life of the previous phase, 1600–1900, were extended another hundred years, the difference to the last term of the series would be negligible. In that case, the Ethereal Phase would last till about 2025. (*RPAH* 308)

Lois Hughson notes that "the naive and arbitrary choices of numbers for his logarithms and square roots" renders the arithmetic embarrassing, but that it must not "obscure for us Adams's . . . attempt to bring the writing of history into relation with what science told the late nineteenth century about the human psyche and the energies that constituted the world" (80). It also must not obscure Adams's prescience about a coming crisis, which he predicted in a 1902 letter to Brooks Adams during the composition of *Chartres*: "I apprehend for the next hundred years an ultimate, colossal, cosmic collapse. . . . My belief is that science is to wreck us, and that we are like monkeys monkeying with a loaded shell. . . . It is mathematically certain to me that another thirty years of energy-development at the rate of the last century, must reach an *impasse*" (*Letters* 5:400).

Adams not only predicted the year of the apocalypse (1917, 1922, or 1927, depending on the calculations) but lived to see at least part of his prediction come true, since World War I "seem[ed] a direct application to human society of the anarchy being unleashed by scientific discovery" (Anderson 130). The image of the loaded shells to which Adams refers had their literal incarnation on the battlefields of France, wreaking four years of death and destruction in the trenches. Provocatively enough, Adams also predicted, in an 1896 letter to his brother Brooks, that the next great movement was "likely to be one of disintegration, with Russia for the eccentric on one side and America on the other" (*Letters* 4:365),

Mother Russia associated with inertial force and America with dynamic energy. As Henry Steele Commager suggests, quoting in part from Adams: "The honest historian might logically 'treat the history of modern Europe and America' as a typical example of energies initiating degradation with 'headlong rapidity' towards 'inevitable death' " (54).

Adams's apocalyptic vision cannot be dismissed as the response of a hysteric or as the knee-jerk response of a reactionary to change, or even as the response of a confirmed cynic. It was the culmination of years of study initiated because of his original fascination, ironically, with the rapid advances in science. Those contemporaries of Adams who embraced the scientific era would no doubt be surprised to learn that they now seem dated because naive, while Adams seems far more modern. Though his original fascination with science marked him as a man of his own time, his eventual suspicion of the changes wrought by science marks him as a peculiarly modern man who speaks directly to us.

Even more strikingly modern is Adams's attitude about the truth value of science. Many of his most advanced contemporaries prided themselves on their unsentimental commitment to scientific truth, but Adams struck a different note, questioning instead its epistemological basis and positing that scientific concepts were both provisional and subjective. If science did not reveal underlying order but imposed a fiction on reality, then the question of what lay beneath the mask became critical, as it was for other nineteenth-century American writers, notably Poe, Hawthorne, and Melville. Adams refers to another version of this question in a 1902 letter to Augustus Saint-Gaudens: "In philosophy, I have gone on studying and reading and thinking for many years without ever finding an answer to the question which is the Absolute, the Ultimate, the Universal;—Infinity or Finity" (*Letters* 5:382). That Adams never answered these questions conclusively is perhaps less important than that he asked them.

Unlike many of his contemporaries, Adams could no longer trust that superficial multiplicity was resolved in underlying unity (though the form of his question implies its existence), instead wavering between a hopeful belief in the objective existence of unity and a growing fear that only chaos lay under the surface. Of course, the general belief in underlying unity had been dealt a severe blow by the nineteenth-century crisis of religious faith. Like Tennyson at the death of Arthur Hallam, Adams had responded to the horrible death in 1870 of his sister Louisa Adams Kuhn with profound doubts about the existence of God, nature having revealed itself not as the perfect handiwork of an omnipotent and omnibenevolent God but as chaos.[11]

Many who found themselves in Adams's position managed to change their commitments, shifting from religion to science. Retaining a belief in unity, absolute meaning, and underlying truth, they simply expected to arrive there by a different route. Adams, however, was less certain that science held the answers: "[There was] evidence of growing complexity, and multiplicity, and even contradiction, in life. . . . He found it in politics; he ran against it in science; he struck it in everyday life, as though he were still Adam in the Garden of Eden between God who was unity, and Satan who was complexity, with no means of deciding which was truth" (EHA 397). Adams's pun on his name turns him into an everyman desperately seeking yet failing to find an absolute truth in science that is no longer available in religion. At best he can affirm only that unity *may* exist, though science cannot prove it. Ironically asserting that "the universe may be—as it has always been—either a supersensuous chaos or a divine unity, which irresistibly attracts, and is either life or death to penetrate" (EHA 487), Adams must conclude with frustration that "modern science guaranteed no unity" (EHA 429).

He thus turned his attention to man's nature. At least here, he hoped, he could discover the truth, though he acknowledged the psychological complexity of man, "the sub-conscious chaos" (EHA 433), that undermined any simple notion of identity—a multiplicity contemporaneously revealed in the fiction of Adams's friend Henry James and the "new psychology" (EHA 433) of William James and Sigmund Freud. Nonetheless, he determined that whatever the nature of reality, man at least could be characterized by his need for unity, since "order was the dream of man" even if "chaos was the law of nature" (EHA 451), and that man could be further characterized by his attempts to impose order on chaos by the creation and manipulation of symbols.[12] Linda Westervelt provocatively argues that Adams "incorporates chaos into the [*Education*] via gaps and puzzles, tension, process, irony, and disillusionment in order to compel the reader to feel the confusion and to enact the failure of the search [for order]," and she suggests that "Adams does not prove that the process is futile . . . [but] that the urge is insistent" (35). By means of the dynamo and the dynamic theory of history, Adams provides a unified system that "momentarily suffices if only because it satisfies an aesthetic desire" (Maine 332), enabling man to function in a modern world marked by fragmentation and multiplicity.[13]

Whether Adams succeeded—indeed, whether it was possible to succeed—is a matter of critical debate, but any discussion must take into account the motif of failure that informs the whole of the *Education*. It is possible that the point of no return—in Adams's symbolic terms, the perihelion of the comet—may have been passed already since the forces that man has unleashed seem no longer to be under his control, developing "spontaneous[ly and] . . . destructive[ly]" (*EHA* 486). But even if Adams has succeeded in imposing order via his symbolic system, the victory is qualified because some forms of order are unattractive: "The mind had thus far adjusted itself by an infinite series of infinitely delicate adjustments forced on it by the infinite motion of an infinite chaos of motion; dragged at one moment into the unknowable and unthinkable, then trying to scramble back within its senses and to bar the chaos out, but always assimilating bits of it, until at last, in 1900, a new avalanche of unknown forces had fallen on it, which required new mental powers to control" (*EHA* 460–61). Repeated efforts at assimilation are revealed to be enervating, as suggested here by the tedious repetitions and the loaded diction.

The mortal danger implicit in such radical assimilation is also revealed since "for human purposes a point must always be soon reached where larger synthesis is suicide . . . [so that] in the last synthesis, order and anarchy were one, but . . . the unity was chaos" (*EHA* 402, 406). The binary opposition is thus deconstructed to the point of a reductio ad absurdum. Yet Adams claimed that it is man's duty to promote this "larger synthesis," arguing in his role as Conservative Christian Anarchist (a mock organization composed of Adams and Bay Lodge) that he had no "duty but to attain the end; and, to hasten it, he was bound to accelerate progress; to concentrate energy; to accumulate power; to multiply and intensify forces; to reduce friction, increase velocity and magnify momentum" (*EHA* 406). Adams again plays a language game since the "end" to be attained is to be understood as both goal and conclusion. The bylaws of this organization are similar to the goals that Adams set for education, which "should try to lessen the obstacles, diminish the friction, invigorate the energy, and should train minds to react, not at haphazard, but by choice, on the lines of force that attract their world" (*EHA* 314). Howard Munford explains the motivation of Adams as Conservative Christian Anarchist: "There is nothing in the new scientific, industrial order a humane and sensitive man would wish to preserve. The impending catastrophe would destroy the new order and give man a chance to return to primitive beginnings" (144)—where he might discover a more productive unity and a more productive multiplicity.

The Virgin Embraced

In the meantime Adams returned to such primitive beginnings in another way. Since "all that a historian won [from studying modern civilization] was a vehement wish to escape" (*EHA* 458), Adams chose to translate himself imaginatively to another time and place, selecting medieval France to study a set of symbols that imposed order on reality in an aesthetically and emotionally appealing fashion. But in escaping to twelfth-century France, Adams did not forget about twentieth-century America:

> Adams [thought] he might use the century 1150–1250, expressed in Amiens Cathedral and the Works of Thomas Aquinas, as the unit from which he might measure motion down to his own time. . . . He began a volume which he mentally knew as "Mont-Saint-Michel and Chartres: a Study of Thirteenth-Century Unity." From that point he proposed to fix a position for himself, which he could label: "The Education of Henry Adams: a Study of Twentieth-Century Multiplicity." With the help of these two points of relation, he hoped to project his lines forward and backward indefinitely. . . . Thereupon, he sailed for home. (EHA 435)

Although this study of medieval French culture was motivated by Adams's aesthetic, historical, and scientific interests, the passage's final line suggests an additional impulse, perhaps the strongest of all. Though Adams was in 1902 literally sailing for home after a long sojourn in Europe, this line (concluding a chapter significantly entitled "The Abyss of Ignorance") has metaphoric import. In committing himself to this study, Adams freed himself emotionally from the present, a liberation that enabled him to reconstruct the medieval civilization imaginatively and then to become, in a manner of speaking, a member of that society—that is, to find a "home" there. For a man who had never felt at home in his own time, the emotional appeal of this enterprise must have been considerable.

Adams's initial attachment to the Middle Ages had begun in boyhood when, like Twain, he had first read the works of Sir Walter Scott:[14] "The happiest hours of the boy's education were passed in summer lying on a musty heap of Congressional Documents in the old farmhouse at Quincy, reading 'Quentin Durward,' 'Ivanhoe,' and 'The Talisman,' and raiding the garden at intervals for peaches and pears" (EHA 39). This nostalgic passage, the brightest and most cheerful in the chapter "Boston," is dense with emotionally charged elements. Summer, Quincy, and the farmhouse are celebrated in these final lines of a chapter focusing on their less attractive opposites. The medievalist texts contrast favorably with the congressional documents, and the "accidental education" (EHA 85, 96, 308, 353) gained from Scott contrasts favorably with formal education. Finally Adams's appreciation of sensory stimulation is subtly evident in his mention of the peaches and pears taken from the garden, samples of which his grandfather used as scientific specimens that inevitably rotted.

Although Adams may be playfully alluding to the Genesis story of Adam in the Garden of Eden eating of the Tree of Knowledge, this mention gains its particular resonance from a passage in an earlier chapter where Adams describes the first two lessons of his life: "He first found himself sitting on a yellow kitchen floor in strong sunlight, . . . this earliest step in education a lesson of color. The second followed soon; a lesson of taste . . . [when] his aunt enter[ed his] sick-room bearing . . . a baked apple" (EHA 5). For Adams, the medievalism of Scott's novels is thus associatively linked with independent learning, pastoral surroundings, and sensual pleasure. This last trait links the child and medieval man, who "had a natural colour-sense" (MSMC 138) and a "restless appetite" manifested as "youthful gluttony" (MSMC 141). Modern society "has reached an age when it can no longer depend, as in childhood, on its taste, or smell, or sight" (MSMC 138).

Adams's next experience of medievalism, as a postgraduate in Europe, was more direct but linked by the same nexus of elements. In the chapter "Berlin," he recounts two experiences that, as in the "Quincy" chapter, provide an implicit contrast. First he describes his journey through the industrialized England of the mid–nineteenth century, hyperbolically alluding to "the plunge into darkness lurid with flames," "the sense of unknown horror in this weird gloom which . . . had existed before [only] in volcanic craters" and "this dense, smoky, impenetrable darkness," concluding that "the boy ran away from it, as he ran away from everything he disliked" (EHA 72–73). Industrial England figured the hellish future that America would share a few short decades later, as Adams describes in his account of a trip west to the St. Louis Exposition in 1904 where he notes that "tall chimneys reeked smoke on every horizon, and dirty suburbs filled with scrap-iron, scrap-paper and cinders, formed the setting of every town" (EHA 466)—a prefiguring of the Valley of Ashes in Fitzgerald's *The Great Gatsby*.

In running away from industrial England, Adams ran for the first time to the medieval past, here symbolized by Antwerp, located in "a landscape that had not changed" (EHA 74) since the thirteenth century: "The taste of the town was thick, rich, ripe, like a sweet wine; it was mediaeval . . . ; but he might as well have drunk out his excitement in old Malmsey, for all the education he got from it. . . . He merely got drunk on his emotions. . . . He felt his middle ages and the sixteenth century alive. . . . As a taste or a smell, it was education . . . but it was education only sensual" (EHA 74). As suggested by the substitution of wine for the peaches, pears, and apples of his "drunken" childhood summers (EHA 8), the sensual appeal of medievalism has intensified, Adams's initiation into the Middle Ages recalling that of the intoxicated "Twain" and his alter-ego Hank Morgan in *Connecticut Yankee*'s frame story.

Adams's next notable encounter occurred in 1864 when he was invited to Wenlock Abbey by the mother of his friend Charles Milnes Gaskell, one of several women to whom Adams attached himself during this period. Older than he, married, and leaders in society, these women provided him with an accidental education that contrasted favorably with the formal or essential education provided by his male teachers. Adams complained that such relationships, their prototype the courtly love relationship, were regarded suspiciously in Puritan America where "women counted for little as models . . . [and where] the idea of attaching one's self to a married woman, or of polishing one's manners to suit the standards of women of thirty, could hardly have entered the mind of a young Bostonian, and would have scandalized his parents" (*EHA* 40). The invitation extended to Adams by this lady was an invitation into the medieval past, for his visit to Wenlock, the first of many over the ensuing decades, introduced him to "a new and charming existence . . . [that would] fit him to act a fairly useful part in life as . . . a contemporary of Chaucer" (*EHA* 207). As in Antwerp and Rome, the Middle Ages seemed still to live at Wenlock.

But Adams no longer merely drinks in this atmosphere through his senses. He imaginatively enters into life in the Middle Ages as though he were at home there. About a later visit in 1867, he notes that "he yearn[s] for nothing so keenly as to feel at home in a thirteenth-century Abbey, unless it were to haunt a fifteenth-century Prior's House, and both these joys were his at Wenlock" (*EHA* 228). By 1870, he feels so comfortable there that he images himself and other houseguests as a group of monks who have withdrawn from the chaos of the Franco-Prussian War into the cloistered "profound peace" (*EHA* 290) of the Middle Ages. Letters written some two decades after these first experiences and more than a decade before his recounting of them in the *Education* testify to the persistence of such fantasies about Wenlock.

Appropriately, it was there that Adams received Harvard president Charles William Eliot's offer of the university's first position in medieval history (concurrent with a position in American history) with responsibility for teaching a course on the period between A.D. 800 and 1649, a gap of almost a thousand years having lain between the classes in classical and modern history because the Dark Ages had been considered unworthy of study. In this regard, Adams's comic account of his interview is particularly revealing: " 'But, Mr. President,' urged Adams, 'I know nothing about Mediaeval History.' . . . Mr. Eliot mildly but firmly replied, 'If you will point out to me any one who knows more, Mr. Adams, I will appoint him'" (*EHA* 293–94). Although Adams characteristically labeled his seven years at Harvard a failure, he was widely admired by students, as were his seminars, an educational reform first introduced by James Russell Lowell (formerly Adams's Dante professor at Harvard and later a colleague who introduced a course in medieval French literature) and embraced by Adams as a sublimation of his frustrated desire for political reform. These years gave Adams the opportunity to engage in a detailed study of the Middle Ages, a task that he considered crucial because no one had yet brought the Middle Ages "into the line of evolution from past to present" (*EHA* 301). He and his graduate students investigated the medieval legal system, acting in accordance with his theory that a thorough knowledge of one aspect would provide a key to the whole culture, this method culminating in *Essays on Anglo-Saxon Law* (1876). Yet however much they had learned about the Middle Ages, he judged his experiment a failure because "its subject was merely antiquarian, [and] . . . the professor could not make it actual" (*EHA* 303).

Adams, however, had defined the problem that he would later address more successfully, the ground having been prepared by these early experiences: first, the sensual awareness of a medieval atmosphere vividly alive to him; next, the ability to absorb himself emotionally into that atmosphere; and finally, the scholarly familiarity with the historical facts of medieval culture. It was these early experiences that later enabled him to make the Middle Ages "actual" for readers of *Chartres*.

But for all his fascination with the Middle Ages and concurrent discomfort at twentieth-century life, Adams did not undertake this task until about twenty years later when impelled by an emotional catalyst that took the shape of a devastating personal tragedy from which he never fully recovered: the suicide in 1885 of his wife of thirteen years, Marian "Clover" Hooper Adams, during a severe depression. Adams was so devastated that he found it difficult to speak of Marian and virtually impossible to write of her. Even his notes in response to condolence letters are remarkable in this respect, for their subject is mentioned only indirectly, Marian's absence from Adams's life replicated in her absence from these notes. More striking still, neither Marian nor his marriage plays any overt role in his autobiography, the death of his sister Louisa serving as a projected version of Marian's death.[15] Instead there is a gap of twenty years—more or less the period of his courtship and marriage—in the white space between the chapters "Failure" and "Twenty Years After." James M. Cox argues that during this gap, which splits the *Education* into two unequal halves, "thus showing in its visible sequence the principle of division multiplying before our eyes" (160), Adams "converts the death of a beautiful woman (whether it be his sister or his 'own' Marian) into the anguished energy that will hurt him into thought" (164).

Marian's death also exacerbated Adams's lifelong impulse to escape. The present era was now associated immediately and personally with self-destruction and death. Throughout the rest of his life he traveled obsessively, making for example several extended trips with John La Farge to the Far East, where they visited Japan, Samoa, Tahiti, and Fiji. While in Japan on his first trip after Marian's death, he tellingly notes in an 1886 letter to Robert Cunliffe that "I ran away from America six weeks ago" (Letters 3:20).

In running away, Adams was hoping to find something that would revive him from his emotionally deadened condition, which is figuratively manifested in the death motif running insistently through Adams's comments about himself during the period following Marian's suicide and which he links more generally to the fin-de-siècle atmosphere of the 1890s. La Farge told an interviewer that he and Adams were traveling to Japan to find nirvana, or spiritual peace. Although La Farge's tone was playful, a serious intent lurks beneath it. But Adams's letters of this period attest that the inspiration for which he yearned was not available to him in the Far East, awaiting him instead in France, his earlier experiences of medievalism having prepared him for whatever visions were still available.[16]

Once again it was a woman who led him to the medieval culture that nourished him emotionally. Mrs. Henry Cabot Lodge extended an invitation that Adams again regarded in the light of a lady's summons to her knight. In 1895 he traveled with the Lodges to Normandy where he visited Caen, Coutances, and Mont-Saint-Michel—the first of many trips, some with the Lodges, others with La Farge (who taught him a refined appreciation for medieval stained glass), and others alone, that Adams took to the sites of medieval pilgrimage.

In a 1901 letter to Henry Osborn Taylor, a former student and the author of Classical Heritage of the Middle Ages (1901), Adams explained his motives for returning at this late date to the study of medieval culture: "I had wandered off to indefinite distances, and only returned, at last, because I was tired, and wanted quiet and solitude and absorption" (Letters 5:247). Later in this letter Adams distinguished his present motives and methodology from those when a young Harvard professor: "Never did any man go blind on a career more virtuously than I did, . . . the reaction . . . [thus] the more violent" (Letters 5:247–48). This blindness refers to Adams's focus on the historical facts of medieval culture and his consequent neglect of its actuality. But during this final stage in his life, Adams chose again to absorb himself emotionally in the medieval atmosphere, responding to the sensual appeal of the Middle Ages that now seemed more vividly real because of his command of historical facts, which he used or transformed as suited his purposes, constructing a history that provides "not accurate information . . . but only a sense of what those centuries had to say, and a sympathy with their ways of saying it" (*MSMC* 61). Adams "says" the Middle Ages in *Chartres* through his many translations of medieval texts and constructed dialogues between medieval figures (notably the debate between Abelard and Guillaume de Champeaux)—making actual by acting out, in a method more sympathetic than Twain's superficially medieval prose.

Many critics have objected to Adams's assertions about the unity of the Middle Ages, pointing out that medieval France was no utopian paradise. Paul Kegel suggests that Adams's view was one-sided and overly generous, and he draws a direct contrast between Adams and Twain in this respect, adopting the conventional view that Twain "flails away at all he finds wrong with medievalism while ignoring the positive aspects" (14–15) while Adams "extolls the beautiful while ignoring the unpleasant" (14). Yvor Winters presents a harsher criticism, insisting that "the thirteenth century as [Adams and his followers] see it never existed, and their conviction that major intellectual and spiritual achievement is possible only in such a Utopia can do nothing but paralyze human effort" (58–59). However, such critics are knocking down a straw man. Adams certainly recognized, as Charles Anderson notes, that medieval unity "was a vision, not a fact, . . . th[e] continuing effort to impose order on chaos, and the faith that it could be done, . . . distinguish[ing] the world of *Chartres* from that of the *Education*" (136). Critics like Kegel and Winters seem to miss the point of Adams's imaginative construction of medieval culture. Rather than a conventional history, *Chartres* is part autobiography, part travelogue, part philosophy, part art appreciation, and part fiction—in addition to part history. It is presented not by an objective and self-effacing narrator, the conventional pose of the historian, but by a subjective narrator who projects himself into the past. The "uncle," an autobiographical projection who functions throughout *Chartres* as both Adams's persona and his narrator, acknowledges and celebrates the symbolic if not the literal unity of the Middle Ages. In a 1905 letter to Henry Osborn Taylor, Adams distinguishes between his work and Taylor's "totally different kind" (*Letters* 5:628): "I have no object but a superficial one, as far as history is concerned. To me, accuracy is relative. I care very little whether my details are exact, if only my *ensemble* is in scale. You need to

be thorough in your study and accurate in your statements. Your middle-
ages exist for their own sake, not for ours" (*Letters* 5:628).

But the criticisms of Kegel and Winters must not be dismissed too
lightly. Though Adams yearned for the transformed medieval France of
his imagination, his imaginative construction bears some of the unattractive characteristics of the actual historical period. Adams's construction is
unselfconsciously marked by the historical limitations of the period he is
idealizing, and these limitations partially mirror those of his own period:
its tolerance for anti-Semitism, which Adams himself embraced;[17] its
support of a social hierarchy, which makes legal justice available only to
the privileged few (a characteristic that Twain had criticized in *Connecticut Yankee*); and its rigid sense of woman's ideal role, which limited the
possibilities for real women in the real world.

Kegel notes that Adams chose to concentrate, however, on largely admirable aspects of the Middle Ages—"its great emphasis on beautiful art
and architecture as preserved in the cathedrals; its maintenance of de-
cency in the good society of the middle ages; its wise administration of
farms and tenants; its encouragement of good manners and chivalric social refinements; and, most importantly, its haven of hope (in the sym-
bolism of Virgin Mary) in an otherwise very dark world" (19). The Virgin
Mary, in Adams's construction, was the most resonant symbol of the
Middle Ages because she expressed the era's energy concept, as the dynamo does for the twentieth century, both felt as "convertible, reversible,
interchangeable attractions on thought" (EHA 383). Paul Hamill provides
a compelling analysis of the relationship between the Virgin and the dynamo according to Adams's dynamic theory of history:

> [Adams's theory] is based on puns; on a literalization of metaphors of
> power, force, momentum. Power in physics is a function of energy, and
> a measure of capacity to perform work. But we also speak of political
> power, personal energy, and the work of civilizations. Comparing the two
> ways of using these words, Adams suggested that the Virgin of medieval
> devotion had done the work of building medieval culture, and that the
> Dynamo would power the construction of modern cultures. Since the
> work performed was similar, the two power-sources, one spiritual and
> one mechanical, could be measured against one another. (8–9)

However similar the work, the civilizations that resulted were quite distinct. Since Adams preferred medieval to modern culture, he necessarily
preferred the Virgin to the dynamo.

In a 1903 letter to Elizabeth Cameron, Adams referred to *Chartres* as
"my great work on the Virgin" (Ford, *Letters* 2:403 n. 1). Indeed the heart

and soul of *Chartres*, the text itself and the cathedral for which it is named, is the Virgin. As Nancy Comley suggests, the Virgin "is the central presence in the text, she is the living part of *Chartres*, and she functions as one of the main characters in the text, whose diachronic movement is towards, and then reluctantly away from her" ("Critical Guide" 66). Adams's escape from the multiplicity or fragmentation of the twentieth century is in one sense, then, a pilgrimage to the medieval shrine of the Virgin.

Unavoidably, however, this pilgrimage has certain peculiarly modern characteristics, as Adams describes in the preface to *Chartres*, which functions as a frame story introducing the uncle's dream vision, much as "A Word of Explanation" does for *Connecticut Yankee*. In the preface Adams translates himself into the uncle, the reader from son into nephew into niece, and both into tourists at the threshold of Mont-Saint-Michel, the modern tourist having supplanted the medieval pilgrim. But Adams preferred the pilgrim, "the idea of a pilgrimage, as opposed to a tour, impl[ying] for 'uncle' a spiritual and imaginative commitment to the life of the past" (Sommer, "Pilgrimage" 34). The uncle thus contrasts the behavior of the stereotypical nineteenth-century American tourist (whom Twain had earlier immortalized in *Innocents Abroad*, subtitled *The New Pilgrims Progress*)—bumbling through the monuments of Europe, snapping photographs with the ever-present Kodak, and judging the worth of everything by how much it cost to produce—with that of the individual who can respond to the beauty and spiritual power of the monuments. He insists that "to feel the art of Mont-Saint-Michel and Chartres we have got to become pilgrims again" (*MSMC* 17).

Thus the uncle takes as one of his principal causes the transformation of his niece from a mere tourist into a pilgrim, teaching her and indirectly his readers by means of a variety of techniques, including imperative commands, explicit advice, exemplary behavior, and even cajolery. According to the uncle, the monuments of medieval culture provide the modern pilgrim with evidence of the Virgin's attraction, energy, and power, for they were constructed by a populace that was inspired by her. The greatest of these monuments is the Gothic cathedral, which expresses "the deepest [emotion] man ever felt,—the struggle . . . to grasp the infinite . . . [as symbolized by] the spire, pointing, with its converging lines, to unity beyond space" (*MSMC* 106). Granting that such evidence will never convince a skeptical tourist, he asserts that it will give pause to the modern pilgrim who is willing to suspend, for the moment, his disbelief.

The paradigmatic movement of *Chartres* begins with the uncle contemplating the cathedral as it stands in the present. Next he undertakes an imaginative reconstruction, imagining it as it must have looked in the Middle Ages, since it is now "a chaos in time" (*MSMC* 149). He then extends his contemplation beyond the cathedral to the force that inspired it, moving beyond the accidental to the essential by climbing a Neoplatonic ladder from the cathedral to the Virgin. Finally he identifies himself with the medieval people worshiping the Virgin in the cathedral. This transformation is signaled by the uncle's shift from third to first person, a shift that Twain had accomplished to similar effect in his description of the coronation day pageant in *The Prince and the Pauper*. This gradual movement, a development and intensification, allows the modern man following the uncle's example to enter into the life and spirit of the Middle Ages. Thus beyond the primary evidence provided by the monuments is an experiential sense transcending such evidence.

Adams, in the guise of his narrative persona, now actually feels the Virgin's attraction. At various points throughout *Chartres* (as in his letters of the period), he imagines himself living in the twelfth century, actively participating in its traditions, and he frequently invites the reader to join him. Adams's revivification of the Middle Ages compels one such reader, Ralph Adams Cram, the neo-Gothic architect and author of *The Gothic Quest* (1907), to identify imaginatively with medieval man, recapitulating in his editor's note to *Chartres*[18] the uncle's shift from third to first person: "Greater, perhaps, even than his grasp of the singular entirety of mediaeval civilization, is Mr. Adams's power of merging himself in a long dead time. . . . It is the very time itself in which we are merged. . . . Seven centuries dissolve and vanish away, being as they were not, and the thirteenth century lives less for us than we live in it" (vii).

To Adams's mind, the child is the antithesis of the professor, for while the professor demands to know, the child's ignorance allows him to feel, and "any one can feel [the Virgin's attraction] who will only consent to feel like a child" (*MSMC* 178). Like Twain, but to different effect, Adams throughout *Chartres* associates childhood with the Middle Ages, noting that "the man who wanders into the twelfth century is lost, unless he can grow prematurely young" (*MSMC* 2)—childhood permitting a vision of unity while adulthood demands an acknowledgment of multiplicity. Cram later echoes this motif in his editor's note, describing the "childlike simplicity and frankness" and the "youthful ardour" of the Middle Ages (vii). Adams forges a further connection between the very young and old, noting that "one needs only to be old enough in order to be as young as one will" (*MSMC* 2). The youthful niece and elderly uncle are thus suited to make the leap of imagination and emotion necessary to carry them from the physical cathedral into the medieval past, first youth and second childhood enabling the translation to this "childlike time" (*MSMC* 290) of unity.

In translating himself into the Middle Ages, modern man escapes from the horrors of the modern world. Adams later used the Middle Ages as an escape from the particular horrors of World War I, as he wrote to Charles Milnes Gaskell in 1915: "Of the war I hear only too much, but I . . . wish only to escape it. I live still only in the 12th century. These mountains echo to the Châtelain de Coucy [a medieval trouvère]. The Crusades are my life, and Coeur de Lion my joy. They are more melodious than 24-inch guns" (*Letters* 6:702). In his last years (after his cerebral thrombosis in 1912 and during the war years 1914–18), he found a purpose in life in the "Scuola Cantorum for the 12th century" (*Letters* 6:598) that he organized, directing others in the search for medieval music in manuscript, which his "niece-in-wish" Aileen Tone would then sing.

The uncle of *Chartres* would have us believe that modern man may use the Middle Ages to escape from the limitations of human life itself, "Mary concentrat[ing] in herself the whole rebellion of man against fate; . . . the whole unutterable fury of human nature beating itself against the walls of its prison-house, and suddenly seized by a hope that in the Virgin man had found a door of escape" (*MSMC* 276). Although Adams had been unsuccessful in discovering nirvana in the Far East, his persona manages to find, if not permanently to grasp, its Western equivalent on his pilgrimage to medieval France:

> The mass of suppliants before the choir [at Chartres] look up . . . and feel there the celestial peace and beauty of Mary's nature and abode. There is heaven! and Mary looks down from it, into her church, where she sees us on our knees, and knows each one of us by name. There she actually is— not in symbol or in fancy, but in person. . . . People who suffer beyond the formulas of expression—who are crushed into silence, and beyond pain—want no display of emotion—no bleeding heart—no weeping at the foot of the Cross—no hysterics—no phrases! . . . There above is Mary in heaven who sees and hears me as I see her. . . . Saints and prophets and martyrs are all very well, and Christ is very sublime and just, but Mary *knows*! (*MSMC* 195–96)

For one sublime moment Adams finds in the Virgin the peace that he had searched for since his wife's suicide crushed him into silence and beyond pain. The profoundly personal nature of this experience is signaled again by the shift from the implicit third-person plural to first-person plural to first-person singular.

Adams devotes much of *Chartres,* especially the central chapters that serve as a fulcrum on which the text balances, to a discussion of the Virgin's attributes that define her "double character" (*MSMC* 73) as both goddess and woman. Since the Virgin's traits, according to the uncle, are intrinsically feminine, they are manifested by all women. In a wonderfully circular movement, the uncle then looks to women, specifically "the great ladies who dictated taste at the Courts of France and England" (*MSMC* 100), to determine what the Virgin is like. But the uncle, while asserting that "the proper study of mankind is woman," also notes that modern man encounters difficulties because "the scientific mind is atrophied, and suffers under inherited cerebral weakness, when it comes in contact with the eternal woman—Astarte, Isis, Demeter, Aphrodite, and the last and greatest deity of all, the Virgin" (*MSMC* 198). The artist alone is privileged to revive "archaic instincts" and thereby to "rediscover the woman" (*MSMC* 198).

Significantly, Adams's earlier journeys to Japan (1886) and the South Seas (1890), journeys he took to recuperate emotionally from his wife's suicide, were marked by just such a search for the eternal woman, as he indicated to Lucy Baxter in 1890: "The position of women—or Woman, if you prefer—in an archaic society has always interested me. . . . I have caught it [in Samoa] all alive" (*Letters* 3:324). Adams obsessively returns in his Polynesian letters to the theme of the Eternal or Archaic Woman[19] and more narrowly to her manifestation in particular Polynesian women, including not only lyrical descriptions of the beauty and sensuality of these women (whose ritualistic fertility dance the *Siva* he admired) but detailed lists of measurements (height, wrist size, head width), thereby approaching the women emotionally and aesthetically, but also scientifically. He ultimately notes in an 1891 letter to Elizabeth Cameron that he has "learned from her [the Tahitian queen about whom Adams wrote the first-person narrative *Memoirs of Marau Taaroa, Last Queen of Tahiti* (1893)] what the archaic woman was" (*Letters* 3:485). Given Adams's subsequent immersion in the culture of the Middle Ages and his concurrent commitment to ideal Woman in the figure of the Virgin and medieval women in the form of ladies at court, it is significant that his descriptions of Polynesian society emphasize its feudal nature. In an 1890 letter he describes the Samoans as "tremendous aristocrats" whose chief is a "feudal lord" (*Letters* 3:321), and in 1891 letters he notes that Polynesian chiefs are "aristocrats with a backing of endless tradition and war" (*Letters* 3:428) and that the civilizations of Samoa and Fiji are "intensely aristocratic" and "perfectly indifferent to everything except woman and war" (*Letters* 3:518).

The feminine attributes that Adams studied in Polynesia became the central focus of his imaginative trip to the Middle Ages. Like C. S. Lewis (who later says of the "new thing" called courtly love that "real changes in human sentiment are very rare . . . but [courtly love] is one of them" [11]), Adams celebrated in medieval culture the revolutionary acknowledgment of woman's power and superiority that was manifested in Mariolatry and courtly love. His sources were both medieval (such as collections of the legendary miracles of the Virgin) and contemporary (such as Gaston Paris's study of medieval French literature).[20]

Noting that Mariolatry and courtly love were two sides of the same coin, Adams indicates in the following remarkable passage that the feminine attributes were perfectly symbolized in the Virgin of Chartres and materialized in the courtly ladies:

> The Queen Mother was as majestic as you like; she was absolute; she could be stern; she was not above being angry; but she was still a woman, who loved grace, beauty, ornament,—her toilette, robes, jewels;—who considered the arrangements of her palace with attention, and liked both light and colour; who kept a keen eye on her Court, and exacted prompt and willing obedience from king and archbishops as well as from beggars and drunken priests. She protected her friends and punished her enemies. She required space . . . because she was liable at all times to have ten thousand people begging her for favours—mostly inconsistent with law—and deaf to refusal. She was extremely sensitive to neglect, to disagreeable impressions, to want of intelligence in her surroundings. She was the greatest artist, as she was the greatest philosopher and musician and theologian, that ever lived on earth, except her Son, Who, at Chartres, is still an Infant under her guardianship. Her taste was infallible; her sentence eternally final. (*MSMC* 90)

Woman is characterized by certain "feminine" attributes. She has great personal beauty and charm. Because her aesthetic sensibility is refined and her taste excellent, she has a civilizing effect on all around her. She has imagination and style, wit and a sense of fun, and she loves to be amused. She is sometimes capricious. Her intelligence is intuitive rather than analytic. Logic impresses her far less than faith. She makes law yet is not constrained by law; thus however much her presence effects unity and order in society, she embodies contradictions. Her mercy is not limited by a strict sense of justice. She loves all who love her, just as a mother loves her child whatever his wrongdoings. She is a coquette who enjoys being courted. She is passionate, a sexual being.

All of these characteristics combine, according to Adams, to create the enormously potent feminine power. John Carlos Rowe suggests that it is as the "ultimate mother, the mythic *Venus geneatrix* . . . [that] the Virgin's creative power is expressed, [for as] the mother of Christ, she is the heart of Western Christianity, a primordial source of energy" (74–75). Adams's Virgin uses this sexual energy to create a dynamic balance in medieval society.[21] This balance is embodied in the figure of Adams's Virgin of Chartres (associated with Gothic architecture, the pointed arch, romances, and courtly love), who, though archetypally feminine (and thereby balancing the archetypally masculine figure of St. Michael of the Mount, associated with Romanesque architecture, the round arch, chansons de geste, and chivalry), paradoxically manifests "quiet, masculine strength" (*MSMC* 195), just as the medieval woman is described by the uncle as "a masculine character" (*MSMC* 199) and the medieval man as "effeminate" (*MSMC* 204). Rigid gender polarity—locating "the female as the essential, the male as the superfluity" (*MSMC* 198)—is briefly revealed to be complex and fluid, allowing the uncle to translate himself at one remarkable point (shifting from third to first person) into a medieval mother praying to the Virgin for her lost baby (see *MSMC* 196).

Feminine power as described by Adams is sometimes manifested in curious forms, however. He notes of the medieval woman that "sometimes [her] husband beat her, dragged her about by the hair, locked her up in the house," but he adds that her husband "was quite conscious that she always got even with him in the end" (*MSMC* 200). He provides examples of such "victorious" women—ladies who as wives have necessarily sunk to the inferior position of mere women, according to C. S. Lewis's reading—noting in particular that history "resounds with . . . [Henry II of England's] battles with Queen Eleanor whom he, at last, held in prison for fourteen years, [but] prisoner as she was, she broke him down in the end" (*MSMC* 200–201). Adams's identification of these female behaviors as powerful is startling, but the emotional intensity of his portraits of medieval women—the Virgin of Chartres, but also courtly ladies such as Blanche of Castile, Mary of Champagne, and Eleanor of Guienne—actually derives from his dissatisfaction with the modern woman, who demanded a different sort of power.

Yet even in the modern age he preferred women to men since he felt that modern women retained at least some of the characteristics of the medieval ideal, that they "were still in touch with the primary sources of vitality, where men, by what they called civilization, law, institutions, and above all, by the exercise of power—had cut themselves away from these sources" (Bell, "Morality" 112). Adams looked particularly to his wife, Marian, and in later years to Elizabeth Cameron—his young, beautiful, and unhappily married Washington neighbor—for contemporary models approaching the medieval ideal, and he borrowed characteristics of these two women in creating his portrait of the Virgin. Joseph Byrnes calls *Chartres* "a tribute to Marian and Elizabeth," describing the Virgin of Chartres chapters as "a consolation-gift that Henry Adams gave to himself to compensate for Marian's absence and Elizabeth's unattainability," the Virgin "a projection of [Adams's] own idealization of his female relationships" (165).

Marian's power was direct, her manner approximating that of the Virgin as empress or the imperious Blanche of Castile, her name recalling both the Virgin Mary and the powerful, energetic, and intelligent Marion of "Li Gieus de Robin et de Marion," a "good-natured" satire by a medieval Adam (de la Halle) "directed wholly against the men" (*MSMC* 242), which Adams translates and interprets in the chapter "Nicolette and Marion." In 1871, shortly before his marriage, Adams wrote to his brother Brooks that Marian "has completely got the upper hand of me, for I am a weak-minded cuss with women, and the devil and all his imps couldn't resist the fascination of a clever woman who chooses to be loved" (*Letters* 2:132).

Elizabeth Cameron, on the other hand, ruled gently, her passivity contrasting with Marian's more active nature. While Marian lived, Adams expressed his admiration for Mrs. Cameron in playful terms, exaggerating his courtly devotion, but after his wife's suicide, Adams increasingly turned for emotional support to the beautiful younger woman. In his many letters to her in the years following his wife's death, he repeatedly expressed his intensifying devotion, though careful of her sense of propriety,[22] as in this 1891 letter: "You have a nature like an opal, with the softest, loveliest, purest lights, which one worships and which baffles one's worship" (*Letters* 3:560). In contrast to Marian Adams's behavior, Mrs. Cameron's manner approximated that of the Virgin as madonna rather than empress: "As for your thinking of me . . . I am . . . as grateful as though I were a ten-year-old boy whom you had . . . put in a rapture of joy at being noticed" (*Letters* 3:510).

Perhaps the shock of his wife's death sharpened his need for the tenderness of a madonna-mother to replace the imperial and imperious woman he had married and who had remained childless.[23] Adams frequently imaged himself at this time as a child, even a babe in arms, as in an 1890 letter where he recounts that the Samoan "women can all carry me in their arms as though I were a baby" (*Letters* 3:293). The letter's recipient (Elizabeth Cameron in her role as madonna) and subject (the Samoan women in their role as archaic women) were led to perceive

Adams as a baby to be nurtured and protected. In his letters to Mrs. Cameron's young daughter Martha, he alternated between two personae: Dr. Dobbitt, an elderly tutor, and Dordy, a helpless little boy even younger than Martha.[24] Adams wrote revealingly to Mrs. Cameron in 1892: "You are as good and kind as a very respectable and eminently devoted mother, and I am very grateful and filially responsive for it, as a good Dordy . . . should be. . . . Women are naturally neither daughters, sisters, lovers nor wives, but mothers" (*Letters* 4:23).

Whether dedicating himself to Marian or to Elizabeth Cameron—to the empress or the madonna—Adams, like the medieval troubadours and the chivalric knights with whom he identified, presented himself as a champion of womanhood. His explicit celebration of the female principle in *Chartres* has made him an apt touchstone for critics interested in making polemical points, hostile or sympathetic, about the feminist movement.

The same assumption about Adams's feminism is made by Edward Saveth (a male critical voice of the 1950s) and Sandra Gilbert (a contemporary feminist voice). Saveth notes that "before it was popular . . . Henry Adams evolved a theory of feminine superiority," but Saveth's contempt for this "theory" is evident in his patronizing tone: "Snob that he was, it would have been small comfort to Adams . . . to have known that he anticipated the conclusions of feature writers in magazines of predominantly feminine readership circa 1956. Nevertheless, long before . . . clubwomen's minds [were filled] with ideas about their superiority, Henry Adams liked to startle his guests by asking which of them believed that he was the equal of, or superior to, his wife" (231). Sandra Gilbert heralds Adams for this same theory in her whimsical "The Education of Henrietta Adams": "Most important from Henrietta's point of view . . . was that in seeking the whole of his education her uncle Henry had focused his attention on just the holes that she had perceived in her own high school curriculum. For when he decided that the Middle Ages were dominated, church and state, by the majestic figure of the Virgin Mother and by the . . . queens—Eleanor and Isolde—who were her earthly surrogates, [he] had asked crucial questions about Western civilization that were curiously similar to her own" (7). Although critics like Saveth and Gilbert may be on opposite ends of the continuum with regard to feminism, they agree that Henry Adams was a doting uncle to the movement.

Yet "stereotyping . . . colors Adams's discussion of the qualities of women, and his reputation as a feminist can be sustained only in part," as William Dusinberre suggests (203). Though Adams certainly celebrated women, his "trick" (*EHA* 442) of affirming women's superiority was constrained by his limited conception of appropriate female behavior. Eugenia Kaledin notes that Adams was "reluctant . . . to support the idea that woman should be independent," believing that education was " 'indispensable if women are at all anxious to adapt themselves for what is demanded of them by men' " (137). Brooks Adams's description of Henry's last years reveals the patronizing element in his celebration: "[Henry] came rather to shun me, seeming to prefer women's society, in which he could be amused and tranquillized" ("Heritage" 102).

It is little wonder, then, that Adams "frequently made insulting remarks about feminists, . . . [calling them] 'a vile gang of women's rights advocates'" (Kaledin 134). Both aspects of Adams's attitudes toward women are evident in his early Lowell Institute lecture "Primitive Rights of Women" (1876),[25] which "challenges received opinions regarding the subjugation of women" but conservatively argues that "women's independence leads to the disintegration of the family and civil anarchy" (Decker 130). Comley notes that "though Adams was a strong proponent of women's legal rights . . . he felt that women had no place in politics, or in the workplace" ("Feminine Fictions" 5). Adams's coarse portrait in *Democracy* of the female lobbyist Mrs. Baker, with its suggestion of sexuality employed in the service of politics, reveals this distaste, recalling Twain's portrait of Laura Hawkins as lobbyist, whose "power of fascination" (*GA* 138, 140–41, 143, 245)—code for sexual appeal—is narratively punished by death at the end of *The Gilded Age*.

Adams's dedication to a medieval ideal of womanhood ironically enabled him to criticize the modern woman, the New Woman of the nineteenth century, with impunity while maintaining his stance as a champion of women. His praise was reserved for those women who served as muses, mother figures, and sexual partners. Only in this last respect did he differ radically from the genteel sentimentalists of the nineteenth century. Yet this difference is certainly significant. His praise of woman as a sexual being and his concomitant criticism of the "monthly-magazine-made American female" (*EHA* 384) derive from his interpretation of the significance of the ideal woman in her medieval manifestation as Virgin, a significance that "history has shown itself clearly afraid to touch" (*MSMC* 261), according to Adams:

> No one has ventured to explain why the Virgin wielded exclusive power over poor and rich, sinners and saints, alike. Why were all the Protestant churches cold failures without her help? Why could not the Holy Ghost—the spirit of Love and Grace—equally answer their prayers? . . . Why did the gentle and gracious Virgin Mother so exasperate the Pilgrim

Father? Why was the Woman struck out of the Church and ignored in the State? These questions are not antiquarian or trifling in historical value; they tug at the very heart-strings of all that makes whatever order is in the cosomos. If a Unity exists, in which and toward which all energies centre, it must explain and include Duality, Diversity, Infinity—Sex! (*MSMC* 261)

While Mariolatry enabled Catholicism to maintain an uneasy relationship with Woman, Puritanism rejected her entirely, Adams argues, seeking "to abolish the woman altogether as the cause of all evil in heaven and on earth" (*MSMC* 277).

Adams's historical shift to the Middle Ages and his concomitant celebration of medieval woman thus offered him a base from which he was able to acknowledge and celebrate female sexuality. Indeed Contosta points out that the original cathedral at Chartres "had been built to house the tunic Mary supposedly had worn at the time of conception," noting that "to the inhibitants [*sic!*] of Chartres she symbolized fecundity, and they prayed to her to grant them children . . . [in] a fertility rite not unlike that Adams and La Farge had witnessed in Samoa" (117). At the same time, this celebration of the eternal woman in the form of the Virgin allowed Adams to suggest an explanation for the decline of religion in the modern age, which Adams personally experienced and regretted, no longer able to commit himself to a church (in this regard like his contemporary heroines Madeleine and Esther) except when imaginatively identifying himself with medieval man. Thus in *Esther,* the artist Wharton (based on La Farge) comments critically of the required design for the neo-Gothic Episcopal Church of St. John's: "I would like . . . to go back to the age of beauty [the twelfth century] and put a Madonna in the heart of their church. The place has no heart" (*E* 262).

Adams's dedication to the medieval ideal provided the dispensation for his attractive celebration of female sexuality, but it also less attractively justified his distaste for the New Woman—concerned with education, employment opportunities, and political power, and willing to compete directly with men—who was increasingly prominent in nineteenth-century America.[26] In an 1875 letter to Robert Cunliffe he writes scornfully of the New Woman's attempt to improve herself for herself: "Our young women are haunted by the idea that they ought to read, to draw, or to labor in some way, not for any such frivolous object as making themselves agreeable to society, nor for simple amusement, but 'to improve their minds.' They are utterly unconscious of the pathetic impossibility of improving those poor little hard thin, wiry, one-stringed instruments which they call their minds, and which haven't range enough to master one big emotion, much less to express it in words or figures" (*Letters* 2:235). Condescension marks an earlier comment to Charles Milnes Gaskell in 1872: "It *is* rather droll to examine women's minds. They are a queer mixture of odds and ends, poorly mastered and utterly unconnected. But to a man they are perhaps all the more attractive on that account" (*Letters* 2:137). By 1905, Adams writes damningly of the modern American woman to Margaret Chanler, implicitly contrasting that contemporary reality with the medieval ideal: "The American woman is a failure . . . [because] she has held nothing together, neither State nor Church, nor Society nor Family. . . . She is a worse failure than the American man who is surely failure enough" (*Letters* 5:701). In escaping from the modern world, Adams was "fly[ing] from the modern woman" (*Letters* 4:213), as he wrote in 1894 to Lucy Baxter, the tongue-in-cheek tone only partially disguising an underlying truth that is also manifested in *Chartres* when the uncle asserts that "historians abhor emancipated women,—with good reason, since such women are apt to abhor them" (*MSMC* 201).

Both Madeleine Lee and Esther Dudley, the heroines of Adams's two novels, share some of the traits of the New Woman.[27] Although the two are characterized (like Marian Adams) by taste, elegance, imagination, and sympathy—all traits of the medieval ideal—they are, like the New Woman (and once again like Marian Adams), also restless, attempting to grasp traditionally male power and to wrestle rationally with intellectual problems rather than grasping them intuitively in the supposedly feminine manner. Independent-minded women both, Madeleine and Esther (like Marian Adams) are bearers of private incomes and decided opinions. Madeleine seems determined to put her traditional life as a wife and mother behind her once she is widowed, and the free-thinking Esther is, according to Wharton, "one of the most marked American types I ever saw" (*E* 222), a characterization that Henry James had earlier made of Marian Adams, as she reports in an 1882 letter to her father: "I seemed to him 'the incarnation of my native land'—a most equivocal compliment coming from him. Am I then vulgar, dreary, and impossible to live with?" (*Letters of Mrs. Henry Adams* 384).

The ultimate fates of Madeleine and Esther are telling, given that both novels were completed before Marian's death, for Adams kills these New Women off by having them kill themselves, at least metaphorically. Though *Democracy* ends with Madeleine running away from America to Egypt after determining that her foray into politics was a failure, the metaphorical pattern of the novel suggests an even worse fate. She confesses that "the fire is burned out [in her]" (*D* 173), and her sister observes that "she would just as lief kill herself as not" (*D* 168). Madeleine's suicidal impulse results initially from a hysterical sense of guilt and self-hatred at having survived the deaths of her husband and child, the plot of *Democracy* functioning on one level as an elaborated attempt to answer the question "whether any life was worth living for a woman who had neither husband nor children" (*D* 220). Though Madeleine attempts to answer this question in the affirmative by reference first to philanthropy (a stereotypically feminine activity) and then politics (a stereotypically masculine pursuit), she ultimately fails since "such a strain could only end in a nervous crisis" (*D* 222), as the narrator sagely observes. From the depths of her collapse, this newly chastened New Woman cries out: "What a vile thing life is! . . . how I wish I were dead! how I wish the universe were annihilated!" (*D* 222). Having failed in her own mind as wife and mother, her sense of intrinsic unworthiness can gain ultimate solace from self-sacrifice alone. Yet whatever its immediate origins, this masochism is, according to the narrator, inherent to the feminine nature, "a woman's natural tendency towards asceticism, self-extinction, self-abnegation" (*D* 120). Little wonder that by the end of the novel Madeleine desires only death, though the wish is masked in metaphor: "What rest it would be to live in the Great Pyramid" (*D* 243)—that is, in a great tomb, a city of the dead.

Adams more thinly disguises the death-directed impulse of his heroine in *Esther*, which climaxes with Esther running away to Niagara Falls where she weeps as she listens to the secret uttered by "the voice of the waters" (*E* 348). Esther's terrible distress results from her inability to believe in the religion of her fiancé, an Episcopal priest, and her inability to marry him without such faith.[28] Despairing that she belongs to "a different world, . . . a new world now" (*E* 368–69), this Puritan descendant who has internalized the "puritan . . . hostility to women" (*MSMC* 202) manifests, like Madeleine, an hysterical self-hatred—"I despise and loathe myself" (*E* 369)—and a complete lack of self-worth: "I am not good enough for you. You must love someone who has her heart in your work. . . . I shall ruin your life!" (*E* 299). Hating herself because unable to sacrifice herself in marriage as society tells her she must, she can do nothing but commit suicide, at least metaphorically, for "a woman who rebels is lost" (*E* 231), according to the omniscient narrator.

Just as Marian Adams's name goes unuttered in condolence letters and in the *Education*, so does the word spoken to Esther at the end of the novel by "the voice of the waters." Such a gap cannot help but intrigue. Yet what could Niagara have said to Esther but "Jump?" A stereotypical honeymoon destination initially imaged as a female "waterfall . . . divinity" (*E* 223), Niagara is soon translated into a masculine energy—appropriately, since in 1881 (some three years before *Esther's* publication) it was first harnessed to a dynamo to generate hydroelectric power (and with poetic justice was later the location of the Adams Station [named after Edward Dean Adams], the world's first large-scale hydroelectric power plant, opened in 1895). As Adams's friend Clarence King (on whom the character Strong was based) wrote after reading the novel, Adams should have ended it with Esther "jump[ing] into the Niagara as that was what she would have done" (quoted by Friedrich 306). Adams admitted to the power of this suicidal impulse in his heroine when he replied to King: "Certainly she would but I could not suggest it" (quoted by Friedrich 306). Only a certain literary propriety and fastidiousness restrained him, causing him to defuse Esther's suicidal impulse by providing an objective correlative and also by luridly projecting this impulse onto a madwoman in the attic—Wharton's insane, drug-addicted, exotically foreign, and socially inappropriate wife.

Propriety and fastidiousness, however, did not restrain Marian Adams, nor did metaphor and projection suffice. Since Madeleine and Esther were both largely based on Marian, the fate of this real-life Adams heroine and representative New Woman is all the more chilling. Seventeen months after the publication of *Esther*, Marian killed herself (on 6 December 1885) by drinking potassium cyanide, a chemical used in the amateur photographic work to which she had committed herself with success since 1883. Until the end of his life some thirty-three years later, Adams saved the bottle of potassium cyanide that he had discovered with his wife's body,[29] and in the years following her death he increasingly saw the camera as a destructive instrument of modern technology and an agent of psychological disturbance, spiritual damnation, and death.[30] Of the novel *Esther*, Adams tellingly wrote to John Hay in 1886, "Now, let it die!" (*Letters* 3:34). In Marian's last letter to her sister Ellen, she wrote, in terms reminiscent of those used by Madeleine and Esther: "If I had one single point of character or goodness I would stand on that and grow back to life" (quoted by Friedrich 318). Her self-hatred is coupled, like that of Madeleine and Esther, with a sense of unworthiness as a woman and wife: "Henry is more patient and loving than words can express. . . . God might envy him. . . . Henry is beyond all words tenderer and better than all of you even" (quoted by Friedrich 318).

Adams's dedication to the medieval ideal of womanhood is, then, linked to his sense of women as limited creatures who would do well to aspire only to certain traditional roles and who attempt to transform those roles—to become New Women (as Marian Adams had done)—

only at their mortal peril. The foils he provides for his two heroines—
Madeleine's sister Sybil Ross and Esther's companion Catherine Brooke
("lovingly modeled on Elizabeth Cameron" [Friedrich 305], who was a
foil of sorts in her own right)—are both simpler girls of a more traditional type—prettier, more frivolous, less intellectual—who, though initially less attractive because less complex, are presented ultimately as appealing children more attractive than the adult heroines. It is particularly
telling that Catherine Brooke, one of the few characters in *Esther* to feel
herself at home in the "older world" (*E* 250) of the Church of St. John's,
is able imaginatively to enter the medieval sensibility to such an extent
that she "would hardly have felt surprised at . . . seeing Michael Angelo
and Raphael, instead of Wharton and Esther, walk in at the side door, and
proceed to paint her . . . as the new Madonna of the prairie, over the high
altar" (*E* 250). Were that to happen, Catherine would imagistically provide the church with the heart that it has lacked, according to Adams, for
centuries. In this regard, she contrasts favorably with Esther, who must
refuse Hazard because she does not "ha[ve] her heart in [his] work"
(*E* 299), and Madeleine, who "ha[s] no heart to give" to Carrington
(*D* 173) because it has turned into "pure steel" (*D* 9).

However, Adams places relatively little explicit blame on his contemporary heroines, Esther or Madeleine (or for that matter, Marian Adams,
whose life and death he expunges from his autobiography), for the
situation in which they find themselves and the problems they must confront. If Esther has, as Wharton indicates, "nothing medieval about her"
(*E* 223), that is because she, like Madeleine—and like Marian Adams—
lives in a rigorously modern world.

Henry Adams also lived in just such a world, except when he could
imaginatively escape to twelfth-century France and kneel before the Virgin in Chartres Cathedral. "As myth," Ronald Martin points out, "*Chartres* records another loss of paradise" (110)—like the loss of Quincy, the
loss of childhood itself. Heir to the eighteenth-century Adams family
traditions, educated in the nineteenth century, and emotionally attracted
to the culture of the twelfth century, Adams, for all his allegiance to the
past, had to adapt himself to the modern world of twentieth-century
America. As he navigated between the centuries on an imaginative journey whose intensity surpassed that of geographical journeys, he confronted basic human questions, recognizing even in the Middle Ages "the
visible effort to throw off a visible strain," discovering there not only
"the delight of its aspirations . . . flung up to the sky" but "the pathos of
its self-distrust and anguish of doubt . . . buried in the earth as its last
secret" (*MSMC* 383), a secret that inevitably emerges over the ensuing cen-

turies as unity gives way to the geometrical progression of multiplicity, Thomas Aquinas's prime motor translating into the dynamo, man translating into machine.

The modern "lost soul" may be able, like Adams, momentarily to "bring the Virgin to life again," yet he inevitably "shatter[s] the whole art by calling into it a single motive of his own" (*MSMC* 178), recognizing that he has constructed this "childlike illusion" (*MSMC* 252) out of a desperate need and hope and faith—the heaven now "deserted," the church "empty," and the faith "dead" (*MSMC* 197).

Adams's triangulation from the Middle Ages and the nineteenth-century world into a twentieth-century wasteland future profoundly affected the next generation of American thinkers and writers. F. Scott Fitzgerald—spokesman for Jazz Age America, chronicler of the failed hero, and courtly celebrant of the glamorous vamp whose sexuality generates destruction and death—owed a particular debt to Adams, whom he had met when a young man.

4

F. Scott Fitzgerald

TENDER IS THE KNIGHT

F. Scott Fitzgerald, like his contemporary Ernest Hemingway and their predecessor Mark Twain, was the product of a troubled marriage between a socially ambitious mother and an ineffectual father, who was a failure in his family's eyes. Fitzgerald was torn in his emotional allegiance, though ultimately identifying, as did Hemingway, most closely with his father, a figure linked to the romantic past by his descent from the aristocratic Scotts and Keys of Maryland, his stories about the Confederacy, and his southern code of manners.[1] Scott Fitzgerald romantically insisted that these lapsed ideals—lost causes all because no longer relevant to progressive America—were more admirable than modern successes, yet he was also embarrassed by his father's business failures, which required the family to live more frugally than their neighbors.

When Fitzgerald moved from the family home in St. Paul, Minnesota, to the East for preparatory school (at Newman, in Hackensack, New Jersey, from 1911 to 1913), he soon attached himself to a surrogate father who combined Edward Fitzgerald's romantic qualities with worldly success. Father (in 1918, Monsignor) Cyril Sigourney Webster Fay was a Catholic priest with a private income and a network of socially prominent friends who shared a love of Catholic ritual, intellectual conversation, and fine living. As a protégé of Fay, whom he had met at Newman in 1912, the young Scott Fitzgerald became a part of this exclusive social circle, which was to shape his attitudes more extensively than has generally been realized. Beginning in late 1914, Fay's friends included Henry Adams, who noted approvingly to Elizabeth Cameron that the "delightful Father Fay . . . has an Irish love for the 12th century and our Châtelain [de Coucy]" (*Letters* 6:670). Fay attended the musical evenings that Adams hosted as head of the "Scuola Cantorum" during his last years. Adams slyly noted in a 1915 letter to Elizabeth Cameron that "Father Fay . . . has an idea that I want conversion, for he directs his talk much to me, and instructs me . . . [but] he had best look out that I don't convert him" (*Letters* 6:681)—a threat that Adams could have pursued had he chosen, since Fay "was very much about the house" (*Letters* 6:781) according to Adams in a 1918 letter.

While visiting Fay in Washington (where Fay lectured at Catholic University), the teenaged Fitzgerald met Adams. Subsequently he "read and studied *The Education of Henry Adams*" (Piper 44). Yet surprisingly little attention has been paid to Adams's influence on Fitzgerald, despite Fitzgerald's acknowledgment in a 1919 letter to his editor, Maxwell Perkins, that Adams appears in his autobiographical first novel *This Side of Paradise* (1920) as one of the minor characters: "Thornton Hancock is Henry Adams—I didn't do him thoroughly, of course—but I knew him when I was a boy" (*Letters* 138). Henry Dan Piper draws only a tenuous connection between Fitzgerald and Adams, asserting that "there is no evidence . . . that Fitzgerald was consciously borrowing from the *Education*" and arguing that "more probably, *This Side of Paradise* reflects . . . assumptions about human nature and human society that Fitzgerald at the time shared with both Adams and Fay" (44).

Prominent among these shared assumptions was the construction of the modern age and the Middle Ages as historical opposites, though Adams's conception was more sophisticated than either Fay's or Fitzgerald's. Like the nineteenth century for Twain, the twentieth century expressed an energy and excitement that exerted a seductive pull on Fitzgerald, who became the spokesman for the time he named the Jazz Age—"the greatest, gaudiest spree in history," as he described it in his 1937 essay "Early Success" (ES 87). While World War I was a culmination for Adams, providing horrible evidence of the validity of his historical theory, it was a commencement for Fitzgerald, who left Princeton in 1917 during his senior year to accept an army commission but was untouched by the horrors of trench warfare, seeing action only on the romantic front at Fort Leavenworth in Kansas, Camp Sheridan in Alabama, and Camp Mills in New York.

For the "restless generation" (TSP 278) that inherited the postwar world, World War I provided a rupture with the past, just as the Civil War had for the generation of Twain and Adams, yet at a geographical remove that foregrounded its social implications. World War I liberated the young from traditional mores, Adams's radical New Woman metamorphosing into the glamorous vamp who grasped not only political and economic power but sexual freedom that hearkened back not to the sexual generativity of the Virgin but forward to the glamorous destruction of the dynamo—sexuality as promiscuity, in Fitzgerald's queasy formulation. Fitzgerald recognized early that the feverish pace of the modern age had a destructive quality, that it used people up, bankrupting them (to appropriate one of his metaphors) emotionally and morally just as it ultimately bankrupted society economically during the Great Depression. Though the young Fitzgerald was powerfully attracted to the possibilities offered by his era, yearning for success in its terms at least as strongly as had Twain, the Middle Ages as celebrated by Adams and Fay provided him with an alternative worldview, a set of standards against which he could compare his own day. As time went on and the destructive aspects of twentieth-century life revealed themselves ever more clearly in his life, Fitzgerald increasingly turned to the earlier period, using it as both nostalgic escape from the present and apocalyptic portent of the future.

The Education of Scott Fitzgerald: Lessons in the Theory of History

In *This Side of Paradise*, Fitzgerald presents a slyly affectionate portrait of Henry Adams as "the Honorable Thornton Hancock, of Boston, ex-minister to the Hague, author of an erudite history of the Middle Ages and the last of a distinguished, patriotic, and brilliant family" (*TSP* 26). In this self-indulgent novel Hancock-Adams is condescendingly praised for his perceptiveness in recognizing the special qualities of Amory Blaine, an autobiographical projection with a vengeance (as suggested not least of all by the omniscient narrator's late lapse into first-person narration [see *TSP* 223]): "'He's a radiant boy,' thought Thornton Hancock, who had seen the splendor of two continents and talked with Parnell and Gladstone and Bismarck—and afterward he added to Monsignor: 'But his education ought not to be intrusted to a school or college'" (*TSP* 26)— this last a self-justifying observation by Fitzgerald, who had failed to graduate from Princeton, alluding to Adams's criticism of educational institutions.

Hancock provides a counterpoint to the more important Monsignor Darcy, the character based on Monsignor Fay, to whom the novel was dedicated. Doubly Amory's soul-father as both priest and onetime true love of Amory's mother, Beatrice, the paternal Darcy contrasts his faith in Catholicism, which he predicts Amory will someday adopt, with the agnosticism of Hancock, who yearns to believe in the religion that provided the foundation on which medieval society constructed itself. "The war . . . ha[ving] made [Amory] a passionate agnostic" (*TSP* 162), at least temporarily separating him from Catholicism, "whose American sponsor was Ralph Adams Cram, with his adulation of thirteenth-century cathedrals" (*TSP* 125), Amory is troubled by the contradiction between Hancock's cynicism and his religious yearnings, considering the ambivalence of this "authority on life," "adviser to Presidents," and "educator of educators" (*TSP* 264) an embarrassing weakness rather than the product of an intellectual integrity that refuses to deny emotional desire. Agreeing with both Darcy and Hancock that Catholicism is "seemingly the only assimilative, traditionary bulwark against the decay of morals," Amory fears that it has become "an empty ritual" (*TSP* 281).

By the end of the novel, book 3 of which is pertinently subtitled "The Education of a Personage," [2] Amory feels that he has outgrown Hancock, along with all his earlier teachers, thereby ironically recapitulating the very responses of the young Adams in the *Education,* yet he identifies both himself and Hancock as types of the "spiritually unmarried man" (*TSP* 271) who is "a part of progress" (*TSP* 272), offering a final proclamation that sounds remarkably like Adams's Conservative Christian Anarchy: "Modern life . . . changes no longer century by century, but year by year, ten times faster than it ever has before—populations doubling, civilizations unified more closely with other civilizations, economic interdependence, racial questions, and—we're *dawdling* along. My idea is that we've got to go very much faster" (*TSP* 272). Torn between Darcy and Hancock, Amory the "mediaevalist" (*TSP* 105)—with his "reverent devotion" (*TSP* 53) to Princeton's neo-Gothic architecture,[3] symbolic of "lofty aspiration" (*TSP* 53)—recapitulates Fitzgerald's unassimilated response to Fay and Adams, medievalists both, though with competing visions.

Despite the explicitness of Fitzgerald's portrait of Adams in *This Side of Paradise* and his metaphoric identification of the autobiographical Amory with the autobiographical Hancock, critics have generally paid only cursory attention to the Adams-Fitzgerald connection. Yet Adams's influence also colors Fitzgerald's second novel, *The Beautiful and Damned* (1922), whose male protagonist, Anthony Patch, is an Adams figure seen through the distortions of a carnival mirror (to appropriate another of Fitzgerald's metaphors). As the grandson of the wealthy Adam Patch— certainly that first name gives pause—Anthony belongs to an American aristocracy with links to Boston, headed by a prominent grandfather whose approval he seeks.

Many of Anthony's early experiences parallel those described in the *Education*. Anthony watches his father's death, accompanied by "much sweating and grunting and crying aloud for air" (*BD* 6), in a Lucerne hotel, just as Adams watched his sister Louisa's horrible death from convulsions in a Bagni di Lucca hotel. Anthony responds initially by falling into "a panic of despair and terror" (*BD* 6); Adams felt "violent emotion" (*EHA* 288) at the "terror of the blow" (*EHA* 287), which is a "personal horror" (*EHA* 289). Like Adams, Anthony visits first Washington and then a historic Virginia house (the Lee mansion standing in for Adams's Mount Vernon) whose atmosphere he prefers to that of the city. Anthony goes to Harvard (not Fitzgerald's Princeton) because "there was no other logical thing to be done with him" (*BD* 7) and it would "give him innumerable self-sacrificing and devoted friends" (*BD* 7); Adams attended Harvard because "custom, social ties, convenience, and . . . economy, kept each generation [of Adamses] in the track" (*EHA* 54). Both Anthony and Adams are disappointed in the matter of friends, though in their senior years both suddenly gain a measure of unexpected success and popularity.

Immediately after their Harvard graduations, both travel to Europe where both fall passionately in love with Rome. Both immerse themselves in the medieval atmosphere, Anthony dallying in architecture, painting, and music, even writing "some ghastly Italian sonnets, supposedly the ruminations of a thirteenth-century monk on the joys of the contemplative life" (*BD* 8). Anthony later decides to write a history of the Middle Ages, but his grandfather, a pragmatic businessman, cannot see the relevance of this study to modern American life: "Why you should write about the Middle Ages, I don't know. Dark Ages, we used to call 'em. Nobody knows what happened, and nobody cares" (*BD* 15). Adam counsels Anthony to write instead about the Civil War or the Revolutionary War—events specifically American in identity (indeed events like those that Adams explored in his American histories).

Anthony briefly contemplates committing himself to science but is put off by the fundamentals of physics and chemistry, and he considers elective politics in order to be "a power upon the earth" (*BD* 55), but the political system of the early twentieth century gains no more respect from him than the Grant administration gained from Adams, who provides no more damning indictment of the transformation of American democracy than the following: "[Anthony] tried to imagine himself in Congress rooting around in the litter of that incredible pigsty with the narrow and porcine brows. . . . Little men with copy-book ambitions who by mediocrity had thought to emerge from mediocrity into the lustreless and unromantic heaven of a government by the people—and the best, the dozen shrewd men at the top, egotistic and cynical, were content to lead [them]" (*BD* 56). Rejecting politics and science as areas where he might "accomplish some quiet subtle thing that the elect would deem worthy" (*BD* 3), Anthony dedicates his limited energy to his historical project on the Middle Ages, ultimately selling a single essay on the twelfth century. Like Adams, though with more reason, Anthony considers himself a failure. Only in the final pages does he change his opinion, having gained fabulous wealth by breaking his grandfather's will, for money has become the measure of success in the Jazz Age. But his delusion is all too evident. However wealthy, he is a broken man.

Adams's influence on *The Beautiful and Damned* is even more significantly evident in the portrait of Maury Noble, whose life does not superficially replicate Adams's, as does Anthony's, but whose attitudes about life do (all three figures associated with the eighteenth century). These beliefs appear in a monologue that Maury introduces by stating, "I think I shall tell you the story of my education" (*BD* 252), culminating as follows: "Experience is not worth the getting. It's not a thing that happens pleasantly to a passive you—it's a wall that an active you runs up against. So I wrapped myself in what I thought was my invulnerable scepticism and decided that my education was complete. But it was too late. Protect myself as I might by making no new ties with tragic and predestined humanity, I was lost with the rest" (*BD* 254). Like Adams, Maury feels that man is caught between two unattractive possibilities: "[I felt] a ghastly dissatisfaction at being used in spite of myself for some inscrutable purpose of whose ultimate goal I was unaware—if, indeed, there *was* an ultimate goal" (*BD* 254).

Ultimately rejecting the notion that life has meaning, Maury acknowledges man's urge toward truth yet fears that the quest will lead to nothingness. At the same time, he celebrates art, which though intrinsically meaningless gives life meaning of a sort, and he acknowledges the power and beauty of Catholicism, which provides an ordered moral system enabling the masses to function. But in spite of these relatively optimistic assumptions, Maury projects a bleak future for humanity. Like Adams, he denies the sovereignty of the human intelligence, his illustrative example noteworthy because it recalls Adams's dynamo: "There are people who say that intelligence must have built the universe—why, intelligence never built a steam engine! Circumstances built a steam engine" (*BD* 257). Maury suspects that man, in his attempts to master the energies of nature, will be destroyed in an apocalypse that partakes of the Adams brothers' racism. According to Gilbert Seldes's astute contemporary review in *The*

Dial, Maury's long speech about the meaninglessness of life and the coming apocalypse "reads like a resumé of *The Education of Henry Adams* filtered through a particularly thick page of *The Smart Set*" (330). Milton Stern suggests that this speech serves as "Fitzgerald's explicit attempt to follow up the self-conscious, lost-generation vision of all wars fought, all faiths shaken, and all gods dead" (134) that concludes *This Side of Paradise.* The apocalypse, or at least its premonitory rumblings, is later given concrete form by an allusion to World War I in a chapter ironically entitled "A Matter of Civilization."

Though Adams's influence on *The Beautiful and Damned* is perceptible in the central characters of Anthony Patch and Maury Noble, it would be a mistake to draw too easy an identification between the views of Fitzgerald and Adams. Particularly as a young man, Fitzgerald's irony and pessimism were more than balanced by an excited optimism at the possibilities offered by modern life, an optimism that Adams seldom felt if we can believe the evidence offered by the *Education.* Indeed this uneasy mixture of pessimism and optimism is often thought to be the central flaw of *The Beautiful and Damned.*[4] Fitzgerald's youthful impatience with Anthony's effete antiquarianism and Maury's exaggerated cynicism is sometimes evident, an impatience consistent with the narrative criticism of Thornton Hancock in *This Side of Paradise.* Much later, Monroe Stahr, the hero of Fitzgerald's unfinished last novel, *The Last Tycoon* (posthumously published in 1941), expresses a similar impatience at the mention of Henry Adams's brother. When told that Charles Francis Adams knew "Gould, Vanderbilt, Carnegie, [and] Astor . . . [and] said there wasn't one he'd care to meet again in the hereafter" (*LT* 16), the pragmatic Stahr dismisses Adams as "a sourbelly" and suggests that "he wanted to be head man himself, but he didn't have the judgment or else the character" even if he did have the "brains" (*LT* 17).

Yet granting the criticism of the Adamses implied in these portraits, Fitzgerald used Henry Adams's pessimistic interpretation of history as a touchstone, as William Wasserstrom rightly notes: "When and how F. Scott Fitzgerald . . . homed in on Adams's autobiography . . . is uncertain. What is almost beyond disproof, however, are the effects on his imagination of Adams's scholarly fusion of his own fate with the general condition of mankind as well as Adams's denunciation of progress, Adams's dogma of degradation—dramatized by womankind and womanhood in America" (166). Particularly relevant to this dogma of degradation is an early title for *The Beautiful and Damned*—"The Flight of the Rocket"—for it suggests not only adventure, aspiration, and the progress associated with modern science but the inevitable degradation of energy that causes the rocket to come crashing back to earth. Like the comet that Adams provides as an objective correlative for human history, Fitzgerald's rocket suggests an accelerating movement that reaches its apex, then reverses itself, descending at speeds beyond man's control. In "The Crack-Up" (1936), one of a series of autobiographical essays about Fitzgerald's emotional breakdown in the thirties, he describes his own ego in metaphorically similar terms as "an arrow shot from nothingness to nothingness with such force that only gravity would bring it to earth at last" (CU 70).

Fitzgerald repeatedly provides rockets in the form of his novels' male protagonists. Not only Amory Blaine and Anthony Patch but Jay Gatsby, Dick Diver, and Monroe Stahr ultimately come crashing back to earth, the novels recounting their decline and fall in painful detail. Diver's name suggests a rapidly accelerating plunge that parallels his life's direction in *Tender Is the Night* (1934), and Stahr is a kind of falling star whose metaphoric as well as literal descents (he is to die in a plane crash) are recounted in *The Last Tycoon*. It is a critical commonplace that Fitzgerald was a master at depicting the Keatsian dying fall, yet however compelling these failures are on the personal level of the protagonists, their larger symbolic resonances are equally significant since "Fitzgerald believed in a one-to-one relationship between personal and historical tragedy" (Lehan, *Craft* 134), seeing his own rise and fall as parallels for the era of the 1920s and 1930s. Fitzgerald was, according to Wasserstrom, "the first of our writers—after Henry Adams—to insist that his private failure to survive his own apocalypse registered intimations of an American disaster" (163–64).

Because Fitzgerald was, according to his daughter Scottie Fitzgerald Smith, "fascinated by the poetic aspects of early times" (496), he read more in history than in any other discipline outside literature, exploring various theories of history. While at Princeton he was "deeply influenced by the Celtic world-historical pessimism . . . in the war books of Shane Leslie" (Sklar 223). Like Fitzgerald, Leslie was a protégé of Father Fay (who had hired him to teach at Newman) whom Fitzgerald first met during a visit to Newman from Princeton in 1917. In "Homage to the Victorians," a 1922 *New York Tribune* review of Leslie's *The Oppidan*, Fitzgerald wrote in detail about his first impressions of Leslie, one of the three men to whom he later dedicated *The Beautiful and Damned*: "He first came into my life as the most romantic figure I had ever known. . . . He was a convert to the Church of my youth, and he and another [Monsignor Fay], since dead, made of that church a dazzling, golden thing, dispelling its oppressive mugginess and giving the succession of days upon gray days, passing under its plaintive ritual, the romantic glamour of an adolescent dream" (HV 134). Shane Leslie had learned his pessimistic philosophy of history in part from Henry Adams, whom he had known for years, visiting him when both were in Paris in 1902 while Adams was rewriting *Chartres* and beginning the *Education*. Leslie's *The Celt and the World* (1917) was "worked out in close harmony with Fay under Adams's influence (perhaps even including some of Adams's dictation)," according to Owen Edwards (204).

Fitzgerald's early assimilation of the historical pessimism in the works of Adams and Leslie (whose *The Celt and the World* Fitzgerald reviewed for the May 1917 *Nassau Literary Review*) was later reinforced by Oswald Spengler's *The Decline of the West*, which Fitzgerald bought and began to read early in 1927 at the suggestion of Max Perkins. Spengler's theory of history, like Adams's, denies the existence of historical teleology. But unlike Adams, who sometimes seems to posit eternal regression and degradation (as his metaphoric appropriation of the second law of thermodynamics would suggest), Spengler suggests that history moves through thousand-year cycles. Kermit Moyer notes that "the distinction between 'Culture' and 'Civilization' is central to Spengler's concept of historical cycle, . . . [with] the biography of any civilization includ[ing] a pivotal shift from Culture to Civilization" (242 n. 11). A culture is "destiny-driven, vibrant, religious, intuitive, and aristocratic"; a civilization is "rigid, irreligious, money-controlled, soulless, moribund" (Moyer 242 n. 11).

In *The Decline of the West*, Spengler celebrates culture, concurrently criticizing civilization, which inevitably develops from and subsumes culture: "Civilizations are the most external and artificial states of which a species of developed humanity is capable. They are a conclusion, the thing-become succeeding the thing-becoming, death following life, rigidity following expansion, intellectual age and the stone-built, petrifying world-city following mother-earth and the spiritual childhood of Doric and Gothic. They are an end, irrevocable, yet by inward necessity reached again and again" (31).

In a 1940 letter to Max Perkins, Fitzgerald expressed the powerful effect Spengler's historical theory had on him: "I read him the same summer I was writing *The Great Gatsby* and I don't think I ever quite recovered from him. He and Marx are the only modern philosophers that still manage to make sense in this horrible mess" (*Letters* 289–90). Though Fitzgerald's memory was probably playing him false—Fitzgerald did not read German, and the English translation of Spengler's first volume did not appear until 1926, several years after *Gatsby*'s 1924 composition[5]—

Fitzgerald's 1940 comment bears witness to Spengler's powerful impact. Some years earlier, Fitzgerald's wife, Zelda, had asked him in a 1931 letter what he would like to be doing, "to be reading Spengler, or what?" (*Correspondence* 256), and she asked him to send *The Decline of the West* to her at Prangins, the Swiss sanatorium where she was being treated for schizophrenia. Fitzgerald declared in a 1932 letter to Mrs. Bayard Turnbull that "if one is interested in the world into which willy-nilly one's children will grow up, the most accurate data can be found in the European leaders, such as Lawrence, Jung, and Spengler" (*Letters* 433). Fitzgerald later made Spengler the centerpiece of the educational program that he created for Sheila Graham,[6] with whom he had an affair beginning in 1937 and ending with his death in 1940, fictionalizing this program in *The Last Tycoon*, where Katherine Moore (based on Graham) recounts the educational program created for her by a lover: "He wanted me to read Spengler. . . . The history and philosophy and harmony was all so I could read Spengler" (*LT* 91).

Fitzgerald was doubtless attracted to Spengler's theory of history because it can be read as embodying a combination of pessimism and optimism, a combination that Fitzgerald himself frequently manifested in unassimilated form. In contrast to Adams's more pessimistic theory of history, Spengler's theory provides some cause for comfort. Just as, according to Spengler, each culture must inevitably give way to civilization in a generational fashion, so must a new culture necessarily spring from the ashes of a civilization that has suffered an apocalypse. Constructed as opposites, cultures and civilizations grow from one another. While despairing at the horrors of civilization, an adherent of Spengler can look forward optimistically to the new culture shining on the horizon, a new spiritual childhood filled with new promise.[7] What could have been more attractive to Fitzgerald, like Twain a celebrant of golden youth, Fitzgerald celebrating not boyhood but young manhood in its first flush of personal power?

Like Spengler, Fitzgerald regarded twentieth-century America as an example of a civilization in its death throes, observing as early as 1920 that "modern American civilization is death," as recorded in his Princeton friend Alexander McKaig's diary (quoted by Milford 103). During a 1927 inverview with Harry Salpeter for the *New York World*, Fitzgerald discussed his Spenglerian views, startling the reporter, who expected something quite different from this quintessentially contemporary figure: "Here was I interviewing the author of *This Side of Paradise*, the voice and embodiment of the jazz age, its product and its beneficiary, a popular novelist, a movie scenarist, a dweller in the gilded palaces, a master of servants, only to find F. Scott Fitzgerald, himself, shorn of these associations, forecasting doom, death and damnation to his generation" (274).

The doom, death, and damnation of modern civilization is particularly evident in *Tender Is the Night*, "a novel about the decline of the West, about the collapse of Western Civilization into Caesarism and moral anarchy" (Moyer 242), in which Fitzgerald explores various Spenglerian themes.[8] The terrible anarchy of World War I serves as a backdrop for the action of the novel, set in Europe some six years after the war's conclusion. Dick Diver is particularly sensitive to the apocalyptic aspect of this war, which has destroyed the genteel civilization of his American youth: "This western-front business couldn't be done again, not for a long time. . . . This took religion and years of plenty and tremendous sureties and the exact relation that existed between the classes. . . . You had to have a whole-souled sentimental equipment going back further than you could remember. . . . All my beautiful lovely safe world blew itself up here with a great gust of high explosive love" (*TN* 57). Climaxing horrifically in a gesture at once sexual and suicidal, the war has created a "new world" (*TN* 101) of love and death, with which Dick identifies himself and his friends, out of the "older America" (*TN* 101), with which he identifies the previous generation, as represented by the Gold Star Mothers and his father.

However intrinsically admirable, the old values—"dignity" and "maturity" (*TN* 100, 101), "honor, courtesy, and courage" (*TN* 204)—are irrelevant in the postwar world of the sons (whose own children have only a shadowy existence, like virtually all children in Fitzgerald's fiction, thereby protecting the essential youthfulness of these postwar fathers and mothers). Dick embraces the excesses of the dawning Jazz Age, a decade that Fitzgerald in his valedictory essay "Echoes of the Jazz Age" (1931) calls "the most expensive orgy in history" (*EJA* 21), an era when the "whole race [was] going hedonistic, deciding on pleasure" (*EJA* 15). *Tender Is the Night* catalogs these pleasures as the Divers move among glamorous resorts, sunning on the French Riviera, skiing at Gstaad, and visiting movie sets in Paris and Rome. Since Fitzgerald in "Echoes of the Jazz Age" images this era as a "carnival" (*EJA* 15), it is singularly appropriate that a pivotal scene in *Tender Is the Night* occurs at a carnival where Nicole, who was "a carnival to watch" (*TN* 149), rides a Ferris wheel while laughing hysterically. An early version of *Tender Is the Night* was entitled "The World's Fair," recalling Adams's claim in *Chartres* that the cathedral has been replaced by the world's fair, which "tends more and more vigorously to express the thought of infinite energy" (*MSMC* 106) with no promise that the energy will be put to constructive use. The Divers are on an endless round of activities (as suggested by the recurring metaphor of the circle) that briefly entertain but lead nowhere. As Dick obsessively seeks the pleasures available in this postwar world, he also experiences a marked sense of loss, expressed in a growing bitterness and uncertainty, which in turn motivates his desperate search for distracting entertainment.

The postwar world is "the broken universe of the war's ending" (TN 245), marked irrevocably by the violence of the war. Fitzgerald's fascination with this violence is suggested by his "collection of World War I pictures depicting executions and corpses" (Diliberto 193), a collection that he showed to Ernest Hemingway at a luncheon in 1925. According to Michael Reynolds, Fitzgerald and Hemingway "talked frequently about the war" during the twenties, and "Scott, who admired Hemingway's scars and damaged knee, felt he had missed the primal experience for his generation" (*Homecoming* 68).

Attempting to incorporate this experience into *This Side of Paradise*— first written at Princeton in 1917, then revised at officer's training camp at Fort Leavenworth in 1917 and in St. Paul after demobilization in 1919— Fitzgerald adopted the characteristic tripartite structure of World War I novels and memoirs but compressed the middle section (characteristically devoted to the war experience) to a mere few pages—its diminished significance aptly suggested by the title "Interlude"—composed exclusively of letters and poems, "this tiresome war" (*TSP* 102) relegated to the white space between a poem written on the night of Amory's embarkation for France and a letter written after the armistice. Drawing the novel's title from a poem by Rupert Brooke, the tragically doomed British golden boy of World War I with whom Amory is repeatedly compared, Fitzgerald offers brief and frequently jejune allusions to the war: Amory's "sporting interest" (*TSP* 55) in military battles that are compared to prizefights and football games; the equation drawn between "another ship sunk" and "somebody flunk[ing] out" (*TSP* 121) of Princeton; the collection ostensibly taken up for French war orphans but used to purchase brandy; the "No Man's Land" (*TSP* 174) of Rosalind's bedroom (a particularly tasteless pun) and the "disastrous battle" (*TSP* 210) that ends their engagement; more powerfully, the death of the aristocratic Humbird, "like those pictures in the Illustrated London News of the English officers who have been killed" (*TSP* 78), in an automobile accident that functions as an objective correlative for the war.

Fitzgerald's stateside army experiences during the war provided him with the material for the lengthy "Matter of Civilization" chapter in *The*

Beautiful and Damned, a depressing account of Anthony's tedious military training and sordid extramarital romance while at "Camp Hooker" somewhere in the Deep South, Anthony's regiment "ignominious[ly] return[ing]" (BD 372) to camp after farcically missing embarkation for France because of the armistice. "This interminable war" (BD 221) is presented largely as a welcome interruption in Anthony and Gloria Patch's marriage, the armistice's greatest impact being the brief "False Armistice" (BD 354) that it initiates for the warring couple.

Not Fitzgerald's army experiences but his postwar expatriate experience in France revealed to him the apocalyptic quality of World War I, which he incorporated into later works. Though " 'I Didn't Get Over' " (1936) is set at a twentieth college reunion and focuses on a couple of alumni whose regiment, like Anthony Patch's, had remained stateside during the war, it is filled with chaos, death, and survivor guilt. In *Tender Is the Night*, Dick Diver, like Fitzgerald, has seen no battle service, but his initial belief that "the war didn't touch him at all" (TN 115) is incorrect, as suggested by his nightmare: "His dream had begun in sombre majesty; navy blue uniforms crossed a dark plaza behind bands. . . . Presently there were fire engines, symbols of disaster, and a ghastly uprising of the mutilated in a dressing station. He turned on his bed-lamp . . . and made a thorough note of it ending with the half-ironic phrase: 'Non-combatant's shell-shock' " (TN 179–80). Dick's irony reveals a deep truth, as does the nightmare, which subverts "the romantic glamour of an adolescent dream" (HV 134) to which Fitzgerald had referred in another context in 1922.

As Carl Jung (Fitzgerald's alternate choice as consulting psychiatrist on Zelda's case) said of his similar nightmare in 1926: "The happenings in the dream suggested that the war, which in the outer world had taken place some years before, was not yet over, but was continuing to be fought within the psyche" (quoted by Fussell 113).

"Symbols of disaster" and "the mutilated" abound in the outer and the inner worlds of *Tender Is the Night.* Just as Eliot's *Waste Land* stands behind *The Great Gatsby's* (1925) "waste land" (GG 24)—the famous valley of ashes—it stands even more insistently behind the sterile modern world of *Tender Is the Night.*[9]

The characters who populate this world are cracking up (to use one of Fitzgerald's characteristic metaphors). Nicole Diver's mental illness, diagnosed as "split personality" (TN 191), is only the most obvious example of what Fitzgerald calls in "Echoes of the Jazz Age" the "wide-spread neurosis . . . evident [by 1927]" (EJA 19), much of the action of the novel taking place at two psychiatric hospitals. Nicole, divided even here in her roles as "half a patient" (*TN* 239) and half the hospital's owner and psychiatrist's wife, is only one of the psychologically wounded characters—the sick in search of a cure, the broken in search of repair. But the supposedly normal characters, those outside the discrete (and discreet) confines of the hospital, are revealed to be abnormal as well, just as the universe that they inhabit is broken by violence unleashed by the war, which reverberates through their lives: Abe North is beaten to death; Jules Peterson is shot to death; Maria Wallis shoots an Englishman, resulting in "assez de sang pour se croire à la guerre" (*TN* 86).[10]

Normal sexuality (in Fitzgerald's terms) is also a casualty of the war: Baby Warren has "something wooden and onanistic about her" (*TN* 152); Royal Dumphry and Luis Campion are homosexuals; Mary North Minghetti and Lady Caroline Sibly-Biers engage in a lesbian transvestite adventure; even Rosemary Hoyt serves to recall Nicole's incestuous relationship with her father, for she stars in the movie *Daddy's Girl* and is attracted to Dick because he reminds her of her father.

Finally, Dick, whose professional and personal task is to fix broken people, is himself a broken man: an alcoholic in need of a "leave of abstinence" (*TN* 256); perhaps a latent homosexual, given his "pansy's trick" of "transparent black lace [swimming] drawers" (*TN* 21) and his "associati[on] with a questionable crowd in Lausanne" that leads some to judge him "a notorious——"[11] (*TN* 272); certainly a man who has gradually suffered a "lesion of his own vitality" (*TN* 222) and whose "morale [has] crack[ed]" (*TN* 285), as suggested by the dissolving of his professional ethics and the unspoken guilt that leads him to admit falsely to the rape of a five-year-old girl; no longer Dick but "Dicole," one half of the Dick-Nicole pairing who can no longer "watch her disintegrations without participating in them" (*TN* 191). Though Dick initially exempts himself from his judgment that the psychiatric profession attracts "the man a little crippled and broken" (*TN* 137), he is revealed to be mutilated in exactly this fashion. While initially able to create for others the illusion of a coherent world by "restating the universe" (*TN* 191), Dick ultimately exhausts his store of energy, as Henry Adams would have predicted. Though he protests against the notion that "everybody is so tender that they have to be handled with gloves" (*TN* 178), the evidence of the novel reveals that individuals living in the modern world are just that tender, "Doctor Diver's profession of sorting the broken shells of . . . egg[s] ha[ving] given him a dread of breakage" (*TN* 177). Broken shells in a broken universe perfectly describes the postwar world of *Tender Is the Night*. When a disastrous dinner party hosted by Dick and Nicole is described by Royal Dumphry as "the most civilized gathering . . . I have ever known" (*TN* 246), the Spenglerian adjective is telling.

If *Tender Is the Night* presents Fitzgerald's pessimistic Spenglerian vision of modern civilization, his next projected long work—*Philippe, Count of Darkness*, an unfinished historical novel begun in 1934 and composed of four short stories—presents his optimistic Spenglerian vision of medieval culture. Just as it had for Twain and especially Adams, the medieval setting provided Fitzgerald with a "feeling of escape from the modern world," as he notes in a 1934 letter to Max Perkins (*Dear Scott* 209). Fitzgerald plunged into historical research for this project.[12] In escaping the modern world, he felt that he was escaping the breakdown of civilization, whose premonitory symptoms were manifested in world war, economic depression, and the immorality of the young. This last is ironic given Fitzgerald's early reputation as an agent of immorality whose fiction had led young people astray, yet Fitzgerald considered himself a moralist, and he was profoundly disturbed by the breakdown of traditional moral values in post–World War I society, presenting himself in the three *Crack-Up* essays as an emblem of the dangers of Jazz Age life.

Rather than choosing to escape into a Keatsian dream world, Fitzgerald chose at a psychologically vulnerable time to escape like Adams to medieval France, specifically the Dark Ages of the ninth century rather than the High Middle Ages of the twelfth and thirteenth centuries that had attracted Adams's attention. Fitzgerald was most interested not in a culture's apex but in a new culture's development and consolidation upon a preceding civilization's disintegration.

Fitzgerald sets his first Philippe story—"In the Darkest Hour, a Poignant Romance of Chaos and Leadership"—in A.D. 872, the title foregrounding his focus on a historical nadir when society is at its lowest ebb after the breakdown of a civilization, and he characterizes the period following the decline and fall of Roman civilization as follows:

> There were two hundred years so brutal, so ignorant, so savage, so dark, that little is known about them. It was the time when Europe was so overrun by Northmen, Moors and Huns that it had fallen into . . . helpless and sub-bestial degradation. Leaderless, the wretched farmers had no protection from the fiercest hordes from the north and the east, or from more skillful and better organized Saracens from the south. You could ride for two days across France without meeting a man who could read, write or count to ten; the inhabitants had nothing to offer to the new

invaders except their scrawny livestock, their scanty grain, their women-folk—their lives. (DH 9)

Because such a situation compels the rise of a new culture, Fitzgerald provides its agent in the person of his protagonist, Philippe, count of Villefranche:

> There are epochs when certain things sing in the air, and certain strong courageous men hear them intuitively long before the rest. This was an epoch of disturbance and change; all over Europe men were thinking exactly like Philippe, taking direction from the arrows of history, that seemed to float dimly overhead. Each of those men thought himself to be alone, but really each was an instrument of response to a great human need. Each knew that the spirit of man was at low tide; each one felt in himself the necessity of seizing power by force and cunning. (DH 94)

At the beginning of "In the Darkest Hour," Philippe rides into the Loire Valley, returning home from Spain after eighteeen years as the prisoner of a Moorish chieftain. The firstborn son of the count of Ville-franche, he is, with his tawny hair and cruel gray eyes, clearly an aristo-crat—one who resembles Fitzgerald, who felt great affection for Philippe, noting in a 1938 letter to Max Perkins that "in spite of some muddled writing, he is one of the best characters I've ever 'drawn.' He should be a long book" (*Letters* 281). The comment about "muddled writing" is an understatement (note the "floating arrows" in the passage above), for the Philippe stories are among the least successful of Fitzgerald's works. Janet Lewis notes that they are "overly-busy in plot, often trite and stilted in diction, inaccurate and inconsistent in detail" (7). Fitzgerald's commit-ment to the project over a period of years is thus noteworthy,[13] suggesting that it performed a psychological rather than aesthetic function. Having cut himself off from the present in these stories, Fitzgerald cut himself off from his artistic gift of being absolutely in tune with his own time—a separation that provided him with a necessary psychological escape, how-ever deleterious its effect on his art.

Fitzgerald was most attracted by his protagonist's rage for order, the very characteristic ascribed to medieval man by Henry Adams. Philippe embodies the "spirit which in the course of the coming century would draw the scattered fragments of civilization into the beginnings of a new order in which would be contained, like a portent, the pattern, the char-acteristic tensions and contradictions of Western Civilization itself," as Moyer suggests (243). In the course of the four stories—"In the Darkest

Hour," "The Count of Darkness," "The Kingdom in the Dark," and "Gods of Darkness"—Philippe establishes a feudal hierarchy that he heads, creates a band of men who are "in effect, his knights" (GD 31), drives out the pillaging bands of Northmen, builds increasingly sophisticated castles, and establishes an economic system based on taxation. Philippe is necessarily tough because he must deal with tough situations, but his toughness enables him to establish the beginnings of an ordered society where in a few centuries chivalric knights will ride.

Fitzgerald based Philippe on Ernest Hemingway, provocatively enough, specifying that the "Mediaval [sic] [novel] . . . shall be the story of Ernest" and querying, "Just as Stendahl's [sic] portrait of a Byronic man made *Le Rouge et Noir* [sic], so couldn't *my* portrait of Ernest as Phillippe [sic] make the real modern man" (*Notebooks* 159). Hemingway was for Fitzgerald the quintessential tough guy, powerful, brave, and adventurous despite the fact that, according to Fitzgerald, "the dark was peopled for him" (*Notebooks* 153). Hemingway's personal darkness and the Dark Ages thus combine in the motif that structures the titles of the Philippe stories and links the Dark Ages and the modern age in a paradoxical whole.

Just as Philippe's prototype was a twentieth-century American tough guy, the dialogue is a pastiche of twentieth-century slang. The effect of a medieval knight speaking like a cowboy (a connection already drawn in Twain's *Connecticut Yankee* and Wister's *Virginian*), a hard-boiled detective (a connection later drawn in numerous detective novels, as signaled by protagonists named Marlowe and Spenser), and a gangster—like a Hemingway caricature, in fact—is certainly incongruous, but Fitzgerald's purpose (however disconcerting the effect) was to draw a linkage between the Dark Ages and modern America, "the Dark Ages serv[ing] as a metaphor for the troubled Thirties," as Janet Lewis points out (17).

If American civilization had reached its apex and was now, as Fitzgerald feared, hurtling toward apocalypse, then a new Dark Ages was about to descend. As the editors of *Redbook* pedantically noted in the blurb accompanying the final story: "Witnessing the barbarities of today and foreseeing the chaos that threatens our world, Fitzgerald turned to the far-away past in search of inspiration and new courage" (appended to "Gods of Darkness" 31). In writing "Philippe, Count of Darkness," Fitzgerald was providing America with a model, a pattern to be followed when those dark days again arrived, just as Twain had projected the return of the Dark Ages in an American context in "The Secret History of Eddypus, the World-Empire" (written in 1901–2 and posthumously published), which like Spengler posited a cyclic movement—between Ages of Light and Ages of Darkness, in Twain's terminology.

Having drawn a series of lessons from various historical theories, Fitzgerald recognized the historical significance of his day and related it to the history of Western civilization. These theories, so different from the meliorism of the nineteenth and early twentieth centuries, gave him a means of understanding and interpreting his experience of diminishing physical energy, personal and professional disappointment, and the degeneration and enervation of American society. Yet for Fitzgerald, Spengler's cyclic theory concurrently held out the glimmer of hope, promising a new beginning where "lost youth" would be regained, offering the "pleasure of losing it again" (*TSP* 258). Famously asserting that in American literature there are no second acts, Fitzgerald desperately clung to the belief that second acts were a historical inevitability.

The Lady or the Vamp? Fitzgerald on Courtly Love

In establishing the beginnings of an ordered society, Philippe is the precursor of the chivalric knight of the High Middle Ages who will have the comparative luxury of acting in accordance with an elaborately defined code of martial behavior. Philippe notes that "there *are* no habits [at present]—I *make* the habits" (CD 21).

Philippe is also the precursor of the courtly knight, Fitzgerald providing several scenes depicting his romantic relationships with medieval ladies, represented by the characters Letgarde and Griselda. Philippe's relationship with Letgarde is disastrous from the first: "She had never, from the most ruthless marauder, received such treatment. . . . She came from a civilized province of old Roman Gaul . . . [and she had been] treated . . . always as a sort of queen. But this man!" (CD 22). Rather than submit to such uncultured treatment, Letgarde commits suicide, Philippe later acknowledging ruefully, "I must be pretty much of a tough" (CD 70, 72). When Philippe meets the aristocratic Griselda, he puts to good use the lessons he has learned about the courteous behavior appropriate with a lady: "'I'm different,' he promised. 'I'm not after you, baby. All I want is to know where you're going. I'm a gentleman—honest, I am—I'm a count'" (KD 58). Such reassurances, coupled with Philippe's promise of protection, attract Griselda, who chooses to become his lady—their relationship a vestigial courtly love relationship that marks a cultural advance. Consistent with the courtly tradition, the lady is revealed to be her knight's superior. Griselda eventually identifies herself as "the chief priestess of the Witches of Touraine" (GD 90). As the leader of a secret cult recalling the Cathars,[14] she is worshiped, even adored. But perhaps as a concession to the rough and primitive times in which she lives, Fitzgerald allows Griselda to remain a vivid physical being rather than a disembodied ideal. Griselda is thus a relatively attractive character, for all the infelicities of dialogue and action that plague these stories.

Fitzgerald is the most romantic of novelists insofar as the courtly love tradition characterizing the apex of medieval culture (vestigially represented in the Philippe stories) is the implicit standard against which he judges the relationships that develop during the decline of modern civilization. To the degree that these modern relationships deviate from the medieval ideal of courtly love, they are presented as failures, with the blame implicitly assigned. André Le Vot notes that Fitzgerald's aesthetic "was based on a keen sense of the past's survival in the present" (193) and that "with *The Great Gatsby* and *Tender Is the Night*, the romance of chivalry for a while dethroned the epic, [with] the woman-idol t[a]k[ing] the place of the traditional bestiary in American literature's coat of arms" (xi).

While writing *The Great Gatsby*, Fitzgerald commented hyperbolically to Thomas Boyd (literary editor of the *St. Paul Daily News*) in 1924: "I'm going to read nothing but Homer + Homeric literature—and history 540-1200 A.D. until I finish my novel . . . [which] grows more + more extraordinary" (*Life in Letters* 68). Yet his joking comment about medieval history reveals a deep truth because in Jay Gatsby, Fitzgerald created an absolutely modern hero who closely approximates the medieval knight, adhering to the medieval conventions of the courtly love tradition insofar as that is possible in the modern world.[15] The courtly knight, according to C. S. Lewis, must manifest humility, practice courtesy, engage his beloved in an adulterous relationship, and practice the religion of love—all requirements that Gatsby meets.

The son of unsuccessful midwestern farmers, Gatsby is acutely aware of his inferior social position relative to the southern debutante Daisy. Gatsby's "palace" (*GG* 49) with its "feudal silhouette against the sky" (*GG* 92), his "high Gothic library . . . transported complete from some ruin overseas" (*GG* 45), his fabulous parties, even his expensive shirts[16]—all are purchased to attract Daisy. When she first visits his house, "he revalued everything . . . according to the measure of response it drew from her well-loved eyes" (*GG* 92), and he stops giving parties because "the whole caravansary had fallen in like a card house at the disapproval in her eyes" (*GG* 114). Gatsby cares about how he appears in Daisy's eyes because in his eyes Daisy is the superior lady who gives meaning to his existence.

In his service to Daisy, Gatsby obeys the rules of courtesy that made love an art in the High Middle Ages. After five years of separation he approaches her in an elaborately indirect way, asking Jordan Baker to ask Nick Carraway to ask Daisy to tea. When Jordan suggests a much simpler plan, Gatsby is horrified, as she reports to Nick: "'I don't want to do anything out of the way!' he kept saying" (GG 80). In preparation for Daisy's visit he makes elaborate arrangements, "dress[ing] for the rendez-vous in a seeming semblance of shining armor," as Elizabeth Morgan points out (167). Gatsby behaves with extraordinary courtesy in his last encounter with Daisy. He shields her from responsibility for Myrtle Wilson's death—first taking the blame upon himself; later saying of the hit-and-run accident, in a revealing locution, "I tried to make her stop, but she couldn't" (GG 145) rather than that she "wouldn't," thereby protecting her even psychologically from responsibility for her behavior (and con-currently protecting himself from knowledge of her callousness).

Gatsby's adulterous relationship with Daisy, like courtly love as de-scribed by C. S. Lewis, is "a 'kind of chastity,' in virtue of its severe stan-dard of fidelity to a single object" (34). After "tak[ing]" Daisy in Louis-ville, Gatsby feels "married to her" (GG 149), though his previous sexual relationships have left him "contemptuous" (GG 99) of women. This dual attitude of commitment and contempt replicates the attitude of the me-dieval knight, who adored his aristocratic lady while scorning women (as given literary form in the courtly romance and the pornographic fabliaux, respectively). Gatsby has been ennobled by his courtly commitment, which is consummated sexually—the dream made flesh, or, rather, the flesh made dream. Meyer Wolfsheim calls him "a perfect gentleman" (GG 72) and offers as evidence Gatsby's "careful[ness] about women," noting that "he would never so much as look at a friend's wife" (GG 73). Although Wolfsheim's comment resonates ironically, given Gatsby's sub-sequent affair with the married Daisy, it nonetheless has the ring of truth because Gatsby does not take advantage of the girls at his parties, waiting for his meeting with Daisy, after which their affair resumes, as evidenced by his attempts at discretion: "'I hear you fired all your servants.' 'I wanted somebody who wouldn't gossip. Daisy comes over quite often—in the afternoons'" (GG 114). This discretion in the service of the lady's reputation is a requirement of the courtly knight, for "no article of the code is so important as this, and none is insisted upon so much" (Dodd 5).

In loving Daisy, Gatsby practices the religion of love,[17] finding that like an Arthurian knight, "he ha[s] committed himself to the following of a grail" (GG 149). Louisville becomes a pilgrimage site, the sun "spread[ing] itself in benediction over the vanishing city where she had drawn her breath" (*GG* 153). Later, "his count of enchanted objects" (*GG* 94) includes the famous green light on the end of Daisy's dock, and he practices a nightly ritual of adoration because the light seems "as close [to her] as a star to the moon" (*GG* 94). Daisy is repeatedly associated with stars and "star-shine" (*GG* 149), for she is the Stella to Gatsby's Astrophel, the star to his star lover in an image first employed by the *stilnovisti* poets of the thirteenth century.[18] After the hit-and-run accident he eagerly stands a "vigil" on her lawn that partakes of the "sacredness" (*GG* 146) appropriate to adoration.

Gatsby is not the only character to be involved in an adulterous relationship with a married woman. Tom Buchanan, in his affair with Myrtle Wilson, provides an illustrative contrast. Rather than manifesting humility, Tom is arrogant to Myrtle, a social inferior to whom he condescends. Rather than practicing courtesy, he is brutal, physically assaulting her. Rather than engaging in an adulterous relationship that is paradoxically faithful, he participates in a series of indiscreet affairs. Rather than practicing the religion of love (with its implication of transcendent meaning), he is interested only in casual and meaningless sexual relationships. Morgan notes that Tom and Myrtle's affair "is the very stuff out of which fabliaux are made" (173), and it thereby offers a peculiarly appropriate contrast to the courtly romance of Gatsby and Daisy.

Because Gatsby functions as a courtly knight, he is ennobled by his adulterous affair rather than diminished, as is Tom. While the illegal activities by which Gatsby earns his wealth cannot be ignored, his "incorruptible dream" ultimately displaces the reality of his "corruption" (*GG* 155, 154) in Nick's judgment, as in that of many readers. This conflict between dream and reality is central to *Gatsby*, just as the related conflict between unity and multiplicity was central to Adams's *Chartres* and the *Education*. *Gatsby* poses the eternal question: Which is truly real—the dream, the ideal, the essential; or the material, the accidental, the existential? Fitzgerald, whose favorite poet was John Keats, was intimately familiar with Keats's climactic formulation in "Ode to a Nightingale" (which also provided the title of *Tender Is the Night*): "Was it a vision, or a waking dream? / Fled is that music:—Do I wake or sleep?" Fitzgerald absorbed much of his romanticism from Keats, whose "La Belle Dame sans Merci" (the title taken from a ballad by medieval poet Alain Chartier) and "Eve of Saint Agnes" are set in the Middle Ages and present relationships between knights and their ladies.

Denis de Rougemont's analysis of the underlying motivation of courtly love provides a revealing gloss on Gatsby's behavior. Rougemont locates in courtly love a commitment to the dream, the ideal, the essential, rather than the material, the accidental, the existential. At its base he locates a desire for mystical transcendence, a wish to escape this world for the absolutely Other world, arguing that implicit in this desire is a death wish. He sees in the beloved lady of courtly poetry the vestiges of a transcendent ideal—"the Lady of Thoughts, the Platonic idea of a feminine principle" (110)—which can never be realized in this world. Since the actual lady is only a substitute for the ideal (which remains as a trace in the poetry), courtly love is "the passion that is tasted and savoured for its own sake, in a kind of indifference to its living and external object" (Rougemont 152). This indifference reveals that "the passion of love is at bottom narcissism, the lover's self-magnification, far more than it is a relation with the beloved" (Rougemont 260). Suffering is necessarily the hallmark of the courtly lover since "to love more than the object of love, to love passion for its own sake, [is] to suffer and to court suffering" (Rougemont 50).

Gatsby's desire for mystical transcendence is manifested in his desire to escape the constraints of time and therefore history[19] (a desire also implicitly manifested in Twain's *Connecticut Yankee*): "He wanted nothing less of Daisy than that she should go to Tom and say: 'I never loved you.' After she had obliterated four years . . . they were to go back to Louisville and be married from her house—just as if it were five years ago. . . . 'I wouldn't ask too much of her,' [Nick] ventured. 'You can't repeat the past.' 'Can't repeat the past?' he cried incredulously. 'Why of course you can!' " (*GG* 111). The vehemence of Gatsby's response to Nick's commonsensical commonplace bears witness to the intensity of his desire. In escaping from time, he hopes to escape to a statically perfect realm, one where he can "fix everything just the way it was before" (*GG* 111). The verb is particularly revealing because it suggests Gatsby's desire both to perfect the imperfect and to arrest time (this desire also metaphorically presented in the famous scene where he almost drops a broken clock during his reunion with Daisy).

Gatsby's desire for mystical transcendence is revealed most powerfully, however, in the truly extraordinary scene of his first kiss with Daisy, worth citing in full:

One autumn night, five years before, they had been walking down the street when the leaves were falling, and they came to a place where there were no trees and the sidewalk was white with moonlight. They stopped here and turned toward each other. Now it was a cool night with that mysterious excitement in it which comes at the two changes of the year. The quiet lights in the houses were humming out into the darkness and there was a stir and bustle among the stars. Out of the corner of his eye Gatsby saw that the blocks of the sidewalks really formed a ladder and mounted to a secret place above the trees—he could climb to it, if he climbed alone, and once there he could suck on the pap of life, gulp down the incomparable milk of wonder. His heart beat faster and faster as Daisy's white face came up to his own. He knew that when he kissed this girl, and forever wed his unutterable visions to her perishable breath, his mind would never romp again like the mind of God. So he waited, listening for a moment longer to the tuning-fork that had been struck upon a star. Then he kissed her. At his lips' touch she blossomed for him like a flower and the incarnation was complete. (*GG* 112)

This scene is extraordinarily rich with images from the courtly literature of the Middle Ages and Renaissance. The blocks of the sidewalk "really" (that is, ideally-essentially rather than materially-accidentally) form a "ladder" of love reminiscent of that appropriated from Plato[20] by the medieval Neoplatonists of Chartres (especially in the work of Alain de Lille, later translated by Henry Adams in *Chartres* [MSMC 357–58], and poetically realized in Dante's *Divine Comedy*). In the sidewalk Gatsby sees the rungs of that ladder, leading in a step-by-step progression from human to divine love. In loving Daisy he stands on the first rung; his desire to climb higher reveals his desire for mystical transcendence. Yet as C. S. Lewis notes of the Neoplatonic original, "The very first step upwards would have made a courtly lover blush, since it consists in passing on from the worship of the beloved's beauty to that of the same beauty in others" (5). Courtly Gatsby thus chooses instead to commit himself absolutely to Daisy, to climb no further. However, in doing so he does not abandon his desire for mystical transcendence, here symbolized as the feminine principle by breast imagery. Instead he embodies mystical transcendence *in* Daisy: "The incarnation was complete."

The several references to the heavens in this passage culminate with a sound akin to the medieval music of the spheres, which metaphorically suggests that this is a moment of perfect harmony, indeed perfection. The stars that "stir and bustle" to witness the lovers are here signaling their approval (at least in the eyes of Gatsby, whose version of this climactic moment Nick recounts). Gatsby's experience of this mysterious night, when lights hum and stars stir and a Daisy blossoms, is completely and mystically transformative, its memory simultaneously transfixing and motivating him. When he locates Daisy after five years, he locates the vestiges of the ideal for which he has lived, whose intensity casts into the shadows his materially real life: "In her actual and astounding presence none of it [his possessions] was any longer real" (*GG* 92).

But because Daisy embodies a transcendent ideal, Gatsby does not so much love her as what she represents. In one sense she is simply a later version of Dan Cody's yacht, which "to young Gatz . . . represented all the beauty and glamour in the world" (*GG* 100–101). Yachts are conventionally designated by the feminine pronoun (hence the imaging of Adams's Esther and Hemingway's Brett Ashley as yachts, and the overdetermined significance of the impoverished Amory Blaine's ejection from the Hudson River Yacht Club). This embodiment of the ideal in the feminine is reinforced by the fact that young Gatz met his "destiny in Little Girl Bay" (*GG* 100). Gatsby's history is one of striving for an ideal embodied in feminine form. As the last and most sophisticated of Gatsby's embodiments, Daisy has elicited the most powerful response. Relishing his passion for the "idea" (*GG* 93) of Daisy, he is disconcerted when the materially real woman threatens to supplant his idealization by "tumbl[ing] short of his dreams" (*GG* 97). Having waited five years to touch her again, he is remarkably disinterested when they finally meet: "Daisy put her arm through his . . . but he seemed absorbed in what he had just said [about the green light on her dock]" (*GG* 94). The materially real Daisy is unable to distract him from the idea of the green light representing her and, more specifically, the idea of her.

Ultimately, however, it is Gatsby's "idea of himself" (*GG* 111) that he wants to recover. The narcissism at the base of his love is thus laid bare (a more sublimated version of Amory Blaine's narcissism, repeatedly revealed in section titles such as "The Romantic Egotist" and "Narcissus Off Duty"). Just as Gatsby "sprang from his Platonic conception of himself" (*GG* 99), he requires a Platonic ideal in the form of a lady whom he can endow with his passion if he is to continue his process of self-realization. James Gatz became Jay Gatsby "at the specific moment . . . when he saw Dan Cody's yacht" (*GG* 98), and Jay Gatsby becomes the Great Gatsby at the moment when he commits himself to the idea of Daisy. She is the vehicle by which he realizes himself. Like Twain's Hank and Sandy and King Arthur intermittently, Gatsby more permanently inhabits a mythical plane, his passion's intensity drawing Daisy into that plane.

Fitzgerald provides several analogues for Gatsby and Daisy, most obviously Nick and Jordan, foils who exist by contrast in the realm of quotidian reality. But a much closer parallel is provided by two minor characters—the Star (also identified, like Daisy, by a flower designation) and her director: "'Perhaps you know that lady,' Gatsby indicated a gorgeous, scarcely human orchid of a woman who sat in state under a white-plum tree. Tom and Daisy stared, with that peculiarly unreal feeling that accompanies the recognition of a hitherto ghostly celebrity of the movies. 'She's lovely,' said Daisy. 'The man bending over her is her director'" (GG 106). The mystical quality of this surreal passage, like their professions as dream makers, suggests that these two also inhabit a transcendent realm. Their entire relationship is encapsulated in a second scene that provides a gloss on Gatsby and Daisy's relationship: "Almost the last thing I remember was standing with Daisy and watching the moving-picture director and his Star. They were still under the white-plum tree and their faces were touching except for a pale, thin ray of moonlight between. It occurred to me that he had been very slowly bending toward her all evening to attain this proximity, and even while I watched I saw him stoop one ultimate degree and kiss at her cheek. 'I like her,' said Daisy, 'I think she's lovely'" (GG 108). In this surreal scene—the white-plum tree, the white faces, the white moonlight all seem to glow—this particular courtly lover chooses to forego consummation of an ideal love in the materially real world, placing an obstacle in its way that recalls the sword placed between Tristan and Iseult. This obstacle enables his dream, the dream that he *directs*, to continue.

Gatsby's dream, however, dies when Daisy, loving Gatsby, is unwilling to eradicate the past by denying her love for Tom. Though "the dead dream fought on" (GG 135) in the face of the complexities of life in the materially real world, it is from this moment doomed: "[Gatsby and Daisy] were gone, without a word, snapped out, made accidental, isolated, like ghosts" (GG 136). And Gatsby cannot be "Gatsby" without his dream. When he must confront "a new world, material without being real" (GG 162), he necessarily and inevitably dies. George Wilson is merely the accidental (in both senses of that word) agent of a death that has already occurred. When Nick discovers Gatsby's body in the swimming pool, he notices only a pneumatic mattress on "its accidental course with its accidental burden" (GG 162), since the ideal and essential "'Jay Gatsby' had [already] broken up like glass" (GG 148).

It is only when Nick willfully chooses not to focus on the material— "One night I did hear a material car [at Gatsby's house] . . . but I didn't investigate" (GG 181)—that he is able truly to confront Gatsby's ideality and his necessary death: "The inessential houses began to melt away until gradually I became aware of the old island here that flowered once for Dutch sailors' eyes—a fresh, green breast of the new world. . . . As I sat there brooding on the old, unknown world, I thought of Gatsby's wonder when he first picked out the green light at the end of Daisy's dock. He had come a long way to this blue lawn, and his dream must have seemed so close that he could hardly fail to grasp it. He did not know that it was already behind him" (*GG* 182).

The excesses of Gatsby's idealism are certainly presented ironically,[21] Fitzgerald recognizing its impractical nature in the real and problematic world and thereby giving dramatic form to Auerbach's observation that when courtly love "has to do with the practical business of the world, it proves inadequate" (136). It is clear, moreover, that Gatsby's idealization of Daisy is misguided. He chooses to love her not because of intrinsic merit but superficial qualities. But despite the ironic undercutting of Gatsby's idealism—a task that narrator Nick Carraway frequently per-forms—he remains the most admirable of the characters, the one who is, in Nick's climactic words, "worth the whole damn bunch put together" (*GG* 154). Fitzgerald's presentation of Gatsby, then, is to a degree ambigu-ous. Gatsby seems a bit of a fool for not recognizing the unsuitability of Daisy as love object, for not recognizing that she is "[in]commensurate to his capacity for wonder" (*GG* 182), yet Gatsby's ability to wonder, to dream, and to quest is presented as admirable. Though Gatsby is culpable for dedicating himself to the wrong object, his dedication itself is pre-sented as praiseworthy. Were Gatsby a Dutch sailor viewing the "breast of the new world" (*GG* 182) for the first time (the essentialized America here identified with the feminine principle, itself identified as essentially ma-ternal, just as for Adams)—or were he a medieval knight serving a true lady as defined by the courtly tradition—his actions would be unqualified by authorial irony.

Fitzgerald's response to a 1925 letter of congratulation about *Gatsby* from novelist Roger Burlingame is relevant here, for he indicates uniron-ically that nostalgia was the motivating emotion of the novel: "I was tre-mendously pleased that it moved you in that way 'made you want to be back somewhere so much' because that describes, better than I could have put it myself, whatever unifying emotion the book has, either in regard to the temperment [*sic*] of Gatsby himself or in my own mood while writing it" (*Correspondence* 159–60). Gatsby is the right man at the wrong time, a tragic victim of history whose romantic quest inevitably fails, though not because of personal culpability. Although Gatsby comes in for his share of ironic undercutting, the strongest criticism is thus reserved for the unworthy object of his knightly quest—Daisy, the tarnished mod-ern lady who, for all that she "gleam[s] like silver" (*GG* 150), is actually a false grail undermining the successful operation of courtly love as a sys-tem of values in modern America (no longer a fresh new world, but now a "faithless land" [*TSP* 243] according to Amory Blaine). The medieval figure whom Daisy Fay Buchanan ultimately most resembles is thus not the courtly lady but the Arthurian "fée" or "fay," who in the person of Morgain la Fée (or Morgan le Fay) "undermin[es] the very foundations of the Arthurian world" (Westoby 385). The Middle Ages are again revealed to be not the opposite of modern America but its mirror image.

One need not be a particularly sensitive reader to recognize that Daisy is fickle and selfish, her moral carelessness perfectly symbolized by her bad driving (a failing shared by Gloria Patch), which has all too literal consequences when she kills Myrtle in a hit-and-run accident. Daisy's flaws are revealed most shockingly after this climactic automobile accident, one of a series in the novel that serve to characterize the accidental rather than the ideal nature of the reality these characters inhabit (much as Louisa Adams Kuhn's fatal carriage accident does in the *Education*). Having allowed Gatsby to take the blame for Myrtle's death, Daisy retreats with Tom to her mansion, where they hold hands over cold fried chicken and ale—the grossness of the meal suggesting authorial evaluation— while they plot their escape from a messy scene.

Gatsby, meanwhile, stands vigil outside the house, ready to come to Daisy's rescue. Yet this modern knight is "watching over nothing" (*GG* 146), as Nick bitterly notes. This truth is metaphorically revealed the next morning when Nick notices in Gatsby's house the "inexplicable amount of dust everywhere" (*GG* 147), thereby linking it with not only the modern Valley of Ashes but also the "foul dust [that] floated in the wake of his dreams" (*GG* 2). When Gatsby finally realizes that he is "watching over nothing"—when he realizes "what a grotesque thing a rose is" (*GG* 162) in the modern world (in contrast to Dante's fourteenth-century world where Beatrice is seated in the celestial rose, or Henry Adams's twelfth-century construction where "the Rose is any feminine ideal of beauty, intelligence, purity, or grace,—always culminating in the Virgin" [*MSMC* 247], the rose being "Mary's emblem" [*MSMC* 115] because she is in Adam de Saint Victor's words "Super rosam rosida" [quoted by Adams, *MSMC* 117])—his death is inevitable.[22]

Like Guillaume de Lorris's thirteenth-century *Roman de la Rose*, which according to Adams owes its "interest only to the constant effort of the dreamer to attain his ideal,—the Rose,—and owes its charm chiefly to the constant disappointment and final defeat," *Gatsby* has "an undertone of sadness" (*MSMC* 248). But *Gatsby* still more closely approximates Jean de Meung's fourteenth-century addition to the *Roman de la Rose*, where, according to Adams, "the Woman and the Rose became bankrupt" (*MSMC* 249–50)—a metaphor with powerful resonance for Fitzgerald.

Most readers of *Gatsby* thus join with the author and the narrator in finally pitying the modern knight manqué and reprehending the bankrupt modern woman who makes his quest unachievable,[23] the Jewish Wolfsheim's tuneless whistling of "The Rosary" (*GG* 171) ironically providing the perfect commentary on Gatsby's death. Such judgments are eminently just in terms of the courtly love tradition. Joan M. Ferrante notes in a paraphrase of a poem by the troubadour Bertran de Born: "Since [the lady's] worth depends on her receptiveness" to the man defined as "best," then "she must not reject him if she would remain worthy" (69). Daisy reveals her lack of such worth when she chooses Tom over Gatsby. Like Adams, Fitzgerald presents this choice as a diminishment or degradation of womanhood. The lady Daisy Fay is revealed to be only superficially distinct from the prostitute Jill Wayne, whom Amory recalls as Jill "Fayne" in the stream-of-consciousness passage at the end of *This Side of Paradise*.

Gatsby does not get the girl, and this failure kills him, despite the lesson offered by the "romanticist" (*BD* 73) Anthony Patch in Fitzgerald's preceding novel: "Things are sweeter when they're lost. I know—because once I wanted something [Gloria] and got it. It was the only thing I ever wanted badly . . . and when I got it it turned to dust in my hands" (*BD* 341). The Patches' marriage becomes a valley of ashes that leaves them empty shells, the blame relatively equally apportioned between Anthony and Gloria because Anthony's Adams-like modernity inhibits his ability to function as a Gatsby-like knight to the flawed Gloria. In Fitzgerald's subsequent novel, a Gatsby-like figure does get the girl, but his success also proves metaphorically fatal.

Dick Diver, of *Tender Is the Night* (at one point subtitled *A Romance*),[24] is a self-described "old romantic" (*TN* 58) who opts for love to the exclusion of his other aspirations upon a transformative kiss from Nicole reminiscent of Gatsby and Daisy's: "Wanting above all to be brave and kind, he had wanted, even more than that, to be loved. So it had been. So it would ever be" (*TN* 302). The tag line suggests a mythic inevitability to this relationship, love "provid[ing] Fitzgerald's idealists, Gatsby and Diver, a way into the timeless, the ideal world" (Callahan 15). Yet however romantic the initial motivations, the relationship between Dick and Nicole is quintessentially modern rather than medieval. Its objective correlative is World War I (just as Fitzgerald described himself and Zelda in 1934 as "war survivals" [*Correspondence* 356] and offered himself to Zelda's psychiatrist in 1938 in the role of a military "topographer" analyzing the "terrain" of his marriage [*Correspondence* 500]).

Before meeting Nicole, Dick is a contemporary incarnation of Grant in Galena, "ready to be called to an intricate destiny" (*TN* 118). Grant's destiny was the Civil War; Dick's parallel destiny is marriage to Nicole. Dick is repeatedly compared to Grant,[25] whose "invent[ion of] mass butchery" (*TN* 57) in the Civil War is presented as a precursor to World War I. Though Dick "didn't see any of the war" (*TN* 119), he certainly sees action on the battleground of his marriage, "scent[ing] battle from afar, and subconsciously . . . hardening and arming himself" (*TN* 100). Nicole is first attracted to him when she sees him in his military uniform (recalling Daisy's initial attraction to the uniformed Lieutenant Gatsby and Zelda's initial attraction to the uniformed Lieutenant Fitzgerald), and he later soldiers on through a marriage that, like World War I, becomes a war of attrition.

The war and the marriage are thus collapsed: Dick's study of the Battle of Thiepval results in a "simplif[ication of] it always until it bore a faint resemblance to one of his own parties" (*TN* 59), like the Villa Diana party, whose outcome is a psychotic episode and a duel; the travels of the Diver contingent are compared to "an infantry battalion" on the move (*TN* 77); in Paris, Dick "march[es] along," his stick at "a sword-like angle" (*TN* 94); Dick frequently gets drunk, just as, according to McKisco, "everybody was drunk all the time during the war" (*TN* 50). The mercenary soldier Tommy Barban makes explicit the connection between the Divers' marriage and modern war: "When I'm in a rut I come to see the Divers, because then I know that in a few weeks I'll want to go to war" (*TN* 30).

Battle in modern wars—whether World War I or the Divers' marriage—leads not to ennobling self-realization, as in chivalric warfare, but to waste and destruction. One of Dick's patients gives voice to the cost of the war between modern men and women:

> "I'm sharing the fate of the women of my time who challenged men to battle."
>
> "To your vast surprise it was just like all battles," [Dick] answered, adopting her formal diction.
>
> "Just like all battles." She thought this over. "You pick a set-up, or else win a Pyrrhic victory, or you're wrecked and ruined—you're a ghostly echo from a broken wall."
>
> . . . "Are you quite sure you've been in a real battle?" [he asked]. . . .
> "You've suffered, but many women suffered before they mistook themselves for men." (*TN* 184)

Though Dick represses the truth of what this woman (who ultimately dies of her "wounds") is saying, denying her meaning "as a symbol of something" (*TN* 185), he too is ultimately a casualty of this modern sexual war.[26] He does battle with the archetypal "American Woman"—most frequently in the person of Nicole but also as incarnated in Baby Warren, Mary North, and Rosemary Hoyt—who is critically described by the omniscient narrator as having "broken the moral back of a race and made a nursery out of a continent" (*TN* 232). Judith Fetterley points out that "here, as in *The Great Gatsby*, Fitzgerald indicts America, identifying the nation as female and blaming the woes of American men on the character of American women and on the feminization of American culture" (121). In the marital arena of battle, the destruction is inevitably sexual: Dick is transformed from "Lucky Dick, you big stiff" (*TN* 116) to a man who "avoid[s] high diving" (*TN* 282) and regards his wife's lover "with a curious impotence" (*TN* 308). His alter-ego is the seedy American war veteran who appears at two critical points in Dick's romantic life—when he first contemplates an affair with Rosemary and when he accepts Tommy's demand that he divorce Nicole. Close to Dick's age, the unnamed veteran is identified with locales (barber shops and theater lobbies) and activities (watching people) with which Dick is also identified. By the end of the novel, Dick is wandering aimlessly around the state of New York just as the veteran has wandered around France since the war ended— failures both.

In direct contrast to Daisy, who twice rejects Gatsby—a rejection that destroys his dream and therefore his very self—Nicole marries Dick. Yet just as Daisy is blamed for Gatsby's destruction, Nicole is blamed for Dick's, a blame that she accepts: "Some of the time I think it's my fault— I've ruined you" (*TN* 267). Nicole is presented throughout the novel as a type of vampire who absorbs from Dick what "she had thought of . . . as an inexhaustible energy, incapable of fatigue" (*TN* 300–301), depleting him to make herself psychologically well and then casting him aside for another man. In her lack of guilt, she is similar to Rosemary, another vampire who wants to "devour" (*TN* 66) Dick. Nicole and Rosemary serve as Keatsian belles dames sans merci for Dick (who shares Fitzgerald's love of Keats's poetry). [27] In this regard they are similar to Gloria Patch, who is identified explicitly as "the beautiful and merciless lady" (*BD* 255) and "*la belle dame sans merci*" (*BD* 329), and who is revealed to be a vamp—defined as "a picker up and thrower away of men, an unscrupulous and fundamentally unmoved toyer with affections" (*BD* 95)— who "struck to kill" (*BD* 80), drawing blood when she bites Anthony's thumb in a gesture of castration.

Like Nicole, Dick absorbs others, but he paradoxically expends his own energy in so doing rather than replenishing it, as does Nicole. In serving Nicole and the other women in his life, Dick recalls the courtly role, but rather than being ennobled, he is weakened and enervated by his service to modern women, just as Anthony Patch is depleted by his service to Gloria. Tender is the knight indeed in the modern world, which offers an inhospitable environment for courtly behavior and unsuitable objects for courtly adoration. Though Dick cannot be a true courtly knight, neither can he successfully act the part of a modern man in the postwar world, for his attempts at casual affairs with other women are always undermined. His initial attempt at an affair with Rosemary is forestalled by Peterson's death; the consummated affair is summarily ended because of his anger at her relationship with another man; and his resumption of the affair is forestalled by his otherwise pointless fight with the cabdrivers. His contemplated fling while in Innsbruck is forestalled by his father's death; his potential fling with an English girl is forestalled when he gets drunk; and his potential affair with Mary North Minghetti is forestalled when he abandons the Riviera. Dick is a man caught between the medieval world of the courtly knight, which endows the romantic relationship with transcendent significance, and the modern world, which accepts meaninglessness as a given and celebrates all sexual activity as a simple marker of existence.

Tommy Barban, Dick's replacement in Nicole's life, seems at first glance the most truly knightly figure that the modern world has to offer. "Heroic and gallant" (*TN* 269–70), he quite seriously takes up the gauntlet in defense of Nicole's honor when the "code duello" (*TN* 44) is casually invoked by McKisco. After Dick agrees to the divorce, Tommy formally proclaims, "I stand in the position of Nicole's protector" (*TN* 310), and he warns Dick not to touch Nicole, just as Gatsby stood vigil to protect Daisy from Tom's touch. Yet Tommy is hardly a true knightly model in the courtly tradition. His duel with McKisco is only slightly less farcical than the later "duels" that a drunken Dick fights with a taxi driver and a cook. His heroism in war is in the service not of idealism but economics. A mercenary whose name suggests "barbarian," Tommy plunders Nicole in barbaric fashion: "She lay across his saddle-bow as surely as if he had wolfed her away from Damascus and they had come out upon the Mongolian plain" (*TN* 297–98). Tommy's success brings honor to neither himself, Nicole, nor the modern world. Like Tom Buchanan, Tommy Barban is yet another harbinger of the decline and fall of Western civilization,[28] just as the barbarians at the gates had foretold the destruction of "The Grandeur that was Rome" (*TN* 207)—notably, the title of the movie in which Rosemary stars.

Like her counterpart in *The Great Gatsby*, the modern American woman of *Tender Is the Night* deviates radically from the medieval courtly ideal. Though superficially different, Daisy and Nicole (like the other female characters in these novels) are united in their inability or unwillingness to serve as ladies. This refusal necessarily undermines the knightly behavior of the male protagonists, rendering it either meaningless (Gatsby) or impossible (Dick). The American woman is thus held largely responsible for the male protagonists' failures. Fetterley notes that "to read *Tender is the Night* is to participate in the evocation of sympathy for Dick Diver, . . . and to engage in the concomitant hostility toward that which has destroyed him" (114), and Mary A. McCay similarly asserts that "there is more hostility underlying *Tender Is the Night* than there is in any other [of Fitzgerald's] work[s]" (319).

Given that the object of that hostility was largely based on Zelda Fitzgerald (as was Daisy), it is clear that *Tender Is the Night* functions at one level as an apologia (as does *Gatsby*), serving to explain the failure of the Fitzgeralds' marriage by apportioning a larger share of the blame to Zelda[29] (whereas the earlier and more evenhanded *Beautiful and Damned* functions as a chillingly accurate prediction of the future of the Fitzgerald marriage, the novel a failed attempt to ward off that future by displacing it into fiction). Just as Daisy chooses Tom over Gatsby, Zelda had become involved with French aviator Edouard Jozan while Fitzgerald was writing *Gatsby*. Just as Nicole undergoes psychological breakdowns that enervate Dick, Zelda suffered psychological breakdowns that drew on Fitzgerald's emotional and financial resources.

It is psychologically telling that when "Zelda began to plan a novel [*Save Me the Waltz*] in 1933 dealing with insanity, it seemed to Scott that she was covering some of the same ground as *Tender Is the Night* in order to justify herself and make him look bad" (Donaldson, *Fool* 84). Fitzgerald was to some degree projecting his own motivations onto Zelda, though she doubtless shared them.[30] Fitzgerald's frustration is evident in a 1934 letter to Dr. Harry M. Murdock, psychiatrist at the University of Maryland School of Medicine in Baltimore: "[Dr. Meyer] could never seem to appreciate that my writing was more important than hers by a large margin. . . . In other words, he encouraged the damn woman's desire to express herself" (*Correspondence* 381). Fitzgerald reserved for himself the right to express Zelda, blocking Zelda's right to express herself and certainly her right to express Fitzgerald. Just as the courtly lyric is a "masculine performance" whose "context is validation by other males" (Cholakian 57), *Tender Is the Night* is a recounting of the Fitzgeralds' story from Scott's male perspective, and he was enormously disturbed at Zelda's attempts to tell their story from "the damn woman's" point of view, since perspective largely determines sympathy.

Insofar as the female protagonists of *Gatsby* and *Tender Is the Night* are blamed, like Zelda, for inhibiting successful knightly behavior, they are similar to female characters in the self-consciously contemporary world of Fitzgerald's first novel, *This Side of Paradise*. In this autobiographical Künstlerroman, female characters mark stages in the development of the male protagonist, whose name suggests that amorous adventures will be the locus of his education. As a young man, Amory decides that sex is "a rather unpleasant overpowering force" (*TSP* 238), associating it explicitly with moral evil, as dramatized by two experiences bringing him into actual contact with the devil—a literalization of his later expressed desire to "let himself go to the devil" (*TSP* 262).

In the first experience, he is saved from sexual temptation by a vision of a man whose "unutterably terrible" (*TSP* 113) feet are cloven—a lurid detail whose significance is eventually clear to Amory and immediately clear to the reader (prepared by this section's title, "The Devil"). His vision is given external validation by his friend Tom d'Invilliers, who notes, "Had a hell of a dream about you last night. . . . I had an idea you were in some trouble" (*TSP* 118), and who suddenly sees "something" (*TSP* 119) looking at Amory.

Amory's second experience occurs when he sees "an aura, . . . a horror, diffusively brooding" (*TSP* 247) over him, his friend Alec Connage, and the prostitute Jill Wayne. This vision is accompanied by another vision of "something else, featureless and indistinguishable, yet strangely familiar" (*TSP* 247), which later is revealed to be Monsignor Darcy's spirit. External validation is again provided since Darcy has unexpectedly died that very evening. In the ensuing psychomachia, the devil and Darcy's spirit battle for Amory's soul. The devil is vanquished when Amory, innocent of sexual sin in this encounter, decides to sacrifice himself in Alec's place. Amory's admission of a false guilt (here anticipating Dick Diver's similar admission) paradoxically reassures him of his sexual innocence, an innocence also valued by Anthony Patch, as evidenced by the talismanic importance he ascribes to his pseudomedieval "Chevalier O'Keefe" allegory, which links sex with death and then damnation. Like the sexual temptation that fatally lures the "romantic" (*BD* 89) Chevalier O'Keefe from his vow of chastity, sexual temptation inevitably returns to Amory: "He felt an overwhelming desire to let himself go to the devil—not to go violently as a gentleman should, but to sink safely and sensuously out of sight. He pictured himself in an adobe house in Mexico, half-reclining on a rug-covered couch, . . . [while] an olive-skinned, carmine-lipped girl caressed his hair. . . . There were so many places where one might deteriorate pleasantly . . . all lands of sad, haunting music and many odors, where lust could be a mode and expression of life" (*TSP* 262).

It is telling that Amory here embodies sexual temptation in an "exotic" woman, just as his visions of the devil appear during his encounters with party girls and prostitutes. Amory thus differentiates between these women, with whom he associates sexual activity and thus evil, and the society girls he dates. But the differentiation does not hold. The debutantes reject the role of belle (a model with roots in the Middle Ages, the lady of the plantation self-consciously styled on the lady of the castle) for that of vamp (a contemporary model with roots in World War I). "The 'belle' had become the 'flirt,' the 'flirt' had become the 'baby vamp.' The 'belle' had five or six callers every afternoon. If the P. D. ["popular daughter," used interchangeably with "vamp"], by some strange accident, has two, it is made pretty uncomfortable for the one who hasn't a date with her. The 'belle' was surrounded by a dozen men in the intermissions between dances. Try to find the P. D. between dances, just *try* to find her" (*TSP* 59).

Unlike the belle, the vamp is associated with sexuality, as Fitzgerald explains in "Echoes of the Jazz Age": "The old standard prevailed until after the War. . . . Only in 1920 did the veil finally fall—the Jazz Age was in flower, . . . the word jazz . . . mean[ing] first sex, then dancing, then music" (*EJA* 15–16).

Rosalind, described several times as a "vampire" (*TSP* 170, 180), offers a historical discourse on this new sexual freedom: "There used to be two kinds of kisses: First when girls were kissed and deserted; second, when they were engaged. Now there's a third kind, where the man is kissed and deserted. If Mr. Jones of the nineties bragged he'd kissed a girl, every one knew he was through with her. If Mr. Jones of 1919 brags the same every one knows it's because he can't kiss her any more. Given a decent start any girl can beat a man nowadays" (*TSP* 181). Amory is certainly titillated by the sexual freedom of these contemporary girls: the kissable thirteen-year-old Myra St. Claire; the "Speed" (*TSP* 62), Isabelle Borgé; the fickle Rosalind Connage, who has kissed dozens of men; and the "Bohemian" (*TSP* 232) Eleanor Savage.

In a 1921 interview with Frederick James Smith, Fitzgerald offered similar observations about his attraction to the contemporary girl: "We find the young woman of 1920 flirting, kissing, viewing life lightly, saying damn without a blush, playing along the danger line in an immature way—a sort of mental baby vamp. . . . I prefer this sort of girl. Indeed, I married the heroine of my stories. I would not be interested in any other sort of woman" (244–45). Yet although Fitzgerald was titillated by watching the modern girl "play along the danger line," he was disturbed by the possibility that she might cross it, wanting her vampishness to remain "mental."

Amory too is ultimately disturbed by the sexual freedom claimed by modern girls. His first kiss provokes initial enthusiasm, then "sudden revulsion, . . . disgust, loathing for the whole incident" (*TSP* 14). The intensity of Amory's response is striking, as is his passionate refusal when the "young witch" (*TSP* 13) Myra demands, "Kiss me again" (*TSP* 14). He later encounters another "witch" (*TSP* 227) in the allegorically named Eleanor Savage, who recites poetry "in a weird chant" (*TSP* 224), reads Amory's mind, and blasphemes. Imaged as a "little devil" (*TSP* 235) and a "lunatic" (*TSP* 227) with "a crazy streak" (*TSP* 240), this Maryland debutante is "evil . . . under the mask of beauty" (*TSP* 222). When she acts upon a "crazy" suicidal impulse and nearly rides her horse over a cliff (thereby anticipating Nicole's suicidal attempt at crashing the Diver car), Amory is horrified. Eleanor is sister to those ladies from medieval romances who are "revealed as devils in disguise," such as the "women who tempt [knights], trying to destroy their chastity so they will fail in the quest," and who when "rebuffed by the knights . . . literally go up in smoke, leaving only a foul odor behind" (Ferrante 119).

Rosalind Connage has an even more powerful impact on Amory's life. The archetypal debutante (as suggested by the title of the chapter devoted to her), she is also a "vampire" who "play[s] with men" (*TSP* 181), devastating Amory when she breaks their engagement because he is too poor: "I can't be . . . cooped up in a little flat, waiting for you. You'd hate me in a narrow atmosphere. . . . I wouldn't be the Rosalind you love" (*TSP* 195). Rosalind's analysis is proved accurate, for Amory later asserts that "the girl really worth having won't wait for anybody" (*TSP* 216). Yet narrative sympathy lies not with Rosalind but Amory, as revealed by several authorial interjections in the form of stage directions: "There is a difference somehow in the quality of their suffering" (*TSP* 195); "Rosalind feels that she has lost something, she knows not what, she knows not why" (*TSP* 197). This scene, a fictionalization of Fitzgerald's experience when Zelda broke their engagement because of his lack of financial prospects prior to the publication of *This Side of Paradise*, had powerful significance for Fitzgerald, who returned to it not only in *Gatsby* (where Daisy cries over Gatsby's love letter but marries Tom the next day) but in various short stories, notably "'The Sensible Thing'" (1924), in which Jonquil Cary breaks her engagement to George O'Kelly.

Though O'Kelly (like Fitzgerald) ultimately succeeds financially and the engagement is resumed, he continues to feel a certain bitterness and loss, emotions that Fitzgerald expressed in the *Crack-Up* essay "Pasting It Together" (1936):

> It was one of those tragic loves doomed for lack of money, and one day the girl closed it out on the basis of common sense. During a long summer of despair I wrote a novel . . . so it came out all right, but it came out all right for a different person. The man with the jingle of money in his pocket who married the girl a year later would always cherish an abiding distrust, an animosity, toward the leisure class—not the conviction of a revolutionist but the smouldering hatred of a peasant. . . . I have never been able to stop wondering where my friends' money came from, nor to stop thinking that at one time a sort of *droit de seigneur* [*sic*] might have been exercised to give one of them my girl. (PT 77)

Though Fitzgerald admits to distrusting the leisure class as a result of this experience, the real focus of his displaced distrust must inevitably have been Zelda, the girl who rejected him when he was poor only to marry him when he was rich. Fitzgerald similarly displaces his sense of transformation, asserting only that he had become a "different person," though Zelda too must have been transformed forever in his eyes. Fitzgerald wrote in an unmailed 1939 letter to Zelda, "I never wanted the Zelda I married" (*Correspondence* 559). Unlike Fitzgerald and his fictional alter-ego George O'Kelly, Amory (like Gatsby) will be forever prevented from getting the girl, no matter how successful he becomes, for Rosalind (like Daisy) marries another man. Fitzgerald's anger at Zelda is manifested in Amory's imaginative murder of Rosalind: "Never again could he . . . [want] her. . . . Amory had wanted her youth, the fresh radiance of her mind and body, the stuff that she was selling now once and for all. So far as he was concerned, young Rosalind was dead" (*TSP* 253).

The modern American girl is thus imaged variously as a witch, a devil, a vampire, a madwoman—seductive and enticing, yet dangerous to the men they encounter. For all of her superficial difference from the prostitutes and loose women whom Amory associates with evil, she is revealed to behave in uncomfortably similar ways. Her sexual freedom allows her to "make love" (in that wonderfully ambiguous Fitzgeraldian phrase) with many men; her sexual favors imply no commitment, nor any special worthiness in her male lover; she often takes an aggressive rather than a passive role in the romance. In rejecting the traditional female role, she has escaped male control (except insofar as the male author has constructed her to serve his purposes) but not male opprobrium. Each of Amory's relationships with these baby vamps ends predictably in disaster for him, an outcome that leaves him bitter about modern women and the "real moral letdown" (TSP 59) their actions suggest.

Yet Fitzgerald also presents a female character who approximates the medieval ideal. Clara Page plays the part to perfection by allowing herself to be idealized and worshiped by the male protagonist. Her given name like that of Astrophel's Stella allegorically suggesting "light," and her sur-name manifesting her primary function as literary material for a male author,[31] Clara is the goddess Amory adores from afar in the paradig-matic courtly love relationship. Residing on the allegorically named Ark Street, the Catholic Clara becomes a locus for Amory's spiritual aspira-tions, his faith in her reviving his faith in God. And his is not the only life that she transforms in her "court" of "adorers" (TSP 139). Clara provokes not sexual temptation but "innocent excitement" in "one of the greatest libertines in that city" (TSP 138). Amory thus figures her forth in a poem as St. Cecilia (the same figure that Catherine Brooke sits for in Adams's *Esther*), where he associates her with the rose (an association inappro-priate to the ironically named Rosalind and later, Rosemary), and he thinks of her as inhabiting a transcendent plane where she partakes of "Mary's eternal significance" (TSP 145). A contemporary madonna to whom Amory proclaims, "I love you—or adore you—or worship you—" (TSP 145), Clara functions as a projection of male desire, satisfy-ing Amory's unspoken nostalgia for courtly love and Mariolatry while garnering narrative celebration.

Yet the section detailing Amory's relationship with Clara is by far the briefest of all those devoted to women in *This Side of Paradise*—perhaps because despite the narrator's protestations of her obsessive fascination for men, this ideal lady is inherently dull, a construct rather than a fully realized character. Even in this last characteristic, ironically, she is true to the medieval model, for the lady that the medieval troubadour adores is also defined by a few conventional attributes: "Feminine characteristics exist principally to inspire and validate the poet, . . . leaving in the text a woman whose unique function is to gratify a love which requires of the male little more than sublimated admiration, and of the female, little more than creative inspiration" (Cholakian 174).

Provocatively enough, Amory at some level seems to recognize these limitations of the medieval ideal. He puzzles over "how coldly we thought of the 'Dark Lady of the Sonnets,' and how little we remembered her, . . . and [how] now we have no real interest in her" (TSP 236), but he is unable to articulate the reason. His unconscious recognition of the limitations of the medieval ideal is expressed more personally in a dream that occurs after he contemplates marrying Clara: "Once he dreamt that it had come true and woke up in a cold panic, for in his dream she had been a silly, flaxen Clara, with the gold gone out of her hair and platitudes falling insipidly from her changeling tongue" (*TSP* 141). Yet the insight embedded in this dream is immediately repressed, covered over by a narrative threnody of praise of Clara's virtues. When Amory does propose to Clara, he learns that she has embraced widowhood and will never remarry. Thus does Fitzgerald spare this ideal lady the test of reality—a test that she would inevitably fail. In a 1924 article for *McCall's* provocatively entitled "Does a Moment of Revolt Come Some Time to Every Married Man?" Fitzgerald wrote: "No sooner does a man marry his reproachless ideal than he becomes intensely self-conscious about her" (*DMR* 185). By negating any possibility of marriage for Clara, Fitzgerald makes it possible for the courtly love tradition to remain intact as a subtextual model in the novel.

The widowed Clara is a dream mother whose unseen "precious babies" (*TSP* 146)—incarnations of Gloria Patch's "ghostly children" (*BD* 393), her "dear dream children" (*BD* 147)—are the result of immaculate conception, at least in Amory's mind, given her confession that she has never been in love. Untouched by "the reality, the earthiness . . . of childbearing" (*BD* 392), which so repels Gloria Patch, who notes with disgust the "*alive, mechanical, abominable*" (*BD* 361) fertility that makes "motherhood . . . also the privilege of the female baboon" (*BD* 393), Clara has nothing of the "feminine animality" (*BD* 389) so abhorrent to Anthony Patch, who identifies "*females,* in the word's most contemptuous sense, [as] breeders and bearers, exuding still that faintly odorous atmosphere of the cave and the nursery" (*BD* 104). While celebrating the emerging sexuality of the postwar vamp, Fitzgerald concurrently feared a promiscuity that would render these girls "unclean" (a metaphor repeatedly employed in his fiction), Anthony and Gloria Patch holding multiple confused conversations in which they attempt to distinguish between "clean" and "unclean" promiscuity. Fitzgerald also found distasteful the "female animality" that gives to childbearing its "earthiness," thereby transforming glamorous dream girls into real women, madonnas into mothers.

Fitzgerald's presentation of onetime dream girls—most notably Rosalind, Gloria, Daisy, and Nicole—reveals his fascination with a particular kind of lost cause. In none of these novels does a romantic relationship work out well. Nor did Fitzgerald's relationship with Zelda, which was marked not only by their fractured engagement but by destructive arguments (the "splits in the skin that won't heal," as Fitzgerald described them [*Notebooks* 192]) and separations resulting from Zelda's psychological breakdowns and Fitzgerald's alcoholism. In a 1938 letter to Dr. Carroll, Zelda's psychiatrist at Highland Hospital in Asheville, North Carolina, Fitzgerald wrote: "Certainly the outworn pretense that we can ever come together again is better for being shed. There is simply too much of the past between us. When that mist falls—at a dinner table, or between two pillows—no knight errant can transverse (*sic*) its immense distance" (*Correspondence* 487).

In acknowledging his own inability to serve as "knight errant" to Zelda, Fitzgerald was relinquishing a role that he had played for years, a role Zelda had alluded to in her autobiographical novel *Save Me the Waltz* (1932) when she named the male protagonist (clearly based on Fitzgerald) first Amory Blaine and then David Knight. Yet Fitzgerald's renunciation of this role is particularly interesting because he tacitly blames Zelda for his inability to function as a knight, as implied by his judgment that "*no* knight-errant" (emphasis mine) could succeed in this task. In Fitzgerald's fictional worlds, the only way that the modern woman can escape criticism is not by accepting the worthy knight (as do Gloria and Nicole), and certainly not by rejecting him for an unworthy knight (as do Rosalind and Daisy), but by rejecting him for some larger ideal (as does Clara) that precludes sexuality and fixes her status as inspiration for knightly self-realization.

When the courtly model fails to operate successfully in the modern world, the blame is laid largely at the feet of modern women who refuse to behave according to the courtly conventions and therefore make it impossible for modern men to be knights—an important source of what John S. Whitley terms the "deep distrust of women" (177) in Fitzgerald's fiction. Aldrich notes "the irony . . . that Fitzgerald, that incessant brooder on women and Woman, was not particularly good at rendering full or convincing women characters in his long fictions" (152). Of *The Great Gatsby* Fitzgerald "confessed" in a letter to Max Perkins before publication that "'it may hurt the book's popularity that it's a *man's book*' [by which] he meant that his best characters were men and that his women faded out of the novel" (Keath Fraser 61). "To Gatsby, to Diver, and to Stahr"—to Blaine and Patch as well—"women are rarely personalities, rarely individuals, rarely human beings; above all, they are rarely women," according to Callahan (211). Certainly the same could be said of the courtly lady, who is in Cholakian's memorable phrase "topos by absence" (188).

In his novels Fitzgerald explores the cost of a modern allegiance to the courtly model. Yet the validity of the model itself is not seriously called into question. Only in Fitzgerald's unfinished last novel, *The Last Tycoon*, does he suggest that the male protagonist perhaps errs in desiring a courtly relationship, that his desire for a courtly lady rather than a modern woman may be misbegotten. Fitzgerald thereby elaborates the insight that Amory expressed in dream form (and that Fitzgerald unconsciously expressed in his limited narrative attention to Clara) so many years before, calling into question the validity of courtly love as a model, however tentatively.

In a 1939 letter to Kenneth Littauer, fiction editor of *Collier's*, Fitzgerald drew an explicit comparison between *The Last Tycoon* and *Gatsby*: "If one book could ever be 'like' another I should say it is more 'like' *The Great Gatsby* than any other of my books" (*Life in Letters* 412). Perhaps in part an expression of his desire to regain the mastery he had exhibited in writing *Gatsby* (and to expunge the painful nine-year experience of writing *Tender Is the Night*), this comparison is nonetheless apt, as a brief survey will reveal. The Gatsby-like main character, Monroe Stahr, is a man of humble beginnings and limited education who succeeds financially and radiates glamour. His story is told by a first-person narrator who offers admiring commentary punctuated by irony. Though Stahr has involved himself in corrupt activities to maintain his position, at the last opportunity he will repudiate a murderous plan, thereby bearing out his mother's judgment, "We always knew that Monroe would be all right" (*LT* 147). Stahr is given mythic significance by the narrator, who describes a metaphoric flight where, Icarus-like, he "fl[e]w up very high to see, on strong wings, . . . [and] looked on all the kingdoms, with the kind of eyes that can stare straight into the sun" (*LT* 20). Fitzgerald's letter to Littauer outlining the novel reveals that Stahr is to die in a plane crash, to come crashing back to earth. But like Gatsby, whose impact on Nick continues after his death, Stahr's impact also continues, to be drawn out in a subtle "parable or moral lesson" (*LT* 157) that Fitzgerald projected in his working notes as the conclusion of his novel.

Before his death, Stahr has two important romantic relationships—with his wife, Minna Davis (recounted solely as memories), and with Kathleen Moore. While Gatsby wants to repeat the past but is unable to do so, Stahr is vouchsafed that unusual opportunity, for Kathleen is virtually the dead Minna's double in appearance—"not Minna and yet Minna" (*LT* 59). When he and Kathleen first make love, he wants "passionately to repeat yet not recapitulate the past" (*LT* 88), a meaningless distinction. Stahr collapses Minna and Kathleen, thus mourning anew for Minna, who "died again" (*LT* 98) when Kathleen breaks off their relationship. Stahr's feelings for Minna are therefore doubly significant: "He had never lost his head about Minna, even in the beginning. . . . She had loved him always and just before she died, all unwilling and surprised, his tenderness had burst and surged forward and he had been in love with her. In love with Minna and death together—with the world in which she looked so alone that he wanted to go with her there" (*LT* 96). Minna's attraction for Stahr was not the attraction of life, then, but death. Stahr embodies his death wish in Minna, also expressed in his "definite urge toward total exhaustion . . . [which] was a perversion of the life force" (*LT* 108) and his persistent transformation of life into film (whether literally in the production of movies, or metaphorically in his treatment of his life as though it were a movie complete with props and dialogue).

Stahr uses his courtship of Minna as a model in courting Kathleen, but his cautiousness causes him to lose the woman who might have saved him (he is in failing health from heart trouble, appropriately), just as Minna had tried to save him from his impulse toward death. A voice—the narrator's? God's? Fitzgerald's?—cries out a warning: "It is your chance, Stahr. Better take it now. This is your girl. She can save you, she can worry you back to life" (*LT* 115). But only when he has lost Kathleen to another man will he commit himself to her, as revealed in Fitzgerald's proposed outline to Littauer: "Realizing how much he needs Thalia [that is, Kathleen], things are patched up between them. For a day or two they are ideally happy. They are going to marry, but he must make one more trip East" (*Life in Letters* 41). Inevitably, he will die before the commitment that would put an end to ideal happiness can be realized.

Like Gatsby, Stahr is "a romantic" (*LT* 114), but more so than Gatsby he seems to recognize at some level that his quest for the lady is not a desire for the corporeal reality (with its life-affirming powers) but for the transcendence that is death, which she symbolizes to him. Stahr, who "had grown up dead cold" (*LT* 97), thinks of Kathleen and is reminded "of the fresh iced fish and lobsters [at a restaurant]" (*LT* 114) in a telling image of luxury and death. Because Minna and Kathleen serve not only as objects of his desire but also as expressions of his death wish, he attempts to transform both Minna and Kathleen into versions of the courtly lady, but neither woman wishes to serve in this role, for they are committed to life. Though Kathleen chooses to marry another man, she does so only because Stahr finds it impossible to make a commitment to *life* with her. Were Stahr to marry her, he would find himself with "a good wife, a real person" (*LT* 111). But he does not want "a real person," as Kathleen comes to realize. He wants the "perfect girl" (*LT* 41) he demands for his movies, where "the dream [is] made flesh" (*LT* 50). He wants his dead wife again, whom he could love only when she was dying.

The Last Tycoon is unique among Fitzgerald's novels in that the male protagonist bears primary responsibility for the failure of the relationship. Though Kathleen is unwilling to be the lady that Stahr has constructed, she is not blamed for this refusal, as so many of Fitzgerald's earlier female protagonists had been. [32] Fitzgerald asserted in the 1939 letter to Littauer, "My present conception of her should make her the most . . . sympathetic of my heroines" (*Life in Letters* 410). Fitzgerald's treatment of the Stahr-Kathleen relationship suggests at least a questioning of the validity of courtly love as a model, but "the full implications of that love affair were still not clear in Fitzgerald's mind" (Piper 280), as evidenced by Fitzgerald's working notes on the novel. Perhaps the implications of his affair with Sheilah Graham were not yet clear either. In 1935 he had told Laura Guthrie, "I am always searching for the perfect love," and when she asked if that was because he'd had it as a young man, he answered, "No, I never had it. . . . I was searching then too" (quoted by Donaldson, *Fool* 110). Donaldson notes that "such a search worked to prevent him from committing himself fully to any one person, for, as common sense dictated and his fiction illustrated, there could be no such thing as the perfect love, up close" (*Fool* 110). Fitzgerald's 1937–40 affair with Graham may have represented in its last stages a renunciation of that search. In any case, it provided a measure of comfort and stability to Fitzgerald in his final years during which he conceived and began writing The Last Tycoon.

Dying at forty-four of heart disease, Fitzgerald wrestled to the end of his life with the nature of love, the courtly love tradition providing an important context within which he explored love—and death—in the modern world. The figure of the knight profoundly attracted Fitzgerald because knighthood offered two ways to win the lady—by birth, to be sure (as Twain obsessively insisted), but also by deeds. Ostensibly aristocratic by birth, Amory Blaine betrays on virtually every page Fitzgerald's middle-class background (however much Fitzgerald insisted upon his father's aristocratic connections). Amory's hatred of the class system (source of his bogus Marxist pronouncements) subsists uneasily with his frank desire to be at the top of a system that would award him the golden girl by right—the droit du seigneur. But the knightly code also offered the opportunity to ennoblement through deeds—a somewhat riskier path to be sure, less certain of rewards, and bifurcated since they could be deeds of courtly love or chivalric valor. This European system had particular attractions for an American audience, now allied with Europe not only by national birth but by martial deeds in World War I, uncertain of its social status in the fluidity of democracy, resenting unwritten rules that inhibited access to the upper reaches yet yearning to attain the heights. Knighthood earned by deeds offered a rarefied version of the Horatio Alger myth, celebrating the power of the individual man who was already part of the American mythology in the figure of the cowboy (beloved by young James Gatz in the person of Hopalong Cassidy). Slight of build, more or less bereft of physical courage except when drunk, and denied access to the martial arena of World War I, Fitzgerald capitalized on his personal attributes—golden good looks, charm, and literary genius—in his quest for knighthood via courtly deeds, becoming the troubadour of the Jazz Age who won the golden girl in the person of Zelda Sayre.

Fitzgerald's literary rival and alter-ego Ernest Hemingway took a different path, not rejecting knighthood but attempting to earn it via deeds of chivalric valor, obsessively seeking out martial arenas in war and blood sport. Whereas Fitzgerald dealt with the primal experience for his generation largely via metaphor, allusion, and objective correlative (his technique of treating romance like war itself rooted in the Middle Ages), Hemingway prided himself on the firsthand experience that enabled the flat descriptive style he made famous. Yet Hemingway, like Fitzgerald, discovered the high cost of an allegiance in the modern world to medieval ideals, a cost that Hemingway felt should be borne with grace under pressure.

5

Ernest Hemingway

KNIGHTHOOD IN OUR TIME

In the character of Nick Adams, Ernest Hemingway constructed a fictional alter-ego who served as a "stalking-horse for exploring his anxieties," in Kenneth Lynn's memorable phrase (405). Hemingway wrote stories about Nick Adams over the course of four decades, from the 1920s through the 1950s, focusing on Nick from boyhood to middle age. The last Nick Adams story—in terms of Nick's age rather than the chronology of composition—is "Fathers and Sons" (1933), in which Nick comes to terms with the death of his father, Henry Adams (so named in "The Doctor and the Doctor's Wife" [1925]), the autobiographical Nick taking his place as Henry Adams's heir in the modern world.[1]

In thinking of his youth, Nick recalls the "virgin forest" (FS 239), which has largely disappeared, destroyed in the service of industrial progress. The adolescent Nick escapes to the "virgin timber" in "The Last Good Country" (an unfinished and posthumously published novel on which Hemingway worked from 1952 to 1958), where he feels "like the way I ought to feel in church" (LGC 74). Having "read about" and "imagine[d]" (LGC 75) the cathedrals that he plans to visit in Europe someday, he asserts that the virgin forest, this last survival from the "olden days" (LGC 74), is "the best one [cathedral] we have around here" (LGC 75). His escape to this natural American cathedral affords him a physical and spiritual safety whose tenuousness is suggested by its gradual disappearance from the American landscape, and by the immediate threat of interlopers searching for Nick, who says his prayers but doesn't know if he still believes in God. Nick's first trip to Europe is occasioned by World War I, and he is grievously and variously wounded (in the spine in Chapter 6, "Nick Sat Against the Wall . . ." [1923], in the leg in "In Another Country" [1927], and in the head in "A Way You'll Never Be" [1933]). His postwar recuperative voyage to the Michigan woods in "Big Two-Hearted River" (1925) takes him through a literal valley of ashes, "hills of burnt timber" (BTHR 159), "the country . . . burned over and changed" (BTHR 161), but deep in the woods he is able to find a measure of security, though even there a swamp threatens tragedy. Whenever Nick is troubled, he comforts himself with participation in or memory of blood sports—fishing and hunting—practiced in a peculiarly ritualistic and code-governed fashion by which he defines himself.

A number of Hemingway's Nick Adams stories appeared first in *In Our Time* (1925), a collection self-consciously presenting the voice of a new generation—the "lost generation" of Gertrude Stein's famous pronouncement (which Hemingway adopted as an epigraph for *The Sun Also Rises* [1926]). The influential Hemingway style—flatly descriptive, employing a few serviceable adjectives in often dichotomous relationship, structured by coordination rather than subordination, and marked by omission (as celebrated in his iceberg theory of writing) and insistent repetition—bears witness to Hemingway's attempt to exert rigorous control over a chaotic universe and to impose linguistic order on emotional chaos, just as Hemingway's bluff persona was a disguise for his vulnerabilities—a result of his physical wounding in World War I (as Philip Young's landmark study suggested) and his psychological wounding in a troubled family (as recent studies by Kenneth Lynn and Mark Spilka suggest).

Representing himself as a hard-boiled proponent of tough, masculine writing, Hemingway has long been regarded as the avatar of antiromanticism. Famously asserting in *Green Hills of Africa* (1935) that "all modern American literature comes from one book by Mark Twain called *Huckleberry Finn*" (22), Hemingway is a writer self-consciously in the tradition of Mark Twain, "trying to do once more 'that good work done by Cervantes' (as Mark Twain put it) by purging our culture of its foolishness again," according to Martin Light (21). Yet just as Twain's attempts to purge America of the medievalist impulse disguise his emotional attraction to it, Hemingway's hard-boiled approach disguises his desperate affection for medieval traditions, traditions that no longer work In Our Time, as Henry Adams had predicted a generation earlier. Unlike Twain,

Adams, or Fitzgerald, Hemingway had direct and extended experiences of war, rendering chivalry a particularly powerful model and contrast in the modern world.

The Chivalric Standard in Hemingway's Novels of Modern War

When *The Sun Also Rises* and *A Farewell to Arms* were published in 1926 and 1929, respectively, these novels helped to crystallize antiwar sentiment in America. In part because of their influence, it became fashionable to regard war cynically, to reject the nobility of battle.[2] The editors of *Scribner's Magazine* drew this moral explicitly, stating in a comment appended to the serialized version of *A Farewell to Arms* that the novel fashioned "such a picture of war as would discourage either victors or the conquered from that terrible solution of international troubles" (quoted by Oldsey 7).

A Farewell to Arms struck an immediate chord with readers and critics alike, who often quoted the bitter words of its protagonist, Frederic Henry, to suggest the horrors of war. The disillusionment of the idealistic young soldier in this best-selling novel came to stand for the disillusionment of the World War I generation: "I was always embarrassed by the words sacred, glorious, and sacrifice and the expression in vain. We had heard them . . . now for a long time, and I had seen nothing sacred, and the things that were glorious had no glory and the sacrifices were like the stockyards at Chicago if nothing was done with the meat except to bury it" (*FA* 184–85). Yet this cynical response seems paradoxical, given Hemingway's reputation as a man obsessed with war. Returning repeatedly to war as the subject of his fiction, he also returned repeatedly to actual wars, voluntarily participating in World War I, the Greco-Turkish War, the Spanish Civil War, the Sino-Japanese War, and World War II, and regretting his absence from the Korean War (where "he said he would gladly serve under [General Charles 'Buck'] Lanham," a friend from his World War II days [Baker, *Life* 415]). Whether functioning as a Red Cross ambulance driver and canteen operator, newspaper correspondent, intelligence operative of sorts, or unofficial leader of troops, Hemingway's insistence on placing himself repeatedly in the thick of battle was legendary. He manifested, then, two seemingly opposed attitudes—cynicism about the nobility of war and obsession with war as an arena for action[3]—a paradox that can be explained by reference to his admiration for medieval chivalry. Not only in *The Sun Also Rises* and *A Farewell to Arms* but also in *For Whom the Bell Tolls* (1940) and *Across the River and into the*

Trees (1950), Hemingway implicitly compares modern technological war-fare with the aesthetically ordered, rule-governed, and self-contained warfare of medieval chivalry. His admiration for chivalry causes him to react against the horror of modern war but to glorify idealized war as a means to self-affirmation and personal improvement.

Hemingway's first personal experience of war was World War I. At the age of eighteen he served as a Red Cross volunteer, driving ambulances and operating a rolling canteen unit that served refreshments to Italian troops. Severely wounded by a trench mortar explosion after only two weeks with the ambulances and a subsequent six days with the canteen unit at the front, he spent about three months in the American Red Cross Hospital in Milan. James Nagel reports that in Hemingway's correspon-dence home "his observations on the dangers of Red Cross work, on the simplicity of dying, on how one offers one's body as a sacrifice, and on how a mother should be proud to lose a son in combat all reflect the romantic idealism of youth," with "little here of war fatigue, cynicism, or the 'separate peace' motifs that pervade Hemingway's mature fiction, nor . . . any sign at any point in the letters of shell shock or psychic trauma" (Villard and Nagel 250).

Hemingway initially heroicized his limited war experience in an at-tempt to read this war in a traditional fashion because "in 1919 the age demanded heroes," as Michael Reynolds observes, "and if his experience did not quite fit the mold, then Hemingway would expand a bit here and there until it did fit" (*Young Hemingway* 21). He found this expansion necessary, according to Reynolds, because "it was not enough to have been a myopic Red Cross ambulance driver blown up while distributing chocolate . . . [so he] invent[ed] his fantasy war, the war he would have fought if only he had been given the chance" (*Young Hemingway* 55). While busily constructing the heroic myth, as evidenced by the discrep-ancies in his many accounts of his wounding, Hemingway also immersed himself in a study of this war, reading histories, memoirs, and fictions. Ironically, as a result of his research he ultimately came to the conclusion that his heroic reading of the war was not tenable, that even if he had been given the chance, World War I was not the war of his heroic fanta-sies. His World War I novels—preeminently *A Farewell to Arms* but also, at a remove, *The Sun Also Rises*—bear witness to his new understanding of the ways modern war deviates from heroic wars of the past.

Modern war is characterized in *A Farewell to Arms* by the mud fill-ing its battlefields. Repeatedly rain falls and the mud increases, trapping the soldiers in its foulness. Hemingway's descriptions are based on the facts of the retreat from the Battle of Caporetto, a battle of which he

had no firsthand knowledge since it had occurred months before his arrival in Italy. Reynolds states that "a close examination of the rain during
the retreat [in the novel] shows . . . that Hemingway was following a
rather exact timetable provided by the [Caporetto] battle accounts. Not
once . . . does fictional rain fall when actual rain did not" (*First War* 116).
But the weather conditions at Caporetto were not unique, for rain fell all
too frequently and with disastrous consequences on the battlefields of
World War I. Paul Fussell notes of the Third Battle of Ypres, for example,
that "the bombardment churned up the ground; rain fell and turned the
dirt to mud. . . . Thousands literally drowned in the mud" (16). Hemingway's contemporary Edmund Blunden, in his memoir *Undertones of War*
(1928), appropriated this literal fact about the World War I landscape to
describe metaphorically a failed attack: "One more brilliant hope, expressed a few hours before in shouts of joy, sank into the mud" (223). Just
as for Blunden (whose book Hemingway owned),[4] so for Hemingway
does the literal mud of World War I become a symbol for all that is ignoble and degraded in this war.

The problems created by the mud were compounded by cumbersome
machinery, so that the massive retreat in which Frederic takes part is literally stalled when the cars, trucks, and ambulances get stuck in the
mud. The machinery was also undependable, often breaking down. More
important, however, the new technology caused a massive machinelike
destruction that made this war impossible to understand in traditional
terms.[5] The horror of World War I was so overwhelming that any discussion of it, no matter how critical, is considered by Hemingway's protagonists to be reductive, even banal.

This "calamity for civilization" (*SAR* 17) negatively affects the lives of
nearly all the characters in *The Sun Also Rises*, Jake Barnes perhaps most
permanently of all. Jake's impotence, the result of a physical wound, is a
horror that is shared, according to Denis de Rougemont, by many others:
"Countless doctors and soldiers testified to the way in which a war of
material was accompanied by a 'sex disaster.' A widespread impotence—
or at least its premonitory symptoms, chronic onanism and homosexuality—was the result vouched for by statistics of a sojourn of four years
in the trenches. That is how it came about that presently for the first time
there was a general revolt of soldiers against war, because war, from being
an outlet for the passions, had become a kind of vast castration of Europe" (266). Rougemont suggests that World War I's special horror resulted from its substitution of a war of material or machines for a war of
men, essentially emasculating them.

This break with the chivalric tradition—in which the strength, courage, and integrity of individual knights largely determined the outcome of battles and enabled the realization of the masculine self—had been developing for centuries but occurred decisively only when modern technological advances took hold in the twentieth century. The ultimate effect of such technological advances, as Hemingway later wrote in an *Esquire Magazine* article, "Notes on the Next War" (1935), was that "in *modern* war there is nothing sweet or fitting in your dying" (quoted by Stephens, *Nonfiction* 304; emphasis mine). Hemingway had earlier testified to this disjunction in a 1918 letter from the Red Cross Hospital in Milan where he was recovering from his own injuries: "When there is a direct hit your pals get spattered all over you. Spattered is literal" (*Letters* 14). Mark Twain had thus proved prescient in *Connecticut Yankee* when he described the knights killed by Hank's modern weapons as not "individuals, but merely . . . homogeneous protoplasm, with alloys of iron and buttons" (*CY* 396). Though in this letter Hemingway asserts that "there isn't anything funny about this war" (*Letters* 14), its horrors were so extreme that laughter in the face of absurdity sometimes seemed the only appropriate response.

Jake's impotence is thus not simply a horror, but also a laughable indignity. It is Jake's bad fortune that he is not only wounded on "a joke front" (*SAR* 31) but that as Brett points out, even his wound "seem[s] like a hell of a joke" (*SAR* 27). Such a wound, however devastating personally, lacks the nobility of glorious death in battle, the kind of sweet or fitting death one might expect to meet in chivalric combat. But even when death comes in World War I, it presents itself in an ignoble guise, Brett's first war love dying of dysentery (just as Catherine Barkley's first love "didn't have a sabre cut," as she had expected, but was blown "all to bits" [*FA* 20]). Survivors of the war often suffer psychological wounds that cause aberrant behavior. After returning from the war, Brett's husband sleeps with a loaded service revolver and threatens to kill her, potentially pulling her into the orbit of war casualties. Others are able to deal with its horror only by treating it lightly. Mike, who never sent for the medals he had earned, "borrows" some medals and passes them out as souvenirs, and Count Mippipopolous is celebrated as "one of us" because he suffered his arrow wounds not while in the army, at present an ignoble occupation, but on a business trip.

The successors to World War I in military history—the Spanish Civil War ("a strange new kind of war," as Hemingway reported in a cable dispatch [quoted by Watson 33]) and World War II—were even more affected by the devastating advances in technology. Though war had been waged before on land and sea, now the air became a battlefield as well, for the airplane, which played a relatively minor role in World War I (aviation then seeming "like the romantic side of the war, of course—like cavalry used to be," according to Fitzgerald's Tom D'Invilliers [TSP 150]), soon became one of the most important machines of war. The sight of planes provokes in Robert Jordan a horrified poetic rumination: "The bombers were high now in fast, ugly arrow-heads beating the sky apart with the noise of their motors. They *are* shaped like sharks, Robert Jordan thought. . . . [But] these do not move like sharks. They move like no thing there has ever been. They move like mechanized doom" (FWBT 87). Death dealt by an animate being is less horrifying to Jordan than the impersonal doom created by modern technology, which has mechanized (at least metaphorically) and thereby depersonalized the arrow, a more traditional weapon. The guerilla leader Pilar admits: "We are nothing against such machines" (FWBT 89). Upon describing the destruction wrought by the Allied bombing raids in World War II, Colonel Cantwell suggests that "if a man has a conscience . . . he might think about air-power some time" (ARIT 224). Other so-called advances in military technology are also available. Cantwell jokes about the atomic bomb, botulism, and anthrax, but nuclear and biological warfare cannot be defused by a joke.

Despite their horrified reactions, these modern soldiers are sometimes excited by modern technology. Robert Jordan feels pride in his skill at blowing up bridges with sophisticated explosives, and Colonel Cantwell, who recognizes that the cavalry is "worthless . . . in our time" (ARIT 232), transfers to a machine the affection that in an earlier century he would have felt for a horse: "Every move she [the engine] makes . . . is a triumph of the gallantry of the aging machine. We do not have war horses now like Old Traveller, or Marbot's Lysette who fought, personally, at Eylau. We have the gallantry of worn-through rods that refuse to break; the cylinder head that does not blow though it has every right to" (ARIT 52). His use of heightened diction to describe a machine is telling. But such adaptations to the increasingly familiar technology, though they implicate the modern soldier in modern war, are largely an attempt to make a virtue of necessity. At base, these men are uneasy at such technological advances, which make war less personal and therefore paradoxically more horrifying.

Modern war is also less personal because of the number of soldiers involved. Paul Fussell suggests that the training of the first British conscript army in 1916 "could be said to mark the beginning of the modern world" (11). That beginning had been marked earlier in America, where during the Civil War the Confederate Congress legislated the first draft in American history and the federal government soon followed suit, leading

Confederate soldier Sam Watkins to note: "From this time on . . . a soldier was simply a machine, a *conscript*. . . . All our pride and valor had gone" (quoted by Burns 129). Units in which individuals cease to have any identity become like a war machine, as a Spanish guerilla in *For Whom the Bell Tolls* says: "What an army. What equipment. What a mechanization. . . . Camion after camion. All uniformed alike. All with casques of steel on their heads" (*FWBT* 415). The confusion of the machine and the soldier in this passage marks a historical shift, military history revealing, as Rougemont suggests, the "transform[ation of] the inspired and magnificent knights into troops disciplined and uniform" like these, "as gradually men serving machines became themselves machines" (254).

By the same token, the more comprehensive the army becomes, the less professional it can be. The Russian adviser Karkov in *For Whom the Bell Tolls* asserts that a conscript army lacks discipline, and Colonel Cantwell notes with regret the increasing lack of professionalism of his army, an army in which, he claims hyperbolically, no one knows how to shoot. Cantwell's driver, Jackson, manifests the very lack of martial skill and professional commitment that Cantwell reprehends. But Cantwell's pride in his own professionalism is mitigated by shame at his involvement in battles against armies of nonprofessionals, causing him to deny that the taking of Paris was a military operation since the occupying army was composed largely of office workers left behind as soldiers. When war is no longer left to a professional elite, civilians are no longer exempt from war.

Robert Jordan is able to avoid some of the problems of this army of the masses by working as a partisan. His independence from a regular army allows him more freedom and responsibility, enabling him to avoid becoming merely one more soldier in a long line but requiring him to cast his lot with untrained peasant rebels. Though Robert admires the Spanish resistance workers, recognizing that they are necessary to a Republican victory, their involvement is one more manifestation of the merging of civilian and military populations. The peculiar horror of such a merging is revealed in Pilar's story about the Republican takeover of a town. Not only did the Republicans, mostly men who worked the surrounding fields, shoot the *guardia civiles*, but they also flailed to death the mayor, the priest, and the landowners. This slaughter, in no traditional sense a battle, garners shame rather than honor for the participants. Its double is the takeover of Maria's town by the Fascists during which Maria is repeatedly raped. In such a war there are no civilians, and the horrors know no limits.

When an army is composed of such masses, efficiency becomes of paramount importance. Cantwell bitterly mocks the mechanical efficiency of modern war by ironically suggesting a refinement: replacements should be shot immediately upon arrival at the rear of the lines because this action would delete those later steps when the replacements are brought forward, wounded or killed, and then removed to the rear. Individual heroism is irrelevant in an efficient war, as Frederic Henry learns when he offers to wait for treatment after being wounded: "Don't be a bloody hero" (*FA* 58). In such a large army, whether functioning as a well-oiled machine or a blundering behemoth, men are expendable commodities. Individual battles may be planned merely as holding actions, and the anonymous men engaged in these battles are considered simply a price to be paid if another battle is to be won. This strategy gains a peculiar horror from the fact that the soldiers never know if their battles are "real" or if they are merely expendable commodities. Frederic Henry is wounded in one such holding action, and Robert Jordan, who knows little about the larger scheme in which his actions figure, assumes desperately that his battle may be merely a holding action. Duval, an officer who has the power to stop Jordan's doomed attack, is paralyzed by indecision because he has not been told the status of this battle, which ironically has not been planned as a holding action and should be canceled. The complicated system of military administration, when coupled with the incompetence of the officers, results in the death of Robert Jordan and many guerillas.

The modern army is often presented as a large, inefficient bureaucracy where important information cannot make it through channels and important orders are given too late. Confusion thus reigns in the huge retreat of the Italian army in *A Farewell to Arms*. Frederic Henry is disgusted by the complete lack of order and discipline that results in the senseless execution of Italian officers by other Italian officers—a breakdown in leadership that as Reynolds points out was true to the facts of the retreat from Caporetto.[6] Frederic deserts from the army at this point, making his famous "separate peace" (*FA* 243). Yet he deserts not from a general horror of war as such, as this action is often interpreted, but because his army is led by men who in turning on their fellows betray the chivalric values of loyalty and comradeship. Frederic's desertion may also testify to a tension between the codes of courtly love and chivalry, both operative for him if not for other modern soldiers. Although these two codes typically functioned in complementary fashion in the Middle Ages, various medieval romances reveal that their harmonious relationship sometimes broke down, as Ferrante notes: "[Courtly] love is often consummated in a strange land, or other world, which offers a new life to the hero, and which attracts him, but to which he cannot totally commit himself. He is drawn back to the old life by personal and chivalric ties or habits. The very activity which, in many cases, has won [his lady]—fighting—takes him away from her or sets up conflicts with his commitment to her which he is unable to resolve" (74). When confronted with a choice between the courtly love relationship he shares in an other world with Catherine on the one hand and the meager possibilities for chivalric behavior offered by World War I on the other, Frederic chooses to commit himself to courtly love, "the disasters of war and the appeals of Catherine . . . gradually combin[ing] to pull Henry from his male bondings until, in Switzerland, he no longer desires to see anyone but Catherine" (Solotaroff 5).

Like Frederic Henry, Colonel Cantwell evinces distaste for the military leadership of his day, insisting that most generals are now mere administrators without actual fighting experience and thus without the necessary experience to lead men well and honorably. Instead such generals order their men to fight battles that result in mere butchery. Cantwell claims that men now rise through the ranks on the basis of political maneuverings rather than merit, the army having become a big business rather than a corps of elite professionals. Though he recognizes the exigencies of modern warfare, he appeals to the lessons of the past, to military history with its legendary war heroes, in his condemnation of contemporary generals, whom he regards as mere politicians and businessmen. Having lost several companies because of the orders of incompetents, he proclaims bitterly: "In our army you obey like a dog" (*ARIT* 242).

The confusion within the army among both officers and men results necessarily in a larger confusion about the relationship of friend and foe. During the retreat, Frederic Henry regards his fellow Italian soldiers as more dangerous than his Austrian and German enemies. His fears prove justified when Aymo (one of the ambulance drivers under Frederic's command) is killed by an Italian bullet and Frederic is almost executed by the Italian battle police. So must Robert Jordan be wary of the guerillas with whom he fights, Pablo switching between friend and foe with such frequency that Robert considers killing him for the good of the group. By the same token, Cantwell aphoristically states that he sometimes loves his enemies more than his friends, and Robert regards his enemies as friends, feeling sharp regret when he kills a young cavalryman (who, astride his horse and with saber hanging, is a clear approximation of the medieval knight).

While these novels overtly depict the horrible reality of modern war, the idealized warfare of medieval chivalry functions as a critical subtext. Subtle allusions and references to chivalry suggest a golden age of aesthetically ordered warfare, rule-governed and self-contained, that the protagonists nostalgically desire and within which they attempt to operate, against all odds. In contrast to the soldiers engaged in modern war, the medieval knight had great independence (*franchesse*), which encouraged self-actualization. The outcome of any battle depended on his skill and bravery (*prouesse*) rather than sophisticated technology. He was set off from the mass of men as a member of an elite group (*noblesse*). Within this special society, however, comradeship and loyalty (*loyauté*) were among the highest virtues, and the "conventional chivalric distinction between combatants and noncombatants" (John Fraser 184) was easily maintained.

The chivalric tradition, when invoked, held great power for Hemingway in his own military life, as testified to by an incident that occurred during World War II when Hemingway functioned officially as a correspondent but acted unofficially as the leader of a small troop of men during the liberation of Paris. On 1 September 1944, Hemingway received from his friend General Buck Lanham a telegram that parodied King Henry IV's sneering comment to the duke of Crillon after a victory at Arques: "We have fought at Landrecies and you were not there" (quoted by Baker, *Life* 533). Instead of laughing off the taunt, Hemingway left the hard-won comfort of the Ritz Hotel and, placing himself and his driver at great risk for no reason other than to pick up the thrown gauntlet, spent several harrowing days and nights crossing territory packed with German soldiers. When he finally caught up with Lanham, there was little to do but turn around and return to Paris. Notably, Hemingway was afraid when he left Paris that his fabled luck had run out but felt that the challenge issued could not be ignored with honor.

The parallel between Hemingway's behavior in this situation and the attitude of the medieval knight toward battle is instructive. Rougemont alludes to the "countless instances where a futile carnage resulted from the [knight's] attempt to fulfil at great peril vows of an overweening arrogance," leading him to conclude that "danger was what knights courted for its own sake" (247). In Froissart's *Chronicles*, a book to which Hemingway later referred in a 1949 letter to his publisher, Charles Scribner (*Letters* 683), similar reference is made to this practice of granting an almost religious validity to military formality. Froissart observes that knights often chose to be killed rather than to infringe chivalric rules.

Hemingway's reading reveals that medieval chivalry was no tempo-
rary interest. Like Twain, Adams, and Fitzgerald, he was exposed during his childhood to Walter Scott's medievalist novels, including *Ivanhoe*
(received as a gift from his Uncle Leicester for Christmas 1909 and later
studied for five weeks at Oak Park High School). Reynolds notes that
the adolescent Hemingway studied *Old English Ballads*, Chaucer's "General Prologue" and "Knight's Tale," the first two books of *The Faerie
Queene*,[7] and Tennyson's *Idylls of the King*. The adult Hemingway read a
number of primary and secondary histories of the Middle Ages, most
notably Villehardouin and DeJoinville's *Chronicles of Crusaders* but also
Coulton's *Life in the Middle Ages*, Lidell Hart's *Decisive Wars of History*,
and Lecky's influential *History of European Morals*. Reynolds notes pointedly that Hemingway's "reading reveals one . . . warrior, little connected
with Hemingway, whom we should have suspected long ago: the medieval knight," and he posits that critics have largely ignored this element
in Hemingway because the chivalric influence "will not be found on
the fiction's surface" (*Reading* 26). Hemingway's literary rival Fitzgerald
feared, however, that Hemingway's interest in chivalry would at some
point explicitly emerge in his fiction, as he indicated in a 1934 letter to
Max Perkins, who served as Hemingway's editor also: "Needless to say I
am highly curious about the setting of his [Hemingway's] novel. I hope
to God it isn't the crusading story that he once had in mind, for I would
hate like hell for my 9th-century novel [*Philippe, Count of Darkness*]
to compete with *that*" (*Dear Scott* 212). Reynolds pointedly states that
Hemingway's reading "suggests that Fitzgerald was not being paranoid"
(*Reading* 26).

In various contexts Hemingway referred easily and naturally to chivalry. In a 1953 letter to Bernard Berenson, he described his relationship to
his work in terms of the chivalric relationship between lord and knight,
asserting that "[work is] the Liege Lord that I had sworn to serve and
would serve always until I die" (*Letters* 801). Even more telling is a comment in a 1952 letter to Bernard Berenson in which he actually imagined
himself as a medieval knight: "Do you ever have the feeling that you lived
at all times in many different countries? Or is that crazy. I can smell the
horses in the morning and I know exactly how the different types of body
armour felt and where you chafed" (*Letters* 785). Hemingway's comment
bears a telling resemblance to the journal entry in which Mark Twain
recorded the germ of *Connecticut Yankee*—"Dream of being a knight errant in armor in the Middle Ages" (*Notebook* 171)—though Twain, unlike
Hemingway, exploited this dream for specifically comic purposes. On a

trip through France's Loire Valley, Hemingway again "amused himself by imagining that he was a medieval knight riding his horse along the riverbank, [and] the notion stayed with him all the way south . . . to Hendaye, where he had worked [on *The Sun Also Rises*] long ago" (Baker, *Life* 648).

Hemingway's first wife, Hadley Richardson, had drawn similar parallels between Hemingway and various knightly figures during their courtship, telling him in a 1921 letter that he "would have been an alchemist in the Middle Ages, or a Galahad" (quoted by Griffin, *Youth* 191) and dubbing him in another 1921 letter "a verry, perfect, gentile knight" (quoted by Griffin, *Youth* 154), echoing the description of the Knight in Chaucer's *Canterbury Tales*. Reynolds observes that "Hadley was right . . . [since] like Chaucer's soldier with his rust-stained armor, Hemingway appreciated the code of honor and service, and like that faithful warrior, Hemingway found the values of his youth outdated in modern times" (*Young Hemingway* 223). Curiously, two of Hemingway's sons also explicitly identified him with knightly figures. Patrick claimed, "When you were with my father, it was the Crusades," and asserted that "he was Richard the Lion-Hearted, and my mother [Pauline Pfeiffer] was the woman you left behind in the castle with the chastity belt" (quoted by Kert 336). Gregory described fishing trips (cum submarine surveillance) with his father during World War II as "Don Quixote vs. the Wolf Pack" (*Papa* 68), noting that his father addressed the crew as "Caballeros" (*Papa* 83). Hemingway's early experience as "Robin Hood in the seventh-grade school play" (Kert 40) was thus a rehearsal for other knightly roles that he would adopt in his adult life. It is little wonder that he "tended or pretended to believe that four of his ancestors had taken part in the Crusades" (Mellow 563)—a fantasy he shared with Henry Adams, at whose "old hang out" Hemingway planned to "hole up and write for 4–5 days," as he wrote in a 1944 letter at Mont-Saint-Michel (*Letters* 563).

One of the most important allusions to chivalry in Hemingway's fiction appears in the title *A Farewell to Arms*, as Bernard Oldsey has discussed at length.[8] This title derives from George Peele's poem of the same name (written in 1590), which was attached to a long commemoration of the tournament held in honor of Queen Elizabeth's birthday. The poem presents Sir Henry Lee's withdrawal from the tournament because he has grown too old to serve as the Queen's champion. The tone is one of resignation rather than defeat, Sir Henry requesting the right to serve the queen through prayers and songs of praise since he can no longer serve her on the mock battlefield of a tournament. The orderliness and aesthetic appeal of this whole proceeding is striking: the battle itself is aesthetically ordered, a theatric spectacle; the champion quietly leaves the spectacle when he can no longer play his role adequately; and his request for retirement appears in an elegantly constructed lyric poem.

The contrast between Sir Henry's farewell to arms and that of Lieutenant Henry is great,[9] for Frederic Henry's involvement in a war characterized by horrible disorder can be ended only by desertion. The Peele poem provides an ethos against which modern warfare and the actions to which it impels modern knights are found wanting. As Hemingway stated in a 1932 letter to Arnold Gingrich: "To Arms should clang more than the book deserves—that title could handle a book with more and better war in it" (*Letters* 378). Hemingway's allusion here to the sound of sword and shield, the weapons of medieval rather than modern war, is telling, as is the exception that he originally drew in manuscript to the "obscene" use of "abstract words such as glory, honor, courage, or hallow" (*FA* 185): "The only things glorious were the cavalry riding with lances" (quoted by Paul Smith 34).

The title drawn from the Peele poem was one of fifteen potential titles drawn from ballads and love songs, particularly the courtly lyrics of the English Renaissance, that Hemingway considered, according to Oldsey (24). Hemingway also considered titles drawn from more modern sources, among them "The Sentimental Education of Frederic Henry," which most critics associate with Flaubert's *L'Education sentimentale* but which is more appropriately linked to *The Education of Henry Adams*, as H. R. Stoneback suggests: "The thrust of the Adams work hits the target dead center, for *A Farewell to Arms* is also a 'Study of Twentieth-Century Multiplicity.' . . . Both works deal with the historical 'broken neck' of modern man, both contrast the chaotic forces of the twentieth century with an age and place of faith" ("'Lovers' Sonnets'" 63).

For a later novel, *Across the River and into the Trees*, Hemingway again considered a title that would allude to chivalric exploits: "A New-Slain Knight." Since 1926 Hemingway had been trying to write a novel that would fit this title, drawn from the medieval ballad the "Twa Corbies," which he judged "a great poem" (quoted by Reynolds, *Reading* 93), having first read it at Oak Park High School. Alluding directly to the chivalric exploits of a medieval knight who has been newly (or recently) slain, the title potentially contained a play on words, for it also could allude to the slaying of a "new" (or modern) knight—exactly the history of Colonel Cantwell as chronicled in *Across the River and into the Trees*. However, Hemingway ultimately chose for this novel a title that alludes to the final words of General Stonewall Jackson. This choice was superior since the Civil War embodies both the chivalric elements of medieval warfare explicitly suggested by the "Knight" title and the technological horrors of modern warfare.

Military historians consider the American Civil War a balance point, embodying yet separating the old and new modes of war, a fact of which Hemingway was certainly aware, given his extensive reading in military history of the American Civil War.[10] Particularly the Confederate soldier—always pictured in the popular imagination as brandishing a sword while astride his horse, the plume of his hat waving in the wind—suggests a late incarnation of the medieval knight, acting within a strict code of honor, sacrificing all to an ideal that has become a lost cause. Yet the experimentation during the Civil War with new methods and technologies of war—conscript armies, ironclad ships, repeating rifles, field entrenchments, flexible assault formations, mined harbors, submarine attacks, mass movement of troops by train, aerial observation—introduced a new era of military history that would culminate in the horrors of the First and Second World Wars.[11] The title that Hemingway chose for this late novel thus suggests, though at a remove, the chivalric exploits of medieval warfare while providing a modern contrast. Hemingway's use of Stonewall Jackson's dying words suggests that the balance has indeed shifted from one mode of war to another. The same shift is implied in the character of Cantwell's driver, Jackson, who, though he shares a surname with the great Confederate general, "was in no sense a soldier but only a man placed, against his will, in uniform" (ARIT 22).

In addition to choosing titles that resonate with chivalric suggestiveness, Hemingway composed pseudomedieval epigraphs to appear at the head of two books—his own *Winner Take Nothing* (1933) and his third wife Martha Gellhorn's *A Stricken Field* (1940). Hemingway was particularly proud of these epigraphs, directing Max Perkins in a 1943 letter to reveal that he had not merely cited them (as implied by his use of quotation marks) but had written them: "I wrote that quotation . . . all same I wrote the other fine medaeval [sic] one in the front of Martha's Stricken Field. I probably would have written pretty well in those times but unfortunately that's been written and these are these so try to write in these. Is far from easy" (*Letters* 553). "These" times are presented in *Winner Take Nothing* by means of a series of remarkably depressing short stories (one of which, "A Way You'll Never Be," presents Nick Adams at his nervous return to the Italian front during World War I, having just recovered from terrible injuries and battle fatigue). The mock medieval epigraph—"'Unlike all other forms of lutte or combat the conditions are that the winner shall take nothing; neither his ease, nor his pleasure, nor any notion of glory, nor, if he win far enough, shall there be any reward within himself'"—bears ironic witness to the inevitable failure of men attempting to function chivalrically in "these" times—that is, In Our Time.

Hemingway's evocation of the chivalric in titles and epigraphs is reinforced by his allusions to famous medieval battles. In an inscription in a copy of *The Sun Also Rises*, he described the novel as presenting "a fishing expedition in the Pass of Roland" (quoted by Stoneback, "Rue Saint-Jacques" 6). Jake Barnes, on his fishing trip, takes special note of Roncesvalles—the home of the medieval monastery ("Roncevaux" in the Old French, which as Stoneback points out is the name that Jake uses in dialogue, as distinct from his usage in narration ["Rue Saint-Jacques" 8 n. 5]) where Roland, the knightly hero of the archetypal chanson de geste, dies after an epic rearguard battle with the Saracens.[12] Roland's great courage, dedication to a lost cause even unto death, loyalty to his fellows, and commitment to his king all serve to identify him as a chivalric knight of the highest order.

Hemingway had studied Roland's exploits at some length, discussing the *Chanson de Roland* with Eric "Chink" Dorman-Smith (a friend from World I) after the 1924 Pamplona festival (Reynolds, *Reading* 93), during which he had gone to mass at the Roncesvalles monastery. He continued familiar enough with the *Chanson* to end a 1956 letter to Harvey Breit with a reference to the climactic line: "Ah que cet cor a long haleine!" (*Letters* 870). In an earlier letter, to General Charles "Buck" Lanham in 1950, Hemingway revealed by reference to Roland's battle his own penchant for rethinking the strategies of famous battles: "But Chink and I used to . . . fight each other at any famous or infamous place like playing chess. . . . I would tell him that I could come through the pass of Roncevaux and he would say, 'You can not.' And I would do it" (*Letters* 687). Robert Jordan, whose "rearguard action [defending a mountain pass] evokes the *Song of Roland*" (Brenner 130), shares his creator's interest in military strategy and one-upmanship, and thinks of Agincourt as he plans his own small battle. Colonel Cantwell also engages in such war games, imagining himself as a fifteenth-century condottiere in the process of deciding which Italian town to capture. On a 1923 walking tour in Italy with Ezra Pound, Hemingway had "show[n] Pound how [Sigismundo] Malatesta probably had fought [at Orbetello]" (Adair 343) in his defeat of Alphonse of Aragon in 1448; and "Malatesta, one-time captain of Venice, *condottiere* (not unlike the modern Arditi young Hemingway so admired), lover, and well-known patron of the arts, may have fired Hemingway's imagination" (Adair 344). Though the condottieri differed from medieval knights because they were mercenaries largely concerned with material gain rather than noble deeds, they nonetheless adopted many of the rules of chivalry, exaggerating them to such an extent that war became more of an art than ever. Hence duels reminiscent of those held in medieval tournaments were arranged between commanders of rival armies, the winner of the duel automatically winning the entire battle. The condottieri rejected the use of firearms not from ignorance of their effectiveness but from a sense that their use was inconsistent with dignity.[13]

Though Cantwell grows happy in his identification with such knights, he later stops playing this war game, mourning that "there aren't any such times any more" (*ARIT* 63). The narrator's comment that "the spell was broken" (*ARIT* 63), a comment reiterated by Cantwell, is telling, for the spell in question is clearly a nostalgic evocation of the chivalric past (perhaps the same spell that had enchanted Hank and the narrator "Mark Twain" in *Connecticut Yankee*). By escaping into this past, this golden age of warfare if not a golden age of peace, Cantwell is able to escape, however briefly, from the horrible memories of modern war that haunt him to such an extent that he must obsessively confess them to Renata.

Cantwell is able to reactivate this chivalric spell by invoking the order of Brusadelli, a mock order he has created in imitation of the medieval orders of chivalry. Two years before the publication of *Across the River and into the Trees*, Hemingway took great pleasure in his induction in Venice into a knightly order, the Knights of Malta, in which he was given the title of Cavaliere di Gran Croce al Merito. The Order of Brusadelli, like the medieval orders serving as its model and that of the Knights of Malta, is noble, military, and religious, and has a select membership composed of knights ("de los Caballeros"). At the mere mention of the order, its members—all men who had fought together in World War I— are transformed, their change in identity signaled by a change in title. Colonel Cantwell becomes the Supreme Commander, the maitre d' becomes the Gran Maestro, and the cook becomes the Commendatore. However whimsical the game, these men gain a measure of dignity and self-confidence from their knightly identities not present in their own lives. While this order is a parodic version of the medieval orders—its supreme secret is mere nonsense and its members proclaim their vassalage not to the king but to a corrupt businessman—the parody is significant only insofar as it underscores the self-consciousness of these modern knights. Their recognition of the inappropriateness of a true chivalric order in the modern world paradoxically frees them to escape into a fantasy of such an order.

Robert Jordan similarly feels the appeal of a knightly order. He initially identifies himself as part of a crusade, a knight fighting with other knights in a great cause: "Crusade . . . was the only word for it although it was a word that had been so worn and abused that it no longer gave its true meaning. You felt, in spite of all bureaucracy and inefficiency and party strife . . . a feeling of consecration to a duty . . . [that] was authentic as the feeling you had when you . . . stood in Chartres Cathedral. . . . You felt an absolute brotherhood with the others who were engaged in it" (*FWBT* 235). But after Robert learns more about the workings of this war—the self-aggrandizing motives for military involvement of various parties, the ignoble political maneuverings, the propagandistic distortions of truth—he no longer feels part of a crusade, though he continues to fight because the cause is just. He is never sure whether this change is for the good or bad, whether he has merely lost his naïveté or been corrupted. Perhaps both are to some extent true. But it is telling that in his final moments, as he lies close to death after his battle, his thoughts revert to memories of his grandfather, a saber-wielding leader of cavalry in the American Civil War.

In comparing his military exploits to those of his grandfather, Robert feels that he has proved himself worthy.[14] Robert's qualified success as a knight in this modern war, a success greater than that achieved by most of Hemingway's other modern knights, is largely due to his unusual independence. He is set off from the mass army as a member of a small if not particularly elite group and feels a sense of real comradeship with a few of his fellows. Most important, he feels that his actions, skill, and bravery can make a significant difference. That they will not ultimately do so—a fact of which the reader is aware, though Robert is not—is a function not of his own personal limitations but of the disorder inherent in modern war.

At base, then, modern war is criticized by Hemingway because unlike chivalric war, it does not provide modern man with an appropriate opportunity to test and define himself in battle and thereby to realize his masculine identity, try though he may to do so[15] (as evidenced by Hemingway's obsessive returns to the battlefield). However, one arena remains in which a few select men can replicate the behavior of the chivalric knight—the bullfight, "the one thing that has, with the exception of the ritual of the church, come down to us intact from the old days," as Hemingway described it in a 1926 letter to Max Perkins (*Letters* 237). In *Death in the Afternoon* (1932), his treatise on bullfighting (like Adams's treatise on medieval cathedrals, part autobiography, part travelogue, part history, part art appreciation, and part fiction), Hemingway asserts that the bullfight is a tragedy that is "well ordered and . . . strongly disciplined by ritual" (*DIA* 8) and that "the aficionado, or lover of the bullfight, may be said . . . to be one who has this sense of the tragedy and ritual of the fight" (*DIA* 9).

Hemingway's sense of the relationship between the bullfight and the tragedy, and his evident admiration for a ritual that aesthetically shapes passion—in particular, the passion for death, which is one of the "things that are necessary for a country to love bullfights" (*DIA* 265)—can be interpreted with an eye to Rougemont's comments about the medieval tournament. Hemingway virtually invites an interpretation of the bull-fighter as a type of the medieval knight when he suggests that bullfighters and "the crusaders in the middle ages" (*DIA* 101) share occupational hazards. Just as Hemingway asserts the relationship between the bullfight and the tragedy, Rougemont suggests that the tournament is a source of the modern tragedy. Just as Hemingway emphasizes that the bullfight is governed by a ritual that aesthetically shapes the passion for death, Rougemont suggests that the tournament is governed by chivalric ritual that functions to order aesthetically the erotic and fighting instincts. For Hemingway, the bullfight is the modern analogue of the medieval tournament. The modern knight who, like the chivalric knight, loves danger for its own sake can there indulge his erotic instinct (performing for his lady) and his martial instinct (killing his enemy) within a rigorously defined set of rituals. In pursuing such adventures—"perilous encounters by which [the knight] can prove his mettle," according to Erich Auerbach (133)—the knight engages in acts of self-definition. He becomes his best self, "a true knight," for "trial through adventure is the real meaning of the knight's ideal existence, . . . [and] the very essence of the knight's ideal of manhood is called forth by adventure" (Auerbach 135).

Pedro Romero is the moral avatar of *The Sun Also Rises* because he takes full advantage of his opportunity[16]—a unique opportunity in the modern world—to behave gracefully within this rigorously defined set of rituals, dedicating himself to his lady and to his enemy, to loving and fighting. Like the "world of knightly proving" described in the courtly romances, the world of the bullfighter "contains nothing but the requisites of adventure [for] nothing is found in it which is not either accessory or preparatory to an adventure" (Auerbach 136). In other words, it is "a world specifically created and designed to give the knight opportunity to prove himself" (Auerbach 136). Romero dedicates his valorous deed to Brett, the lady who in true courtly fashion sits above him observing his knightly adventure. But Romero's knightly service is not selfless: "He did it all for himself inside, and it strengthened him, and yet he did it for her, too. But he did not do it for her at any loss to himself. He gained by it all through the afternoon" (*SAR* 216). Romero's action suggests the knightly behavior that Auerbach describes when he calls into question the supposed selflessness of the medieval knight, arguing that though love served as the immediate motivation for knightly adventure, the focus in the romances was most often on the adventures themselves and the knight's self-actualization through adventures.

Hemingway's own approximation of this knightly adventure was his participation in the amateur fights and the running of the bulls at Pamplona. In a 1924 letter inviting Howell Jenkins (with whom he had driven ambulances in Italy during World War I) to participate in this adventure, Hemingway describes "six bull fights on six successive days and every morning an amateur fight in which will take part . . . Ernest de la Mancha Hemingway representing the Stock Yards of Chicago" (*Letters* 130). Like Cervantes's Don Quixote (though with more self-consciousness about the implications), Hemingway attempted to function as a knight in a rigorously nonchivalric age, characterized here by the Chicago stockyards, inevitably suggesting a parodic and debased version of the bullfight—these same "stockyards at Chicago" (*FA* 185) later famously invoked as an objective correlative for modern war in *A Farewell to Arms*.

In the final analysis, however, we might call into question an ethic that condemns the horrors of modern war only to celebrate the beauties of ritualized chivalric warfare. However true it may be that limited and ordered war is preferable to the increasingly unlimited chaos of modern war, it is also true that the chivalric sensibility, with its central concept that man realizes his masculine identity in the context of glorious battle, encourages the very existence of war. Hence the final irony: those modern wars so criticized by Hemingway's protagonists—and by Hemingway himself—because they deviate from the chivalric ideals are themselves the logical extension of a continued celebration of chivalry in the modern era. As Mark Girouard notes of the origins of World War I, "Opinions will always differ as to whether the Great War could or should have been prevented. But one conclusion is undeniable: the ideals of chivalry [as assimilated and acted upon by the class of English gentlemen] worked with one accord in favour of war" (276). The assimilation of these ideals by Ernest Hemingway caused him to seek obsessively, and ultimately futilely, in his life and art for a war that would enable his self-realization as a modern American man in the mold of the medieval knight. When no such war appeared, Hemingway had to content himself with the blood sports around which he elaborated a set of codes, obedience to which enabled him in a limited way to function as a knight in the modern world.

Hemingway's famous nonfiction texts of the 1930s, *Death in the After-noon* and *Green Hills of Africa*, resonate in peculiar ways with his late novel *The Old Man and the Sea* (1952). All three focus on blood sports—bullfighting, big-game hunting, and big-game fishing. Yet in pitting man against beast, Hemingway is not constructing a naturalistic world so much as a mythic world—The Last Good Country. Spain, Africa, and Cuba, unlike the United States, continued to provide last good countries for Hemingway, havens where knightly behavior remained at least possible for individual men willing to commit themselves to a code of prow-ess (*prouesse*) in one-on-one jousts with noble antagonists they respect as brothers. Santiago is one such knight—unlikely because of his age, poverty, and lack of sophistication, yet proving himself a member of the "natural aristocracy" (Sylvester, "Extended Vision" 136) in the lyrical chanson de geste that is *The Old Man and the Sea*. In a sense, *Death in the Afternoon* and *Green Hills* provide a gloss on Hemingway's late novel, foregrounding motifs that might otherwise go unnoticed.

Santiago is named after Saint James, or Santiago de Compostela, the saint who "carried Mary's worship . . . to Spain" as Henry Adams notes (*MSMC* 171) in his discussion of the complementary windows at Chartres focusing on Saint James's pilgrimage and the *Chanson de Roland*. When Santiago "lift[s] the harpoon as high as he c[an] and dr[i]ve[s] it down with all his strength" (*OMS* 93) into the marlin, he resembles Roland's suzerain Charlemagne, who, directed by Saint James in a dream, travels to "Pampeluna," as Henry Adams notes, and "transfixes with his lance the Saracen chief" (*MSMC* 170)—rather like Romero at Pamplona's bull-ring thrusting "the hilt of the sword . . . between the bull's shoulders" (*SAR* 218). Inevitably, Santiago, who keeps on the wall of his shack a pic-ture of the Virgin of Cobre, "promise[s] to make a pilgrimage to the Virgin of Cobre if [he] catch[es the marlin]" (*OMS* 65)—just as Heming-way presented his 1954 Nobel (Noble?) Prize to "the Virgen of Cobre, Cuba's national saint, to be kept in the shrine of Our Lady at Santiago de Cuba" (Baker 669). Santiago proceeds to say multiple "Hail Marys [which] are easier to say than Our Fathers" (*OMS* 65).

Of course, Santiago's fishing trip is a pilgrimage—or more accurately, a quest. Like the Fisher King of ancient vegetation myths—his most re-cent incarnation in Eliot's *The Waste Land*—Santiago is identified with "a fishless desert" (*OMS* 10), a sterility that awaits redemption.[17] His one-on-one victory over a worthy antagonist, whose "sword was . . . tapered like a rapier" (*OMS* 62), enables him to prove himself via a chivalric test and thereby to bring back knowledge that will result in potency and fertility after a dry spell of eighty-four days. Santiago's frequently noted identification with Christ, whose Passion he replicates in his three-day voyage, aligns him with the Christian version of such vegetation myths. Yet Santiago's end, the great marlin landed but mutilated by the sharks, is more equivocal than the ultimately optimistic conclusion of Christ's Passion in Resurrection—in this regard more like Eliot's equivocal conclusion to his modernist *Waste Land.*

Santiago's statement "I am not religious" (*OMS* 64) and his "mechanical" (*OMS* 65) repetition of the Hail Marys reveal that though he is in more than one sense an old man, he is also inevitably marked by the modern era. Though he continues to fish in the old way, in contrast to the "younger fishermen" with their "motorboats" (*OMS* 29) and radios, he recognizes that his way is inevitably disappearing—hence his desire for a radio and more important, his equivocal relationship with the squirelike Manolin. He has taught Manolin to fish in the old way, and Manolin's loyalty (*loyauté*) paradoxically maintains Santiago's own faith. But he counsels Manolin to stay with the lucky modern fisherman, who fishes successfully if ignobly, though Manolin ultimately decides to reject such counsel and fish again with Santiago, who passes to him the marlin's "spear" (*OMS* 124) in a critical rite of passage.

In a curious refrain, Santiago returns repeatedly to a dream of his youthful past "before the mast on a square rigged ship that ran to Africa," where he saw "lions on the beaches" (*OMS* 22) whom "he loved" (*OMS* 25). This dream, revisited again and again, inevitably aligns the marlin with the lion, big-game fishing with big-game hunting, the "gray blue hills" of Cuba (*OMS* 35) with the green hills of Africa, the "long green line" of Cuba's coast (*OMS* 35) with Africa's "long golden beaches" (*OMS* 24), indeed Cuba with Africa. Just as Cuba reminds Santiago of Africa, in *Green Hills* Africa reminds Hemingway of Spain and the Michigan woods of his boyhood—mythic places, each last good country where chivalric behavior remains potentially operative. But even in Africa Hemingway is forever pulling out for "a new country" (*GHA* 146), attempting to keep ahead of the sterility and destruction that results when modern man inevitably imports the modern era into these mythic places: "When [man] quits using beasts and uses machines, the earth defeats him quickly. The machine can't reproduce, nor does it fertilize the soil, and it eats what he cannot raise" (*GHA* 284). The motif of failure informs *Green Hills* as surely as *The Education of Henry Adams*, lending poignance to Hemingway's question "What is the dynamo driving?" (*GHA* 20).

Santiago notes that "the dark water of the true gulf is the greatest healer that there is" (*OMS* 99), the old man always "th[inking] of the sea as *la mar* which is what people call her in Spanish when they love her"—like Adams's Virgin a "feminine [being] . . . that gave or withheld great favours" (*OMS* 29, 30). Santiago's triumph over the marlin—like all other fish, generically referred to as male—is thus fought over the very body of the female ocean, which witnesses this joust between noble antagonists.

Just as Santiago dedicates his marlin to the Virgin of Cobre, Spanish bullfighters dedicate their bulls to "the *Virgen de la Soledad,*" who is, as Hemingway states in *Death in the Afternoon,* "the patron of all bullfighters" (*DIA* 448). *Green Hills* similarly links big-game hunting and bullfighting, as suggested by the white hunter's nickname for Hemingway—"you damned bullfighter" (*GHA* 213, 290)—and the "yellow-and-black-labelled German beer with the horseman in armor on it" that Hemingway ritually drinks in commemoration of successful hunting adventures (distributing the labels to the knightly Masai) to "remember the place better and even appreciate it more" (*GHA* 159). With Santiago, Hemingway comes full circle, from Michigan to Spain to Africa to Cuba, finding again in the New World an arena for knightly behavior while acknowledging that such behavior is inevitably in the process of being transformed into a nostalgic dream. Santiago, who must repeatedly remind himself that his long battle with the marlin was "not a dream" (*OMS* 98), realizes this inevitable transformation, the last line of *The Old Man and the Sea* specifying that he "was dreaming about the lions" (*OMS* 127) once again.

Courtly Love among the Lost Generation

In *The Sun Also Rises,* Hemingway composed an archetypally modernist novel whose general outline is remarkably reminiscent of a medieval romance: Brett Ashley, a beautiful married woman of title, is at the center of a group of men who love and serve her, and whose suffering recalls that of the courtly knight in its inevitability and severity. However, the many parallels between the events in this novel and the courtly love tradition are skewed, revealing the breakdown of romantic love in the modern world. Lady Ashley's title betokens no moral superiority, as in the medieval tradition, but only a socioeconomic superiority, and her promiscuity undermines the courtly quality of her position at the center of a group of enamored men. She neither remains faithful to her husband while granting her love to a single other nor deceives her husband because of the "fault" of love—a single grand passion for a worthy knight, as Rougemont describes it, which is enjoined yet is more magnificent than the strictures of conventional morality. She engages in casual affairs that ultimately frustrate and dissatisfy the men who serve her.

In the literary criticism of *The Sun Also Rises* much is made of the degrees of romanticism exhibited by the male protagonists. Robert Cohn is typically identified as the most romantic, the other male characters located at various points along the continuum. Earl Wilcox argues that Robert Cohn is a deluded romantic in the tradition of Tom Sawyer and Jake Barnes a realist in the tradition of Huck Finn (322–24). With similar intent though appealing to a different set of literary archetypes, both Robert O. Stephens and Martin Light suggest that Cohn is the Don Quixote to Jake's Sancho Panza. Stephens argues that "quixotic delusion by romance" ("Hemingway's Quixote" 216) is undercut by realism. Robert W. Lewis argues that "romantic love is examined and rejected" (*On Love* 20), and Mark Spilka argues that Robert Cohn's function is to illustrate, "through the absurdity of his behavior, that romantic love is dead" ("Death of Love" 241). A figure of fun, Cohn follows Brett about in a perversion of the knightly quest, even tracking her and Mike to San Sebastian, where as Mike states, "He hung around Brett and just *looked* at her . . . ma[king] me damned well sick" (*SAR* 143). Cohn has earlier had what he so eagerly desired, sexual consummation, but his mistake is that like Gatsby, "he can't believe it didn't mean anything" (*SAR* 181), as Brett points out.[18]

Unlike Brett, Robert Cohn is operating within a tradition that insists that passionate sexual consummation with one's lady transcends even morality, necessarily demanding profound commitment. Mike mocks the sentimentality of Cohn's assumptions and by extension a tradition that no longer works: "Then Cohn wanted to take Brett away. Wanted to make an honest woman of her, I imagine. Damned touching scene" (*SAR* 201). Mike thereby presents himself as a hard-boiled realist, a man who rejects the illusions that weak or foolish men like Cohn require. Jake and Bill do the same when they deride Cohn's grooming efforts, which are consistent with the pattern of self-improvement resulting from adherence to the courtly love tradition. Scaglione describes the frequent "allusions to personal hygiene," scenes of bathing and washing, in the medieval romances as a "symptom of the feeling for social refinement that both courtliness and chivalry embodied and promulgated" (161).

The attitude toward Cohn of most critics is governed by Jake's cynical judgment: "Somehow he seemed to be enjoying it. The childish, drunken heroics of it. It was his affair with a lady of title. . . . He stood . . . proudly and firmly waiting for the assault, ready to do battle for his lady love" (*SAR* 178). Arthur Mizener calls Cohn a "high-school Lancelot" ("*Sun*" 138), and Stephens asserts that Cohn "wants credit for having had a mistress as the courtly and literary traditions demand" ("Hemingway's Quixote" 217). Though Jake's cynical judgment of Cohn's behavior is typically read as an indictment of the courtly love tradition itself, it is more properly a criticism of Cohn's naïveté in believing that the modern world will reward such behavior with the hand of the lady. Each of the other male protagonists, including the ironic Jake, behaves in as courtly a manner as possible in the modern world, but each is also sufficiently sophisticated to recognize that this behavior will reap at best some momentary pleasures rather than the grand passion of medieval days.

Jake's cynical comments to Cohn about Brett do not prevent him from responding to her in much the same fashion,[19] but the glorious "fault" of love is not possible for him. His impotence paradoxically transforms him into the kind of ideal knight described by C. S. Lewis and Denis de Rougemont, who grant that while consummation was the goal of many courtly knights, chaste love was honored more highly. Jake is transformed into the ideal knight by an accident of modern war rather than a moral choice, his wound causing him to serve his lady without sexual reward. The sexual behavior still possible for him is similar to the love *par amours* and pure love that according to D. W. Robertson was considered acceptable for a knight: love *par amours* was "a love for the sight of the beloved [that] may lead to a kiss or a chaste (not nude) embrace, . . . [but whose] chief satisfaction arises from the contemplation of the beauty of the beloved" (454); pure love was "the kiss, the embrace, and contact with the nude beloved, but with the final solace omitted" (437). After kissing and caressing Brett, Jake asks, "Couldn't we just live together? . . . Couldn't we go off in the country for a while?" (*SAR* 55). The wistfulness of Jake's request is touching, his desire for a pastoral idyll (not unlike that shared by Frederic and Catherine in Switzerland) an escape into a fantasy validated by the courtly love tradition yet doomed to failure in the real world because Brett is unwilling to be satisfied with the love *par amours*, the pure love, that Jake is offering. Unlike the medieval lady, she rejects his love in favor of sexual experience: "I don't think so. I'd just *tromper* you with everybody. . . . It's my fault, Jake. It's the way I'm made" (*SAR* 55).

Though Jake is certainly foolish for trying to actualize this fantasy (if not for momentarily escaping into it), Brett nonetheless bears the burden of the blame, blaming herself for making such pure love impossible and thus taking the onus of accusation from Jake, who need only acquiesce silently (just as Fitzgerald's Dick Diver will later quietly acquiesce in Nicole's similar assumption of blame). Earlier, Brett had judged herself similarly when Jake offered to leave her because of her sexual frustration:

"'We'd better keep away from each other,' [Jake said]. 'But, darling, I have to see you. It isn't all that you know,' [Brett replied]. 'No, but it always gets to be.' 'That's my fault,' [she said]" (SAR 26).

The modern woman thus reveals herself as made differently from the medieval lady, and this difference makes the pure love offered by Jake, and so valued by the courtly lady, valueless to the modern woman. Since even Brett blames herself, the narrative generates sympathy not for her, despite her evident sexual frustration, but for Jake, who wishes that Brett could be satisfied with the love he can offer her. Jake continues to serve Brett, though with the full consciousness that she is not the lady he would like her to be, the lady who would reward his pure love with her love and fidelity. Jake's confusion of Brett with Georgette, the prostitute he had picked up at a café, thus serves as an implicit judgment of Brett, whose promiscuity is a rejection of not only sexless love but faithful sexual love, as is clear from her relationships with Mike, Cohn, and Romero: "I heard Brett's voice. Half asleep I had been sure it was Georgette. I don't know why" (SAR 32). Though Jake is somewhat ingenuous here, it is clear that the similarity in voices and the rhyming names are designed to betray a yet more important similarity between the women, the correlation between the modern woman and the courtly lady replaced by a correlation between the modern woman and the whore.

However disillusioned Jake may be about Brett—and he takes great pains to disillusion Robert Cohn as well—he nonetheless persists in his knightly service, leading him paradoxically to pimp for Brett (just as Nick Carraway had pandered for Gatsby in an action rich with homoerotic suggestiveness), proving that he loves Brett by sacrificing his feelings and betraying his *aficion* for bullfighting to arrange an affair between Brett and Romero. Jake's final service follows upon the end of this affair when he responds to Brett's request for help by mounting the modern equivalent of the knight's horse, a train, to go to her rescue. Though Jake's ironic commentary on his action signals a recognition of his degradation in performing this degraded version of knightly service, this commentary also signals a recognition of Brett's degradation.

Unlike the medieval lady, whose influence serves to ennoble the knight, to spur him to self-improvement, Brett influences her knights for ill, spurring them to moral degeneration. As Robert Cohn so aptly puts it, Brett is Circe, turning men not into the chivalric knights they desperately want to be but into swine. Jake must take the affair between Brett and Cohn "as a matter of course" (SAR 99) only because Brett is incapable of fidelity—whether to him in a sexless relationship or to any one of the lovers with whom she is involved sexually. Jake's recognition results in a contempt that is curiously mingled with his love for her (or perhaps not so curiously, given the courtly linkage between adoration of ladies and contempt for women): "To hell with Brett. To hell with you, Lady Ashley. . . . I suppose she only wanted what she couldn't have" (*SAR* 30, 31). Of course, Jake's accusation can be turned on himself, for he too wants what he cannot have: not merely a sexual relationship that is physically impossible for him but fidelity from Brett, who has herself been wounded, psychologically and emotionally, by the war, which undermined any sense of permanence, certainty, and therefore commitment—indeed, the viability of the old values in the new world.

Pedro Romero's service to Brett closely approximates the archetypal knightly service, since in slaying the bull he slays the modern equivalent of a dragon for her. Romero is the most successful of Brett's knights because the context of the bullfight offers him an appropriate locus in which to approximate the ideals of courtly and chivalric behavior.[20] Yet when Romero presents Brett with the bull's ear as a token of his adventure, her response is a damning self-indictment (just as she had earlier revealed her moral carelessness by flicking her cigarette ashes onto Jake's rug, in a gesture linking her to Daisy Buchanan). She leaves the ear, along with some cigarette stubs, in a hotel drawer, revealing herself to be unworthy of the noble deed performed by Romero and dedicated to her, the deed by which he proves himself a courtly lover and a chivalric knight.

Montoya recognizes the harm that would ultimately result to Romero's bullfighting from Brett's influence, and Brett herself acknowledges, with some self-congratulation at her moral astuteness, the problems she causes Romero. Brett ultimately rejects Romero to protect him from her bad influence, she claims, but this stated motive for a presumably selfless moral act is qualified by her repeated self-congratulations, and her rejection of Romero conforms to her pattern of behavior with other men. Just as she rejected the increasingly lovesick Cohn only after satisfying her sexual curiosity, she chooses to protect Romero only after their sexual relationship leads him to demand love from her. Romero wants their relationship to be permanent, and he demands that Brett be "more womanly" (*SAR* 242) by letting her hair grow long—a telling request given the magical powers attributed to hair by the chivalric tradition[21] and the powerful emotional valence of hair for Hemingway. The nearest approximation to the courtly and chivalric knight in the modern world, Romero wants Brett more nearly to approximate the ideal lady. When Brett rejects Romero, this modern woman implicitly rejects the courtly tradition itself, thereby revealing herself as unworthy of knightly adoration. Her inability to remain sexually faithful to this most worthy knight suggests that she is fooling herself when she claims at the end of the novel that all would have been well if only Jake, that other worthy knight, had not been rendered impotent. As Jake comments in the famous conclusion, "Isn't it pretty to think so?" (*SAR* 247). However, by presenting Brett's rejection of Romero offstage, merely describing rather than dramatizing it, Hemingway highlights Romero's brief moments of glory when in dedicating himself to his lady he becomes his best self, a true knight in the courtly and chivalric traditions.

Just as the courtly love tradition fails in the modern world of *The Sun Also Rises,* so too is Christianity largely irrelevant. The only one of Brett's knights who declares a religious affiliation, Jake is a nominal Catholic, but despite his attendance at mass, his religion has little consequence for his life.[22] Brett is clearly not at home in church. She asks Jake if she can listen when he gives his confession to a priest but is told that "it would be in a language she did not know" (*SAR* 151), and later she acknowledges cheerfully that she is "damned bad for a religious atmosphere" (*SAR* 208). She is much more at home with the riau-riau dancers—a remnant of a pagan tradition that shares the fiesta with the Catholic Church. When Brett is prevented from entering the church because she has no hat, Bill and Jake choose to follow her rather than remain inside, and the three stand with the dancers, who recognize in Brett a power they do not acknowledge to the church, forming a circle around her and using "her as an image to dance around" (*SAR* 155).

But it is telling that another image—a "framed steel-engraving of Nuestra Señora de Roncesvalles" (*SAR* 109)—presides over one of Jake's few periods of peace, while he is in Burguete on a fishing trip, far from Brett's disturbing influence. Jake later chooses to abandon another place of peace, San Sebastian, like Pamplona one of the "stops along the medieval pilgrimage route to the shrine of Santiago de Compostela" (Balassi 140). Jake leaves San Sebastian to rescue Brett, choosing to commit himself to her rather than to the Virgin, to courtly love (however distorted in the modern world) rather than to Mariolatry (just as Romero dedicated his bullfight to Brett rather than the *Virgen de la Soledad*).

Jake thereby fulfills his membership in a modern version of a courtly order of love—C. S. Lewis arguing that courtly orders were originally a reflection of the religious orders of the period, and Denis de Rougemont arguing that religious orders were a retort to the already-existing orders of love. Of course, secret societies are a constant in Hemingway's fiction, occurring in several oft-noted manifestations in this novel. The society of men who love Brett is suggestive of a courtly order, but this distorted modern order differs in significant ways from the courtly original. Though a number of medieval knights might dedicate themselves to a single lady and thereby enroll in a courtly order of love, she must grant only the most worthy knight the favor of her love. The favored knight has the duty of secrecy because her reputation is of great concern. And the knights enrolled in a courtly order feel themselves set off, as members of an elect society, from the mass of common humanity.

The modern order of love dedicated to Brett deviates radically from these three principles. Brett's promiscuity denies the worth of any particular knight since her choice of men depends largely on sexual curiosity rather than any determination of particular merit. Moreover, her lack of compunction about revealing her sexual liaisons makes any secrecy on the part of the knights irrelevant. Brett even goes so far as to provide Mike with Cohn's love letters, but Mike reports with pride that he refused to read them. Jake's reply—"Damned noble of you" (SAR 143)—is ironic only because such nobility is totally out of keeping with Brett's lack of discretion. While speaking with Jake and Bill, Mike is not so discreet about his relations with Brett. Brett's comment—"Don't be indecent, Michael. Remember there are ladies at this bar" (SAR 79)—distinguishes her from ladies who, like the medieval lady, would demand secrecy about such a liaison. The ultimate result of Brett's promiscuity and indiscretion is that her knights have no sense of being members of an elite society. Their scorn at the undesired presence of Robert Cohn in this order of love undercuts any sense of personal superiority deriving from membership: "[Mike said,] 'What if Brett did sleep with you? She's slept with lots of better people than you'" (SAR 142). Although these modern knights, like their medieval counterparts, are enrolled in an order of love, their order is unsatisfying, in part because they act badly but more importantly because Brett, refusing to act as a lady as defined by the medieval code, necessarily undermines the worth of behavior in accordance with those rules.

Hemingway's attraction to the courtly love tradition thus provided him with a dispensation for criticism of the modern woman, just as it did for Henry Adams and F. Scott Fitzgerald. In creating Brett Ashley, Hemingway created a vivid portrait of a modern woman who rejects the role of the medieval lady—ironically, a rejection caused by the destruction of medieval patterns occasioned by World War I, which has wounded Brett, a war nurse, as surely as it has wounded any of the male characters. The power that Brett wields over her own life, and the lives of the men who love her, derives not from the courtly love tradition (which is fundamentally androcentric, as Cholakian has argued) but from her rejection of that tradition, which in the context of World War I has failed her as it has failed the male characters. In willfully stepping outside that tradition, she has freed herself from conventions that would constrain her behavior to what would be acceptable to the men who wish paradoxically to "serve" her.

Though the very vividness of Brett's portrait makes her a compelling character, her rejection of the role of medieval lady results in an implicit narrative indictment. Like World War I itself, she is blamed for the destruction of the courtly love tradition as a viable system of values and behaviors in the modern world, a system that each of the male characters wishes to maintain. Their regret at its loss, though often disguised by cynicism or flippant irony, is nonetheless painfully palpable. When Jake thinks in an unguarded moment, "To hell with Brett. To hell with you, Lady Ashley" (*SAR* 30), he speaks for all the male characters and ultimately for Hemingway himself. In revealing the ineffectuality of knightly behavior in the modern world, Hemingway is exhibiting a nostalgia for the days when the courtly love tradition operated successfully as a system of values, when courtly ladies rewarded the adventures of worthy knights and thereby inspired them, enabling them to realize their ideal masculine identities.

Love, Death, and the Lady in the Mirror

In contrast to the male protagonists of *The Sun Also Rises*, the modern knights of *A Farewell to Arms, For Whom the Bell Tolls,* and *Across the River and into the Trees* gain a measure of satisfaction from their courtly behavior. They are given the opportunity to dedicate themselves to ladies who approximate the medieval ideal, thereby distinguishing themselves from other modern women—both fictional characters in Hemingway's novels and many of the women in Hemingway's life. Catherine Barkley, Maria, and Renata, the heroines of these three novels, all passively accept the devotion of those worthy modern knights who have chosen to serve them.

Catherine Barkley is described by Frederic Henry's friend Rinaldi as an English goddess to be worshiped. Rinaldi's comment echoes Hemingway's comment to Bill Horne in 1919 about Agnes von Kurowsky, the nurse with whom he had fallen in love while recovering from his wounds in World War I and on whom he largely based his portrait of Catherine: "I've loved Ag. She's been my ideal, and . . . I forgot all about religion and everything else because I had Ag to worship" (quoted by Griffin, *Youth* 114). Agnes ultimately threw Hemingway over for another man, breaking their engagement by letter, but her fictional alter-ego remains true to Frederic Henry. Like the "delineation of the woman in the courtly discourse" whose voice is appropriated, according to Cholakian, "to say what the poet would like the fictionalised woman to tell him" (74), Agnes's voice was appropriated by Hemingway in his representation of Catherine.[23] As T. S. Matthews approvingly noted in a 1929 review of *A Farewell to Arms*, Catherine Barkley is that "lovely creature whom men, if they have never found, will always invent" (quoted by Beversluis 22). Catherine's "objectification functions to negate what might be seen as [Agnes] von Kurowsky's asserted female subjectivity," according to Jamie Barlowe-Kayes, as manifested by "her initial rejection of Hemingway and her continuing desire to distance herself from association with Catherine Barkley" (32).

Maria, whose very name Robert Jordan loves, is identified with the Virgin Mary, just as in courtly love poetry the worship of the idealized and idolized lady is often indistinguishable from Mariolatry,[24] a parallelism disjoined in *The Sun Also Rises*. Robert Jordan moves in a stream-of-consciousness passage between Maria, "Spanish chivalry," and Spain's "own special idol worship within the Church," which he apostrophizes as "*Otra Virgen más*" (*FWBT* 354–55). In physical appearance, Maria was based on Martha Gellhorn, whom Hemingway married three weeks after the publication of this novel (which was dedicated to her). But in personality, "Maria is a portrait of Martha as Hemingway would have liked her to be," as Jeffrey Meyers observes (319). Whereas Martha's ambition, independence, and success as a writer threatened Hemingway and therefore their marriage, Maria's commitment to Robert Jordan is absolute.

Countess Renata, a rich lady of title, is proclaimed the sun, the moon, Cantwell's "last and only and true love" (*ARIT* 94), and the "Queen of Heaven" (*ARIT* 83). Her model was Adriana Ivancich, a young woman Hemingway transformed into a muse during a period of literary and personal difficulties. During their "sentimentally Platonic" relationship (Baker, *Life* 604), Adriana lived in a guest house at the Finca Vigía—the home of Hemingway and his fourth wife, Mary Welsh—spending hours at the top of the Finca's tower like a princess in a medieval romance. The symbolic suggestiveness was not lost on Hemingway, who "told her that they were equal partners in a firm called White Tower, Incorporated, and that when he saw her it made him feel that he could do anything, including writing better than he could possibly write" (Baker, *Life* 619). Hemingway justified his attentions to Adriana and his humiliating neglect of Mary by referring to the literary benefits that accrued. According to Baker, he felt that "true creativity . . . came to full flowering only from being in love" (*Life* 614), like the courtly poet who adored a lady so that he might write of his experience. Baker reports that after the dual plane

crashes in which Hemingway and Mary were injured—Hemingway seriously and Mary less so—"[Hemingway] assured Adriana that both times
he had 'died' his only regret had been that it would make her sad, and
[he] made sentimental allusions to Petrarch and Laura, Héloïse and Abelard" (*Life* 662). Only within the context of the courtly love tradition is
it not strange that his primary concern should be for his "lady," Adriana,
and not his injured wife, Mary. As Jeffrey Meyers notes in his paraphrase of letters that Hemingway wrote to Adriana, he knew that he could
not marry her and "wished only to serve her well, like a chivalric
knight" (443).

Catherine, Maria, and Renata each initially keeps herself aloof from
her circle of admiring men, but each ultimately grants the favor of her
love to the most worthy knight. In contrast to most courtly romances and
lyrics, which focus on the early courtship during which the medieval lady
is cruel and distant, these novels focus on the relationships after the lady
has granted her love, when she remains faithful and committed to her
knight, serving him as well as being served. Though the lady may command her knight, such power is actually granted, as in the medieval
tradition, by the knight rather than assumed by the lady. As Cholakian
says of a lyric by the troubadour Guiraut Riquier, "He concedes to the
woman's control . . . only because she has already capitulated to him"
(176). The "ultimate irony in the idealisation of the woman," as Cholakian points out, is that "her accreditation as intercessor from whom the
male begs for pardon (and love) comes from him and finally returns to
him" (178)—an accreditation for which Brett cares not at all, in contrast
to the conventionally ideal ladies of these later novels.

Unlike Fitzgerald with his squeamishness about sex, Hemingway represents sexuality as a vital aspect of his ideal ladies. Catherine makes love
with Frederic to allay her guilt at having sexually refused her doomed first
lover (despite Agnes von Kurowsky's claim that her affair with Hemingway had never been consummated). Maria is healed from her rape
trauma through sexual intercourse with Robert (in a psychologically unconvincing response). And Renata participates in mysterious sexual activities with Cantwell in a gondola (despite Adriana Ivancich's insistence
that a real Venetian girl of that age and social station would not have so
compromised herself). Just as "the romance lady appears to be a separate
being, but . . . [is] a figure he has somehow fashioned to his desires"
(Ferrante 66), Hemingway's ideal ladies are a projection of the male protagonists' desires, identifying absolutely with them. As Catherine says,
"There isn't any me any more. Just what you want" (*FA* 106). Maria goes
a step further, asserting her wish to become Robert, to take on his very

identity: "If thou should ever wish to change I would be glad to change. I would be thee because I love thee so" (*FWBT* 263). Renata asks Cantwell, "Couldn't I be you?" (*ARIT* 156).

This desire for absolute identification with the male protagonists links these Hemingway heroines with the lady beloved by the medieval poet, who functioned as "a mirror in which he sees his ideal self, what he might be" (Ferrante 67). "The romance hero falls in love with his own image . . . in the person of a woman who is a mirror image of himself" (Ferrante 73–74), and Frederic Henry, Robert Jordan, and Colonel Cantwell fall in love with women who function as their mirror images. This mirroring is often effected by similar hairstyles, as so many critics have noted. Gioia Diliberto further points out that Hemingway often "presents lovers as so physically and spiritually alike that they are almost identical," noting that his "experimentation with merging sexual identities culminated in the posthumously published *The Garden of Eden*" (79), the 1,500-page manuscript that Hemingway began in 1946 and that appeared in a much-abbreviated and edited version in 1986.

Various critics—most notably, Kenneth Lynn in his psychobiography *Hemingway*, Mark Spilka in *Hemingway's Quarrel with Androgyny*, and Nancy Comley and Robert Scholes in *Hemingway's Genders: Rereading the Hemingway Text*—have attempted to grapple with the androgyny implied in novels like *A Farewell to Arms* and *For Whom the Bell Tolls*, especially since the explicit transsexual fantasies of *The Garden of Eden* have placed it in high relief. Lynn provides a psychoanalytic explanation, focusing on Hemingway's childhood during which his mother frequently dressed him in girl's clothing and engaged in an elaborate pretense that he and his older sister Marcelline were twins. Spilka contextualizes Hemingway, placing him within a nineteenth-century culture whose definition of manliness was shifting from that supplied by the feminine genteel tradition of the Victorian era to that supplied by the masculine imperialist tradition. Comley and Scholes contextualize him differently, noting that "the complexity of human sexuality—especially the potential bisexuality of all humans—had been given a prominent place in the cultural text by Fliess, Freud, and Weininger . . . [so that] these issues were in the air that Hemingway . . . w[as] breathing" (144). The medieval courtly love tradition, however, might provide yet another cultural context for Hemingway's fictional representation of androgynous lovers. According to Ferrante, various courtly romances—*Floire et Blancheflor, Aucassin et Nicolette, Erec et Enide*—present lovers in whom "the identity of the two is so strong that even sexual distinctions are blurred" (78). In some cases, this identity is "so strong that one can be mistaken for the other" (78) and may be manifested in "the reversal of sexual roles" (80). In providing androgynous lovers who mirror not only each other's appearance but each other's sexual roles, Hemingway is employing a convention sanctioned by the courtly love tradition (and appropriated by Fitzgerald in his portraits of the twinlike Amory and Eleanor, Amory "ha[ving] loved himself in Eleanor" and discovering at the end of their relationship that "what he hated was only a mirror" [*TSP* 240]).

The transformation of the lady into a projection of the male's desires may be accompanied by another transformation validated by the courtly love tradition. Since courtly love is an art practiced by a knight, the lady of such a tradition may be presented as an art object. Renata, upon presenting Cantwell with her portrait, notes perceptively: "While it is not truly me, it is the way you like to think of me" (*ARIT* 97). Cantwell is thus a modern incarnation of Tristan. Just as "the only figure from which Tristan can derive satisfaction without danger or pain is the statue he has had made of Isolt, the image he created of his love as he wanted her to be" (Ferrante 94), Cantwell takes extraordinary satisfaction in the portrait of Renata, though self-consciously emphasizing that he recognizes the distinction between the portrait and the woman: "I love you, portrait, very much. . . . But I love the girl better" (*ARIT* 174). Yet he seems to protest too much, for the distinction between Renata and her portrait becomes increasingly blurred. The tone, content, and manner of his confessional conversations with the portrait differ not at all from his conversations with Renata. He treats the portrait as if it were Renata, and he treats Renata as if she were a portrait, asking her to pose, requesting that she sometimes stand "frontally and formally" (*ARIT* 201), at other times in profile. By obliging him, Renata passively allows herself to be turned into an art object, and he celebrates her for it: "He looked and saw the profile . . . and he said, 'Yes. I like it' " (*ARIT* 201). The pronoun is revealing. Renata ceases to be a real woman and becomes an ideal object, just as the troubadour Marcabru "objectified the female Other into a passive, unmoving creation . . . [by] 'paint[ing]' a simulacrum of her" (Cholakian 74) in his lyric. Renata's effect on Cantwell is the same, whether as woman or portrait, for in either case she exists only to serve as a locus for his aspirations.[25] It is noteworthy that in the chapters where Cantwell speaks to the portrait he also speaks repeatedly to one other object, a mirror.

Despite the relative success of the courtly relationships in these three novels, each relationship is doomed because one of the partners dies. Were the relationships to continue, the courtly aspect would be undermined by the eventual marriage of the lovers. As C. S. Lewis indicates (and as Hemingway testified in his life), courtly love cannot be granted by a necessarily inferior wife but only a superior lady (necessarily outside the bounds of marriage). Were these ideal ladies to undergo the strains that real life in the guise of marriage and children must provide, they would reveal their one-dimensionality—a fate from which Hemingway protects them,[26] just as Fitzgerald protected Clara Page. The lady of the medieval tradition is often a mere collection of attributes, an occasion for the troubadour to demonstrate his skill as a poet and his increasing worth as a man. And the modern lady who develops from this model is similarly flawed. In calling for "feminist critical and theoretical rereadings of Hemingway's female characters [in order to] expose cultural codes and attitudes about women which continue to haunt and limit their lives" (33), Jamie Barlowe-Kayes would do well to pay particular attention to Hemingway's representation of the internalized codes of courtly love and chivalry.

Critics have long been troubled by Hemingway's ideal female characters. Robert W. Lewis suggests that Catherine "is a woman who has no self and very little depth as a fictional character" (*On Love* 48). Robert Solotaroff agrees that Catherine "only has meaning in terms of Henry's needs and responses" (4), and Millicent Bell makes the same point more polemically by characterizing her as "a sort of inflated rubber woman available at will to the onanistic dreamer" ("Pseudoautobiography" 114). Edmund Wilson calls Catherine an abstraction and Maria "amoeba-like" (239 n. 1), and A. Robert Lee asserts that Maria "amounts to no more than a cipher, a figure out of barely disguised supremacist male fantasy" ("Everything" 82–83).

Philip Young suggests that Catherine is the first in an unfortunate series of Hemingway heroines who become increasingly unconvincing as real women: "Idealized past the fondest belief of most people, and even the more realistic wishes of some, compliant, and bearing unmistakable indications of the troubles to come, Catherine Barkley has at least some character in her own right, and is both the first true 'Hemingway heroine,' and the most convincing one" (91). Asserting that Maria "becomes more and more a vision until ultimately she ceases to be a person at all" (109), Young argues that the heroine in her incarnation as Renata "was never less real, being more than ever the girl who exists so for her lover that she ceases to exist for herself" (118). This impulse in Hemingway's characterization of women is consonant with his nostalgia for the courtly love tradition, since that tradition is far more concerned with the knight's adventures than the lady's emotions, however much it claims to be a celebration of the lady. Similarly, Hemingway's heroines, though celebrated as ideals, are important only insofar as they promote by their mere existence the development of the heroes.

In serving these ideal ladies, the male protagonists are able to approximate the actions of the courtly knight far more closely than the male protagonists of *The Sun Also Rises*. Unlike Jake, who is degraded by procuring Romero, they are ennobled by their service. Frederic Henry grows "purer and sweeter" (*FA* 66) when he is with Catherine, according to the cynical Rinaldi. Although Frederic is "embarrassed by the words sacred, glorious, and sacrifice" (*FA* 184) when applied to modern war, he is not, to Rinaldi's surprise, embarrassed when they refer to Catherine: "All my life I encounter sacred subjects. But very few with you. I suppose you must have them too" (*FA* 169). Because Catherine is a sacred subject, Frederic behaves discreetly, in keeping with the courtly code, growing uncharacteristically angry at Rinaldi's sexual innuendoes and defending Catherine's honor. But even the cynical modern man, Rinaldi, admits to envy of the courtly relationship that Frederic shares with Catherine. Because cheap liquor and promiscuous sex, the accepted escapes from modern war, bring Rinaldi no happiness, he jokingly suggests that he too will find an English girl to serve and worship, but his self-destructiveness precludes such an attempt.

Colonel Cantwell is also a cynical modern man, but in contrast to Rinaldi he attempts desperately to save rather than destroy himself. Aware that his unsatisfying life is drawing to a close, Cantwell turns to Renata as the ideal woman who will cure his metaphoric if not his literal broken heart. In this regard she is like the courtly lady who was apostrophized as the only physician able to cure her lover's ills, a "perform[er of] miracles, substituting for God's Grace" (Scaglione 214). Cantwell's attempts to be gentle, particularly when in Renata's presence, lead him to ponder the relationship between the words "gentle" and "gentleman," a telling concern since gentility (that is, *gentilesse*) is one of the primary requirements of the medieval knight. When Renata calls him a good man, he promises to try to be one. As Robert W. Lewis suggests, "Renata is like the lady of *stilnovisti* love poetry whose influence on her lover was very great; she radiated charity and led the way to his salvation. She was perfect and led the true lover to strive for perfection in order to become worthy of her" (*On Love* 187).

Renata is Beatrice to Cantwell's Dante, the lady to his knight, as the many allusions to Dante in the novel suggest. Though Cantwell boastfully insists at one point, "I am Mister Dante" (*ARIT* 246), his identification with the medieval poet, "whose figure comes in the course of the novel to flood Cantwell's consciousness" (Verduin, "Hemingway's Dante" 634), is undercut by his rueful recognition that "Dante isn't around" (*ARIT* 125) in the modern world.[27] Cantwell's self-transformation for Renata's sake—the focus of much of the novel—culminates in his behavior on the duck shoot. Though his boatman is sullen and uncooperative, Cantwell thinks of Renata and restrains his anger, behaving with unexpected gentleness. Cantwell's transformed behavior is implicitly validated when the boatman's response is explained and excused on the basis of his terrible past. Just as for the knightly hero of the medieval romance, so too for Cantwell, "love means a rebirth, . . . awaken[ing] the hero to a new sense of himself, inspiring him not so much to greater deeds as to a higher purpose and responsibility, . . . reveal[ing] qualities in the hero which the lady sees and which the world often does not, but . . . also enhanc[ing] those qualities" (Ferrante 73). Like the courtly lady, Renata "could not love [her knight] if he were not worthy, but he is to some extent worthy because she loves him, . . . her presence in his life symboliz[ing] his potential excellence" (Ferrante 73).

Cantwell's transformation is triggered by his memory of a chivalric service that he once rendered Renata. When two sailors whistled at her, he picked a fight (as Hemingway did upon similar occasions),[28] triumphing though outnumbered and earning the epithet "Richard the Lion-Hearted" that Renata had earlier bestowed on him. In supposedly fighting for her honor, he actually fought for his own, thereby actualizing his knightly identity. Cantwell's memory of this fight elicits a powerful response because it embodies the two essential activities that define the courtly and chivalric knight: "Except feats of arms and love, nothing can occur in the courtly world—and even these two are of a special sort. . . . They are permanently connected with the person of the perfect knight, they are part of his definition, so that he cannot for one moment be without adventure in arms nor for one moment without amorous entanglement. If he could, he would lose himself and no longer be a knight" (Auerbach 140).

Hemingway's nostalgia for the courtly love tradition has profound results for his characterization of women in the modern world. Like Hemingway's prose style, with its dependence on dichotomous adjectives such as "good" and "bad" placed in binary opposition, his characterization of women is also dichotomous, resulting in either the creation of a Catherine Barkley, a Maria, a Renata—modern women who are one-dimensional though presented sympathetically—or the creation of a Brett Ashley—a modern woman who is vividly real though presented unsympathetically.[29] The medievalist impulse suggests why Hemingway's women are caught in this double bind, why they are seldom both fully realized and sympathetic.

The very mixture of adoration and contempt that Denis de Rougemont and Leslie Fiedler identify in the medieval troubadour's attitudes toward ladies and women, respectively, is manifested in Hemingway's fictional representations of women and his attitudes toward the women in his life: "[Hemingway] liked to show off his skill in verbal fencing . . . in the presence of women. In his treatment of those he liked or loved there was often something of the chivalric; [but] once he had turned against them he could be excessively cruel and abusive. When drunk or sufficiently provoked he sometimes slapped or cuffed them. He was unchivalrously outspoken . . . about his internal domestic affairs" (Baker, *Life* 4–5). Hemingway's initial need to see each of his four wives as an ideal figure contributed to the destruction of these marriages, for no real woman could always behave as such an ideal must.[30] This pattern of initial adoration for the lady and subsequent contempt for the wife was manifested in a 1952 letter to Bernard Berenson written shortly after the breakup of Hemingway's marriage to his third wife, Martha Gellhorn: "Anyone confusing a handsome and ambitious girl with the Queen of Heaven should be punished as a fool [n]ot to mention [as a] here[tic]" (*Letters* 789).

But after each failed marriage Hemingway began again his search for the Queen of Heaven, the ideal woman, a search that he justified by nostalgic reference to the golden age of his relatively brief first marriage with Hadley Richardson, who "of all the women in his many lives . . . best understood his romantic streak, his admiration of Chaucer's medieval knight" (Reynolds, *Paris Years* 20). In his posthumously published memoir, *A Moveable Feast* (1964), Hemingway described in loving detail their marriage, which he had chosen to end to marry his second wife, Pauline Pfeiffer. In retrospect, Hadley loomed as his "ideal of womanhood," and "his belief in her perfection—and his continued need to draw on it in creating his heroines"—is documented by Gioia Diliberto in her biography *Hadley* (173, 283). Hemingway's relationships with women thus seesawed between chivalric adoration of the supposed ideal and subsequent contempt when the woman proved other than ideal. However much Hemingway's nostalgia for courtly love may have sharpened his contempt for modern women, the very mixture of adoration and contempt is ironically a legacy of the courtly love tradition.

In celebrating the courtly and chivalric traditions, Hemingway celebrated in the largest sense the medieval attempt to make an art out of love and war. Hemingway's nostalgia for the traditions of courtly love and chivalry thus suggests the appeal that aestheticism held for him, in spite of the surface realism of his novels.[31] His aestheticism is a manifestation of his attempt to compel order and maintain control in the modern age, an age marked by rapid changes in the role of women, the horrors of modern technological war, and the decreasing power of Christianity.[32] Of course, every artist transmutes life into art, but too absolute a transmutation can result in an art that is absolutely lifeless.

Hemingway is thus most successful when he represents deviations from the medieval ideal (whatever the worth of that ideal) rather than modern approximations of the ideal (as in his gallery of idealized ladies). Hemingway's male protagonists do their best to act as courtly and chivalric knights in the modern world but fall short of the ideal with depressing regularity, responding with cynicism, self-pity, and masochistic self-hatred. Perhaps because of such self-criticism, these knights manqué, two of whom are first-person narrators, remain largely sympathetic. Their flaws, failures, and self-pity are justified because these are men with the expectations and sensibilities of the Middle Ages who must nonetheless live In Our Time.

In *Green Hills of Africa*, Hemingway had proclaimed, in language strangely reminiscent of the conclusion of *The Great Gatsby*, "Let the others come to America who did not know that they had come too late. Our people had seen it at its best and fought for it when it was well worth fighting for. Now I would go somewhere else" (*GHA* 285). The somewhere else to which he explicitly refers is the "virgin country" (*GHA* 218) in Africa, its green hills the most recent incarnation of the "green breast of the new world" (*GG* 182), for in Hemingway's eyes America had become "an older country . . . [where] the biggest game was gone" (*GHA* 250). Yet in metaphorically associating his love of Africa "with a woman that you really love" and ultimately with his desire to make "time stand still" (*GHA* 72), in creating a narrator who, by "pursuing beauty personified in the greater kudu, is on a knight's quest" (Reynolds, *Reading* 27), Hemingway unconsciously reveals that on another level the somewhere else for which he wants to leave the "bloody mess" (*GHA* 285) of modern America is the Middle Ages, as it was for Henry Adams, F. Scott Fitzgerald, and even Mark Twain, who proclaims in the epigraph to the final chapter of *Pudd'nhead Wilson* (attributed to Pudd'nhead's "Calendar"): "*October 12, the Discovery.* It was wonderful to find America, but it would have been more wonderful to miss it" (*PW* 165).

Yet the final irony remains, an irony of which Adams was most sharply aware. Just as chivalry led to the excesses of technological war and courtly love to contempt for women, so did the Middle Ages lead to modern America. In yearning for the Middle Ages as the supposed opposite of

American culture, these American writers were looking into one more mirror that reflected their culture with its attributes and limitations. Fitzgerald's Nick Carraway articulates this realization in the famous last line of *The Great Gatsby*, his retrospective act of narration evidence of the validity of his observation: "So we beat on, boats against the current, borne back ceaselessly into the past" (*GG* 182). For Hemingway, the current that "has gone by the shoreline of that long, beautiful, unhappy island since before Columbus sighted it" (*GHA* 149) sweeps into the past the effluvia of the present, "the palm fronds of our victories, the worn light bulbs of our discoveries and the empty condoms of our great loves float[ing] with no significance" (*GHA* 150).

Like the sun that always rises, the current is thus represented as itself unchanged and unchanging. Yet Hemingway's works and life—indeed the work of his life in his constructed Hemingway persona—testify that as the present is swept into the past, it inevitably dissolves into the future, altering in often unexpected ways the flow of the stream of history. As Wright Morris notes, "The territory ahead lies behind us" (14), though the territory behind was a golden past that never existed as a natural part of American culture, an invention that shapes present reality. Twain, Adams, Fitzgerald, and Hemingway all mourn in their different ways a lost land that is always already before them.

Notes

Works Cited

Index

Notes

Chapter 1 / The Once and Future America

1. See Block, *The Uses of Gothic*, for a comprehensive pictorial study offering a detailed analysis of the rationale for and realization of the Collegiate Gothic architectural plan at the University of Chicago. Block emphasizes that the literal construction of the Gothic campus was intimately bound up with the construction of the "raw young University['s]" identity, serving to "stabilize, solidify, and perpetuate it" (60), so that "while Gothic seemed to refer to the past, it was, in actuality, a commitment to the future" (xviii).

2. See, for example, Parrington (7), who argues that Virginia was actually settled largely by members of the English middle class rather than Cavaliers loyal to the Stuart king.

3. For a more complete discussion of John Fraser, see my review of *America and the Patterns of Chivalry*.

4. Lears argues that antimodernism was a blend of accommodation and protest. He criticizes the accommodation to society that sometimes resulted from the medievalist impulse; for example, he notes of the crafts movement that many bourgeois businessmen became weekend woodworkers not as a protest against the sterility of capitalist ventures but as a means of fortifying themselves for the workweek ahead. However, the focus of his text and the emotional center of his argument is that antimodernism served as a form of rebellion against modern society; since he clearly sympathizes with this protest, he celebrates medieval traditions whenever possible. John Fraser grants the "seeming vulnerability of the chivalric" (14) to rational analysis, and at

several points he offers the view of "a hostile analyst of chivalric transformations" (29), thereby providing some cogent criticisms of this medieval tradition. However, the body of his text refutes this vulnerability, and his argument derives its considerable emotional power from a celebration of chivalry.

5. The annual conference of SUNY-Binghamton's Center for Medieval and Early Renaissance Studies focused in 1984 on "Medievalism in American Culture"; eighteen papers out of a total of forty-three focused specifically on American literature. Bernard Rosenthal and Paul Szarmach later edited *Medievalism in American Culture* (1989), a collection of essays drawn from this conference, a number of which focus on American literature. Janet Goebel and Rebecca Cochran edited *Selected Papers on Medievalism* (1988), in which they included three essays focusing on American literature out of twenty, all drawn from papers first presented at the 1986 and 1987 general conferences sponsored by the journal *Studies in Medievalism*. The same journal published special issues focusing on "Medievalism in America" (spring 1982) and "Twentieth-Century Medievalism" (fall 1982); these special issues (the first introduced by journal editor Leslie Workman, the second by Workman and special editor Jane Chance) include essays on medievalism in American literature, as do some later issues. In other journals, an occasional article has focused on medievalism and some aspect of American literature— for example, Elizabeth Morgan's "Gatsby in the Garden: Courtly Love and Irony" in *College Literature* (1984) and Rebecca Cochran's "Edwin Arlington Robinson's Arthurian Poems: Studies in Medievalisms?" in *Arthurian Interpretations* (1988). I recently learned of a 1989 dissertation by Margaret Ellen O'Shaughnessey, "The Middle Ages in the New World: American Views and Transformations of Medieval Art and Literature."

6. See, however, Verduin, "Medievalism and the Mind of Emerson." Melville's "Knights and Squires" chapters in *Moby-Dick* might also bear consideration.

7. See Vanderbilt's biography, *Charles Eliot Norton* (130–31), for a discussion of Norton's attempts to reconcile the antagonism in American society between the claims of culture, historically associated with the aristocracy, and those of democracy. Norton feared that democracy brought artistic standards down to the lowest level, a lesson he drew from the decline of art after the Middle Ages. He also thought that the increasing wealth of the modern world, emerging first during the Renaissance, resulted in cheapened taste and a diminishment of the artist's spiritual faith and devotion to craft. Implicit here is Norton's criticism of the values of the Gilded Age, particularly as contrasted with those of the golden medieval past. Hence for Norton, the Middle Ages served as both present contrast and future model.

8. Howard insightfully embodies the identification of, and contrast be-

tween, the medieval and the modern in the title of his biography of Lowell, *Victorian Knight-Errant.*

9. See Kelly for a useful discussion of this seminal article. Like Scaglione (66–67, 91–92), Kelly demurs from the generally accepted view that the term "courtly love" is a modern invention.

10. Among the most controversial of Rougemont's theses, the Catharist hypothesis has attracted much critical attention since the 1939 publication of *L'Amour et l'occident*, translated in 1940 as *Love in the Western World.* Having corrected in the 1956 edition a number of errors, Rougemont offers both a qualification and a spirited defense of the Catharist hypothesis in his appendix to the 1983 edition (which first appeared in French in the 1972 Librarie Plon edition).

11. See Jaeger, *The Origins of Courtliness*, for a broader definition of "courtesy" or "courtliness," which he sees not as deriving from courtly love and the knight (whether in his role as lover or warrior) but as an "ethical and social code" (113) originating in the educator-statesman trained at the cathedral school. Unlike Keen and Scaglione, Jaeger locates the earliest evidence for the origins of courtesy in Germany (specifically the imperial court of Otto the Great) rather than France, emphasizing, however, that "to locate the exact beginnings of this ideal in earlier medieval Europe has not proven possible here" (259) and that "the architects of medieval courtesy were Germans, Frenchmen, and Italians" (272). Jaeger's extensive study draws from an impressive array of primary sources, privileging biography, history, chronicle, and polemic over courtly romance and lyric. Though he largely succeeds at keeping "the phenomenon of courtliness quite separate from what is called 'courtly love'" (157), he ultimately acknowledges that "there is much in the Latin sources that connects courtliness with love" (157–58).

12. Rougemont points to the underlying connection between the over-refined treatment of love in courtly literature and the pornographic fabliaux of the period, as exemplified in the thirteenth-century satire *L'Évangile des femmes*—"a sequence of quatrains, the first three lines of each extolling woman in the courtly manner, and the last being brutally depreciatory" (187). Similarly, Fiedler points out that the troubadour William of Poitou is "a strange, double-faced figure: the author of phallic poems full of male arrogance . . . and contempt for women, and, at the same time, the first of the poets of domnei—the service of ladies" (49). Scaglione notes this "puzzling insistence on a seemingly contradictory code of conduct that made men both worship and despise women" (311). Cholakian also focuses on "these paradoxical attitudes toward the woman," noting that earlier critics such as Jeanroy (1934) imposed a binary opposition on the troubadours, assigning them the category of *idéalistes* or *réalistes*. Cholakian argues, however,

that "what is new and important in the more recent criticism is its awareness that antithetical postures permeate virtually all of this courtly literature" (4) and "that ambivalence underlies the entire courtly discourse" (181). According to Cholakian, this ambivalence is expressed at times intentionally, at other times unconsciously, covertly, subtextually.

13. John Fraser unintentionally makes the same point. He straightforwardly offers the conventional interpretation in his brief celebratory comments about courtly love—"the woman received the services of the man and was given power over him . . . but she returned his power to him and enabled him to increase his honor more than he could have done unaided, thereby enhancing her own as well" (76)—yet he notes at a later point (addressing the issue of paternalistic management practices in American business) that "implicit in possessing the power to grant is the power to withhold" (166).

Chapter 2 / Mark Twain

1. See Cummings for a discussion of how the nineteenth-century weekly *Scientific American* drew an equivalence between science and technology to celebrate the machine.

2. Four years after their marriage, Twain wrote to Olivia from England, his thoughts shifting from the religious to the domestic in a progression natural for the sentimental nineteenth-century husband: "I attended the grand Christmas service in Salisbury Cathedral . . . and then we drove by Old Sarum—all day I was thinking lovingly of my 'Angel in the House'—for Old Sarum and Salisbury recal [*sic*] Coventry Patmore's books" (quoted by Harris 117–18).

3. Whereas Huck Finn voices Twain's hostility toward the influence of family and "sivilization," Hank Morgan speaks for Twain's sentimental attitudes. Emerson notes that "[Huck] finds uncomfortable what Clemens himself had sought when he married Olivia, . . . wr[i]t[ing] to her in January 1869, 'You will break up all my irregularities when we are married, and civilize me . . . won't you?' " (129). The sentimentalism implicit in Twain's plaintive question was even more evident in a letter to Mary Fairbanks written a year after his engagement: "You never saw such a serenely satisfied couple of doves. . . . Yet she has attacked my tenderest peculiarities [identified as "drinking," "smoking," "slang and boisterousness," and "carrying my hands in my pantaloon pockets"] & routed them. She has a way of instituting [reforms] that swindles one into the belief that she is doing him a *favor* instead of curtailing his freedom & doing him a fatal damage. She is the best girl that ever lived" (*To Mrs. Fairbanks* 112–13).

4. Williams notes that there is some controversy over when Twain marked his copy of Lecky's text ("Use of History" 103). Davis, who edited the notations, judged that they were all made in 1906. Blair asserted in his *Mark*

Twain and Huck Finn that some, and perhaps all, of the notations were made much earlier. In any case, Twain probably first read Lecky's *History of European Morals* in the summer of 1874 (see Cummings 59).

5. Wisbey indicates that Twain made marginal notations in the Petrarch chapter of *Memoirs of the Lives of the Poets*, a volume in the Langdon family library. Arguing that this book "probably was marked for Livy in 1868 or 1869" (21) during their courtship, Wisbey suggests that the vehemence of the notations derived from Twain's identification with the husband figure of "Mr. Laura."

6. Twain reported in his *Autobiography* that he was familiar with the southern version of this tradition (96). Alexander Jones notes that "as an adolescent he was an amused observer of, if not a participant in, certain scenes of low comedy . . . during which Wales McCormick, a fellow apprentice, made indecent proposals to an attractive mulatto girl—while her old mother protested halfheartedly, realizing 'that by the customs of slaveholding communities, it was Wales's right to make love to that girl if he wanted to' " (599). There is no evidence that Twain indulged in such a "right" at this time, and he later harshly criticized it.

7. See Hill (xxvi-xxvii, 127–28, 195–96) for a provocative discussion of Twain's attitude toward young girls, which makes clear why he responded so regretfully to the news that Mollie Fairbanks had made her debut: "So you have 'come out' my sweet little sister! I learned it with a pang . . .—I did not want you to 'come out', ever, I wanted you to remain always just as you were when I saw you last, the dearest bud of maidenhood in all the land" (*To Mrs. Fairbanks* 193). See also *Mark Twain's Aquarium*, where he begs one of his young female correspondents: "Don't get any older—I can't have it. Stay always just as you are" (21).

8. In Twain's posthumously published burlesque of utopian novels, "The Secret History of Eddypus, the World Empire" (written in 1901–2), the "pre–Civil War South in which [the character "Twain"] was born is equated with the European Middle Ages" (Marotti 48).

9. See Smith (*Fable* 83) and Pettit (206) for discussions of one of Twain's most important sources, Charles Ball's *Fifty Years in Chains, or the Life of an American Slave* (1860).

10. Twain's attitude toward the southern tradition of the duel hardened considerably over time. As a young man in 1864, he had once even challenged a man to a duel in Virginia City. See Krauth for a discussion of Twain's personal experience with the duel and his complex and ambivalent response to it. See also Twain's *A Tramp Abroad* (22–44), where his description of the Heidelberg student duels—"invest[ed] . . . with a sort of antique charm" (29) yet resulting in the "grisly spectacle" (28) of surgery—and his immediately subsequent burlesque of a French duel have occasioned some critical debate.

11. Cummings carefully traces Twain's intellectual journey, noting particularly the influence of French philosopher Hippolyte Taine, whose *The Ancient Regime* Twain purchased in 1876 and read by 1877. While Lecky's "intuitive" philosophy posited an innate intuition regarding good and evil that compels man to act morally, Taine argued that "man is insignificant in the cosmic perspective, that he displays much stupidity and cruelty, that he is animalic, and that he is the pawn of deterministic forces" (78). Cummings argues that Twain's reading in Paine, Holmes, Darwin, and Taine moved him from "the heroic old world of moral drama to one that made only mechanical sense" (156). In contrast, Berkove attributes Twain's pessimism to his early Calvinistic training, arguing that it "has unmistakably theological associations despite his avowed attraction to determinism" (11) and that this Calvinistic pessimism, surfacing most clearly in the works of his last two decades, made it impossible for him to believe in the progress of civilization.

12. Ironically, Twain's financial disaster (precipitated by the Paige typesetter fiasco and the bankruptcy of Twain's own publishing house, Charles L. Webster and Company) and his arduous recovery caused him to empathize with Walter Scott (who had similarly recovered from serious financial reverses), as reported in a 1902 newspaper interview (see Gribben, *Library* 613). More characteristically, Twain had earlier compared his bankruptcy and recovery to that of Ulysses S. Grant, who in 1885 wrote himself out of financial ruin and public shame with his *Memoirs* (published by Webster and Company). Upon Grant's death, Twain wrote a newspaper eulogy in which he quoted "his favorite passage from the *Morte d'Arthur*, Sir Ector de Maris's lament for Launcelot" (Lauber, *Inventions* 232)—the same passage that he cited almost twenty years later in a 1904 letter about Olivia's death (see Hill, *God's Fool* 86).

13. In an effort to refute the "'soft' critics who have read [*Connecticut Yankee*] as either ambivalent or as an attack on technology and the American faith in material progress" (418), Carter provides compelling external and internal evidence in support of his argument that Twain identified with the Yankee, whom he self-consciously presented sympathetically. More controversial is Carter's assertion that the novel's apocalyptic ending "was both planned by and was untraumatic for its author" (432), that the carnage of the conclusion was "no aberration but a conventional mode of frontier hyperbole" (437). Yet even Carter must grant that in the final pages "Twain's rage . . . got out of hand" (437), though he suggests that it was directed only against aristocratic privilege and not, as the "soft" critics would have it, against technology. Carter's argument breaks down when he argues that Hank's culpability in the Battle of the Sand-Belt lies in the fact that "he was too humane in his [earlier] efforts to reform an evil society" (433).

14. See especially Harris, who suggests that certain "preferred images"—

space, water, childhood, good women, and dreams—yield "a landscape at once removed from human time and preserved in it through the power of the written word" (157). Harris suggests that "Twain's quest for an escape from history" (137) was in turn a manifestation of his desire to escape the tragic human condition. Salomon, to whom Harris's analysis is indebted, had earlier noted that Twain had "a passionate desire to escape the moral and aesthetic implications" of the conflict between his progressive view of history and his pessimistic view of human nature by means of "some sort of transcendent dream" (4). Stahl, indebted to both Harris and Salomon, states that "the aesthetic experience of history in Mark Twain's works is itself often, paradoxically, a moment of stasis, outside or beyond history, . . . a moment accompanied by the *frisson* of contact with the totally other, a brush with death and transcendence" ("Female Power" 52).

15. See especially Marotti (137–38), who uses Roland Barthes's trivalent approach to myth to engage in a semiotic analysis of Twain's use of myth in his life and work (particularly in his later unpublished writing). She argues that Twain functions as a producer (constructing new myths in his literary works), a mythologist (interpreting the myths of nineteenth-century America from a critical distance), and a reader (applying myths to his own purposes).

16. "Mark Twain, A Biographical Sketch" appeared at the end of volume 22 of *The Writings of Mark Twain*, a signed and numbered twenty-two-volume edition published during 1899 and 1900. Twain wrote fourteen manuscript pages, then sent them to his nephew, Samuel E. Moffett, who revised the sketch and signed it for publication. Twain had final approval.

17. Sellers was also based on James Lampton, a cousin of Jane Clemens. Another cousin, Jesse Madison Leathers, also served as a model for *The American Claimant*'s Beriah Sellers. Leathers, convinced that he was the rightful earl of Durham, asked Twain to underwrite the expenses necessary to lay claim to the estate. Twain refused but encouraged him to write an autobiography, entitled "An American Earl."

18. See Baetzhold, "England's Advocate," for a discussion of Twain's Anglophilia in the 1870s. See also Williams, who notes that "during the late 1880's [Twain] went through a phase of extreme hostility to England—especially to English aristocracy" (288), arguing, however, that this Anglophobia had "shallow roots" since in 1883 "he had seen England as the greatest of all nations" (297).

19. See Gribben, "Robin Hood 'By the Book' " (201–4).

20. Gribben suggests that Twain's "animosity toward Scott may well have been a reaction against—and an attempt to obliterate—the worshipful view of Scott he held in his youth" (*Library* 612).

21. Schleiner suggests persuasively that Twain probably read Tasso's *Jerusalem Delivered* and Ariosto's *Orlando Furioso*. She also notes that the adult

Twain owned a copy of *The Chronicle of the Cid* and suggests that Twain, "in an effort to read the *Canterbury Tales* of Chaucer (mentioned in 'Capt'n Stormfield's Visit to Heaven,' an early work) . . . [may have] penetrated to the tale of Palamon and Arcite, or to the burlesque romance begun by the squire" (332).

22. Schleiner (332–33) provides a list that includes such works as Kiefer's *Legends of the Rhine from Basel to Rotterdam* (mentioned in *A Tramp Abroad*), Bäring-Gould's *Curious Myths of the Middle Ages* (containing a discussion of the Arthurian legends), Cervantes's *Don Quixote*, Shakespeare's romances, Scott's "Lady of the Lake" and *The Talisman*, Tennyson's *Idylls of the King* and "Bugle Song," Goethe's play *Götz von Berlichingen*, William Morris's "Shameful Death" (which, according to Howells, Twain loved to read aloud in the early 1870s and which appeared in a volume entitled *"The Defense of Guinevere" and Other Poems*), Thackeray's *The Legend of the Rhine*, Browning's poetry (which Twain read intensively in 1884–85), and Wagner's operas. Further, Williams (see his "Use of History") provides evidence suggesting that by 1884 Twain had read the chronicles collected in the Bohn Library: *The Anglo-Saxon Chronicles*, *Bede's Ecclesiastical History of England*, *The Chronicles of the White Rose of York*, *Chronicles of the Crusades*, Joinville's *Memoirs of Saint Louis*, and Froissart's *Chronicles*.

23. Kordecki extends this duality of motives to the structure and style of the novel, noting that "*Connecticut Yankee*'s structure, the *forma tractatus* of medieval rhetoric, is that of an Arthurian romance [while] the style or *forma tractandi* is that of a nineteenth-century, rationalistic anti-romance" (329).

24. Cummings's discussion of Taine's influence is relevant to this disjunction between the realistic and mythic approaches. Cummings argues that "from Taine and others [Twain] learned the clinical approach to personality and society—an approach that sporadically conflicted with the mythical or heroic views of life that he had previously absorbed" (xi).

25. See Marshall for a discussion of another of Twain's dream-vision fictions, "A Curious Dream" (1870), which Marshall links to Dante's *Inferno* and Berkove similarly links to *Connecticut Yankee*.

26. Marotti notes a similar strategy in the first chapter of two of the three versions of "The Mysterious Stranger" manuscripts, where "narrative levels interact through the use of two codes of language, referential and mythical" (103). She points out that in the posthumously published "The Enchanted Sea-Wilderness" (written in 1896), once again "the rational frame of mind is set against a mythical mentality" but that in this text "the former uses the language of genteel society [while] the latter is oral and vernacular" (79). See also Zlatic, "Language Technologies," for a detailed analysis of the two "forms of thought and expression" (454) extant in *Connecticut Yankee*—

identified as "orality" (associated with the medieval world and characters) and "literacy" (associated with the nineteenth century and Hank).

27. See Harris for a thorough and provocative analysis of water imagery in Twain's works. Harris points out that "in his early work Twain's most lyrical passages tend to combine images of water with references to escape, daydreams, or contentment" (72). Arguing that "together, water and space are possibly the most central of Twain's preferred images," she suggests that "he uses them, first, to express his ambivalence about the tensions he perceived between himself and the community and, second, as a means to escape the restrictions of the human condition" (72).

28. Cummings suggests that Twain chose Hendon's first name for its symbolic significance, as explicitly defined early in Taine's *The Ancient Regime*: "The noble, in the language of the day, is the man of war, the *soldier* (miles)" (quoted by Cummings 18).

29. The Don Quixote–Sancho Panza relationship is repeatedly invoked by critics to describe the relationship of Tom and Huck. But such critics tend to interpret Cervantes's novel with surprising naïveté, assuming that Sancho is the undisputed hero and Quixote merely the satirical butt. Just as such a reading completely ignores Cervantes's affection for Quixote while excessively elevating Sancho, it leads to a one-sided and simplistic reading of Twain's novels (particularly *Tom Sawyer*, though to some degree *Huck Finn* as well). For a recent version of this interpretive stance, see Harkey (6–13). For a sympathetic interpretation of Tom as a "quixotic hero," see Welsh (94–97, 141–42).

30. Another version of this "talking by the book" exists in Twain's working notes for *The Prince and the Pauper* where he "copied a few dozen words and phrases from *Henry IV*, Part I, and hundreds from *Ivanhoe, Kenilworth,* and *Quentin Durward*, by way of practicing sixteenth-century English" (Cummings 121). That Twain spent hours copying out passages from Scott suggests the complexity of his attitude toward the man he repeatedly reviled. Twain practiced still another version of "talking by the book"—or as he also termed it, "practic[ing] my archaics" (*Autobiography* 292)—in *1601*, where "though he indubitably parodies the Euphuists, his imitation is skillful enough . . . to represent a form of tribute to its ingenuity" (Stahl, "Female Power" 58).

31. See Walker for an exploration of this merger of the courtly love tradition and genteel sentimentalism in *Huckleberry Finn* where Mary Jane Wilks functions as "'damsel in distress'" to Huck's "gallant knight" while also functioning as the "sentimental stereotype of the pure, innocent young woman" (82).

32. See Stahl, *Culture and Gender,* for a detailed exploration of Twain's

complementary if tentative deconstruction of the binary opposition between male and female, specifically in his European novels and travel writing. Stahl argues that "the Otherness of European culture represented . . . a convenient staging ground for exploring his fears, desires, and ideas" (177) about gender. Then, too, the many female disguises adopted by boys in novels like *Huckleberry Finn* and *Pudd'nhead Wilson* point to Twain's exploration of gender identity in the context of American settings.

33. See Emerson (195) and Lauber (*Making* 37). For a revisionist reading of this account, see Zwarg (63).

34. In a provocative if not ultimately convincing feminist reading of *Joan of Arc*, Zwarg makes the startling claim that "Twain assumes a feminist attitude toward history that situates his novel at the center of the theoretical problem engaging feminists today" (52). Asserting that "it is neither a sentimental nor transcendent attempt to inscribe the innocent female into history, as has been supposed," Zwarg argues that "it is rather a study of the way in which Joan of Arc, as representative woman, has been written out of history by this very act of inscription" (60). In a neat rhetorical flourish, she undercuts potential objections by asserting that "critical responses denying this necessarily reenact the patriarchal 'reading' of Joan of Arc's life subverted by Twain's text" (60). For a more persuasive reading that borrows at points from Zwarg, see Stahl (*Culture and Gender* 121–50).

35. See Merritt for a detailed discussion of the aesthetic and symbolic significance of processions and pageants in Twain.

36. See Cooper for a fascinating psychoanalytic reading of Twain's complex response to the death of his brother. Cooper argues that Twain felt guilty not simply for surviving Henry but more specifically for "instilling Henry with the sham of romance, so that Henry follows him onto the river, only to die before he can unlearn the fatal allure of false appearances" (86). Twain's felt responsibility for Henry's death is an exact parallel for "the monstrous way that he blames Walter Scott for the Civil War" (86). In contrast to my reading, Cooper then argues more conventionally that *Life on the Mississippi* provides "a virtual aesthetic of anti-romanticism" (78).

37. The foundering steamboat in *Huckleberry Finn* is named the *Walter Scott*, following the tradition of the St. Louis and Keokuk Packet Line, which served Hannibal during the 1850s and "named their steamboats exclusively from Scott's fictional nomenclature" (Gribben, *Library* 612). Twain's choice of the name *Walter Scott* has been the object of much critical interest (see, for example, Krause). Though typically interpreted as a negative comment about the medievalist impulse in America, this name identifies Twain's beloved steamboats with the medieval period; in *Innocents Abroad*, Twain similarly compared the medieval Cathedral of Milan, which he admired, to a steamboat.

Chapter 3 / Henry Adams

1. Hughson calls into question the generic identification of the *Education* as autobiography, arguing that Adams "wrote a history of his period in the form of a biography, and in it expressed the bankruptcy of history as biography" (1). See also Cox (144–67) for a provocative discussion of Adams's experiments in autobiography in the *Education*.

2. Westervelt argues that "Adams juxtaposes these poles, not to synthesize them, but to hold them at the same time, in order to see how each constitutes the other" (23), just as Kronick argues that "Adams' desire to reconcile the opposing principles of unity and chaos leads him to Hegel . . . [which] leads not to some higher synthesis but to a larger contradiction and the ironic awareness that to be a Hegelian is to be aware that the larger synthesis lies outside one's grasp" (391). Westervelt's deconstructive reading reveals that "Adams denies hierarchy" (35) and that "the division [into doubles is not] entirely reliable as a principle upon which to base value judgments" (24).

3. Chalfant devotes much of his biography to an examination of Adams's years in England as private secretary to his father, arguing that Henry's contributions to the elder Adams's diplomatic success have been little recognized because Henry created a "carefully fostered illusion . . . [designed] to augment his father's stature" (445 n. 32), downplaying his own contributions to benefit his father's reputation.

4. See John Martin for a detailed discussion of Adams's analysis of the Civil War and the political and social changes it effected. Martin focuses on Adams's essay "The Great Secession Winter of 1860–61" (written in 1861, though not published until 1910) where Adams confronts the fact "that if the values of his father had force, the war itself should never have occurred" (327). In response to the war, Adams had to develop a revised view of history, crafting an explanation that "the inability of ideals to prevent the war . . . led to the opportunity to extricate the last sore spot in American life" (328). Martin argues that "as the interpretation was a make-shift one . . . it inevitably did not satisfy Henry Adams . . . and as [he] . . . contemplated the realities of war, [he] became aware of the contradictions built into [his] faith" (328).

5. See Zlatic, "Mark Twain's View of the Universe."

6. See Lyon for a discussion of Washington's symbolic significance for Adams.

7. Carney argues that Adams was not alone in "recogniz[ing] Darwinism as a mere metaphor and fiction [rather than] a law of nature or fact of life" but that he was unique in choosing "*not* to argue against it or to reject it, but to embrace it (as a fiction) anyway, . . . even incorporat[ing] a set of evolutionary metaphors and concepts into his own argument" (513).

8. Henry Adams was here influenced by Brooks Adams, whose *Law of Civilization and Decay* he first read in draft in 1893. J. C. Levenson et al. note that this book "proposed a new science of history that could explain by economic and statistical analysis the rise of commercial power and the decline of 'the emotional, the martial, and the artistic types of manhood' " (*Letters* 4:xviii-xix). Adams wrote in an 1895 letter to Elizabeth Cameron that he "st[oo]d in awe" of Brooks because he "has done for [history] what only the greatest men do, . . . creat[ing] a startling generalization which reduces all history to a scientific formula" (*Letters* 4:336). However, Ronald Martin points out that "the idea that reality was in essence a system of forces was widely popular and influential in America around the turn of the century . . . deeply infus[ing] . . . American culture and literature" (xi).

9. Some sixty-three years after Adams wrote the *Education*, Howard Mumford Jones attempts to find a "leading principle that might serve to make sense out of American development as a whole from . . . Andrew Johnson to . . . Woodrow Wilson," and he "hit[s] upon the idea of energy as being central" (xii). Asserting that his massive *Age of Energy* addresses what is only "hint[ed] at in the concluding chapters of *The Education of Henry Adams*," Jones gives Adams short shrift, arguing that he "confined himself to the effects of science, invention, and industry upon the creation and control of physical (mechanical) energy" (xiii). Having grossly oversimplified the *Education*, Jones states, "My guess is that the conflict was more complicated" (xiii). However irritating his treatment of Adams, Jones offers a wide-ranging and provocative discussion, with sections on such elements as "The Release of energy in style," "Energy as individualism: personality as activity," and "Energy as mobility: restlessness, expansion, urbanization."

10. Levenson et al. use textual evidence to argue persuasively that "Me— the dead Atom-King!" should actually read "Me—the dead Atom—King!" (*Letters* 5:211 n. 8). Just as "Atom" recalls Adams, so does "King" recall Clarence King.

11. On a recuperative trip after Louisa's untimely death from tetanus after an accident, Adams had a terrifying vision: "Mont Blanc for a moment looked to him what it was—a chaos of anarchic and purposeless forces" (*EHA* 289). Comley notes Adams's shift from a "Wordsworthian view of nature as invested with a divine unity which included man, to a sense of nature as a careless Other, a realm of chaos" ("Critical Guide" 4), pointing out other allusions to Wordsworth in the *Education* and *Chartres*. Carney provocatively asserts that "it is entirely appropriate that Wordsworth, even more than the Virgin, should be the patron saint of most of *Mont Saint Michel and Chartres*" (508). Some eight years after Adams's experience, Twain had his own vision of the Alps after a period of depression and writer's block, but his was reassuringly Wordsworthian rather than terrifying. In a letter to his companion

on that trip, Joseph Twichell (pastor of the Asylum Hill Congregational Church in Hartford), Twain later wrote: "Those mountains had a soul; they thought; they spoke. . . . Alp calleth unto Alp!—that stately old Scriptural wording is the right one for God's Alps and God's ocean. How puny we were in that awful presence—and . . . how fitting and right it seemed, and how stingless was the sense of our unspeakable insignificance. And Lord how pervading were the repose and peace and blessedness that poured out of the heart of the invisible Great Spirit of the Mountains" (quoted by Cummings 90).

12. Bishop suggests in his reading of Adams that "man in his capacity as symbol-maker conceived the idea of the unity of the universe" (117). Carney less optimistically argues that Adams imagines a universe in which "individuals have been dethroned as the originators and creators of value and meaning and replaced by a field of forces, a network of discursive, social, and intellectual systems beyond the mere individual's control or perhaps even knowledge, . . . inescapably limit[ing] his deployment of new personal fictions" (517).

13. Adams's frequently avowed intention to turn history into a science must be interpreted with an eye to his sense that science was a system of symbols rather than a repository of truth. Bishop states that Adams was "interested in the metaphoric relationship of history to science" (121). Colacurcio makes the important point that "one's reaction to Adams' various essays in search of a theory of history will depend on whether one believes he is reading science or a poetic vision; it seems entirely possible that Adams was consciously using the most technical diagrams and formulae not as a perverse science . . . but as metaphors of apocalypse" (697).

14. Brooks Adams was also fascinated by the Middle Ages, and during a depression lasting from 1880 to 1881 he did little but read Scott. Henry later adopted this practice, an extension of his childhood reading, as did many others during the Scott revival in the 1880s and 1890s. Doubtless some of them read *The Complete Poetical Works of Sir Walter Scott* (1894), containing an introduction by Henry's Harvard colleague Charles Eliot Norton. Henry long retained his affection for Scott, comparing him with Shakespeare to Scott's advantage in a 1911 letter to Ward Thoron where he proclaimed *Ivanhoe* "an enormous work of instinctive comprehension and genius" (*Letters* 6:416).

15. Decker draws a compelling relationship between the deaths of Louisa (1870) and Marian (1885): "The horror of Louisa's death is compounded in the telling by the fact that her instance . . . must absorb the horror of Marian's. . . . Adams establishes his sister's mortality as the first in an unwritten, but (at least for the 1907 readership) understood, sequence. . . . Having burdened his text with the task of accounting for the absurd deaths of two

brilliant American women in the flower of life, we can hardly wonder that the rest of the *Education* should prove womanless" (265).

16. See Lears for a study of the links drawn by the American imagination between the European Middle Ages and the Orient.

17. Many critics have noted Adams's anti-Semitism. Even a cursory reading of his letters reveals its pervasive presence. Decker rightly observes that "the dismaying spectacle of brilliant language expended upon racist perception and hateful sentiment intensified in the midnineties but was an established dimension of his correspondence long before" (97). Levenson et al. note that "his was not an abstract anti-Semitism, but a deep-felt anarchic impulse" (*Letters* 4:xix). Most significant for my study is Lears's perceptive observation that Adams's anti-Semitism was linked to his admiration for the medieval knight, "the Adams brothers [Henry and Brooks] merg[ing] capitalist, usurer, and international Jew, declaring a plague on all their houses and exalting the Christian knight of the Middle Ages as an untainted alternative" (275). The Knights of the Ku Klux Klan declared a similar "plague" and promoted "untainted" alternatives in their racist philosophy.

18. Cram was not the closest of Adams's personal contacts with the Gothic Revival architects, Adams's cousin Caroline Smith DeWindt—like Henry, a great-grandchild of John Adams—having married Andrew Jackson Downing.

19. See O'Toole for a discussion of the obsessive attraction of Adams's friend Clarence King to the "primaeval woman" (quoted by O'Toole 186). Adams's contribution to the *Clarence King Memoirs* states that "it was not the modern woman that interested [King]; it was the archaic female, with instincts and without intellect" (quoted by O'Toole 367). King's "intimates knew, in a general way, of his attraction to dark-skinned women" (186)—contemporary manifestations for King of the primaeval woman—though they did not know the particulars of his sexual adventures with Native American and African American women, nor did they know of his secret fourteen-year marriage (from 1888 until his death in 1901) to a black nursemaid, Ada Copeland, who bore him five children. King contrasted these "natural women" (quoted by O'Toole 184) with "the modern female, whom he saw as badly educated, overly talkative, and sexually inhibited" (186). King promised Adams on their 1894 trip to Cuba and the Bahamas that they would discover the "ideal negro woman" (quoted by O'Toole 273).

20. See Byrnes (138–50) for a detailed discussion of Adams's medieval and modern sources for *Chartres.*

21. Samuels suggests that Adams "discover[ed] sex as a universal energy" (*Middle Years* 304) during his second journey to the Far East. In *Memoirs of Marau Taaroa* (1893) and the later version *Memoirs of Arii Taimai* (1901), Adams insists that "the key to [the Tahitian queen's] social and political au-

tonomy lay in . . . her sexual freedom" (Decker 230). Comley notes that Adams later stresses "female sexuality and fecundity" in his portrait of the Virgin because "this is one form of energy that endures and does not change" ("Critical Guide" 75).

22. See Byrnes (84–85) for a discussion of Adams's travels as an attempt to put geographical if not epistolary distance between himself and the sexually inaccessible Elizabeth Cameron. See also O'Toole for a detailed description of their relationship.

23. Marian's last social call, only two days before her suicide, was to the pregnant Mrs. Cameron, who gave birth to her only child, Martha, shortly after Marian's death. Many critics have suggested that grief at her childlessness may have contributed to Marian's suicide. Henry's probable grief has also attracted critical attention, his letters revealing his devotion to the children of siblings and friends. Samuels notes that "Adams had the intensest sense of family ties and pride of family, and it must have been deeply disquieting to realize that he would have no descendants to honor his memory as he so filially honored that of his ancestors" (*Middle Years* 160). Lears suggests that "the deepest source of Adams's anxiety was his childlessness" (267). This grief and anxiety, when coupled with sorrow at Marian's death, led Adams not only to an intensification of his affection for Elizabeth Cameron but also to his intense attraction to the figure of the Virgin as madonna. With newborn babe in arms, Elizabeth Cameron served as a powerful contemporary manifestation of the Virgin or Eternal Woman. In an 1891 letter to Elizabeth Cameron, Adams drew an explicit identification between the madonna and Elizabeth: "As I grow older I see that all the human interest and power that religion ever had, was in the mother and child, and I would have nothing to do with a church that did not offer both. There you are again! you see how the thought always turns back to you" (*Letters* 3:561). Samuels points out that Adams "had found his Madonna [in Elizabeth Cameron], and in his symbol-haunted mind, she had fulfilled, as his own marriage had tragically failed to fulfill, his vision of the highest role of women in the world, maternity" (*Major Phase* 70). In later years, Elizabeth "Bessy" Davis Lodge, wife of Adams's young friend George Cabot "Bay" Lodge and a young mother of two, would serve as "a type Madonna" (*Letters* 5:540) for Adams, as he wrote to Elizabeth Cameron in 1904. After Bay Lodge's untimely death in 1909, Adams wrote movingly in a condolence letter to Bessy: "I doubt whether all the genius that ever lived has ever produced poem or figure that could rival you when you produced the children. . . . This is no new notion of mine, for I said it all, years ago, in print [in *Chartres*], and in solemn seriousness. The woman and the child are the wonder of my old age. You are the true poems, the best [Bay] ever did" (*Letters* 6:279). For all the power that Adams self-consciously attributes to Bessy, he repeatedly characterizes her as "the

subject/object for male discourse" (Cholakian 57) while characterizing Bay as the "the creator-poet who possesses her" (Cholakian 99), a relationship normalized by the courtly love tradition.

24. See Chalfant for a fascinating if labored argument that these nicknames are "an encoded form of George Washington" (52).

25. Comley notes that Adams's "Primitive Rights of Women" may be "read as an admonitory lesson addressed to women suffragists such as Susan B. Anthony, who lectured in Boston the night following Adams' lecture" ("Feminine Fictions" 4–5).

26. Adams was not alone in his distaste. Samuels reports that "the most controversial subject [of the day] was the women's rights question and the future of the family. The [Washington] Star asked, 'Are We Dying Out?' . . . The medical expert warned of the growing physical degeneracy of American women, the increase of nervous diseases, the loss of muscle, the dying out of the maternal instinct" (Middle Years 39). Adams noted the "extreme nervous sensitiveness" (Letters 3:471) of modern women, observing at another point: "The women's-rights people have however made themselves so odious that I think we are rid of them for ever" (Letters 2:204). In 1903 he offered a litany of complaints to Anne Palmer Fell: "You cannot conceive how the American woman has changed. . . . The U. S. female is now a portentous bore. She can't take a joke; she isn't pretty, she carries herself like a globe-trotter; and she is more ignorant than ever, besides affecting to have no morals. She bores me as none other" (Letters 5:531).

27. Decker states that Adams "felt his historiography's failure to account for the woman's part in historical process and so turned to the novel as a means to consider the great questions of human society from the perspective of female protagonists" (146). Comley suggests that "Primitive Rights of Women" is "an Ur-text to Adams' novels, Democracy and Esther, in that both the essay and the novels reflect an age much concerned with women's rights and women's place in society" ("Feminine Fictions" 6). Donoghue posits that "the two novels amount to one," excepting the details, arguing that this single story "raise[s] the larger question of what women have to do, or may be allowed to do, in a world ordained for the most part by men" (186).

28. Sommer draws a contrast between the Virgin and Esther, which is in another sense a contrast between medieval and modern womanhood: "[The Virgin's] role in the medieval church was representative of woman's potential role in society. Yet Esther has little hope of establishing even the tenuous relationship with the church that the Virgin maintained, and therefore her efforts dissolve into an invisible martyrdom" ("Feminine Perspectives" 142–43).

29. O'Toole reports that after Adams's death, his companion Aileen Tone

found in his desk "a partially filled bottle of potassium cyanide, the instrument of Clover's suicide" (399).

30. See my "Photo Killeth" for a discussion of Marian's photographic work where I explore the contrast that Henry ultimately draws between photography (rejected as a destructive instrument of modern technology) and painting (a vehicle for the recuperation and regeneration of his emotional and psychological balance); his embrace of painting was a stepping-stone to the medieval aesthetic because he came to associate painting with medieval glasswork.

Chapter 4 / F. Scott Fitzgerald

1. Donaldson notes that "Edward Fitzgerald's sympathies, and Scott's, rested with the Confederacy, . . . [for both were] imbued with the romance of the lost Southern cause" ("Romance" 15). Kuehl suggests that Fitzgerald's "financially inept but 'Old American stock' father came to symbolize pre–Civil War southern aristocracy while his mother's financially successful but 'black Irish' relatives came to represent post–Civil War northern *nouveaux riches*" (*Apprentice Fiction* 35).

2. West states that "the title *The Education of a Personage* may have been suggested by Adams's *The Education of Henry Adams*" (44 n. 4).

3. Princeton's coolness to Fitzgerald's success paradoxically reinforced his "idealized picture" (Donaldson, *Fool* 40). Fitzgerald acknowledged in his 1929 essay "Princeton" that it "had become for him a 'myth', . . . situated enrapturingly amid 'the loveliest riot of Gothic architecture in America' " (Lee, *Promises* 8). In a 1935 letter he suggested new lyrics for a Princeton song, "the idea being, of course, that Princeton to Princeton men lies outside of time and space" (*Correspondence* 400). While dismissing his own conception as "over-sentimental," he suggested that it "might mean something to the older alumni," of whom he was one (*Correspondence* 400).

4. See, for example, Lehan, *Craft of Fiction* (82).

5. Whitley points out that Fitzgerald "could have been alerted [to Spengler's *Decline of the West*] earlier [than 1926] through his relationship with [a] Princeton professor, Christian Gauss, or through various magazine articles about Spengler prior to the first English edition" (158). See also Lehan ("Romantic Destiny") and Gross.

6. Eble notes that "the curriculum he set up for Sheilah Graham in 1939 was both a recapitulation of his own reading and a considered judgment of what books would best serve Sheilah Graham's beginning and his own continuing education" (83–84). For a firsthand account, see Graham, *The Rest of the Story* and *College of One*.

7. Moyer speaks for this optimistic reading: "Spengler had not only cor-

roborated Fitzgerald's sense that the West was in a state of decline; he had also suggested that world history was like the story of the phoenix. . . . If it was the fate of every Civilization to die, it was also certain that . . . a new Culture would inevitably rise from the dead ashes of Civilization" (253). However, Kirby offers a more pessimistic reading, arguing that "Spengler's delineation of the development and evolution of any given culture is rectilinear" but acknowledging that since "he sees all civilizations as following this pattern, his concept of history is often called circular" (163). This "circular" aspect of Spengler's theory provides the basis for the optimistic reading.

8. For a detailed discussion of these themes, see John Lewis, Stern (289– 462), Lehan ("Romantic Destiny"), Donaldson ("Short History"), Moyer, Kirkby, Gross, and Whitley.

9. See Audhuy for a discussion of Eliot's influence on Fitzgerald. Parker reminds us, however, that "the image of the waste land was as much a possession of the Victorian sensibility as it is of the modern" (33) in an essay comparing *Gatsby* to Browning's "Childe Roland to the Dark Tower Came."

10. Fitzgerald provides a similar list drawn from his own experience in "Echoes of the Jazz Age" (see *EJA* 20).

11. Fitzgerald employed the same locution without the dashes in a 1933 letter to Dr. Adolf Meyer, Zelda's psychiatrist at the Phipps Clinic of Johns Hopkins Hospital: "*For a month Zelda had Dr. Forel* [her psychiatrist at Prangins Clinic] *convinced that I was a notorious Parisien homo-sexual*" (*Correspondence* 306).

12. See Janet Lewis for a listing of his sources, ranging from Gibbon's *Rise and Fall of the Roman Empire*, Belloc's *Europe and the Faith*, Weston's *From Ritual to Romance*, and Murray's *The Witch-cult in Western Europe* to the *Encyclopaedia Brittanica* where "he checked articles on armour, castles and Charlemagne, on feudalism, fortification and Viking ships" (9).

13. Fitzgerald wrote regretfully in a 1940 letter to Neal Begley of having had to abandon his original intention "to carry Philippe through a long life covering the latter part of the ninth and early part of the tenth century, a time that must simply be vibrant with change and would be intensely interesting in view of new discoveries (such as the new data on the witch cult) and the new Marxian interpretation" (*Correspondence* 590). Only his editors' lack of interest led to his decision to stop work on the series. But he continued to play with the possibility of "publish[ing] a shorter book to begin with" (*Correspondence* 590).

14. Catharism differed in many respects from Griselda's witch cult, but each was "a secret society" (GD 33) with a "secret lingo" (GD 88), "a powerful underground league" (GD 90) that the Roman Catholic Church wanted to suppress. Both the witch cults and Catharism were also associated with women, as were other heretical movements of the era. Unlike Roman Ca-

tholicism, which severely limited the role of women in the church, sects like the Cathars "encouraged them to take part and to preach" (Ferrante 8). Whereas Griselda's witch cult is "pagan worship—left over from the days before we had the Holy Word" (GD 33), Catharism (also known as the Albigensian heresy) developed as a dualistic reaction against Christianity; it was characterized by an absolute split between this world (regarded as absolutely evil) and the Other world (regarded as absolutely good). In contrast to Christianity, Catharism insisted that salvation could not come through this world (as symbolized by the incarnation of Jesus Christ) but only by transcendence of this world. The threat of Catharism and other heretical cults was such that the Pope preached a crusade, beginning in 1209 and lasting for twenty years, with enormously destructive consequences for Provence, "its native aristocracy largely dispossessed, its courtly society almost destroyed, its independence destined to disappear at the death of the reigning count of Toulouse and the Inquisition established to root out the Cathar heresy" (Topsfield 241). Denis de Rougemont identifies courtly love poetry as the secret means, necessitated by the repressive power of Roman Catholicism, by which Catharism was spread. The "Lady" of such poetry was thus the symbol for the mystical ideal—the uncreated light of that wholly Other world—toward which the soul strove, according to Rougemont.

15. Noting that English literature is "full of ballads and songs about squires of low degree who long for the love of a great lady" (122), Morsberger offers a suggestive if not well-documented discussion of possible literary influences on Fitzgerald. Kuehl argues in an early influential article that Fitzgerald largely derived his romanticism from the English romantic poets and the Victorian romanticists, and he suggests that "Fitzgerald thought of [Gatsby] as a hero in the older sense of demigods and knights of myth, romance, and fairy tale" ("Romantic" 413). He explains the enduring appeal of *Gatsby* by reference to "the memories of legend and fairy tale that permeate the book, lift[ing it] out of time and place as if the novel were a story celebrated for ages in song, folklore, and literature, a story deeply rooted in the psyche of the western world" ("Romantic" 414). Most important for my purposes, Morgan places *Gatsby* squarely within the medieval courtly love tradition, elucidating parallels between Fitzgerald's novel and the medieval romance, concluding that "the residual romantic depths of Western culture are revealed [by Fitzgerald] to be bankrupt" (176). Morgan's interpretation differs from mine insofar as she finds in *Gatsby* a criticism of courtly love, whereas I find a criticism of the modern world that makes courtly love impossible.

16. Mandel notes that "medieval romance is flush with splendid descriptions of gorgeous clothes" (547 n. 10).

17. Mandel regards the "obvious vigils, quests, and grails" as "the visible

portions of a medieval iceberg that lies beneath the surface of the novel" (544). He makes no attempt to present "a 'new' reading of *The Great Gatsby*" (544 n. 4), instead offering a suggestive list of parallels with medieval romance—some convincing, others far-fetched. Mandel concludes, rather tentatively: "We may never know the extent to which Fitzgerald conceived *The Great Gatsby*—either consciously or unconsciously—as the myth of America retold as medieval romance. We can only identify the medieval trappings with which he dressed the tale" (555–56). These medieval trappings are identified even more specifically by Hoffman, who argues that "Gatsby's grail quest is influenced directly or indirectly by the tradition of Troilus" (156), which Fitzgerald had doubtless studied in his 1916 Princeton course, "Chaucer and His Contemporaries." After elucidating structural and thematic similarities, she argues that "Troilus' lesson for Gatsby is that the pursuit [of Daisy] is pointless, for even the Troiluses of this world (if there are any) can never long possess the Criseydes" (157). She asserts that "the meaning of Troilus' epilogue [is] that all human endeavor comes to nothing when potential for greatness, when *gentilesse*, is wasted on that which is unworthy of it," and she more tentatively concludes that "this is possibly the meaning too of *Gatsby*" (157). Hoffman's interpretation of *Troilus* clearly derives from patristic exegesis; in applying the same interpretive method to *Gatsby*, she inevitably draws from Fitzgerald's novel the lesson that one must reject "the medieval courtly love code, and the seeds of corruption that it spawned within itself" (149).

18. See Ferrante (3, 123, 126–27) for a discussion of the "image of the lady as a star" (148) in *stilnovisti* poetry. In a comment also true of *Gatsby*, she notes that in *stilnovisti* poetry "women are separate entities, instruments of greater forces which work on man's inherent nobility or weakness to save or destroy him" and that "the union of man and woman, whether literal or figurative, has little importance in this literature" (127).

19. See Budick for a discussion of Gatsby's desire "to unwrite history and to replace it with an ideal vision or myth" (143).

20. See Chambers (8–82, 142, 186) for an exploration of Plato's influence on Fitzgerald.

21. Gatsby's bizarre comment about Daisy's admitted love for Tom—"It was just personal" (*GG* 217)—is one manifestation of his idealism, for he regards his love for Daisy as suprapersonal or transcendent. Although the excessiveness of this claim may signal an ironic intention on Fitzgerald's part, Fitzgerald often denigrated the merely personal, writing, for example, to Scottie in 1939: "I am not a great man, but sometimes I think the impersonal and objective quality of my talent and the sacrifices of it, in pieces, to preserve its essential value has some sort of epic grandeur" (*Letters* 62). The motif of the impersonal recurs with some frequency in the letters that Fitzgerald and

Zelda exchanged. Zelda alludes, for example, to a discussion about this issue in a 1934 letter to Fitzgerald: "Besides, *anything* personal was never the objective of our generation—we were to have thought of ourselves heroicly [*sic*]" (*Correspondence* 337).

22. This puzzling assertion has attracted various other critical explanations. Noting that "roses are particularly associated with Daisy" (43), Langman suggests that late in the novel "the rose ceases to be regarded as an emblem, a conventional image of passion, romance, glamour, and is seen as simply itself, an object, unlike any preconceived notion, and therefore grotesque" (44). Mandel rightly notes that "the 'locus classicus' for the Middle Ages is *Le Roman de la Rose*, . . . which Fitzgerald may have known in Chaucer's translation," and he points out that "the poem epitomizes courtly love and the longing of the lover for the beloved, who appears in the poem as a literal rose in an allegorical garden" (556). Mandel suggests that "without the dream of love, the rose is grotesque" (556).

23. Bewley offers a particularly harsh criticism of Daisy, whose "emptiness . . . we see curdling into the viciousness of a monstrous moral indifference as the story unfolds" (19). For a rare sympathetic reading, see Fryer, who argues that Daisy "is a victim of a complex network of needs and desires [who] deserves more pity than blame" ("Beneath the Mask" 165).

24. Fitzgerald announced in a telegram to Max Perkins on 9 November 1933: "I have definitely decided on title please spread the word around as widely as seems necessary" (*Correspondence* 321). Perkins wrote on the telegram, "Tender is the Night A Romance" (*Correspondence* 321).

25. Giddings sees in the Diver-Grant comparison the influence of Adams: "[Fitzgerald] shows that [Diver], like Adams's failed hero, succumbed to temptation when he found himself surrounded with the wealthy and socially distinguished. Like Grant, Diver is a dreamer destroyed by realities which he is too frail to combat" (88).

26. See Pitcher for an examination of "Fitzgerald's effort to make [Nicole] the representative of the twentieth century" (76). He notes, for example, that "she is born in 1901 and therefore enters her tenth year in 1910, her twentieth in 1920, and her thirtieth in 1930" (76), and he correlates the major events of her early life with modern historical events.

27. See Tuttleton for a discussion of the motif of female vampirism in *Tender Is the Night*, a constant in Fitzgerald's fiction that "expresses one of Fitzgerald's recurrent anxieties about woman's consuming power [and that] takes its form from a literary source—the poetry of John Keats" (238). Tuttleton argues that in *Tender Is the Night* Fitzgerald merged Keatsian vampirism (in the form of la belle dame sans merci) with his faulty understanding of the psychoanalytic process of transference.

28. Wasserstrom identifies the power shift from Dick to Tommy as

evidence of social degradation: "Against a background of war talk, pogroms, purge trials, he deposed Diver and installed Barban as the master spirit of modern times" (178). Callahan suggests more specifically that "Diver and Barban bear some resemblance to the weakening, self-indulgent, self-deceiving Western democracies between the wars on one hand and the emerging fascist coalitions of ruthless, recessive power on the other" (174). He "explain[s] the transfer of dominion from Dick Diver to Tommy Barban" by proposing that the Diver-Barban shift is "a male version of Henry Adams's notion of the evolution of historical energy from virgin to dynamo" (164).

29. In a provocative feminist reading, Fetterley points out that "the story Fitzgerald told [in *Tender Is the Night*] differs significantly from what actually happened" (113), and she argues that this "self-serving" novel "intends toward the perpetuation of male power" (114).

30. Fryer compares *Tender Is the Night* and *Save Me the Waltz*, arguing that "because *Save Me the Waltz* is a woman's creation, critics are inclined to view it from a feminine perspective—sympathizing with Alabama, resenting David," while "*Tender is the Night*, a man's creation, generally evokes sympathy for Dick Diver and distrust—if not outright hostility toward Nicole" ("Threshold" 319). While acknowledging the criticisms of Nicole, she offers a more sympathetic analysis, arguing that Nicole "takes small but important steps toward her own personal freedom in a world dominated by men" and further arguing for a reconsideration of the common critical view that Fitzgerald was "extremely unsympathetic toward his female characters" ("Threshold" 325).

31. Aldrich notes that "*This Side of Paradise* ostensibly chronicles the progress of its hero . . . but with remarkable self-consciousness the novel confesses . . . its real subject: the use of women in the making of a writer" (134). She states that each female character "can contribute more . . . by her absence (causing the sick heart that enables the page of words); her service . . . is to impress and attract by her beauty and then to be gone" (134).

32. Fairey correctly notes that Stahr "loses the girl through the complicity of his own reservations—unlike Gatsby or any of Fitzgerald's sad young men who are so totally at their ladies' bidding and mercy," but she proceeds to blame Kathleen in familiar terms: "Kathleen's elusiveness and her failure to wait for Stahr . . . may indicate some resemblance to Fitzgerald's undependable flappers, [and] it can be said that Kathleen lets Stahr down just as Daisy lets down Gatsby" (71). Fairey ends by essentially absolving both Stahr and Kathleen: "We have such a clear sense of the conflict in *both* lovers between attraction and caution, that we move beyond Fitzgerald's earlier notion of men being destroyed by their women to a more impartial and judicious sense of life simply being very difficult" (71).

Chapter 5 / Ernest Hemingway

1. Monteiro points out that "Nick's family name is . . . Adams. His father's given name is Henry. And Nick's 'journey' as chronicled from story to story can be, and has been, seen as one of 'education'" ("Education of Ernest" 213). Robert W. Lewis notes that Nick Adams's father shares "the name of the greatest of our medieval admirers" ("Long Time Ago" 209), and he compares Hemingway's chronological primitivism (manifested in "his interest in medievalism and his tendency to idealize the frontier past of America" ["Long Time Ago" 209]) with his cultural primitivism (manifested in his representations of "the Indians of Michigan, . . . the Gypsies and peasants of Spain and the natives of East Africa" ["Long Time Ago" 207]). Positing that Hemingway's interest in "chronological primitivism . . . seem[s] to have emerged later than his cultural primitivism, which was less consciously sought out and more naturally learned" ("Long Time Ago" 209), Lewis suggests that Hemingway's works of cultural primitivism are superior to those of chronological primitivism.

2. Lynn observes that 1929 represented "the high-water mark of postwar revulsion . . . and it was the big year as well for antiwar books" (385). Way notes that "in [Hemingway's] correspondence he expresses the hope that [*A Farewell to Arms*] will supplant Erich Maria Remarque's *All Quiet on the Western Front* as the leading anti-war novel of the 1920s" (166).

3. Stephens notes that "the ambivalences and the ambiguities of Hemingway's thinking [about war]" (*Nonfiction* 84) are manifested in his introduction to the 1948 edition of *A Farewell to Arms*, as follows: "Some people used to say: why is the man so preoccupied and obsessed with war. . . . It is the considered belief of the writer of this book that wars are fought by the finest people that there are . . . but they are made, provoked and initiated by straight economic rivalries and by swine that stand to profit from them." McNeely observes that Hemingway's vision of war is "polarize[d] . . . in an almost schizophrenic way," as follows: "Necessary, of ultimate simplicity, and even beautiful, war [for Hemingway] is also barbarity personified and horror unrestrained" (21).

4. Reynolds notes that Blunden's *Undertones of War* was listed on a book inventory made at Key West in 1955 (*Reading* 100). According to Reynolds, books listed on this inventory were "probably in the Key West library in 1940 when Hemingway packed for Cuba" (75), and "for books published in the 1930s, it seems safe to assume that [Hemingway] got his copy soon after publication" (73). Given Hemingway's intense interest in World War I texts and the 1928 publication date of Blunden's memoir, it is at least possible that he read it while writing *A Farewell to Arms* (begun in early March 1928 and

completed [except for the last paragraphs] by the end of January 1929). Hemingway read another World War I memoir listed on the 1955 Key West inventory—Robert Graves's *Goodbye to All That: An Autobiography* (1929)— shortly after its publication, completing it at some point before 5 January 1930, which would have been shortly after the period of composition of *A Farewell to Arms*. Graves's and Hemingway's differing agendas are suggested by the titles they chose—synonymous yet connotatively quite different. For Hemingway's comments about Graves's autobiography, see his 1930 letter to Fitzgerald (*Letters* 320).

5. Fussell notes that "the machine gun alone makes [World War I] so special and unexampled that it simply can't be talked about as if it were one of the conventional wars of history" (153). Ellis notes that the machine gun "was a dire threat to assumptions about the nature of war, . . . undermin[ing] the old certainties of the battlefield—the glorious charge and the opportunities for individual heroism" (17).

6. See Reynolds for a detailed comparison of the fictional and historical retreats from Caporetto (*First War* 105–34).

7. Griffin points out that Hemingway later drew on his knowledge of *The Faerie Queene*—"one of [his] favorite romances"—in a 1925 letter to Fitzgerald, parodically "casting himself in the role of the quester for truth, the Red Cross Knight" (*Treason* 108).

8. See Oldsey (10–34), Reynolds (*First War*), Fleming, and Stoneback ("'Lovers' Sonnets'" 64–65).

9. Oldsey queries: "[Was] Sir Henry Lee . . . destined by strange literary karma to become Lieutenant Henry?" (27).

10. Reynolds notes that "during the thirties [Hemingway] began to study the American Civil War" (*Reading* 25), and he lists fifteen relevant books in Hemingway's library. Meyers indicates that Hemingway "maintained a life-long interest in the war and had twenty-six books on the subject in his library" (3).

11. Ross notes that General Sherman concluded from the Civil War "that the impact of increased firepower meant that field entrenchments had to become a critical tactical element in all combats" (183), a prophecy borne out in World War I's trenches.

12. See particularly Wagner-Martin and Curtis for discussions of parallels between the medieval *Chanson de Roland* and Hemingway's modern novel. See also Stoneback, "Rue Saint-Jacques" (6–10) and "Road to Roncevaux."

13. For a discussion of the role of the condottieri, see Rougemont (251–54) and Scaglione (30, 222, 229–30).

14. Noting that the bridge Jordan blows up becomes, as the novel records, "'a dream bridge,'" Lee argues that it is "not only his designated target, . . .

but the place where finally his boyhood dreams of heroic Civil War and Western frontier derring-do become for a moment utterly real, romance literally
transformed into historic actuality" ("Seeing" 89). Lee suggests that "behind
[the novel's] surface lies the appeal to a discernibly larger, mythic paradigm
of heroic action, . . . whether the picture book chivalry of childhood classics,
or the epic moments from actual history" ("Seeing" 89).

15. Flores points out that Frederic Henry and Robert Jordan's motivations
for becoming involved in their wars are largely psychological, Frederic engaging in "an unconscious search" and Jordan "want[ing] to prove himself in
the face of danger . . . [and to engage in] the search for his own self" (29).
McNeely posits that Frederic's motivation is "cover[ed] up" (24) by both
Frederic and Hemingway: "It is that he is a romantic. He cannot articulate
this, naturally, because his own creed rejects romance. . . . He is a permanently divided personality: coming to the war a romantic, . . . he has been
devastatingly disillusioned" (24). McNeely argues that "the numerous chivalric and martial motifs planted carefully through the book, especially the
early part, are not primarily either satire or parody; they are the fragments
precisely of Henry's pre-fall world. . . . As emphatically ironic as his presentation of these images is, it cannot conceal the permanent fascination and
appeal they nevertheless retain for him, . . . confirming the picture of Henry
as a chronic romantic as regards war" (24).

16. Josephs notes that "all the characters who make the pilgrimage to the
fiesta at Pamplona are measured—morally or spiritually—around the axis of
the art of *toreo* . . . [and] Romero . . . comes closest to perfection" (92).
Stoneback asserts that "the bullfight is meant to convey an emblem of moral
behavior" and that "the behavior of every important character except perhaps
Romero is found wanting" ("Road to Roncevaux" 149). See also Kinnamon
(59–61).

17. See Sylvester for commentary on "the Fisher King legend as interpreted" ("Italian *Waste Land*" 90) in various Hemingway works, including
The Old Man and the Sea.

18. Hemingway's parodic comment in a 1926 letter to Fitzgerald—"I have
tried to follow the outline and spirit of the Great Gatsby [in *The Sun Also
Rises*] but feel I have failed somewhat because of never having been on Long
Island" (*Letters* 200–201)—contained a kernel of truth.

19. Lauter argues that Cohn is a "romantic idealist" (339) and that Jake
must fight against the seductive pull of just such idealism. Spilka perceives
Jake, a "restrained romantic," as even closer to the position of Cohn but
assumes that such a position is misguided, specifying that Jake "share[s] with
Cohn a common (if hidden) weakness" ("Death of Love" 242). Mizener
("*Sun*" 140) regards these similarities in the most positive light for romanticism, arguing that both Cohn and Jake are romantic but that Cohn is falsely

so because his values are maintained by a literary distortion of the actual conditions of his life, while Jake's values are earned.

20. For a detailed discussion of Pedro Romero's role as knight, see my "Hemingway's Medievalist Impulse." See also Josephs.

21. Robert W. Lewis (*On Love* 46) refers to Huizinga's discussion of the significance of hair in medieval traditions.

22. Balassi argues, however, that "though Jake may be a 'rotten Catholic' . . . it is not for lack of trying" (140). See also Stoneback for a description of Jake as "a quite specifically Catholic pilgrim on a specific pilgrimage route, very much in touch with the history, the ritual, the discipline, the moral and aesthetic and salvific legacy of the great medieval pilgrimage to Santiago de Compostela" ("Rue Saint-Jacques" 4). See Budick for a somewhat different version of the same argument where Jake is the "inheritor of an American Puritan past" who is ultimately "release[d] . . . from his Puritan prejudices and allow[ed] . . . to resume his Roman Catholic identity . . . [which] will return him to an incarnational view of the universe" (173).

23. For Agnes von Kurowsky's own voice, see Villard and Nagel, *The Lost Diary of Agnes von Kurowsky.*

24. See Robert W. Lewis (*On Love* 7) for a discussion of the relationship between Maria and the Virgin Mary. See also Carpenter for a discussion of Maria as "a symbol of the traditional mariolatry of the Spanish Catholic Church" (285).

25. Hemingway's relationship with Adriana Ivancich provides an important parallel to the fictional relationship between Cantwell and Renata, for even in the actual relationship the reality and the fantasy, the real woman and the ideal, merged in his mind: "Adriana is so lovely to dream of, and when I wake I'm stronger than the day before and the words pour out of me" (quoted by Meyers 447). In this observation Hemingway unselfconsciously revealed that it was the *dream* of Adriana that inspired him. Meyers notes that "she was his fictional creation—in life as well as in art" (452) and that Hemingway "preferred to keep their relationship on an imaginative rather than a realistic plane" (447).

26. In the case of Catherine Barkley's death, Hemingway was also wreaking revenge on Agnes von Kurowsky for jilting him by providing her fictional alter-ego with a painful and drawn-out death. Solotaroff emphasizes that "the author killed the heroine as surely as the hemorrhages he created" (12). Hemingway wrought a different revenge on Agnes in his "A Very Short Story" (1923), which recounts the jilting of a young soldier by a nurse named Luz, who "comes through as one of his earliest 'bitch' heroines" (Kert 131). Scholes offers an insightful semiotic analysis of the story, noting that "the good, loyal, reticent male character is supported by the discourse, through its covert first-

person perspective and the complicity of its style with those values, . . . [while] the bad, treacherous, talkative female is cast out" (42). See also Pullin.

27. See Verduin for a complete discussion of the many references to Dante in this novel ("Hemingway's Dante"). See also Brenner (151–63), who devotes a chapter of his book to demonstrating that *Across the River and into the Trees* is "A Dantesque 'Imitation' " and that this novel is a dream vision.

28. Because Hemingway took seriously his self-imposed role as knight, one constant was his exaggerated sense of protectiveness toward ladies. Baker reports that in the early years in Paris, Hemingway "was notably truculent whenever he squired Ada [MacLeish] to prizefights or bike races [and] if anyone even remotely jostled her, he would be invited to stand up and be slugged" (*Life* 226). Aronowitz and Hamill note that years later Hemingway wanted to fight a duel for Ingrid Bergman (172), who played Maria in the screen version of *For Whom the Bell Tolls.*

29. See Whitlow for a critique of this dichotomous perspective, which he terms "the most popular critical manner of categorizing Hemingway's women" (11) and derides for limiting both discussion and appreciation of these female characters. Whitlow offers brief discussions of female characters in this slight book, ultimately concluding that "Hemingway has presented interesting, dramatic characters" in his "portrayals of female trauma, . . . victimized women, . . . [and] deeply loving women" (113). While Whitlow's argument is unpersuasive and insubstantial, he presents a useful survey of critical perspectives on Hemingway's female characters. For a more compelling critique of the dichotomous perspective, at least as it affects interpretations of Catherine Barkley, see Spanier, who provides a survey of the major critical views of Catherine, taking her own idiosyncratic place in the debate as one who "read[s] Catherine Barkley . . . as the one character in the novel who, more than any other, embodies the controls of courage and honor that many have called the 'Hemingway code' " (80). One need not agree with Spanier's reading of Catherine to appreciate her careful placement of Catherine Barkley in the context of World War I. See also Beversluis for another attack on the dichotomous perspective as it affects readings of Catherine Barkley. However, in contrast to Spanier, who sees Catherine "as the truly heroic figure of the novel, . . . a model of courage and stoic self-awareness" (76), Beversluis sees Catherine as a woman whose "suffocating omnipresence" (21), "unyielding possessiveness and . . . desire to control even from beyond the grave" (24) make her ultimately a burden to Frederic.

30. See Kert for a detailed and sympathetic discussion of Hemingway's four wives and other important women in his life, including the much-maligned Grace Hall Hemingway.

31. Monteiro discusses "the ways aestheticism . . . permeate[s]" *Across the*

River and into the Trees ("Hemingway's Colonel" 40). McNeely argues more generally that "the aesthetic emotion is the highest and most authentic response to experience [the Hemingway hero] can have" (16). See also Gaggin, who argues that "the themes of aestheticism . . . inform [Hemingway's] fiction throughout his career, . . . underscoring [his characters'] sense of detachment, the importance they place on observation, and at times, their poignant sense of living in a dessicated culture" (3). For a discussion of how aestheticism informs Hemingway's nonfiction, see Brenner (67–106), who explores the "preoccupation with esthetics" (106) found in *Death in the Afternoon* and *Green Hills of Africa.*

32. See, however, Stoneback, " 'Lovers' Sonnets,' " for a provocative if ultimately unpersuasive discussion of what he terms the "Catholic sub-text of *A Farewell to Arms*" (57). Calling for "a thoroughgoing examination of Hemingway under a new rubric, the Catholic novel" (70), Stoneback argues that "the religious issue is central" in *A Farewell to Arms* "as everywhere else in Hemingway," and he makes the startling claim that *A Farewell to Arms* is "a moving record of the progress of the soul, a hymn of love, and a prayer for the whole state of the world" (74 n. 3). Though Stoneback's argument is overstated here and in his "Rue Saint-Jacques" (which focuses on *The Sun Also Rises*), he performs an important service in foregrounding Hemingway's conversion to Catholicism (which Hemingway claimed dated from his battlefield wounding in 1918 but which he did not publicly proclaim until his 1927 marriage to the Catholic Pauline Pfeiffer required it).

Works Cited

Adair, William. "Hemingway's 'Out of Season': The End of the Line." In *New Critical Approaches to the Short Stories of Ernest Hemingway*, ed. Jackson J. Benson, 341–46.

Adams, Brooks. "The Heritage of Henry Adams." In *The Degradation of the Democratic Dogma*, by Henry Adams, ed. Brooks Adams, 1–122.

Adams, Henry. *The Degradation of the Democratic Dogma*. Ed. Brooks Adams. New York: Macmillan, 1919.

——. *Democracy: An American Novel*. New York: Farrar, Straus, and Young, [1952?]. Reprint, New York: Harmony Books, 1981.

——. *The Education of Henry Adams*. New York: Random House, 1931.

——. *Esther: A Novel*. In his *"Democracy" and "Esther," Two Novels by Henry Adams*, 207–371. Gloucester, Mass.: Peter Smith, 1965.

——. *The Letters of Henry Adams*. Ed. Worthington Chauncey Ford. 2 vols. Boston: Houghton Mifflin, 1930–38.

——. *The Letters of Henry Adams*. Ed. J. C. Levenson, Ernest Samuels, Charles Vandersee, and Viola Hopkins Winner. 6 vols. Cambridge: Harvard Univ. Press, 1982–88.

——. *Mont-Saint-Michel and Chartres*. Princeton: Princeton Univ. Press, 1981.

——. "Prayer to the Virgin of Chartres." In his *Letters to a Niece and Prayer to the Virgin of Chartres*, ed. Mabel La Farge, 125–34. Boston: Houghton Mifflin, 1920.

―――. "The Rule of Phase Applied to History." In his *The Degradation of the Democratic Dogma*, ed. Brooks Adams, 267–311.

―――. "The Tendency of History." In his *The Degradation of the Democratic Dogma*, ed. Brooks Adams, 125–33.

Aldrich, Elizabeth Kaspar. "'The most poetical topic in the world': Women in the Novels of F. Scott Fitzgerald." In *Scott Fitzgerald: The Promises of Life*, ed. A. Robert Lee, 131–56.

Anderson, Charles R. "Henry Adams, 1838–1918" (1965). In *Critical Essays on Henry Adams*, ed. Earl N. Harbert, 115–39.

Aronowitz, Alfred, and Pete Hamill. *Ernest Hemingway: The Life and Death of a Man*. New York: Lancer Books, 1961.

Audhuy, Letha. "The *Waste Land* Myth and Symbols in *The Great Gatsby*" (1980). In *F. Scott Fitzgerald's "The Great Gatsby,"* ed. Harold Bloom, 109–22.

Auerbach, Erich. "The Knight Sets Forth." In his *Mimesis*, trans. Willard R. Trask. Princeton: Princeton Univ. Press, 1953.

Baetzhold, Howard G. "Mark Twain: England's Advocate." *American Literature* 28 (1956): 328–46.

Baker, Carlos. *Ernest Hemingway: A Life Story*. New York: Avon, 1980.

Balassi, William. "Hemingway's Greatest Iceberg: The Composition of *The Sun Also Rises*." In *Writing the American Classics*, ed. James Barbour and Tom Quirk, 125–55.

Barbour, James, and Tom Quirk, eds. *Writing the American Classics*. Chapel Hill: Univ. of North Carolina Press, 1990.

Barlowe-Kayes, Jamie. "Re-Reading Women: The Example of Catherine Barkley." *Hemingway Review* 12, no. 2 (1993): 24–35.

Bassett, John E. "Tom, Huck, and the Young Pilot: Twain's Quest for Authority." *Mississippi Quarterly* 39 (1985–86): 3–19.

Bell, Millicent. "Adams' *Esther*: The Morality of Taste" (1962). In *Critical Essays on Henry Adams*, ed. Earl N. Harbert, 104–14.

―――. "*A Farewell to Arms*: Pseudoautobiography and Personal Metaphor." In *Ernest Hemingway: The Writer in Context*, ed. James Nagel, 107–28. Madison: Univ. of Wisconsin Press, 1984.

Benson, Jackson J., ed. *New Critical Approaches to the Short Stories of Ernest Hemingway*. Durham: Duke Univ. Press, 1990.

Berkove, Lawrence I. "The Reality of the Dream: Structural and Thematic Unity in *A Connecticut Yankee*." *Mark Twain Journal* 22, no. 1 (1984): 8–14.

Beversluis, John. "Dispelling the Romantic Myth: A Study of *A Farewell to Arms*." *Hemingway Review* 9, no. 1 (1989): 18–25.

Bewley, Marius. "Scott Fitzgerald's Criticism of America" (1954). In *F. Scott Fitzgerald's "The Great Gatsby,"* ed. Harold Bloom, 11–27.

Bishop, Ferman. *Henry Adams.* Boston: Twayne, 1979.

Blackmur, R. P. *Henry Adams.* Ed. Veronica A. Makowsky. New York: Harcourt Brace Jovanovich, 1980.

Block, Jean F., ed. *The Uses of Gothic: Planning and Building the Campus of the University of Chicago 1892–1932.* Chicago: Univ. of Chicago Library, 1983.

Bloom, Harold, ed. *F. Scott Fitzgerald's "The Great Gatsby."* New Haven: Chelsea House, 1986.

Blunden, Edmund. *Undertones of War.* Garden City, N.Y.: Doubleday, Doran, 1929.

Boase, Roger. *The Origin and Meaning of Courtly Love: A Critical Study of European Scholarship.* Manchester: Manchester Univ. Press, 1977.

Brenner, Gerry. *Concealments in Hemingway's Works.* Columbus: Ohio State Univ. Press, 1983.

Brooks, Van Wyck. *The Ordeal of Mark Twain.* Cleveland: World, 1955.

Bryer, Jackson R., ed. *The Short Stories of F. Scott Fitzgerald: New Approaches in Criticism.* Madison: Univ. of Wisconsin Press, 1982.

Budick, Emily Miller. *Fiction and Historical Consciousness: The American Romance Tradition.* New Haven: Yale Univ. Press, 1989.

Bulfinch, Thomas. *The Age of Chivalry.* Boston: J. E. Tilton, 1858.

Burgess, Glyn S., and Robert A. Taylor. *The Spirit of the Court.* Cambridge: D. S. Brewer, 1985.

Burns, Richard, and Ken Burns. *The Civil War.* New York: Knopf, 1990.

Byrnes, Joseph F. *The Virgin of Chartres: An Intellectual and Psychological History of the Work of Henry Adams.* London: Associated Univ. Presses, 1981.

Callahan, John F. *The Illusions of a Nation: Myth and History in the Novels of F. Scott Fitzgerald.* Urbana: Univ. of Illinois Press, 1972.

Carney, Raymond. "The Imagination in Ascendance: Henry Adams' *Mont Saint Michel and Chartres.*" *Southern Review* 22 (1986): 506–31.

Carpenter, Frederick I. "Hemingway Achieves the Fifth Dimension" (1955). In *Ernest Hemingway: Five Decades of Criticism,* ed. Linda Welshimer Wagner, 279–87.

Carter, Everett. "The Meaning of *A Connecticut Yankee.*" *American Literature* 50 (1978): 418–40.

Chalfant, Edward. *Both Sides of the Ocean: A Biography of Henry Adams, His First Life, 1838–1862.* Hamden, Conn.: Archon, 1982.

Chambers, John B. *The Novels of F. Scott Fitzgerald.* New York: St. Martin's Press, 1989.

Chance, Jane, and Leslie Workman, eds. "Twentieth-Century Medievalism." *Studies in Medievalism* 2, no. 1 (1982).

Chandler, Alice. *A Dream of Order: The Medieval Ideal in Nineteenth-Century English Literature.* Lincoln: Univ. of Nebraska Press, 1970.

Cholakian, Rouben C. *The Troubadour Lyric: A Psychocritical Reading.* Manchester: Manchester Univ. Press, 1990.

Cochran, Rebecca. "Edwin Arlington Robinson's Arthurian Poems: Studies in Medievalisms?" *Arthurian Interpretations* 3, no. 1 (1988): 49–60.

Colacurcio, Michael. "The Dynamo and the Angelic Doctor: The Bias of Henry Adams' Medievalism." *American Quarterly* 17 (1965): 696–712.

Collins, Carvel. Introduction to *Mayday,* by William Faulkner. Notre Dame: Univ. of Notre Dame Press, 1977.

Comley, Nancy Rich. "A Critical Guide to the Literary Journey and Henry Adams' *Mont-Saint-Michel and Chartres.*" Ph.D. diss., Brown University, 1978.

———. "Henry Adams' Feminine Fictions: The Economics of Maternity." *American Literary Realism, 1870–1910* 22, no. 1 (1989): 3–16.

Comley, Nancy R., and Robert Scholes. *Hemingway's Genders: Rereading the Hemingway Text.* New Haven: Yale Univ. Press, 1994.

Commager, Henry Steele. "Henry Adams" (1937). In *Critical Essays on Henry Adams,* ed. Earl N. Harbert, 50–62.

Contosta, David R. *Henry Adams and the American Experiment.* Boston: Little, Brown, 1980.

Cooper, Stephen. "'Good Rotten Material for Burial': The Overdetermined Death of Romance in *Life on the Mississippi.*" *Literature and Psychology* 36 (1990): 78–89.

Cox, James M. *Recovering Literature's Lost Ground: Essays in American Autobiography.* Baton Rouge: Louisiana State Univ. Press, 1989.

Cram, Ralph Adams. Introduction to *Mont-Saint-Michel and Chartres,* by Henry Adams. Boston: Houghton Mifflin, 1933.

Cummings, Sherwood. *Mark Twain and Science: Adventures of a Mind.* Baton Rouge: Louisiana State Univ. Press, 1988.

Curtis, Mary Ann C. "*The Sun Also Rises*: Its Relation to *The Song of Roland.*" *American Literature* 60 (1988): 274–80.

Decker, William Merrill. *The Literary Vocation of Henry Adams.* Chapel Hill: Univ. of North Carolina Press, 1990.

Denton, L. W. "Mark Twain on Patriotism, Treason, and War." *Mark Twain Journal* 17, no. 2 (1974): 4–7.

Diggins, John Patrick. "'Who Bore the Failure of the Light': Henry Adams and the Crisis of Authority." *New England Quarterly* 58 (1985): 165–92.

Diliberto, Gioia. *Hadley.* New York: Ticknor and Fields, 1992.

Dodd, William George. "The System of Courtly Love" (1913). In *Chaucer Criticism,* ed. Richard J. Schoeck and Jerome Taylor, 2:1–15. Notre Dame, Ind.; Univ. of Notre Dame Press, 1961.

Donaldson, Scott. *Fool for Love: F. Scott Fitzgerald*. New York: Congdon and Weed, 1983.

———. "Scott Fitzgerald's Romance with the South." *Southern Literary Journal* 5, no. 2 (1973): 3–17.

———. "A Short History of *Tender Is the Night*." In *Writing the American Classics*, ed. James Barbour and Tom Quirk, 177–208.

———, ed. *Critical Essays on F. Scott Fitzgerald's "The Great Gatsby."* Boston: G. K. Hall, 1984.

———, ed. *New Essays on "A Farewell to Arms."* Cambridge: Cambridge Univ. Press, 1990.

Donoghue, Denis. "Henry Adams' Novels." *Nineteenth-Century Fiction* 39 (1984): 186–201.

Dusinberre, William. *Henry Adams: The Myth of Failure*. Charlottesville: Univ. Press of Virginia, 1980.

Eble, Kenneth E. "*The Great Gatsby* and the Great American Novel." In *New Essays on "The Great Gatsby,"* ed. Matthew J. Bruccoli, 79–100. Cambridge: Cambridge Univ. Press, 1985.

Edwards, Owen Dudley. "The Lost Teigueen: F. Scott Fitzgerald's Ethics and Ethnicity." In *Scott Fitzgerald: The Promises of Life*, ed. A. Robert Lee, 181–214.

Ellis, John. *The Social History of the Machine Gun*. New York: Random House, 1975.

Emerson, Everett. *The Authentic Mark Twain: A Literary Biography of Samuel L. Clemens*. Philadelphia: Univ. of Pennsylvania Press, 1984.

Fairey, Wendy. "*The Last Tycoon*: The Dilemma of Maturity for F. Scott Fitzgerald." In *Fitzgerald / Hemingway Annual, 1979*, ed. Matthew J. Bruccoli, 65–78.

Faulkner, William. *Knight's Gambit*. New York: Vintage, 1978.

———. *Mayday*. Notre Dame: Univ. of Notre Dame Press, 1977.

Ferrante, Joan M. *Woman as Image in Medieval Literature: From the Twelfth Century to Dante*. New York: Columbia Univ. Press, 1975.

Fetterley, Judith. "Who Killed Dick Diver? The Sexual Politics of *Tender Is the Night*." *Mosaic* 17, no. 1 (1984): 111–28.

Fiedler, Leslie. *Love and Death in the American Novel*. Rev. ed. New York: Stein and Day, 1966.

Fitzgerald, F. Scott. *The Beautiful and Damned*. New York: Scribners, 1922.

———. *Correspondence of F. Scott Fitzgerald*. Ed. Matthew J. Bruccoli and Margaret M. Duggan. New York: Random House, 1980.

———. "The Count of Darkness." *Redbook Magazine*, June 1935.

———. "The Crack-Up." In *The Crack-Up*, ed. Edmund Wilson, 69–74.

———. *The Crack-Up*. Ed. Edmund Wilson. New York: New Directions, 1956.

―――. *Dear Scott / Dear Max: The Fitzgerald-Perkins Correspondence*. Ed. John Kuehl and Jackson R. Bryer. New York: Scribners, 1971.

―――. "Does a Moment of Revolt Come Some Time to Every Married Man?" In *F. Scott Fitzgerald in His Own Time: A Miscellany*, ed. Matthew J. Bruccoli and Jackson R. Bryer, 184–86.

―――. "Early Success." In *The Crack-Up*, ed. Edmund Wilson, 85–90.

―――. "Echoes of the Jazz Age." In *The Crack-Up*, ed. Edmund Wilson, 13–22.

―――. "Gods of Darkness." *Redbook Magazine*, November 1941.

―――. *The Great Gatsby*. New York: Scribners, 1925.

―――. "Homage to the Victorians." Review of *The Oppidan*, by Shane Leslie. In *F. Scott Fitzgerald in His Own Time: A Miscellany*, ed. Matthew J. Bruccoli and Jackson R. Bryer, 134–35.

―――. "In the Darkest Hour." *Redbook Magazine*, October 1934.

―――. "The Kingdom in the Dark." *Redbook Magazine*, August 1935.

―――. *The Last Tycoon*. New York: Scribners, 1941.

―――. *The Letters of F. Scott Fitzgerald*. Ed. Andrew Turnbull. New York: Scribners, 1963.

―――. *A Life in Letters: F. Scott Fitzgerald*. Ed. Matthew J. Bruccoli. New York: Simon and Schuster, 1994.

―――. *The Notebooks of F. Scott Fitzgerald*. Ed. Matthew J. Bruccoli. New York: Harcourt Brace Jovanovich, 1978.

―――. "Pasting It Together." In *The Crack-Up*, ed. Edmund Wilson, 75–80.

―――. *Tender Is the Night*. New York: Scribners, 1933.

―――. *This Side of Paradise*. New York: Scribners, 1920.

Fleming, Robert E. "Hemingway and Peele: Chapter I of *A Farewell to Arms*." *Studies in American Fiction* 11 (1983): 95–100.

Flores, Olga Eugenia. "Eros, Thanatos and the Hemingway Soldier." *American Studies International* 18, nos. 3–4 (1980): 27–35.

Fraser, John. *America and the Patterns of Chivalry*. Cambridge: Cambridge Univ. Press, 1982.

Fraser, Keath. "Another Reading of *The Great Gatsby*" (1979). In *F. Scott Fitzgerald's "The Great Gatsby,"* ed. Harold Bloom, 57–70.

Freeman, Douglas Southall. *R. E. Lee: A Biography*. Vol. 1. New York: Scribners, 1934.

Friedrich, Otto. *Clover*. New York: Simon and Schuster, 1979.

Fryer, Sarah Beebe. "Beneath the Mask: The Plight of Daisy Buchanan." In *Critical Essays on F. Scott Fitzgerald's "The Great Gatsby,"* ed. Scott Donaldson, 153–66.

―――. "Nicole Warren Diver and Alabama Beggs Knight: Women on the Threshold of Freedom." *Modern Fiction Studies* 31 (1985): 318–26.

Fussell, Paul. *The Great War and Modern Memory.* Oxford: Oxford Univ. Press, 1975.

Gaggin, John. *Hemingway and Nineteenth-Century Aestheticism.* Ann Arbor, Mich.: UMI Research Press, 1988.

Geismar, Maxwell, ed. *Mark Twain and the Three R's: Race, Religion, Revolution and Related Matters.* Indianapolis: Bobbs-Merrill, 1973.

Giddings, Robert. "*The Last Tycoon*: Fitzgerald as Projectionist." In *Scott Fitzgerald: The Promises of Life*, ed. A. Robert Lee, 74–93.

Gilbert, Sandra. "The Education of Henrietta Adams." In *Profession 84*, 5–9. New York: MLA, 1984.

Girouard, Mark. *The Return to Camelot: Chivalry and the English Gentleman.* New Haven: Yale Univ. Press, 1981.

Goebel, Janet, and Rebecca Cochran, eds. *Selected Papers on Medievalism.* 2 vols. Indiana: Indiana Univ. of Pennsylvania Press, 1988.

Graham, Sheilah. *College of One.* New York: Viking, 1966.

———. *The Rest of the Story.* New York: Coward-McCann, 1964.

Gribben, Alan. "How Tom Sawyer Played Robin Hood 'By the Book.' " *English Language Notes* 13 (1976): 201–4.

———. *Mark Twain's Library: A Reconstruction.* Vol. 2. Boston: G. K. Hall, 1980.

———. " 'The Master Hand of Old Malory': Mark Twain's Acquaintance with *Le Morte D'Arthur*." *English Language Notes* 16 (1978): 32–40.

Griffin, Peter. *Along with Youth: Hemingway, the Early Years.* Oxford: Oxford Univ. Press, 1985.

———. *Less than a Treason: Hemingway in Paris.* Oxford: Oxford Univ. Press, 1990.

Gross, Dalton. "F. Scott Fitzgerald's *The Great Gatsby* and Oswald Spengler's *The Decline of the West*." *Notes and Queries* 17 (1970): 476.

Hamill, Paul J., Jr. "The Future as Virgin: A Latter-Day Look at the Dynamo and the Virgin of Henry Adams." *Modern Language Studies* 3, no. 1 (1973): 8–12.

Harbert, Earl N., ed. *Critical Essays on Henry Adams.* Boston: G. K. Hall, 1981.

Harkey, Joseph H. "Mark Twain's Knights and Squires." *Mark Twain Journal* 20, no. 3 (1981): 6–13.

Harris, Susan K. *Mark Twain's Escape from Time, a Study of Patterns and Images.* Columbia: Univ. of Missouri Press, 1982.

Harrison, Stanley R. "Mark Twain's Requiem for the Past." *Mark Twain Journal* 16, no. 2 (1972): 3–10.

Hemingway, Ernest. *Across the River and into the Trees.* New York: Scribners, 1950.

———. "Big Two-Hearted River." In *The Nick Adams Stories*, 159–80.

———. *Death in the Afternoon.* New York: Scribners, 1932.

————. *Ernest Hemingway: Selected Letters, 1917–1961.* Ed. Carlos Baker. New York: Scribners, 1981.

————. *A Farewell to Arms.* New York: Scribners, 1929.

————. "Fathers and Sons." In *The Nick Adams Stories,* 234–45.

————. *For Whom the Bell Tolls.* New York: Scribners, 1940.

————. *Green Hills of Africa.* New York: Scribners, 1935.

————. *In Our Time.* New York: Scribners, 1925.

————. "The Last Good Country." In *The Nick Adams Stories,* 56–114.

————. *A Moveable Feast.* New York: Scribners, 1964.

————. *The Nick Adams Stories.* New York: Scribners, 1972.

————. *The Old Man and the Sea.* New York: Macmillan, 1952.

————. *The Sun Also Rises.* New York: Scribners, 1926.

————. *Winner Take Nothing.* New York: Scribners, 1933.

Hemingway, Gregory H. *Papa: A Personal Memoir.* Boston: Houghton Mifflin, 1976.

Hill, Hamlin. *Mark Twain: God's Fool.* New York: Harper and Row, 1973.

Hoffman, Nancy Y. "*The Great Gatsby: Troilus and Criseyde* Revisited?" In *Fitzgerald / Hemingway Annual, 1971,* ed. Matthew J. Bruccoli, 148–58.

Howard, Leon. *Victorian Knight-Errant, a Study of the Early Literary Career of James Russell Lowell.* Berkeley: Univ. of California Press, 1952.

Howell, Elmo. "Mark Twain, William Faulkner, and the First Families of Virginia." *Mark Twain Journal* 13, no. 2 (1966): 1–3, 19.

Howells, William Dean. *My Mark Twain: Reminiscences and Criticisms.* Ed. Marilyn Austin Baldwin. Baton Rouge: Louisiana State Univ. Press, 1967.

Hughson, Lois. *From Biography to History: The Historical Imagination and American Fiction, 1880–1940.* Charlottesville: Univ. Press of Virginia, 1988.

Huizinga, Johan. *The Waning of the Middle Ages: A Study of the Forms of Life, Thought, and Art in France and the Netherlands in the Fourteenth and Fifteenth Centuries.* Trans. F. Hopman. Harmondsworth, England: Penguin, 1955.

Jaeger, C. Stephen. *The Origins of Courtliness: Civilizing Trends and the Formation of Courtly Ideals, 939–1210.* Philadelphia: Univ. of Pennsylvania Press, 1985.

Jones, Alexander E. "Mark Twain and Sexuality." *PMLA* 71 (1956): 595–616.

Jones, Howard Mumford. *The Age of Energy: Varieties of American Experience, 1865–1915.* New York: Viking, 1971.

Josephs, Allen. "*Toreo:* The Moral Axis of *The Sun Also Rises.*" *Hemingway Review* 6, no. 1 (1986): 88–99.

Kaledin, Eugenia. *The Education of Mrs. Henry Adams.* Philadelphia: Temple Univ. Press, 1981.

Kaplan, Justin. *Mr. Clemens and Mark Twain, a Biography.* New York: Simon and Schuster, 1966.

Keen, Maurice. *Chivalry*. New Haven: Yale Univ. Press, 1984.

Kegel, Paul L. "Henry Adams and Mark Twain: Two Views of Medievalism." *Mark Twain Journal* 15, no. 3 (1970): 11–21.

Kelly, Henry Ansgar. "Gaston Paris's Courteous and Horsely Love." In *The Spirit of the Court*, ed. Glyn S. Burgess and Robert A. Taylor, 217–23.

Kert, Bernice. *The Hemingway Women*. New York: Norton, 1983.

Kinnamon, Keneth. "Hemingway, the *Corrida*, and Spain" (1959). In *Ernest Hemingway: Five Decades of Criticism*, ed. Linda Welshimer Wagner, 57–74.

Kirkby, Joan. "Spengler and Apocalyptic Typology in F. Scott Fitzgerald's *Tender Is the Night*" (1979). In *F. Scott Fitzgerald: Critical Assessments*, ed. Henry Claridge, 3:153–69. East Sussex, England: Helm Information, 1991.

Kordecki, Lesley C. "Twain's Critique of Malory's Romance: *Forma tractandi* and *A Connecticut Yankee*." *Nineteenth-Century Literature* 41 (1986): 329–48.

Koretz, Gene H. "Augustine's *Confessions* and *The Education of Henry Adams*" (1960). In *Critical Essays on Henry Adams*, ed. Earl N. Harbert, 63–75.

Kraft, Stephanie. *No Castles on Main Street*. Chicago: Rand McNally, 1979.

Krause, Sydney J. "Twain and Scott: Experience versus Adventures." *Modern Philology* 62 (1965): 227–36.

Krauth, Leland. "Mark Twain Fights Sam Clemens' Duel" (1980). In *Critical Essays on Mark Twain, 1910–1980*, ed. Louis J. Budd, 225–35. Boston: G. K. Hall, 1983.

Kronick, Joseph G. "The Limits of Contradiction: Irony and History in Hegel and Henry Adams." *CLIO* 15 (1986): 391–410.

Kuehl, John. "Scott Fitzgerald: Romantic and Realist." *Texas Studies in Literature and Language* 1 (1959): 412–26.

———, ed. *The Apprentice Fiction of F. Scott Fitzgerald*. New Brunswick, N.J.: Rutgers Univ. Press, 1965.

Langman, F. H. "Style and Shape in *The Great Gatsby*." In *Critical Essays on F. Scott Fitzgerald's "The Great Gatsby*," ed. Scott Donaldson, 31–53.

Lauber, John. *The Inventions of Mark Twain*. New York: Hill and Wang, 1990.

———. *The Making of Mark Twain: A Biography*. New York: American Heritage, 1985.

Lauter, Paul. "Plato's Stepchildren, Gatsby and Cohn." *Modern Fiction Studies* 9 (1963–64): 338–46.

Lears, T. J. Jackson. *No Place of Grace: Antimodernism and the Transformation of American Culture, 1880–1920*. New York: Pantheon, 1981.

Lee, A. Robert. " 'Everything Completely Knit Up': Seeing *For Whom the Bell Tolls* Whole." In his *Ernest Hemingway: New Critical Essays*, 79–102.

———. "F. Scott Fitzgerald and Romantic Destiny." *Twentieth Century Literature* 26 (1980): 137–56.

———, ed. *Ernest Hemingway: New Critical Essays*. London: Vision, 1983.

———, ed. *Scott Fitzgerald: The Promises of Life*. London: Vision, 1989.

Lehan, Richard D. *F. Scott Fitzgerald and the Craft of Fiction*. Carbondale: Southern Illinois Univ. Press, 1966.

Le Vot, André. *F. Scott Fitzgerald: A Biography*. Trans. William Byron. Garden City, N.Y: Doubleday, 1983. Originally published as *Scott Fitzgerald* (Paris: Julliard, 1979).

Lewis, C. S. *The Allegory of Love*. London: Oxford Univ. Press, 1936.

Lewis, Janet. "Fitzgerald's 'Philippe, Count of Darkness.' " In *Fitzgerald / Hemingway Annual, 1975*, ed. Matthew J. Bruccoli, 7–32.

Lewis, Robert W. *Hemingway on Love*. Austin: Univ. of Texas Press, 1965.

———. " 'Long Time Ago Good, Now No Good': Hemingway's Indian Stories." In *New Critical Approaches to the Short Stories of Ernest Hemingway*, ed. Jackson J. Benson, 200–212.

Light, Martin. "Sweeping out Chivalric Silliness: The Example of *Huck Finn* and *The Sun Also Rises*." *Mark Twain Journal* 17, no. 3 (1974): 18–21.

Lowell, James Russell. *The Poetical Works of James Russell Lowell*. Vol 5. Boston: Houghton Mifflin, 1904.

Lowrey, Robert E. "The Grangerford-Shepherdson Episode: Another of Mark Twain's Indictments of the Damned Human Race." *Mark Twain Journal* 15, no. 1 (1970): 19–20.

Lucas, John. "In Praise of Scott Fitzgerald." *Critical Quarterly* 5 (1963): 132–47.

Lynn, Kenneth S. *Hemingway*. New York: Simon and Schuster, 1987.

Lyon, Melvin. *Symbol and Idea in Henry Adams*. Lincoln: Univ. of Nebraska Press, 1970.

Maine, Barry. "*The Education of Henry Adams*: 'Music for Ourselves Alone.' " *New England Quarterly* 61 (1988): 325–40.

Mandel, Jerome. "The Grotesque Rose: Medieval Romance and *The Great Gatsby*." *Modern Fiction Studies* 34 (1988): 541–58.

Marotti, Maria Ornella. *The Duplicating Imagination: Twain and the Twain Papers*. University Park: Pennsylvania State Univ. Press, 1990.

Marshall, W. Gerald. "Twain's 'A Curious Dream' and *The Inferno*." *Mark Twain Journal* 21, no. 3 (1983): 41–43.

Martin, John S. "Henry Adams on War: The Transformation of History into Metaphor." *Arizona Quarterly* 24 (1968): 325–41.

Martin, Ronald E. *American Literature and the Universe of Force*. Durham, N.C.: Duke Univ. Press, 1981.

McCay, Mary A. "Fitzgerald's Women: Beyond Winter Dreams." In *American*

Novelists Revisited: Essays in Feminist Criticism, ed. Fritz Fleischmann, 311–24. Boston: G. K. Hall, 1982.

McNeely, Trevor. "War Zone Revisited: Hemingway's Aesthetics and *A Farewell to Arms*." *South Dakota Review* 22, no. 4 (1984): 14–38.

Mellow, James R. *Hemingway: A Life Without Consequences*. Boston: Houghton Mifflin, 1992.

Merritt, Chris. "'The Greatest Spectacle': Processions in the Works of Mark Twain." *American Literary Realism, 1870–1910* 17 (1984): 180–92.

Meyers, Jeffrey. *Hemingway: A Biography*. New York: Harper and Row, 1985.

Milford, Nancy. *Zelda*. New York: Avon, 1970.

Mizener, Arthur. *The Far Side of Paradise, a Biography of F. Scott Fitzgerald*. Boston: Houghton Mifflin, 1949.

———. "*The Sun Also Rises*." In his *Twelve Great American Novels*, 120–41. New York: World, 1969.

Monteiro, George. "'The Education of Ernest Hemingway'" (1974). In *Critical Essays on Henry Adams*, ed. Earl N. Harbert, 211–19.

———. "Hemingway's Colonel." *Hemingway Review* 5, no. 1 (1985): 40–45.

Moreland, Kim. "Courtly Love in America: Ernest Hemingway and F. Scott Fitzgerald Present the Lady and the Vamp." In *Selected Papers on Medievalism*, ed. Janet E. Goebel and Rebecca Cochran, 2:19–32. Indiana: Indiana Univ. of Pennsylvania Press, 1988.

———. "The Education of Scott Fitzgerald: Lessons in the Theory of History." *Southern Humanities Review* 19 (1985): 25–38.

———. "Hemingway's Medievalist Impulse: Its Effect on the Presentation of Women and War in *The Sun Also Rises*." *Hemingway Review* 6, no. 1 (1986): 30–41.

———. "Henry Adams, the Medieval Lady, and the 'New Woman.'" *CLIO* 18 (1989): 291–305.

———. "The Photo Killeth: Henry Adams on Photography and Painting." *Papers on Language and Literature* 27 (1991): 356–70.

———. "Plumbing the Iceberg: A Review Essay on Recent Hemingway Biographies." *Southern Humanities Review* 23 (1989): 145–64.

———. Review of *America and the Patterns of Chivalry*, by John Fraser. *Southern Humanities Review* 18 (1984): 374–76.

Morgan, Elizabeth. "Gatsby in the Garden: Courtly Love and Irony." *College Literature* 11 (1984): 163–77.

Morris, Wright. *The Territory Ahead*. New York: Harcourt, Brace, 1957.

Morsberger, Robert E. "The Romantic Ancestry of *The Great Gatsby*." In *Fitzgerald / Hemingway Annual, 1973*, ed. Matthew J. Bruccoli, 119–30.

Moyer, Kermit W. "Fitzgerald's Two Unfinished Novels: The Count and the Tycoon in Spenglerian Perspective." *Contemporary Literature* 15 (1974): 238–56.

Munford, Howard M. "Henry Adams: The Limitations of Science" (1968). In *Critical Essays on Henry Adams*, ed. Earl N. Harbert, 140–49.

Norton, Charles Eliot. *Letters of Charles Eliot Norton*. Ed. Sara Norton and M. A. DeWolfe Howe. 2 vols. Boston: Houghton Mifflin, 1913.

O'Brien, Patricia. "Michel Foucault's History of Culture." In *The New Cultural History*, ed. Lynn Hunt, 25–46. Berkeley: Univ. of California Press, 1989.

Oldsey, Bernard. *Hemingway's Hidden Craft: The Writing of "A Farewell to Arms."* University Park: Pennsylvania State Univ. Press, 1979.

O'Shaughnessey, Margaret Ellen. "The Middle Ages in the New World: American Views and Transformations of Medieval Art and Literature." Ph.D. diss., Duke University, 1989.

O'Toole, Patricia. *The Five of Hearts: An Intimate Portrait of Henry Adams and His Friends, 1880–1918*. New York: Clarkson Potter, 1990.

Paine, Albert Bigelow. *Mark Twain: A Biography*. New York, 1912.

Parker, David. "Two Versions of the Hero" (1973). In *F. Scott Fitzgerald's "The Great Gatsby,"* ed. Harold Bloom, 29–44.

Parkison, Jami. "A Woman's Mark Twain." *Mark Twain Journal* 21, no. 4 (1983): 32–33.

Parrington, Vernon L. *The Romantic Revolution in America, 1800–1860*. Vol. 2 of *Main Currents in American Thought*. New York: Harcourt Brace Jovanovich, 1927.

Pettit, Arthur G. *Mark Twain and the South*. Lexington: Univ. Press of Kentucky, 1974.

Piper, Henry Dan. *F. Scott Fitzgerald: A Critical Portrait*. New York: Holt, Rinehart and Winston, 1965.

Pitcher. E. W. "*Tender Is the Night*: Ordered Disorder in the 'Broken Universe.'" *Modern Language Studies* 11, no. 3 (1981): 72–89.

Pullin, Faith. "Hemingway and the Secret Language of Hate." In *Ernest Hemingway: New Critical Essays*, ed. A. Robert Lee, 172–92.

Reynolds, Michael S. *Hemingway: The American Homecoming*. Oxford: Blackwell, 1992.

———. *Hemingway: The Paris Years*. Oxford: Blackwell, 1989.

———. *Hemingway's First War: The Making of "A Farewell to Arms."* Princeton: Princeton Univ. Press, 1976.

———. *Hemingway's Reading, 1910–1940: An Inventory*. Princeton: Princeton Univ. Press, 1981.

———. *The Young Hemingway*. Oxford: Blackwell, 1986.

Robertson, D. W. *A Preface to Chaucer: Studies in Medieval Perspective*. Princeton: Princeton Univ. Press, 1963.

Rosenthal, Bernard, and Paul E. Szarmach, eds. *Medievalism in American Culture*. Binghamton: State Univ. of New York Press, 1989.

Ross, Steven. *From Flintlock to Rifle: Infantry Tactics, 1740–1866*. London: Associated Univ. Presses, 1979.

Rougemont, Denis de. *Love in the Western World*. Trans. Montgomery Belgion. Rev. ed. with preface and postscript. Princeton: Princeton Univ. Press, 1983. Reprint, New York: Schocken, 1983.

Rowe, John Carlos. *Henry Adams and Henry James: The Emergence of a Modern Consciousness*. Ithaca: Cornell Univ. Press, 1976.

Salomon, Roger B. *Twain and the Image of History*. New Haven: Yale Univ. Press, 1961.

Salpeter, Harry. "The Next Fifteen Years Will Show How Much Resistance There Is in the American Race" (originally published as "Fitzgerald, Spenglerian"). In *F. Scott Fitzgerald in His Own Time: A Miscellany*, ed. Matthew J. Bruccoli and Jackson R. Bryer, 274–77.

Samuels, Ernest. *Henry Adams: The Major Phase*. Cambridge: Harvard Univ. Press, 1964.

———. *Henry Adams: The Middle Years*. Cambridge: Harvard Univ. Press, 1958.

Saveth, Edward N. "The Heroines of Henry Adams." *American Quarterly* 8 (1956): 231–42.

Scaglione, Aldo. *Knights at Court: Courtliness, Chivalry, and Courtesy from Ottonian Germany to the Italian Renaissance*. Berkeley: Univ. of California Press, 1991.

Schinto, Jeanne M. "The Autobiographies of Mark Twain and Henry Adams: Life Studies in Despair." *Mark Twain Journal* 17, no. 4 (1975): 5–7.

Schleiner, Louise. "Romance Motifs in Three Novels of Mark Twain." *Comparative Literature Studies* 13 (1976): 330–47.

Scholes, Robert. "Decoding Papa: 'A Very Short Story' as Work and Text" (1982). In *New Critical Approaches to the Short Stories of Ernest Hemingway*, ed. Jackson J. Benson, 33–47.

Seldes, Gilbert. "*The Beautiful and Damned*: This Side of Innocence." Review of *The Beautiful and Damned*, by F. Scott Fitzgerald. In *F. Scott Fitzgerald in His Own Time: A Miscellany*, ed. Matthew J. Bruccoli and Jackson R. Bryer, 329–31.

Sklar, Robert. *F. Scott Fitzgerald: The Last Laocoön*. New York: Oxford Univ. Press, 1967.

Smith, Frederick James. "'I'm Sick of the Sexless Animals Writers Have Been Giving Us'" (originally published as "Fitzgerald, Flappers and Fame"). In *F. Scott Fitzgerald in His Own Time: A Miscellany*, ed. Matthew J. Bruccoli and Jackson R. Bryer, 243–45.

Smith, Henry Nash. *Mark Twain's Fable of Progress: Political and Economic Ideas in "Connecticut Yankee."* New Brunswick, N.J.: Rutgers Univ. Press, 1964.

————. "A Sound Heart and a Deformed Conscience." In *Mark Twain: A Collection of Critical Essays*, ed. Henry Nash Smith, 83–100.

————, ed. *Mark Twain: A Collection of Critical Essays*. Englewood Cliffs, N.J.: Prentice-Hall, 1963.

Smith, Paul. "The Trying-out of *A Farewell to Arms*." In *New Essays on "A Farewell to Arms,"* ed. Scott Donaldson, 27–52.

Smith, Scottie Fitzgerald. "The Colonial Ancestors of Francis Scott Key Fitzgerald." In *Some Sort of Epic Grandeur: The Life of F. Scott Fitzgerald*, by Matthew J. Bruccoli, 496–509. New York: Harcourt Brace Jovanovich, 1981.

Solotaroff, Robert. "Sexual Identity in *A Farewell to Arms*." *Hemingway Review* 9, no. 1 (1989): 2–17.

Sommer, Robert F. "The Feminine Perspectives of Henry Adams' *Esther*." *Studies in American Fiction* 18 (1990): 131–44.

————. "*Mont-Saint-Michel and Chartres*: Henry Adams's Pilgrimage into History." *Centennial Review* 33 (1989): 32–51.

Spanier, Sandra Whipple. "Hemingway's Unknown Soldier: Catherine Barkley, the Critics, and the Great War." In *New Essays on "A Farewell to Arms,"* ed. Scott Donaldson, 75–108.

Spengler, Oswald. *The Decline of the West: Form and Actuality*. Trans. Charles Francis Atkinson. Vol. 1. New York: Knopf, 1926.

Spilka, Mark. "The Death of Love in *The Sun Also Rises*." In *Twelve Original Essays on Great American Novels*, ed. Charles Shapiro, 238–56. Detroit: Wayne State Univ. Press, 1958.

————. *Hemingway's Quarrel with Androgyny*. Lincoln: Univ. of Nebraska Press, 1990.

Stahl, John Daniel. "Mark Twain and Female Power: Public and Private." *Studies in American Fiction* 16 (1988): 51–63.

————. *Mark Twain, Culture and Gender: Envisioning America Through Europe*. Athens: Univ. of Georgia Press, 1994.

Steinbeck, John. *The Acts of King Arthur and His Noble Knights*. New York: Avenel, 1976.

————. *Travels with Charley in Search of America*. Harmondsworth, England: Penguin, 1980.

Stephens, Robert O. "Hemingway's Don Quixote in Pamplona." *College English* 23 (1961): 216–18.

————. *Hemingway's Nonfiction: The Public Voice*. Chapel Hill: Univ. of North Carolina Press, 1968.

Stern, Milton R. *The Golden Moment: The Novels of F. Scott Fitzgerald*. Urbana: Univ. of Illinois Press, 1970.

Stevenson, Elizabeth, ed. *A Henry Adams Reader*, by Henry Adams. Gloucester, Mass.: Peter Smith, 1968.

Stoneback, H. R. "From the rue Saint-Jacques to the Pass of Roland to the 'Unfinished Church on the Edge of the Cliff.' " *Hemingway Review* 6, no. 1 (1986): 2–29.

———. "Hemingway and Faulkner on the Road to Roncevaux." In *Hemingway: A Revaluation*, ed. Donald R. Noble, 135–63. Troy, N.Y.: Whitston, 1983.

———. " 'Lovers' Sonnets Turn'd to Holy Psalms': The Soul's Song of Providence, the Scandal of Suffering, and Love in *A Farewell to Arms*." *Hemingway Review* 9, no. 1 (1989): 33–76.

Sylvester, Bickford. "Hemingway's Extended Vision: *The Old Man and the Sea*." *PMLA* 81 (1966): 130–38.

———. "Hemingway's Italian *Waste Land*: The Complex Unity of 'Out of-Season.' " In *Hemingway's Neglected Short Fiction: New Perspectives*, ed. Susan F. Beegel, 75–98. Ann Arbor, Mich.: UMI Research Press, 1987.

Tanner, Tony. "The Lost America—the Despair of Henry Adams and Mark Twain" (1961). In *Mark Twain: A Collection of Critical Essays*, ed. Henry Nash Smith, 159–74.

Topsfield, L. T. *Troubadours and Love*. Cambridge: Cambridge Univ. Press, 1975.

Turner, Arlin. *Mark Twain and George W. Cable: The Record of a Literary Friendship*. East Lansing: Michigan State Univ. Press, 1960.

Tuttleton, James W. "Vitality and Vampirism in *Tender Is the Night*." In *Critical Essays on F. Scott Fitzgerald's "Tender Is the Night*, " ed. Milton R. Stern, 238–46. Boston: G. K. Hall, 1986.

Twain, Mark. *Adventures of Huckleberry Finn*. Ed. Henry Nash Smith. Boston: Houghton Mifflin, 1958.

———. *The Adventures of Tom Sawyer*. New York: Bantam, 1981.

———. *The Autobiography of Mark Twain*. Ed. Charles Neider. New York: Harper and Row, 1959.

———. *A Connecticut Yankee at King Arthur's Court*. London: Penguin, 1986.

———. *The Innocents Abroad*. Hartford: American, 1895.

———. *Life on the Mississippi*. New York: New American Library, 1961.

———. *The Love Letters of Mark Twain*. Ed. Dixon Wecter. Westport, Conn.: Greenwood Press, 1976.

———. *Mark Twain, Business Man*. Ed. Samuel Charles Webster. Boston: Little, Brown, 1946.

———. *Mark Twain in Eruption: Hitherto Unpublished Pages about Men and Events by Mark Twain*. Ed. Bernard De Voto. New York: Harper, 1940.

———. *Mark Twain to Mrs. Fairbanks*. Ed. Dixon Wecter. San Marino, Calif.: Huntington Library Publications, 1949.

———. *Mark Twain's Aquarium: The Samuel Clemens–Angelfish Correspondence, 1905–1910*. Ed. John Cooley. Athens: Univ. of Georgia Press, 1991.

————. *Mark Twain's Letters.* Ed. Albert Bigelow Paine. 2 vols. New York: Harper, 1917.

————. *Mark Twain's Letters to His Publishers, 1867–1894.* Ed. Hamlin Hill. Berkeley: Univ. of California Press, 1967.

————. *Mark Twain's Letters to Will Bowen.* Ed. Theodore Hornberger. Austin: Univ. of Texas Press, 1941.

————. *Mark Twain's Notebook.* Ed. Albert Bigelow Paine. New York: Harper, 1935.

————. *Mark Twain's Speeches.* New York: Harper, 1923.

————. "The Mysterious Stranger." In *The Complete Short Stories of Mark Twain,* ed. Charles Neider, 602–79. New York: Doubleday, 1957.

————. *Personal Recollections of Joan of Arc by The Sieur Louis de Conte.* 2 vols. New York: Harper, 1896.

————. "Plymouth Rock and the Pilgrims." In *Mark Twain and the Three R's: Race, Religion, Revolution and Related Matters,* ed. Maxwell Geismar, 110–14.

————. *The Prince and the Pauper.* New York: Penguin, 1980.

————. *Selected Mark Twain–Howells Letters, 1872–1910.* Ed. Frederick Anderson, William M. Gibson, and Henry Nash Smith. New York: Atheneum, 1968.

————. *The Tragedy of Pudd'nhead Wilson.* New York: Penguin, 1964.

————. *A Tramp Abroad.* New York: Heritage Press, 1966.

————. "The United States of Lyncherdom." In *Mark Twain and the Three R's: Race, Religion, Revolution and Related Matters,* ed. Maxwell Geismar, 33–40.

————. *"What Is Man?" and Other Essays.* New York: Harper, 1917.

Vanderbilt, Kermit. *Charles Eliot Norton.* Cambridge: Harvard Univ. Press, 1959.

Verduin, Kathleen. "Hemingway's Dante: A Note on *Across the River and into the Trees." American Literature* 57 (1985): 633–40.

————. "Medievalism and the Mind of Emerson." In *Medievalism in American Culture,* ed. Bernard Rosenthal and Paul E. Szarmach, 129–50.

Villard, Henry Serrano, and James Nagel. *Hemingway in Love and War: The Lost Diary of Agnes von Kurowsky, Her Letters, and Correspondence of Ernest Hemingway.* Boston: Northeastern Univ. Press, 1989.

Wagner, Linda Welshimer, ed. *Ernest Hemingway: Five Decades of Criticism.* East Lansing: Michigan State Univ. Press, 1974.

Wagner-Martin, Linda W. "Hemingway's Search for Heroes, Once Again." *Arizona Quarterly* 44 (1988): 58–68.

Walker, Nancy. "Reformers and Young Maidens: Women and Virtue" (1985). In *Modern Critical Interpretations: Mark Twain's "Adventures of Huckleberry Finn,"* ed. Harold Bloom, 171–85. New York: Chelsea House, 1986.

Wasserstrom, William. *The Ironies of Progress: Henry Adams and the American Dream.* Carbondale: Southern Illinois Univ. Press, 1984.

Watson, William Braasch. "Hemingway's Spanish Civil War Dispatches." *Hemingway Review* 7, no. 2 (1988): 4–92.

Watt, Ian. *The Rise of the Novel.* Berkeley: Univ. of California Press, 1957.

Way, Brian. "Hemingway the Intellectual: A Version of Modernism." In *Ernest Hemingway: New Critical Essays,* ed. A. Robert Lee, 151–71.

Welsh, Alexander. *Reflections on the Hero as Quixote.* Princeton: Princeton Univ. Press, 1981.

West, James. L. W. III. *The Making of "This Side of Paradise."* Philadelphia: Univ. of Pennsylvania Press, 1983.

Westervelt, Linda A. "Henry Adams and the Education of His Readers." *Southern Humanities Review* 18 (1984): 23–37.

Westoby, Kathryn S. "A New Look at the Role of the Fée in Medieval French Arthurian Romance." In *The Spirit of the Court,* ed. Glyn S. Burgess and Robert A. Taylor, 373–85.

Whitley, John S. "'A Touch of Disaster': Fitzgerald, Spengler and the Decline of the West." In *Scott Fitzgerald: The Promises of Life,* ed. A. Robert Lee, 157–80.

Whitlow, Roger. *Cassandra's Daughters: The Women in Hemingway.* Westport, Conn.: Greenwood Press, 1984.

Wilcox, Earl. "Jake and Bob and Huck and Tom: Hemingway's Use of Huck Finn." In *Fitzgerald / Hemingway Annual, 1971,* ed. Matthew J. Bruccoli, 322–24.

Williams, James D. "Revision and Intention in Mark Twain's *Connecticut Yankee.*" *American Literature* 36 (1964): 288–97.

———. "The Use of History in Mark Twain's *Connecticut Yankee.*" *PMLA* 80 (1965): 102–10.

Wilson, Edmund. "Hemingway: Gauge of Morale." In his *The Wound and the Bow: Seven Studies in Literature,* 214–42. New York: Oxford Univ. Press, 1929.

Wilson, Robert H. "Malory in the *Connecticut Yankee.*" *University of Texas Studies in English* 27 (1948): 185–205.

Winters, Yvor. "Henry Adams, or the Creation of Confusion." In his *The Anatomy of Nonsense.* Norfolk, Conn.: New Directions, 1943.

Wisbey, Herbert A., Jr. "Mark Twain on Petrarch: More Quarry Farm Marginalia." *Mark Twain Journal* 24, no. 1 (1986): 21–23.

Workman, Leslie, ed. "Medievalism in America." *Studies in Medievalism* 1, no. 2 (1982).

Young, Philip. *Ernest Hemingway: A Reconsideration.* Rev. ed. University Park: Pennsylvania State Univ. Press, 1966.

Zlatic, Thomas D. "Language Technologies in *A Connecticut Yankee.*" *Nineteenth Century Literature* 45 (1991): 453–77.

———. "Mark Twain's View of the Universe." *Papers on Language and Literature* 27 (1991): 338–55.

Zwarg, Christina. "Woman as Force in Twain's *Joan of Arc*: The Unwordable Fascination." *Criticism* 27 (1985): 57–72.

Index

"A Way You'll Never Be" (Hemingway), 162, 175

Abelard, Pierre, 36–37, 77, 81, 101, 192. *See also* Héloïse; Scholastic Philosophy

Across the River and into the Trees (Hemingway), 163–64, 174, 177; Colonel Cantwell, 167; —on conscript army, 168; —, on modern warfare, 170, 176; —, identity as modern knight, 174, 177, 197; —, and Countess Renata, 191–94, 195, 197; —, as modern incarnation of Tristan, 194; —, as Dante, 196–97, 229 n. 27; —, as Richard the Lion-Hearted, 197; Jackson, 168, 175; Countess Renata, 177, 190; —, modeled on Adriana Ivancich, 191, 228 n. 25; —, as art object, 194; —, as Beatrice, 196; and courtly love, 190; and lovers as mirror images, 193

Acts of King Arthur and His Noble Knights, The (Steinbeck), 22, 26

Adair, William, 176

Adam de la Halle, 109

Adams, Brooks: *The Law of Civilization and Decay*, 6, 88, 92, 109, 111; influence on Henry Adams, 214 n. 8; fascination with Middle Ages, 215 n. 14

Adams, Charles Francis, 81, 124; minister to England, 82

Adams, Charles Francis, Jr., 89; in *Last Tycoon*, 124

Adams, Henry, character in *What Is Man?* 77

Adams, Henry, character in "The Doctor and the Doctor's Wife," 161

Adams, Henry, 6, 25, 26, 27, 76, 125, 131, 178; and New England Puritan families, 11; and medievalist impulse, 77–117; and dynamo as symbol of modern age, 76, 87–88; and Virgin, 76, 102–9, 111–12, 117, 144, 183, 217 n. 23; as model for "Henry Adams" in *What Is Man?* 77; and courtly love, 77; view of nineteenth century and Middle Ages compared with Twain's, 77–79; and medieval Virgin as sexual-maternal dynamo, 77, 78, 79, 216 n. 21; his dynamic theory of history, 78, 88–89, 92, 94, 214 n. 9, 215 n. 13; and triangulation, 78, 79, 117; and Immaculate Conception, 79; allegiance to eighteenth century, 80–81, 116; and Twain, 81, 83, 85, 87, 88, 98, 101, 102, 104; and political life, 81–85, 213 n. 3; and immigrants, 82; and U. S. Grant, 82, 83, 84, 85, 86, 122, 145–46; and Civil War, 82–83, 213 n. 4; and Darwin's theory of evolution, 83, 84, 86–87, 213 n. 7; and American democracy, 85–86, 122; and Lyell, 86–87; and modern science, 86, 87, 90, 93–94; and problem of origins, 88; and railroad as symbol of industrial age, 89–90; and Elizabeth Cameron, 89, 102, 106, 108–10, 116, 119, 214 n. 8, 217 n. 23; and atom-Adam-Adams conflation, 90, 214 n. 10; and atomic

Adams, Henry (*cont.*)
  age, 90–91; on Roman Empire and
    American society, 91–92; and wife's sui-
    cide, 93, 99–100, 122, 144, 214 n. 11,
    215 n. 15, 217 n. 23, 218 n. 29; on chaos and
    order, 94, 215 n. 12; and French medieval
    culture, 95–96; experiences of medieval-
    ism and attachment to Middle Ages, 96–
    98; influenced by Sir Walter Scott, 96–
    97, 172, 215 n. 13; and industrial England,
    97; and career at Harvard, 98–99; and
    sister's death, 99–100, 214 n. 11, 215 n. 15;
    and study of Middle Ages, 99, 100–101;
    and construction of medieval unity, 101–
    2; and anti-Semitism, 102, 216 n. 17; and
    pilgrimage, 103; association of childhood
    with Middle Ages, 104–5; and Middle
    Ages as escape from modern horrors,
    105; on eternal-archaic woman as ideal,
    106–8, 110, 115–16, 217 n. 19, 217 n. 23; on
    medieval culture and feminine power,
    107–8; and courtly love, 107–10; his
    feminism, 110; criticism of New Woman,
    111–13, 115–16, 120, 218 n. 26; friend of Fa-
    ther Fay, 118–19; as model for Thornton
    Hancock in *This Side of Paradise*, 119–21;
    influence on Fitzgerald, 119–25, 132, 133,
    141, 143, 223 n. 25; as model for Anthony
    Patch and Maury Noble in *The Beautiful
    and Damned*, 121–24; and Shane Leslie,
    126; theory of history contrasted with
    Spengler's, 127; and bankruptcy, 144; on
    the rose and the feminine ideal, 144,
    223 n. 22; as model for "Henry Adams"
    in "The Doctor and the Doctor's Wife,"
    161; and Hemingway, 161–63, 172–74, 178,
    181, 188, 199, 200; influenced by Words-
    worth, 214 n. 11
Adams, John, 80, 216 n. 18; *Novanglus and
    Massachusettensis*, 81
Adams, John Quincy, 80
Adams, Louisa. *See* Kuhn, Louisa Adams
Adams, Marian ("Clover") Hooper, 99, 114,
    115, 116; suicide, 99–100, 215 n. 15,
    217 n. 23, 218 n. 29; as contemporary
    model of medieval ideal, 108–9, 110;
    compared to Blanche of Castile and Vir-
    gin as empress, 109; as New Woman, 113;
    as photographer, 115, 219 n. 30
Adventures of Huckleberry Finn (Twain), 50,
    51, 61, 64, 65, 66, 73, 212 n. 37; Huck Finn,
    33, 45, 51, 61, 72, 184; —, refusal to play
    Don Quixote, 66; Colonel Grangerford,
    44, 45, 64; Colonel Sherburn, 44, 51, 64;
    Boggs, 44, 51; feuds, 44–45; Duke and
    Dauphin, 51; Jim, 61, 68; child as pro-

tagonist, 65; child as knight, 66–68, 73;
    slave as child, 68; slave as knight, 68; Tom
    Sawyer, 73; —, as courtly knight, 66–67,
    184; —, courtship of Becky, 67–68; im-
    pact on Hemingway, 162. See also *Adven-
    tures of Tom Sawyer, The*
Adventures of Tom Sawyer, The (Twain), 43,
    65, 66, 67, 70, 73; Becky Thatcher, 66;
    Huck Finn, 66; Tom Sawyer, 66, 67; —,
    courtship of Becky, 67; child as knight,
    67–68, 73; child as slave, 68. See also *Ad-
    ventures of Huckleberry Finn*
Aestheticism, 198–99, 219 n. 30, 230 n. 31
Africa, 181, 183; dream of, 182; compared to
    Cuba and Spain, 182
Agincourt, Battle of, 176
Albigensian heresy, 16, 136, 138–39, 205 n. 10,
    220 n. 14
Alcoholism, 83, 131, 156
Aldrich, Elizabeth Kaspar, 156; and female
    absence, 224 n. 31
Alger, Horatio, 160
America, mid-nineteenth-century transfor-
    mations, 1–27
American Claimant, The (Twain), 52; Beriah
    Sellers, modeled on Jesse Madison Leath-
    ers, 209 n. 17
Anderson, Charles, 92, 101
Androgyny: in Adams, 108; in Fitzgerald and
    Hemingway, 193–94
Angel in the House, 31, 33, 77, 79, 206 n. 2
Anglade, Joseph, 20
Anspacher, Louis K.: *Tristan and Isolde*, 21
Anthony, Susan B., 218 n. 25
Antimodernism, 7–8, 203 n. 4
Antiromanticism, 162, 212 n. 36
Anti-Semitism: and Adams, 102, 216 n. 17
Aronowitz, Alfred, 229 n. 28
Aroux, Eugène, 16
Arques, Battle of, 171
Arthur, King, 12, 34, 39; in Steinbeck, 22–23;
    in Twain, 61–64, 141; in Fitzgerald, 144.
    See also Arthurian England; Arthurian
    legends; Camelot; Guinevere; Knights,
    medieval; Launcelot
Arthurian England, 31, 32, 43
Arthurian legends, 4, 5, 60. *See also* Arthur,
    King; Camelot
Arts and Crafts movement, 3, 203 n. 4,
    204 n. 7
Atlantic Monthly, 4, 55
Atomic power, 90, 167
Audhuy, Letha, 220 n. 9
Auerbach, Erich, 15; and courtly love, 17, 20,
    143; and knightly *avantures*, 74, 179–80,
    197

Autobiography of Mark Twain, The, 31, 32, 34, 71, 86; and slavery, 29, 35, 70, 207 n. 6

Baetzhold, Howard, 209 n. 18
Baird, Helen, 24
Baker, Carlos, 163, 181, 191–92; on Hemingway as knight, 173, 198, 229 n. 28
Balassi, William, 228 n. 22
Ball, Charles, 44; influence of his *Fifty Years in Chains* on Twain, 207 n. 9. *See also* Slavery
Bankruptcy: and Twain, 46, 208 n. 12; and Fitzgerald, 120, 144; and Adams, 144; and Grant, 208 n. 12; and Scott, 208 n. 12
Barlowe-Kayes, Jamie, 191, 195
Barnard, Edward W.: "Ballade of Chivalry," 21
Barthes, Roland, 209 n. 15
Bassett, John, 67
Baxter, Lucy, 84, 106, 113
Beard, Daniel, 49, 60
Beatrice. *See* Dante
Beautiful and Damned, The (Fitzgerald), 121–23, 124, 125, 129; Adam Patch, 121–22; Anthony Patch, 121, 145, 147, 148; —, based on Henry Adams, 121–23; —, military training, 130; —, inhibited knightly qualities, 145; —, tender is the knight, 148; dedicated to Shane Leslie, 125; Gloria Patch, 130, 144, 145, 147, 155, 156; —, as dream girl, 155; and Fitzgerald marriage, 149; and Chevalier O'Keefe allegory, 150; and female sexuality, 155
Begley, Neal, 220 n. 13
Bell, Millicent, 108, 195
Berenson, Bernard, 172, 198
Berkove, Lawrence, 46, 208 n. 11, 210 n. 25
Beversluis, John: on Catherine Barkley, 229 n. 29
Bewley, Marius: on Daisy Buchanan, 223 n. 23
"Big Two-Hearted River" (Hemingway), 162
Bishop, Ferman, 83, 215 n. 12, 215 n. 13
Blaine, James G., 84, 85; as model for Ratcliffe, 84
Blanche of Castile, 108, 109
Block, Jean: Gothic Revival and University of Chicago, 203 n. 1
Blunden, Edmund: *Undertones of War*, 165, 225 n. 4
Boase, Roger, 14–15
Bowen, Will, 65
Boyd, Thomas, 136
Brackenridge, Hugh Henry: *Modern Chivalry*, 21

Breit, Harvey, 176
Brenner, Gerry, 130, 229 n. 27; and Hemingway's aestheticism, 230 n. 31
Brooke, Rupert, 129
Brooks, Van Wyck, 80
Budick, Emily Miller, 222 n. 19; on Jake Barnes and Puritan-Catholic identity, 228 n. 22
Bulfinch, Thomas: as popularizer of Arthurian tales, 5; *The Age of Chivalry*, 5, 20
Bullfight, 181, 186, 227 n. 16; as analogue of medieval tournament, 40, 179; and tragedy, 178–79; bullfighter as chivalric knight, 178–79, 186, 187; Hemingway as bullfighter, 181, 183; and dedication of bulls to Virgin, 183. *See also* Fishing; Hunting; Pamplona
Burlingame, Roger, 143
Byrnes, Joseph, 109, 216 n. 20, 217 n. 22

Cabell, James Branch: *Line of Love*, 21; *Jurgen*, 21; *Chivalry*, 21
Cable, George Washington, 45, 55, 66; *The Cavalier*, 21; introduces Twain to *Morte Darthur*, 57–58
Callahan, John F., 145, 156, 223 n. 28
Calvinism, 41, 208 n. 11
Camelot, 10, 63, 73. *See also* Arthur, King
Cameron, Elizabeth: correspondence with Adams, 89, 102, 106, 119, 214 n. 8; as contemporary model of medieval ideal, 108–9, 110, 116, 217 n. 23; and meeting with Marian Adams before suicide, 217 n. 23
Cameron, Martha, 110, 217 n. 23
Capitalism, laissez-faire: boom-or-bust cycles, 1–2; labor unrest, 1–2, 51–52; exploitation of workers, 3, 50; dangers of, 48–49; methods of, 89. *See also* Mobs; Robber barons; Tramp menace
Caporetto, Battle of, 164, 165, 169; comparison of fictional and historical versions, 226 n. 6
Caritas, 15
Carlyle, Thomas, 6
Carney, Raymond, 213 n. 7, 214 n. 11, 215 n. 12
Carnival: as world's fair, 87, 97; in Adams and Fitzgerald, 128–29
Carpenter, Frederick, 228 n. 24
Carpenter Gothic. *See* Gothic Revival
Carter, Everett, 208 n. 13
Caruthers, William Alexander: *The Cavaliers of Virginia*, 21; *The Knights of the Horse-Shoe*, 21
Catharism. *See* Albigensian heresy
Cathedral, The (Lowell), 6, 11
Cathedral. *See* Gothic architecture

Catholicism, Roman, 10–11, 220 n. 14; and chivalry, 13–14; and courtly love, 37; and Twain, 37, 41–42, 77; and Adams 77, 95–117; and Fitzgerald, 118, 120–21, 123, 125–26, 220 n. 14; and Hemingway, 182, 188, 228 n. 22, 228 n. 24, 230 n. 32

Cavalier: myth of Old South, 5, 203 n. 2; as knightly cowboy, 53

Cervantes, Miguel de, 162, 180, 211 n. 29. See also Don Quixote

Chalfant, Edward, 213 n. 3, 218 n. 24

Chambers, John: influence of Plato on Fitzgerald, 222 n. 20

Chance, Jane, 204 n. 5

Chandler, Alice, 9, 12

Chanler, Margaret, 113

Chanson de Roland, 176, 181; compared to The Sun Also Rises, 226 n. 12

Chartier, Alain, 138

Chaucer, Geoffrey, 98, 198, 209 n. 21, 221 n. 17, 223 n. 22; "General Prologue," 172; "Knight's Tale," 172; Canterbury Tales, 173

Chaytor, H. J., 20

Chivalry, 6, 26, 203 n. 3, 203 n. 4; America's attachment to, 8; and sentimentalism, 10–11, 12, 20–24; defined, 14; courage (prouesse), 14, 171; independence (franchesse), 14, 171; loyalty (loyauté) 14, 171, 182; generosity (largesse), 14; nobility (noblesse), 14, 171; courtesy (courtoisie), 14; and Twain, 39, 42–45, 47–49, 53–75; and Fitzgerald, 132–36; and Hemingway, 163–83; and combat, 166; and modern soldier, 170–75; chivalric and modern war contrasted, 175–80; Roland as archetypal knight, 176; condottieri and rules of chivalry, 176–77, 226 n. 13; bullfighter as knight, 178–79; and modern man, 183–200; gentility (gentilesse), 196, 221 n. 17. See also Auerbach, Erich; Boase, Roger; Courtly love; Fraser, John; Jaeger, C. Stephen; Knights, medieval; Lewis, C. S.; Paris, Gaston; Robertson, D. W.; Rougemont, Denis de; Troubadour; Watt, Ian

Cholakian, Rouben, 18–19, 191; feminist critique of courtly love, 19, 20, 37, 149, 189, 192, 205 n. 12; courtly lady as absence, 154, 156, 190–91; and troubadour lyric, 192; courtly lady as art object, 194

Chrétien de Troyes: Lancelot du Lac, 38

Christianity, 16, 40, 182, 188, 199, 220 n. 14. See also Catholicism, Roman

Circus, 72–73

Civil War, 5, 48, 65, 73; effects of, 1; and slavery, 2, 85–86; and Twain, 29, 40, 44–45;

postbellum period, 30; and southern aristocracy, 44–45; and Adams, 82–83, 84; and Fitzgerald, 119, 122, 146; and Hemingway, 167–68, 174–75, 178, 226 n. 10; elements of medieval and modern warfare, 174–75, 226 n. 5; new methods and technologies, 175, 226 n. 11. See also North, the; South, the

Clemens, Henry, 74, 212 n. 36

Clemens, Jane, 52

Clemens, John Marshall, 52

Clemens, Olivia Langdon, 29, 31, 53, 55, 66, 67, 79

Clemens, Orion, 52, 53

Clemens, Samuel Langhorn. See Twain, Mark

Clemens, Susy, 57, 71

Clinton, President Bill, 10

Cochran, Rebecca, 204 n. 5

Code duello, 44, 148. See also Duel

Colacurcio, Michael, 215 n. 13

Coleridge, Samuel Taylor: "Christabel," 9

Collective memory. See Cultural memory

Collegiate Gothic. See Gothic Revival

Colliers, 157

Collins, Carvel, 24

Colt Arms Factory, 47, 60

Comley, Nancy, 103, 193, 214 n. 11, 216 n. 21; on Adams and women's rights, 111, 218 n. 25, 218 n. 27

Commager, Henry Steele, 93

Condottieri: and rules of chivalry, 176–77; role of, 226 n. 13

Confederacy, 219 n. 1; congress of, 167; and soldiers, 167–68, 175. See also Civil War; South, the

Connecticut Yankee at King Arthur's Court, A (Twain), 31–35, 37–41, 43–51, 56–63, 68, 70–73, 75, 81, 87, 102, 103, 139, 166, 172, 208 n. 13; as celebration of Middle Ages, 29, 31, 32; Hank Morgan, 31–34, 37–41, 43–49, 57, 59–63, 71, 72, 81, 87, 98, 177; ——, as archetypal common man, 31, 32, 33; and Arthurian England, 32, 40, 49; as satire of Middle Ages, 33, 34; Sandy (Alisande la Carteloise) 33, 61; and aristocrat as slaveholder, 34–35; and women, 37–40; Launcelot and Guinevere, 38–39; King Arthur, 39, 61–64; and droit du seigneur, 39, 207 n. 6; and Catholicism, 41; and medievalist South, 43–45; and modern technology, 47–48; and knight-errantry, 49; and western cowboy as knight, 53, 134; and southern slave and medieval slave-freeman, 68; and knight as child, 70–73, 75

Conscription, 167, 168, 175
Conservative Christian anarchy, 95, 121
Contosta, David R., 112
Cooper, Stephen, 212 n. 36
Copeland, Ada, 216 n. 19
Coronation Day pageant, 71–72, 104. *See also* Pageants, medieval
Coulton, George Gordon: *Life in the Middle Ages*, 172
"Count of Darkness, The" (Fitzgerald), 134–35
Courtly ladies, 38–39, 108. *See also* Blanche of Castile; Eleanor of Guienne; Guinevere; Mary of Champagne
Courtly love, 6, 15–24, 26, 205 n. 12, 206 n. 13; and sentimentalism, 10–11, 12; term's origin, 14; theories of origin, 14–15; theories of meaning, 15; critics of, 15; defined, 16; as religious dissent, 16; and Christianity, 16; and Twain, 33–40, 66–68; and Adams, 77, 100, 106–10; and Fitzgerald, 135–60; and Hemingway, 183–200; and love *par amours*, 185; secret societies and courtly orders, 188–89. *See also* Courtly ladies; Troubadours
Courtoisie, 14, 205 n. 11
Cowboy, knightly, 53, 134, 160
Cox, James M., 99–100, 213 n. 1
"Crack-Up, The" (Fitzgerald), 125, 132, 153
Cram, Ralph Adams, 3, 7, 11, 104, 121, 216 n. 18; *The Gothic Quest*, 104. *See also* Davis, Alexander J.; Downing, Andrew Jackson; Gothic Revival
Crusade, 14, 40, 54–55, 56, 105, 173, 178, 220 n. 14. *See also* Pilgrimage; Quest
Cuba, 181, 183, 225 n. 4; compared to Africa, 182
Cultural memory, and medievalism, 4
Cummings, Sherwood, 90, 206 n. 1, 208 n. 11, 210 n. 24, 211 n. 28
Cunliffe, Robert, 100, 112
Curtis, Mary Ann C., 226 n. 12

Dante, 4, 99, 196–97, 210 n. 25, 229 n. 27; *Divine Comedy*, 140; and Beatrice, 144, 196–97
Dark Ages. *See* Middle Ages
Darwin, Charles, 2; theory of evolution and Adams, 83, 84, 213 n. 7; theory of evolution and Twain, 86, 208 n. 11; *Origin of Species*, 86; *Voyage of the "Beagle,"* 86; *The Descent of Man*, 86
Davis, Alexander J., 3. *See also* Cram, Ralph Adams; Downing, Andrew Jackson; Gothic Revival
De Leon, T. C., 5

Death in the Afternoon (Hemingway), 178, 181, 183
Decker, William Merrill: on historiography, 46, 84, 85, 215 n. 15, 216 n. 17; on Adams and woman's role, 111, 218 n. 27
Deism, 87
DeJoinville: *Chronicles of Crusaders*, 172
Democracy (Adams), 84, 85, 111, 113, 114, 116; Senator Ratcliffe, 84, 85; —, modeled on James D. Blaine, 84; Madeleine Lee, 85; —, on Washington, D.C., and Mount Vernon, 85–86; —, as New Woman, 113–16; Carrington, 85, 116; Mrs. Baker, 111; Sybil Ross, 116
Denton, L. W., 39–40
DeWindt, Caroline Smith, 216 n. 18
Dial, The, 123–24
Diggins, John, 88
Diliberto, Gioia, 129, 193, 198
Divine right of kings, 35
"Doctor and the Doctor's Wife, The" (Hemingway), 161
Dodd, William George, 137
"Does a Moment of Revolt Come Some Time to Every Married Man?" (Fitzgerald), 155
Domnei: as flower, 67; as bull's ear, 187
Don Quixote, 23, 66, 173, 180, 184, 211 n. 9
Donaldson, Scott, 149, 159, 219 n. 1, 220 n. 8
Donnoi. See Domnei
Donoghue, Denis, 218 n. 27
Dorman-Smith, Eric, 176
Downing, Andrew Jackson, 3, 6, 43, 216 n. 18. *See also* Cram, Ralph Adams; Davis, Alexander J.; Gothic Revival
Draft. *See* Conscription
Dream, 32, 52, 132; and Arthurian world, 22, 60–61, 63; of courtly lady, 24; of Middle Ages and American Dream, 26, 199–200; and medievalist revival, 42; as germ of Twain's *Connecticut Yankee*, 58, 172; and writing, 58; and enchantment imagery, 59–60, 177; and Mississippi River, 61; and triumph over reality, 63; and Twain's childhood, 74; and nightmare, 90, 130, 155, 157; of order versus chaos of nature in Adams, 94; and Catholicism, 125–26; and ideal contrasted with material and accidental, 138–45; and evil, 150; and mothers and children, 155; and modern girls, 155, 195, 228 n. 25; and movies, 159; of last good countries, 181–82; as escape from history, 208 n. 14, 211 n. 27; and war, 226 n. 14. *See also* Dream vision
Dream vision: in Faulkner, 24; in Twain, 59–63, 210 n. 25; in Hemingway, 229 n. 27

Droit du seigneur, 39, 69, 153, 159, 207 n. 6
Duel: in Twain, 40, 42, 44, 64–65, 69,
    207 n. 10; in Fitzgerald, 146, 148, 153, 159;
    in Hemingway, 177, 229 n. 28. *See also*
    Code Duello; Feud
Dusinberre, William, 110
Dynamo: as symbol of age of technology, 30,
    87; and Twain, 48, 76, 87; and Adams,
    76–79, 87–88, 92, 94, 102, 117; as mascu-
    line principle, 79; and Fitzgerald, 120, 123;
    and Hemingway, 182. *See also* Electricity;
    Niagara Falls

"Early Success" (Fitzgerald), 119
Eble, Kenneth, 219 n. 6
"Echoes of the Jazz Age" (Fitzgerald), 128,
    130, 151, 220 n. 10
Education of Henry Adams, The, 78, 80–89,
    94, 98–101, 114, 174; and Fitzgerald, 119–
    26, 138, 144; and Hemingway, 182
Edwards, Owen, 126
Eleanor of Guienne (or Aquitaine), 108
Electricity: and Twain, 48, 74, 75, 76; and Ad-
    ams, 79–80, 87–88, 89, 115. *See also* Dy-
    namo; Niagara Falls
Eliot, Charles William, 98
Eliot, T. S.: *The Waste Land,* 130, 181, 182; in-
    fluence on Fitzgerald, 220 n. 9
Ellis, John: machine gun and modern war,
    226 n. 5
Emerson, Everett, 206 n. 3, 212 n. 33
Esquire Magazine, 166
Essays on Anglo-Saxon Law (Adams), 99
Esther (Adams), 83, 87, 112, 114, 115, 116, 154;
    Stephen Hazard, 83, 114, 116; George
    Strong, 87; —, modeled on Clarence
    King, 115; Wharton, 112, 116; Esther Dud-
    ley, 113–16, 141, 218 n. 28; Catherine
    Brooke, 116, 154
Eternal-archaic woman, 106–8, 115–16,
    217 n. 23; Clarence King's obsession with,
    216 n. 19. *See also* Adams, Henry; *Mem-
    oirs of Marau Taaroa*

Fairbanks, Mary, 31, 54, 58, 62, 206 n. 3
Fairbanks, Mollie, 54, 207 n. 7
Fairey, Wendy, 224 n. 32
Farewell to Arms, A (Hemingway), 163, 164–
    65, 169, 173, 180; Frederic Henry, and
    horrors of war, 163, 165, 169, 170, 174,
    227 n. 15; —, and courtly love, 169–70,
    185, 190, 192; —, and chivalry, 169–70,
    190; Catherine Barkley, 166, 170, 185, 191,
    192, 195, 196, 197, 229 n. 29; —, modeled
    on Agnes von Kurowsky, 190, 228 n. 26;
    Aymo, 170; and Adams, 174, 230 n. 32;

Rinaldi, 190, 196; and lovers as mirror
    images, 193; and androgyny in, 193–94
Fascism, 168, 223 n. 28
"Fathers and Sons" (Hemingway), 161
Faulkner, William, 26; *Mayday,* 23–24, 26;
    Knight's Gambit, 24; *The Sound and the
    Fury,* 24
Fay, Father Cyril Sigourney Webster, 118–19,
    120, 121, 125, 126
Fell, Anne Palmer, 218 n. 26
Feminist critique, and courtly love, 2, 18, 20,
    110, 205 n. 12. *See also* Cholakian,
    Rouben; Ferrante, Joan
Ferrante, Joan, 18; and courtly love, 19, 20,
    169–70, 192, 197; and troubadours, 145;
    and lady as devil, 152; and lady as mirror,
    193–94; and lady as star, 222 n. 18
Fetterley, Judith, 147, 149, 224 n. 29
Feud: and Twain, 44–45, 64. *See also* Code
    duello; Duel
Fiedler, Leslie, 11, 198, 205 n. 12
Fisher King, 181–82
Fishing, 162; big-game, 181–83. *See also* Bull-
    fight; Hunting
Fitzgerald, Edward, 118, 219 n. 1
Fitzgerald, F. Scott, 25, 27, 52, 117; early
    family life and education, 118–19, 120;
    and Mark Twain, 118, 119, 120; influence of
    Henry Adams, 119–25, 133, 219 n. 2; char-
    acters in *The Beautiful and Damned* and
    This Side of Paradise based on Adams,
    119–24; and Middle Ages, 119–20, 122,
    123; military career, 119, 129–30; Jazz Age
    life, 119, 123, 127, 128, 132, 151, 160; and
    Princeton, 119, 120, 121, 122, 125, 127, 129,
    219 n. 3, 221 n. 17; and bankruptcy, 120,
    144; influenced by Keats, 125, 132, 138,
    147, 223 n. 27; and Shane Leslie, 125–26;
    and Spengler's theory of history, 126–27,
    135, 219 n. 5, 219 n. 7; and Zelda, 127, 145,
    146, 149, 150, 160, 222 n. 21; and Zelda's
    mental illness, 127, 130, 149, 156, 220 n. 11;
    and Sheila Graham affair, 127, 159,
    219 n. 6; and view of twentieth-century
    America, 127–32, 134; his marriage, 127,
    145, 146, 149, 152–53, 155–56, 160; and
    Hemingway, 129, 134, 141, 160, 163, 172,
    189, 192, 194, 199, 200, 227 n. 18; and
    mental illness of characters, 130–31; and
    sexuality as casualty of war, 131;
    views of medieval versus modern cul-
    tures, 132–60; and historical research,
    132, 220 n. 12; medieval setting, 132–35;
    figure of knight, 134, 159–60; on courtly
    love, 135–60; and romanticism, 136,

Fitzgerald, F. Scott (*cont.*)
221 n. 15; and connection between modern marriage and war, 146–47, 160; female protagonists and women compared
to courtly ideal, 147–60; belle-vamp binary, 151, 223 n. 27; and modern woman's
sexual freedom, 151–53, 223 n. 27; as failed
knight-errant, 156; as troubadour of Jazz
Age, 160; influenced by Sir Walter Scott,
172; influenced by T. S. Eliot, 220 n. 9;
influenced by English romantic poets,
221 n. 15
Fitzgerald, Scottie. *See* Smith, Scottie
Fitzgerald
Fitzgerald, Zelda, 127, 145, 146, 160, 222 n. 21;
mental illness, 127, 130, 149, 156, 220 n. 11;
as model for Rosalind, Daisy, Jonquil,
and Nicole, 149–53, 155; *Save Me the
Waltz*, 149, 156; —, compared to *Tender
Is the Night*, 224 n. 30
Flaubert, Gustave: *L'Education sentimentale*,
174
Flores, Olga Eugenia, 227 n. 15
For Whom the Bell Tolls (Hemingway), 163,
168, 226 n. 14; and courtly love, 190; lady
as mirror image, 193; androgyny in, 193–
94; chivalric and martial motifs in, 227 n.
15; Pilar, 167, 168; Robert Jordan, 167, 168,
169, 170, 176, 191, 227 n. 15; —, success as
knight, 177–78; Karkov, 168; Maria, 168,
190, 191, 192, 195, 197, 228 n. 24; Duval,
169; Pablo, 170
Foucault, Michel, 88
France, medieval, and Adams, 95–96, 102;
and Fitzgerald, 132
Franchesse, 14, 48, 171
Franco-Prussian War, 98
Fraser, John, 7–8, 171, 203 n. 3, 203 n. 4,
206 n. 13
Fraser, Keath, 156
Freeman, Douglas Southall, 5
Free-Soil Party, 81. *See also* Slavery; Adams,
Charles Francis
Freud, Sigmund, 94, 193
Friedrich, Otto, 116
Froissart, Jean: *Chronicles*, 171
Fryer, Sarah Beebe, 223 n. 23; and compari-
son of *Save Me the Waltz* and *Tender Is
the Night*, 224 n. 30
Fussell, Paul, 165, 167; machine gun and
modern war, 226 n. 5

Gaggin, John, 230 n. 31
Galahad, Sir, 63, 173
Garden of Eden, The (Hemingway), 193; an-
drogyny in, 193–94

Gaskell, Charles Milnes, 98, 105, 113
Gauss, Christian, 219 n. 5
Gellhorn, Martha, as model for Heming-
way's Maria, 191; *A Stricken Field*, 175; as
Queen of Heaven, 198
Genre critique, and courtly love, 15–18. *See
also* Auerbach, Eric; Watt, Ian
Gentilesse, 196, 211 n. 31, 221 n. 17
Giddings, Robert, 223 n. 25
Gilbert, Sandra, 110
Gilded Age, The (Twain and Warner), 43, 48,
52, 54, 74–75, 83, 85, 89, 111; Colonel Ber-
iah Sellers, 52, 85; —, modeled on James
Lampton, 209 n. 17; Senator Dilworthy,
54, 85; Senator Noble, 54; Henry Worley,
74; —, modeled on Twain's brother
Henry, 74; Laura Hawkins, 85, 111; Col-
onel Selby, 85; Philip Sterling, 85; Ruth
Bolton, 85
Gingrich, Arnold, 174
Girouard, Mark, 12, 13, 14, 20; and World
War I, 180
"Gods of Darkness," 134–35, 220 n. 14
Goebel, Janet, 204 n. 5
Gothic architecture, 126; cathedrals, 3, 6, 77,
89, 96, 103–4, 108, 128; Wenlock Abbey,
98; forest as cathedral, 161–62. *See also*
Gothic Revival
Gothic Revival, 3, 7; Princeton University, 7,
121, 219 n. 3; Walpole's Strawberry Hill, 9;
and Twain, 43, 55; and Adams, 77, 89,
108, 112, 216 n. 18; and Fitzgerald, 121;
University of Chicago, 203 n. 1. *See also*
Cram, Ralph Adams; Davis, Alexander J.;
Downing, Andrew Jackson
Gould, Jay, 49, 89, 124. *See also* Robber
barons
Graham, Sheila: affair with Fitzgerald, 127,
159, 219 n. 6; as Katherine Moore, 127; *The
Rest of the Story*, 219 n. 6; *College of One*,
219 n. 6
Grant, President Ulysses S., 54, 55, 82, 83, 86,
122; compared to Adams's Old Granite,
84, 85; compared to Dick Diver, 145–46,
223 n. 25; and bankruptcy, 208 n. 12
Grapes of Wrath, The (Steinbeck), 23
Graves, Robert: *Goodbye to All That*, and
Hemingway, 225 n. 4
Great Depression, 120
Great Exposition of 1900, 87
Great Gatsby, The (Fitzgerald), 97, 126, 130,
136, 147, 149, 152, 156, 157, 199, 200; Jay
Gatsby, 52, 125, 145, 153, 157, 158; —, as
courtly knight 136–47, 184; —, as Great
Gatsby, 141; —, on mythical plane, 141;
—, as James Gatz, 141, 160; —, as mod-

Great Gatsby, The (cont.)
ern knight, 144–45; —, blamed for Myrtle's death, 144, 184; —, as inhibited knight, 149, 150; and Eliot's *Waste Land*, 130; and chivalry, 136, 138; American women compared to courtly ideal, 136–44, 147, 149; Jordan Baker, 137, 141, 191–92; Nick Carraway, 137, 138, 139, 141, 143, 157, 186, 200; Myrtle Wilson, 137; —, affair with Tom Buchanan, 138; —, death, 144; Meyer Wolfsheim, 137; and contrast between ideal and accidental, 138–44, 222 n. 21; as example of courtly literature, 140, 221 n. 17; Dan Cody, 141; Star and director, 141–42; Tom Buchanan, 142, 144, 145, 148; —, affair with Myrtle Wilson, 138; George Wilson, 142; and Fitzgerald marriage, 149; Daisy Buchanan, 152, 153, 156, 187, 223 n. 23; —, as courtly lady, 136–44, 145, 147; —, as transcendent ideal of feminine, 139–43, 222 n. 21; —, as Arthurian "fay," 144; —, as unwilling courtly lady, 149; —, as dream girl, 155; and courtly love in, 221 n. 15
"Great Secession Winter of 1860–61, The" (Adams), 213 n. 4
Greco-Turkish War, 163
Green Hills of Africa (Hemingway), 162, 181–83, 199
Gribben, Alan, 57, 209 n. 19, 209 n. 20
Griffin, Peter, 226 n. 7
Gross, Dalton, 219 n. 5, 220 n. 8
Guerilla Soldiers, 167, 168, 169, 170
Guillaume de Champeaux, 79, 101
Guillaume de Lorris: *Roman de la Rose*, 144, 223 n. 22
Guinevere, 38–39. *See also* Chivalry; Courtly love; Arthur, King; Launcelot
Gunsaulus, Frank Wakely, 7
Guthrie, Laura, 159

Hallam, Arthur, 93
Hamill, Paul, Jr., 87, 102, 229 n. 28
Hammond, L. H.: "Knights Errant," 21
Harkey, Joseph, 211 n. 29
Harper's Monthly, 4
Harris, Joel Chandler, 45
Harris, Susan, 208 n. 14, 211 n. 27
Harrison, Stanley, 65
Hart, Lidell: *Decisive Wars of History*, 172
Harvard University, 98, 122
Hawthorne, Nathaniel, 93
Hay, John: correspondence with Adams, 12, 115; as secretary of state, 91–92
Hegel, G. W. F., 213 n. 2
Héloïse, 36–37, 77, 192; as eternal woman, 78. *See also* Abelard, Pierre

Hemingway, Ernest, 25, 26, 27, 40, 53, 118; and Fitzgerald, 129, 141, 160, 172, 189, 192, 194, 199, 200, 225 n. 4, 227 n. 18; as model for Fitzgerald's Philippe, 134; as Nick Adams's alter-ego, 161–62; forest as cathedral, 161–62; and medievalist impulse, 161–200; World War I, 162, 163, 164, 165, 167, 175, 176, 177, 180, 189, 190, 225 n. 4; physical war wounds, 162, 164, 190; psychological war wounds, 162; iceberg theory of writing, 162; antiromanticism, 162; and Twain, 162–63, 199, 200; and Adams, 162, 163, 172, 173, 174, 178, 181, 188, 199, 200; affection for medieval traditions, 162; medieval chivalry and modern warfare, 163–83; military experiences, 163, 164; Red Cross volunteer, 163, 164; ambivalence toward war, 163, 225 n. 3; World War II, 163, 166, 171, 173; influence of war experience on fiction, 164–80; influence of Blunden, 165, 225 n. 4; Civil War, 167–68, 174–75, 178, 226 n. 10; medieval knights and modern soldier, 170–75; his own chivalric behavior, 171–73, 192, 198; medieval influences, 172; early education and study of the Middle Ages, 172; Chaucer, 172; Sir Walter Scott, 172; marriages, 173, 175, 191, 198, 229–30 n. 30; chivalric influence on sons, 173; chivalry and courtly love in fiction, 173–200; pseudomedieval epigraphs, 175–76; induction in Knights of Malta, 177; bullfighting, tragedy, and modern chivalric knight, 178–79, 181, 186, 187; as modern knight, 180, 191, 229 n. 28; Ernest de la Mancha, 180; hunting, bullfighting, and blood sports, 181, 183; modern and medieval women contrasted, 186–88; secret societies and courtly orders, 188–89; nostalgia for courtly love tradition, 189–200; and modern woman, 189–200; and Agnes von Kurowsky, 190, 191, 192, 228 n. 23, 228 n. 26; and Adriana Ivancich, 191, 192, 228 n. 25; and sexuality of ideal courtly ladies, 192–93; androgyny and mirroring between lovers, 193–94; and sister Marcelline, 193; criticism of ideal female characters, 195–96; search for Queen of Heaven, 198; and Ada MacLeish, 229 n. 28; conversion to Catholicism, 230 n. 32
Hemingway, Grace Hall, 229–30 n. 30
Hemingway, Gregory, 173
Hemingway, Marcelline, 193
Hemingway, Patrick, 173
Henry II of England, 108
Henry IV, 171

Hill, Hamlin, 207 n. 7
Hoffman, Nancy: *Gatsby* and Troilus, 221 n. 17
Holiday, 23
"Homage to the Victorians" (Fitzgerald), 125
Homosexuality, 131, 165; and homoeroticism, 186; Zelda accusing Fitzgerald of, 220 n. 11
Hooker, Bryan: "Ysobel de Corveaux," 21; "Swanhild," 21
Hooper, Ellen, 115
Horne, Bill, 190
Horton, Chase, 22, 23
Hovey, Richard: *The Marriage of Guenevere*, 21
"How Sir Launcelot Slew Two Giants, and Made a Castle Free" (Malory), 60
Howard, Leon, 204 n. 8
Howell, Elmo, 53, 65
Howells, William Dean, 46, 53, 55
Hughson, Lois, 88, 92, 213 n. 1
Huizinga, Johan: *The Waning of the Middle Ages*, 13, 14, 228 n. 21
Hundred Years' War, 40, 163
Hunting, 162; big-game, 181–83. *See also* Bullfight; Fishing

"I Didn't Get Over" (Fitzgerald), 130
Immaculate Conception, 79, 155
Impotence, and war, 146–47, 165–66
In Our Time (Hemingway), 162
"In the Darkest Hour" (Fitzgerald), 132–34
Industrial Revolution, 2, 97
Innocents Abroad, The (Twain), 34, 56, 103, 212 n. 37; on Abelard and Héloïse, 36–37, 39; on Petrarch and Laura, 36–37, 39; and Catholicism, 41; medieval history, literature, and architecture in, 55; and childhood, 66
Inquisition, 41
Iseult. *See* Tristan
Ivancich, Adriana, 192; as model for Countess Renata, 191, 228 n. 25
Ivanhoe (Scott), 9, 42, 56, 172

Jackson, General "Stonewall," 174; dying words, 175. *See also* Civil War
Jaeger, C. Stephen, 14, 205 n. 11
James, Henry, 94, 113
James, William, 94
Japan, 106
Jazz Age, 119, 123, 127, 128, 132, 151, 160
Jean de Meung: *Roman de la Rose*, 144, 223 n. 22
Jeanroy, Alfred, 20, 205 n. 12
Jenkins, Howell, 180
Jones, Alexander, 207 n. 6
Jones, Howard Mumford, 21, 214 n. 9

Josephs, Allen, 227 n. 16, 228 n. 20
Jung, Carl, 130

Kaledin, Eugenia, 111
Kaplan, Justin, 47, 52, 54, 55, 71
Keats, John: "The Eve of St. Agnes," 9, 138; "La Belle Dame Sans Merci," 9, 138, 147; influence on Fitzgerald, 125, 132, 138, 223 n. 27; "Ode to a Nightingale," 138
Keen, Maurice, 12–14, 205 n. 11
Kegel, Paul, 101, 102
Kelly, Henry Ansgar, 205 n. 9
Kennedy, John Pendleton: *Rob of the Bowl*, 21
Kert, Bernice, 173, 229–30 n. 30
King, Clarence: as model for George Strong, 115; attraction to dark-skinned women, 216 n. 19; *Clarence King Memoirs*, 216 n. 19. *See also* Copeland, Ada
"Kingdom in the Dark, The" (Fitzgerald), 134–35
Kinnamon, Keneth, 227 n. 16
Kirkby, Joan, 219 n. 7, 220 n. 8
Knights, medieval, 4, 6, 14, 17–24, 47, 74, 180; in Twain's fiction, 33–44, 49, 60, 172; of Round Table, 40, 72; cowboy as knight, 53, 134, 160; as mythic figures in Twain, 64; female version of, 64; childhood and knighthood, 66–68, 70–71, 75; slave as, 68; and Adams, 110; and Fitzgerald's Philippe, 134, 135; chivalric-courtly and inhibited, in Fitzgerald, 135, 143, 148, 149, 150, 156; C. S. Lewis on, 136; Arthurian, 137; Fitzgerald as failed knight-errant, 156; and Hemingway, 163–200; and modern warfare, 168; cavalryman as, 170–75; and modern soldier, 170–75; Hemingway's own chivalric behavior, 171–73, 192, 198; Roland as archetypal, 176; Hemingway's induction in knightly order, 177; Hemingway characters as, 177; Robert Jordan as, 177; bullfighter as, 178–79; Pedro Romero and knightly service, 179–80, 228 n. 20; Hemingway as, 180, 191; and modern man, 183–200. *See also* Chivalry; Courtly love
Knight's Gambit (Faulkner), 24
Knights of Malta, 177
Knights of the Round Table, 40, 49, 72. *See also* Knights, medieval; Arthur, King; Lanier, Sidney; Launcelot; Malory, Sir Thomas
Kordecki, Lesley, 59, 210 n. 23
Korean War, 163
Koretz, Gene, 87
Krause, Sydney J., 212 n. 37
Krauth, Leland, 207 n. 10

Kronick, Joseph G., 213 n. 2
Ku Klux Klan, Knights of, 216 n. 17
Kuehl, John, 219 n. 1, 221 n. 15
Kuhn, Louisa Adams: effect of suicide on Adams, 93, 99, 100, 122, 144, 214 n. 11, 215 n. 15, 217 n. 23, 218 n. 29
Kurowsky, Agnes von, 192, 228 n. 23; as model for Catherine Barkley, 190–91, 228 n. 26; *The Lost Diary of Agnes von Kurowsky*, 228 n. 23

La Belle Dame Sans Merci: Keats's poem, 9, 138, 147; Nicole, Rosemary, and Gloria as, 147, 223 n. 27
La Farge, John, 3, 100; model for Adams's Wharton, 112
Lancelot du lac (Chrétien de Troyes), 38
Langdon, Olivia. *See* Clemens, Olivia Langdon
Langley, Samuel Pierpont, 90
Langman, F. H., 223 n. 22
Lanham, General Charles, 163, 171, 176
Lanier, Sidney: *The Boy's Froissart*, 4; *The Boy's King Arthur*, 4, 57; *The Boy's Mabinogion*, 57
Largesse, 14
"Last Good Country, The" (Hemingway), 161
Last Tycoon, The (Fitzgerald), 124, 125, 127, 157, 159; Monroe Stahr, 124, 125, 157, 224 n. 32; —, romance with Minna, 157–58; —, romance with Kathleen, 157–58; Kathleen Moore, 127, 157–59; —, modeled on Sheila Graham, 127; Minna Davis, 157–59
Lauber, John, 30, 57, 72, 212 n. 33
Launcelot, 14, 38–39, 60, 63, 184. *See also* Guinevere; Arthur, King
Laura. *See* Petrarch
Lauter, Paul: on Robert Cohn, 227 n. 19
Lears, T. J. Jackson, 7–8, 203 n. 4, 216 n. 16; on Adams's anti-Semitism, 216 n. 17; on Adams's childlessness, 217 n. 23
Leathers, Jesse Madison, 209 n. 17
Lecky, William Hartpole, 33, 81, 172, 206 n. 4, 208 n. 11. *See also* Meliorism
Lee, A. Robert, 195; on *For Whom the Bell Tolls*, 226 n. 14
Lee, General Robert E., 5. *See also* Civil War
Lee, Sir Henry, 173, 174, 226 n. 9
Lehan, Richard, 125, 219 n. 4, 219 n. 5, 220 n. 8
Leslie, Shane, 125; *The Oppidan*, 125; and Adams, 126; *The Celt and the World*, 126
"Letter to American Teachers of History, A" (Adams), 83
Levenson, J. C., 214 n. 8, 214 n. 10, 216 n. 17
Le Vot, André, 136

Lewis, C. S., 15, 20, 37, 41; and courtly love, 16–18, 19, 107, 108, 194–95; and ideal courtly knight, 136, 137, 185; and Neoplatonic ladder of love, 140; and religious and courtly orders, 188
Lewis, Janet, 133, 134, 220 n. 12
Lewis, John, 220 n. 8
Lewis, Robert, 184, 195, 196, 228 n. 21; on Nick Adams and Henry Adams, 225 n. 1; on Hemingway's Maria and Virgin Mary, 228 n. 24
Life of Albert Gallatin, The (Adams), 85
Life on the Mississippi (Twain), 43; postbellum middle class, 30; and Middle Ages, 37; Richard the Lion-Hearted, 39; medievalist revival and Scott, 42; and slavery, 45; criticism of Mardi Gras, 72; steamboat pilot as knight, 73
Light, Martin, 162, 184
Lille, Alain de, 140
Littauer, Kenneth, 156, 159
Lodge, Elizabeth "Bessy" Davis, 217 n. 23. *See also* Lodge, George Cabot "Bay"
Lodge, George Cabot "Bay," 95
Lodge, Mrs. Henry Cabot, 100
Longfellow, Henry Wadsworth, 4
Louis IX, king of France, 78
Love, "fault" of, 38, 183
Love, pure, 185, 186
Love *par amours*, 185, 186
Lowell, James Russell, 4, 11, 99, 204 n. 8; *The Cathedral*, 6, 11; "A Legend of Britanny," 21
Lowrey, Robert, 44
Loyauté, 14, 171, 182
Lyell, Charles, 86–87; *Principles*, 86
Lynn, Kenneth, 161, 162, 193, 225 n. 2
Lyon, Isabel, 55
Lyon, Melvin, 213 n. 6

McCay, Mary A., 149
McKaig, Alexander, 127
MacLeish, Ada, 229 n. 28
McNeely, Trevor, 225 n. 3, 227 n. 15
Madonna, 112, 155; Elizabeth Cameron as, 109–10, 217 n. 23; and Clara Page, 154
Maine, Barry, 94
Major, Charles: *When Knighthood Was in Flower*, 21
Malatesta, Sigismundo, 176
Malory, Sir Thomas: *Morte Darthur*, 22, 23, 57, 58, 60, 66, 68; "How Sir Launcelot Slew Two Giants, and Made a Castle Free," 60. *See also* Arthur, King; Knights, medieval; Knights of the Round Table; Launcelot

Mandel, Jerome, 221 n. 16, 223 n. 22; *Gatsby* as medieval romance, 221 n. 17
Mardi Gras, 72. *See also* Pageants, medieval
Mariolatry, 107, 112, 154, 188, 191; and Hemingway's Maria, 228 n. 24
Marotti, Maria Ornella, 63, 209 n. 15, 210 n. 26
Marshall, W. Gerald, 210 n. 25
Martin, John: on Adams and Civil War, 213 n. 4
Martin, Ronald, 116, 214 n. 8
Mary of Champagne, 108
Marx, Karl, 126, 220 n. 13
Matthews, T. S., 191
Maugham, Henry: *The Husband of Poverty,* 21
Mayday (Faulkner), 23–24, 26
McCall's, 155
"Medieval Romance, A" (Twain), 55
Meliorism, 28–30, 83, 86, 135. *See also* Lecky, William Hartpole
Mellow, James, 173
Melville, Herman, 93, 204 n. 6
Memoirs of Marau Taaroa, Last Queen of Tahiti (Adams), 106
"Mental Telegraphy" (Twain), 53
"Mental Telegraphy Again" (Twain), 53
Mercenaries: Tommy Barban as, 146, 148. *See also* Condottieri
Merritt, Chris, 212 n. 35
Meyer, Dr. Adolf, 220 n. 11
Meyers, Jeffrey, 191, 192, 226 n. 10; on Hemingway and Adriana Ivancich, 228 n. 25
Michigan, 161–62; compared to Spain, Africa, and Cuba, 182–83
Middle Ages, 3; as historic link between America and Europe, 5; as direct contrast to American life, 6, 134; as model, 6–7; as cautionary exemplum, 7; texts set in, 21–22; and Twain, 28–76; Dark Ages, 45, 58, 98, 122, 132–34; and Adams, 77–117; and Fitzgerald, 118–60; High Middle Ages, 132, 137; and Hemingway, 169, 173, 199–200
Miscegenation. *See* Droit du seigneur
Misogyny, 18, 19, 37, 108, 137, 155, 198, 205 n. 12; and revenge, 24, 153, 228 n. 26
Mizener, Arthur, 184; on Robert Cohn and Jake Barnes, 227 n. 19
Mobs, 50, 51, 52, 64, 82. *See also* Capitalism, laissez-faire; Tramp menace
Moffett, Samuel E., 209 n. 16
Monteiro, George, 225 n. 1, 230 n. 31
Mont-Saint-Michel and Chartres (Adams), 7, 20, 78–81, 87, 92, 99, 101–13, 116–17, 126, 138, 173; association of childhood with

Middle Ages, 104–5; and Virgin 106–9; and Marian Adams, 109
Morgan, Elizabeth, 137, 138, 204 n. 5; on *Gatsby* and courtly love, 221 n. 15
Morris, Wright, 200
Morsberger, Robert E., 221 n. 15
Morte Darthur (Malory), 22, 23, 57, 58, 66
Moveable Feast, A (Hemingway), 198
Moyer, Kermit, 126, 128, 133, 219 n. 7, 220 n. 8
Munford, Howard, 91, 95
Munsey's, 4
Murdock, Harry, 149
"Mysterious Stranger, The" (Twain), 40, 43, 48, 50, 51, 56; child as protagonist, 65
Mythic-psychological critique, and courtly love, 15–18. *See also* Rougemont, Denis de

Nagel, James, 164, 228 n. 23
Narcissism, 18–19, 139, 141
Nassau Literary Review, 126
Neo-Gothic. *See* Gothic Revival
Neoplatonism, 104, 140
"New-Slain Knight, A" (Hemingway), 174–75
New Woman, 111, 112–16, 120, 218 n. 26
New York Tribune, 125
New York World, 127
Newman School, 118, 125
Niagara Falls, 114; and hydroelectric power and dynamo, 115. *See also* Dynamo; Electricity
"Nick Sat Against the Wall . . ." (Hemingway), 162
Noblesse, 14, 171
Norris, Frank: "Grettir at Drangey," 21; *Yvernelle,* 21
North, the, 1, 5, 45, 82. *See also* Civil War; South, the
Norton, Charles Eliot, 3, 4, 6, 10, 204 n. 7, 215 n. 13, 215 n. 14; and New England Puritan families, 11
"Notes on the Next War" (Hemingway), 166
"Notorious Jumping Frog of Calaveras County, The" (Twain), 54

Oak Park High School, 172, 174
O'Brien, Patricia, 88
Of Mice and Men (Steinbeck), 23
Old Man and the Sea, The (Hemingway), 181, 183; Santiago, 181–83; identity with Christ, 182; Manolin, 182
Oldsey, Bernard, 173, 174, 226 n. 9
Osgood, James R., 37
O'Shaughnessey, Margaret Ellen, 204 n. 5
Otis, Elizabeth, 22

O'Toole, Patricia, 216n. 19, 218n. 29; on Adams-Cameron relationship, 217n. 22

Pageants, Medieval: and Twain, 71–73, 212n. 35. See also Carnival; Circus; Coronation Day pageant; Mardi Gras; Pamplona; Prince and the Pauper, The
Paget, Violet, 20
Paige typesetter, and Twain, 30, 46–47, 208n. 12
Paine, Albert Bigelow, 57
Pamplona, 181; festival at, 176, 180, 227n. 16. See also Bullfight; Pageants, medieval; Sun Also Rises, The
Paris, Gaston, and courtly love, 14, 19–20, 107
Parker, David, 220n. 9
Parkison, Jami, 67
Parrington, Vernon L., 203n. 2
Partisan Leader, 5
Pas d'armes, 14
Patristic exegesis, and courtly love, 15, 20–21, 221n. 17. See also Robertson, D. W.
Peele, George: "A Farewell to Arms," 173, 174
Péladan, Joseph, and Albigensian heresy, 16
Percy, Walker: Lancelot, 26; The Last Gentleman, 26
Perkins, Maxwell: correspondence with Fitzgerald, 119, 126, 132, 156, 172, 223n. 24; and Hemingway, 175, 178
Personal Recollections of Joan of Arc (Twain), 34, 35, 40, 56, 58, 212n. 34; and courtly lover, 36; as mixture of mythic and historical, 64; knight as child, 70–71; Charles VII of France, 35; Joan, as female knight, 40, 64; —, church's treatment of, 41–42; —, as child; —, 65, 66; —, and desexualization of, 71; Cauchon, 42
Petrarch, 36–37, 192, 207n. 5
Pettit, Arthur, 207n. 9
Pfeiffer, Pauline, 173, 198, 230n. 32
Philippe, Count of Darkness (Fitzgerald), 26, 132–35, 172, 220n. 13, 220n. 14; Philippe, 133–35; —, and his knights, 134; —, modeled on Hemingway, 134; —, as precursor of chivalric knight, 135; —, as precursor of courtly knight, 135–36; Letgarde, 135; Griselda, 135–36, 220n. 14
Pilgrimage: in Steinbeck, 23; in Adams, 85–86, 103; in Fitzgerald, 137–38; in Hemingway, 181, 188, 227n. 16, 228n. 22. See also Crusade; Quest
Piper, Henry Dan, 119, 159
Pitcher, E. W., 223n. 26
Plato, 140–41; influence on Fitzgerald, 222n. 20
"Plymouth Rock and the Pilgrims" (Twain), 31

Poe, Edgar Allan, 21, 93
Politics: machines, 2, 54, 82–86, 122–23; and reform, 32, 83–84; and lobbying, 111
Pound, Ezra, 176
"Prayer to the Dynamo" (Adams), 90, 214n. 10
"Prayer to the Virgin of Chartres" (Adams), 90, 214n. 10
"Primitive Rights of Women" (Adams), 111, 218n. 25
Prince and the Pauper, The (Twain), 34–35, 50, 56, 62; Yokel, 34, 50; Henry VIII, 35; Tom Canty, 35, 50; Edward, 50; Miles Hendon, 50, 211n. 28; as mixture of mythic and historical, 63–64; child as protagonist, 65; and medieval aristocrat and slavery, 68; and medieval pageants, 71, 104
Princeton University, 119, 120, 122, 125, 127, 129; and Gothic Revival, 7, 121, 219n. 3
"Private History of a Campaign That Failed" (Twain), 40
Protestantism, 2; dissolution in nineteenth century, 8, 112
Prouesse, 14, 171, 181
Pudd'nhead Wilson. See Tragedy of Pudd'nhead Wilson, The
Pullin, Faith, 228n. 26
Puritanism, 2; colonists as ancient Israelites, 5; characteristics of, 10; and Brahmin New England, 10–11; decline of hegemony, 11; and work ethic, 30; and examination of conscience, 41; Twain as descendant of, 52; suspicion of courtly love, 98; and Mariolatry, 111–12
Putnam, Emily James: "The Lady of the Castle," 21
Pyle, Howard, 4

Queen of Heaven, 198
Quest: in Faulkner, 24; in Twain, 38, 40, 49; in Fitzgerald, 137–38, 140–41, 143–45, 160, 221n. 17; in Hemingway, 199. See also Crusade; Pilgrimage

Rahn, Otto, and Albigensian heresy, 16
Railroad, 1, 2, 73; as symbol of industrial age, 89–90; Union Pacific, 89; and Adams, 90; as modern knight's horse, 186
Redbook, 134
Remarque, Erich Maria: All Quiet on the Western Front, 225n. 2
Revolutionary War, 122, 163
Reynolds, Michael, 129, 164, 165, 169, 172, 173, 176, 198, 199, 225n. 4, 226n. 6, 226n. 10
Richard the Lion-Hearted: and Twain, 39, 57; and Adams, 105; and Hemingway, 173, 197

Richardson, Hadley, 173; as Hemingway's ideal woman, 198
Robber barons, 2, 49, 124. *See also* Capitalism, laissez-faire; Gould, Jay
Robertson, D. W., 15; and courtly love, 16–18, 20; and pure love and love *par amours*, 185–86
Robin Hood, 4, 56, 65–66, 173
Robinson, Edwin Arlington: *Lancelot*, 21–22; *Merlin*, 21–22; *Modred*, 21–22; *Tristram*, 21–22
Roland: as archetypal chivalric knight, 176, 181
Roman de la Rose, 144
Roman Empire, 91, 132. *See also* Rome
Romanesque architecture, 89, 108
Romania, 14
Roncesvalles (or Roncevaux), 176. See also *Chanson de Roland*; Roland
Rosenthal, Bernard, 204 n. 5
Ross, Steven: on trench warfare, 226 n. 11
Rougemont, Denis de, 24, 41, 47, 165, 168, 183, 205 n. 10, 205 n. 12; mythic-psychological criticism and courtly love, 15; courtly love, 16, 17, 18, 20, 220 n. 14; on "fault" of love, 38, 183; as gloss on Fitzgerald's *Gatsby*, 138–39; on chivalric rules, 171; and medieval tournament, 179; and ideal knight, 185; religious and courtly orders, 188; troubadours, 198; on condottieri, 226 n. 13
Rowe, John Carlos, 108
"Rule of Phase Applied to History, The" (Adams), 92
Ruskin, John: *The Stones of Venice*, 3

St. Cecilia, 154
Saint-Gaudens, Augustus, 93
Saint James. See Santiago de Compostela
St. Louis, 32; and Twain, 77; and Adams, 77–78; and 1904 Exposition, 97
St. Michael of the Mount, 108
St. Paul Daily News, 136
Saint Victor, Adam de, 144
Salomon, Roger, 41, 208 n. 14
Salpeter, Harry, 127
Samuels, Ernest, 216 n. 21, 217 n. 23; on women's rights and Adams, 218 n. 26
Santiago de Compostela, 181, 228 n. 22
Save Me the Waltz (Fitzgerald, Zelda), 149; Fitzgerald as model for David Knight, 156; compared to *Tender Is the Night*, 224 n. 30
Saveth, Edward, 110
Scaglione, Aldo, 13, 14, 62, 64, 184, 196, 205 n. 9, 205 n. 11, 205 n. 12, 226 n. 13
Schleiner, Louise, 56, 57, 209 n. 21, 210 n. 22

Scholastic philosophy, 79, 87. *See also* Abelard, Pierre; Guillaume de Champeaux
Scholes, Robert, 193, 228 n. 26
Scollard, Clinton: "Taillefer the Trouvère," 21
Scott, Sir Walter: *Ivanhoe*, 7, 9, 42, 56, 172; *The Lay of the Last Minstrel*, 9; and Twain, 28, 42–45, 172, 208 n. 12, 209 n. 20, 211 n. 30; and Adams, 96–97; and Fitzgerald, 172, 219 n. 1; and Hemingway, 172; and bankruptcy, 208 n. 12; and steamboat in *Huck Finn*, 212 n. 37
Scribner, Charles, 171
Scribner's Magazine, 163
Scudder, Vida Dutton, 4
Scuola Cantorum, 119
Second law of thermodynamics, 83–84
"Secret History of Eddypus, the World-Empire, The" (Twain), 134, 207 n. 8
Seldes, Gilbert, 123–24
"Sensible Thing, The" (Fitzgerald), 152; Jonquil Cary, 152; George O'Kelly, 152–53
"Sentimental Education of Frederic Henry" (Hemingway), 174
Sentimentalism, 10–11, 20; displaces religion, 30; and marriage, 31–39, 67–68; and genteel values, 33; and Twain's portraits of Héloïse and Laura, 37, 39, 77; and Twain's portrait of Hank, 37; contrast between sentimental and courtly ladies, 38; and Twain's portrait of Launcelot, 39; and Twain's presentation of motherhood, 51; and Twain, 206 n. 3
Servant d'amour, 20
Shakespeare, William, 215 n. 14
Simms, William Gilmore: *Life of the Chevalier Bayard*, 4
Sino-Japanese War, 163
1601, or Conversation as It Was by the Social Fireside, (Twain), 37
Sklar, Robert, 125
Slavery, 1, 29, 45, 75, 81; in Twain, 34–35, 68–70, 207 n. 9; childlike slave and medieval knight, 68, 75; relationships between child, knight, aristocrat, and slave, 68; and Adams, 85, 86. *See also* Ball, Charles; Civil War; Free-Soil Party; South, the; Twain, Mark
Smith, Frederick James, 151
Smith, Henry Nash, 32, 49, 68, 207 n. 9
Smith, Scottie Fitzgerald, 125
Sociohistorical critique, and courtly love, 15–18, 19–20. *See also* Bulfinch, Thomas; Lewis, C. S.
"Sold to Satan" (Twain), 90
Solotaroff, Robert, 170, 195; on Hemingway and Kurowsky, 228 n. 26

Sommer, Robert, 103; and contrast between Virgin and Esther, 218 n. 28

Song of Roland. See *Chanson de Roland*

Sound and the Fury, The (Faulkner), 24

South, the, 1, 5, 10, 28, 53, 82; medievalism in architecture, 42; hierarchical class structure of, 42–45; Twain's comparison to Middle Ages, 43, 207 n. 8; and slavery 44–45, 69, 75; in Fitzgerald, 130. *See also* Civil War; North, the

Spain, 181, 183; compared to Africa, 182

Spanier, Sandra Whipple: on Catherine Barkley, 229 n. 29

Spanish Civil War, 163, 166

Spanish resistance workers, 168

Spengler, Oswald: influence on Fitzgerald, 126, 132; *The Decline of the West*, 126, 127; theory of history and Fitzgerald, 126–27, 135, 219 n. 5, 219 n. 7; theory of history and Twain, 134–35

Spenser, Edmund: *The Faerie Queene*, 16, 172; and Hemingway, 226 n. 7

Spilka, Mark, 162, 184, 193; on Jake Barnes, 227 n. 19

Stahl, John Daniel, 208 n. 14, 211 n. 30, 211 n. 32, 212 n. 34

Steamboat: pilot as knight, 73–75; and explosion, 74, 212 n. 36; and association with romance, 75; compared to cathedral of Milan, 212 n. 37

Stein, Gertrude: and lost generation in Hemingway's fiction, 162

Steinbeck, John, 26; *The Acts of King Arthur and His Noble Knights*, 22, 26; *The Grapes of Wrath*, 23; *Of Mice and Men*, 23; *Tortilla Flat*, 23; *Travels with Charley*, 23

Stendhal: *Le Rouge et le Noir*, 134

Stephens, Robert, 184; Hemingway's ambivalence toward war, 225 n. 3

Stern, Milton, 124, 220 n. 8

Stilnovisti, 138, 222 n. 18

Stoneback, H. R., 174, 176, 226 n. 12; on bullfight and moral behavior, 227 n. 16; on Catholicism and Hemingway, 228 n. 22, 230 n. 32

Stones of Venice, The (Ruskin), 3

Suicide: of southern aristocracy, 45; of Hank and Arthurian civilization, 47–48, 73; of Marian Adams, 93, 99–100, 122, 144, 214 n. 11, 215 n. 15, 217 n. 23, 218 n. 29; of Madeleine and Esther, metaphorically, 113–16; and attempts by Eleanor and Nicole, 152; and death wish of Monroe Stahr, 158–59

Sun Also Rises, The (Hemingway), 162, 163, 164, 173, 176, 191, 196; Count Mippipopolous, 166; Mike, 166, 184, 186, 189; Brett Ashley, 166, 184–89, 192; —, as courtly lady, 179; —, as rejecting role of courtly lady, 183–90; —, as Circe, 186; —, as modern woman, 189; —, Jake Barnes, 176, 184–89, 190, 196, 227 n. 19, 228 n. 22; —, choosing Brett over Virgin, 188; —, and horrors of war, 165–66; —, as restrained romantic, 227 n. 19; romanticism and antiromanticism, 183–85; and medieval romance, 183–90; and failure of courtly love in modern world, 183–88; Bill, 184, 188, 189; Robert Cohn, 186, 189; —, as courtly lover, 184–87, 227 n. 19; Pedro Romero, 186, 196; —, as chivalric and courtly knight, 179–80, 187, 228 n. 20; —, as bullfighter, 187, 188; Georgette, 186; Montoya, 187

Sylvester, Bickford, 181, 227 n. 17

Szarmach, Paul, 204 n. 5

Taine, Hippolyte: influence of his *Ancient Regime* on Twain, 208 n. 11, 210 n. 24, 211 n. 28

Taylor, Henry Osborn: *Classical Heritage of the Middle Ages*, 100, 101–2

Technology, modern: and warfare, 1, 47–48, 168, 175, 199, 226 n. 5, 226 n. 11; dynamo as symbol of, 30, 48, 206 n. 1; as representative of progress, 46–47, 73–74

"Tendency of History, The" (Adams), 86

Tender Is the Night (Fitzgerald), 125, 128, 130, 131, 132, 136, 145–50, 157, 223 n. 27; Dick Diver, 125, 128, 129, 131, 150; —, and view of war, 130; —, as romantic, 145; —, compared to U. S. Grant, 145–46, 223 n. 25; —, modern romance with Nicole, 145–49, 185, 223 n. 26; —, as courtly knight, 148; —, and Tommy Barban, 223 n. 28; once entitled "The World's Fair," 128; and Fitzgerald's view of twentieth-century America, 128–29; postwar world of, 130–32; Nicole Diver, 130, 145–49, 156, 185, 224 n. 30; —, as unwilling courtly lady, 149; —, suicide attempt, 151; —, as dream girl, 155; Luis Campion, 131; Royal Dumphry, 131; Abe North, 131; Jules Peterson, 131; Rosemary Hoyt, 131, 147, 148; Mary North Minghetti, 131, 147, 148; Lady Caroline Sibly-Biers, 131; Maria Wallis, 131; Baby Warren, 131, 147; and chivalry, 136; modern romance between Dick and Nicole compared with courtly ideal, 145–49; Tommy Barban, 146; —, as knightly figure, 148, 223 n. 28; and code duello, 148; and Fitzgerald marriage, 149; subtitled "A Tragedy," 223 n. 24

Tennyson, Alfred, Lord, 93; *Idylls of the King*, 9, 172

This Side of Paradise (Fitzgerald), 119, 120, 121, 124, 127, 129, 145, 150, 152, 154, 224 n. 31; Thornton Hancock, 119, 120, 121, 124; Monsignor Darcy, 120, 121, 150; Amory Blaine, 120, 125, 129, 141, 144, 145, 156, 157, 159, 194; —, as medievalist, 121; —, narcissism of, 141; —, and sexual temptation, 150–52; Jill Wayne, 145, 150; Alec Connage, 150; Isabelle Borge, 151; Myra St. Claire, 151; Eleanor Savage, 151, 194; —, as precursor of Nicole Diver, 152; Clara Page, 154–55, 157, 195; —, as medieval ideal of womanhood, 154–55, 156; Rosalind Connage, 154, 156; —, as archetypal debutante and vamp, 151–53; —, as dream girl, 155; Tom D'Invilliers, 167

Thomas Aquinas, 96, 117

Tiffany, Louis Comfort, 3, 55

Thoron, Ward, 215 n. 14

Tone, Aileen, 105, 218 n. 29

Tortilla Flat (Steinbeck), 23

Tournament, 14, 20, 38, 40, 45; and jousting, 183. *See also* Bullfight

Tragedy of Puddn'head Wilson, The (Twain), 62, 64, 65, 68–70, 75, 199; modeled on Virginia society, 53; Judge York Leicester Driscoll, 64; Percy Northumberland Driscoll, 64, 69; Pembroke Howard, 64; Colonel Cecil Burleigh Essex, 64, 69; Roxana, 64, 69–70, 75; and complex equation of child, knight, and slave, 68–70, 73, 75; and deconstruction of white-black binary and master-slave binary, 68–70; Tom and Chambers as twins, 69–70; Capello twins, 70

Tramp Abroad, A (Twain), 55, 207 n. 10

Tramp Menace, 2. *See also* Capitalism, laissez-faire; Mobs

Travels with Charley (Steinbeck), 23

Tristan, 21, 194; and Iseult, 142

Trobar Clus, 19

Troubadours, 17, 18, 19, 195, 198; and chivalry, 19; Guillaume d'Aquitaine, 19; Arnaut Daniel, 19; Jaufré Rudel, 19; Marcabru, 19, 194; Guiraut Riquier, 19, 192; and Adams, 110; and Fitzgerald, 145; Bertran de Born, 145; William of Poitou, 205 n. 12. *See also* Cholakian, Rouben; Courtly love; Knights, medieval

Tucker, Nathaniel Beverley, 5

Turnbull, Mrs. Bayard, 127

Tuttleton, James: on female vampirism, 223 n. 27

"Twa Corbies," 174

Twain, Mark, 25, 26, 27, 207, 208 n. 13; and medievalist impulse, 28–76; and "Angel Fish," 28; and childhood, 28–29; and Sir Walter Scott 28, 42–45, 172, 208 n. 12, 209 n. 20, 211 n. 30; opposition to medievalism, 29; celebration of Middle Ages, 29, 31, 32; and child, knight, and slave, parallels, 29, 66–70; commitment to age of technology, 30; and nineteenth-century common man, 30, 31–33, 50–52; and Paige typesetter, 30, 46–47; sentimental relationship with wife, 31, 206 n. 2, 206 n. 3, 208 n. 12; women in his life, 31; and criticism of medieval political structure, 34–35; criticism of aristocratic social conventions, 35; and courtly love, 35–39, 66–67, 77; and female sexuality, 37–39; and Launcelot, 38–39; and droit du seigneur, 39, 207 n. 6; and religious conditions of Middle Ages, 40–42; influence of Calvinism on, 41, 208 n. 11; on Middle Ages as compared to American South, 43, 207 n. 8; and slavery, 44, 45, 66, 68–70, 207 n. 9; and medievalist impact on language and literature, 45; and nineteenth-century culture, 46–52; and bankruptcy, 46, 208 n. 12; and Anglo-Saxon ancestry, 52–53; as Sir Mark Twain and use of medieval English, 52, 66, 311 n. 30; and desire to transcend history, 52, 139, 208 n. 14, 209 n. 15, 211 n. 27; and southern aristocratic ancestry, 53–54; and travels abroad, 54; nickname "King," 55; Middle Ages as setting, 55–56; evidence of medieval influence, 55–73; and Anglomania-Anglophobia periods, 55–73, 209 n. 18; medieval history, literature, and architecture in fiction, 55–73; as duke of Hartford, 55; and research on Middle Ages, 55–73, 209 n. 21, 210 n. 22; acquaintance with Malory's characters, 57; and two Middle Ages, 59–60, 210 n. 23; and dream vision in, 59–63, 210 n. 25; and King Arthur, 61–64; shift between mythic and historical, 63–65; and escape into childhood, 65–68; and blurring of male-female binary, 69, 211 n. 32; and knight as child, 70–71; and medieval pageants, 71–73, 212 n. 35; and steamboat pilots, 73–75, 212 n. 37; and Adams, 77–79, 81, 83, 87, 88, 101, 102, 104, 111; and Darwin and Lyell, 86–87; atomic power and "Sold to Satan," 90; and Fitzgerald, 118, 120, 127, 132; influence on Hemingway, 162–63, 166; and Hemingway, 172, 199, 200; and Lecky, 206 n. 4, 208 n. 11; and literary influences, 207 n. 5, 208 n. 11, 208 n. 12, 209 n. 21; attitude to-

Twain, Mark (*cont.*)
  ward young girls, 207 n. 7; influence of
    Taine on, 208 n. 11, 210 n. 24; and Webster
    and Company, 208 n. 12; and Grant's eu-
    logy, 208 n. 12; and impact of brother
    Henry's death, 212 n. 36
Twichell, Joseph, 214 n. 11

"United States of Lyncherdom" (Twain), 51

Vamp, 117, 120, 147, 151–52, 153–54; con-
    trasted with belle, 151, 223 n. 27; female
    vampirism, 223 n. 27
Vanderbilt, Kermit, 6, 204 n. 7
Verduin, Kathleen, 197, 204 n. 6; on Dante
    and Robert Cantwell, 229 n. 27
"Very Short Story, A" (Hemingway), 228 n. 26
Villard, Henry Serrano, 228 n. 23
Villehardouin and DeJoinville: *Chronicles of
    Crusaders*, 172
Virgin, 78, 120, 188; Mary, 41, 102–9, 111–12,
    117, 144, 154, 191, 228 n. 24; as sexual-
    maternal dynamo in Adams, 77–79, 89,
    144, 216 n. 21, 218 n. 28; of Chartres, 78, 79,
    107, 108; of Dreux, 79; as feminine prin-
    ciple in Adams, 79; of France, 79; of
    Greece, 79; of Cobre, 181, 183; and "Hail
    Mary," 181, 182; *Virgen de la Soledad*, 183,
    188; and Nuestra Señora de Roncesvalles,
    188. *See also* "Prayer to the Virgin of
    Chartres"
Virginia, and Twain, 53. *See also* South, the
Virginian, The (Wister), 53, 134
Voyage of the "Beagle" (Darwin), 86

Wagner-Martin, Linda, 226 n. 12
Walker, Nancy, 211 n. 31
Walpole, Horace: *The Castle of Otranto*, 9
"War Prayer, The" (Twain), 40
Warner, Charles Dudley: *The Gilded Age*, 43,
    48, 52, 54. *See also* Twain, Mark
Washington, President George, 84, 85; and
    slavery, 86; symbolic significance for Ad-
    ams, 213 n. 6, 218 n. 24
Wasserstrom, William, 124, 125, 223 n. 28
Wasteland, 97, 117; and Fitzgerald's valley of

  ashes, 130, 144, 145, 220 n. 9; in Heming-
    way, 162, 181
Watt, Ian, 15, 18
Way, Brian, 225 n. 2
Webster, Charles L., 58
Welsh, Alexander, 211 n. 29
Welsh, Mary, 191–92
West, James L. W., III, 219 n. 2
Westervelt, Linda A., 94, 213 n. 2
Westoby, Kathryn, 144
Wharton, Edith: "Ogrin the Hermit," 21
What Is Man? (Twain), 77
Whitley, John, 156, 219 n. 5, 220 n. 8
Whitlow, Roger, 229 n. 29
Whitman, Stephen French: "The Noble
    Family of Beaupertys," 21
Wilcox, Earl, 184
Williams, James, 58, 206 n. 4, 209 n. 18,
    210 n. 22
Wilson, Edmund, 195
Wilson, Robert, 57
Winner Take Nothing (Hemingway), 175
Winters, Yvor, 101, 102
Wisbey, Herbert A., 207 n. 5
Wister, Owen, 53; *The Virginian*, 53, 134
Wordsworth, William: and Adams, 214 n. 11
Workman, Leslie, 9, 204 n. 5
World War I, 11, 48; and no-man's-land, 48,
    129; and trench warfare, 48, 92, 226 n. 11;
    and Adams, 92, 105; and Fitzgerald, 119,
    120, 124, 128, 129–30, 132, 145, 146, 151,
    160; and shell shock, 130, 150, 175; and Hem-
    ingway, 162, 163, 164, 165, 167, 175, 176,
    177, 180, 189, 190, 225 n. 4, 229 n. 29; and
    machine gun, 226 n. 5
World War II, and Hemingway, 163, 166, 171,
    173, 175; allied bombing raids, 167

Yachts: as feminine, 141
Young, Philip, 162, 195
Ypres, Third Battle of, 145
"Ysobel de Corveaux" (Hooker), 21
Yvernelle (Norris), 21

Zlatic, Thomas, 210 n. 26, 213 n. 5
Zwarg, Christina, 212 n. 33, 212 n. 34